From Desert
to Town

DEDICATION

To all the Bedouin and Fellahin who live
together in mixed villages and towns
in the Galilee

From Desert to Town

The Integration of Bedouin into Arab Fellahin Villages and Towns in the Galilee, 1700–2020

Tomer Mazarib

Brighton • Chicago • Toronto

Copyright © Tomer Mazarib, 2022.

The right of Tomer Mazarib to be identified as Author of this work has been asserted in accordance with the Copyright, Designs and Patents Act 1988.

2 4 6 8 10 9 7 5 3 1

First published 2022 in Great Britain by
SUSSEX ACADEMIC PRESS
PO Box 139
Eastbourne BN24 9BP

Distributed in the United States of America by
Independent Publishers Group
814 N. Franklin Street
Chicago, IL 60610

All rights reserved. Except for the quotation of short passages for the purposes of criticism and review, no part of this publication may be reproduced, stored in a retrieval system, or transmitted, in any form or by any means, electronic, mechanical, photocopying, recording or otherwise, without the prior permission of the publisher.

British Library Cataloguing in Publication Data
A CIP catalogue record for this book is available from the British Library.

Library of Congress Cataloging-in-Publication Data
To be applied for.

Hardcover ISBN 978-1-78976-153-5

Typeset & designed by Sussex Academic Press, Brighton & Eastbourne.
Printed by TJ Books Ltd, Padstow, Cornwall.

Contents

Preface	vi
Acknowledgments	viii
List of Maps, Figures, Graphs and Tables	x
List of Abbreviations	xii

	Introduction: A View from the Field	1
1	Historical Background: The Bedouin in Palestine, 1700–1918	28
2	Galilee Bedouin under British Rule, 1918–1948	53
3	Impact of the 1948 War on the Bedouin	85
4	Israeli Military Rule, 1948–1966: Chain Migrations and Government Plans	113
5	Governmental and Civilian Events, 1966–2020: Bedouin Settlement in Fellahin Villages and Towns	133
	Summary and Conclusions	163
	Appendix	167
	Notes	177
	Bibliography	222
	Index	242

Preface

Official history has always lacked data on the Bedouin population. There are two reasons for this: Firstly, the historians' perspectives whose narratives tend to focus on political, social, and economic elites, or on wars. Secondly, the mindset of the Bedouin themselves, who both as a small minority and a pastoral people whose lifestyles ran counter to the standards and expectations of the majority culture, have historically preferred to remain unaccounted for and below the radar of the powers-that-be. Thus, they refrained from being recorded in any government registries – Ottoman, British, or Israeli – and remain absent from the narrative and the research literature.

Consequently, the book at hand fills a lacuna in the research literature, providing a wealth of information gathered from both my interviews with Bedouin, and compilation and integration of multiple sources of relevant input extracted from existing historical documents. I am an "outsider and an insider" straddling two worlds: both a Bedouin, and an anthropologist and scholar of Middle Eastern and Islam Studies.

Combining historical information retrieved piece-by-piece from archives, with oral histories from interviews with Galilee Bedouin, enabled me to analyze and distil much information about Bedouin population in the Galilee that has escaped the academic community to date. The findings shed light on the pattern of sedentarizaion and integration of Bedouin living in Fellahin villages and towns in the Galilee between the years 1700 and 2020, by analyzing the dynamics, factors, and circumstances that led to migration of Bedouin communities into towns and villages of Fellahin, in contrast to unique, specifically Bedouin settlements (hereinafter: "Bedouin-only") in the Galilee.

This work's fundamental underlying assumption, which arises from the research, is that the process of settling Bedouin in the Galilee was "glocally" structured – that is, both global factors and local circumstances set the pattern. To further clarify: This development was not primarily the product of governmental settlement programs – whether Ottoman, British, or Israeli – all of which perceived Bedouin as cultural exceptions, whose "needs" (as authorities perceived them) should be treated separately from other communities. There is no denying that while it was government policy (Ottoman, British, and Israeli) to settle Bedouin in permanent locales, this policy was fueled by and designed to serve only the interests of the state. While at best, this policy constituted, indirectly, a force contributing to Bedouin settlement, its main impetus was internal. Secondly, (and a platform for the first), the social categorization of Bedouin and Fellahin populations is based on flexibility, construction, and formation, rather than on a dichotomy or on a linear and inevitable process of total assimilation of the Bedouin population and their transformation into Fellahin over time. While there are essential differences that are becoming more and more blurred over time, construction processes of similarity and separateness operate alongside one another.

For all three ruling regimes during the centuries under study, the promotion of sedentarizaion of Bedouin was merely a vehicle for the realization of each regime's goals and priorities, with all three governing powers hoping that sedentarizaion would enhance their control and governance. The Ottomans viewed Bedouin as a tiny part of a grander scheme to modernize the Ottoman Empire as a path to becoming a major player in the international power matrix; the British Empire acted out of its interest in being an occupying colonial power, and sought to free up pastoral lands for Jewish settlement as part of their commitment to the Balfour Declaration; and Israel aspired to concentrate Bedouin on less land toward realization of national priorities to "Judaize" (*leYahed*) the Galilee. Betterment of Bedouin life, or which type of settlement was most appropriate for them, was of little interest to Ottoman, British, and Israeli authorities. Yet the research reveals that the actual impact of such programmes on this process was in any case very important.

Despite "larger objectives" of all three ruling powers, governmental policy vis-à-vis the Bedouin should be viewed as cultural exceptions, and ought to be treated by scholars separately from other populations: The research reveals that social organization of Bedouin and Fellahin populations in shared spaces was primarily self-generated – based on internal motivations and needs that exhibit remarkable flexibility, construction and formation. Moreover, it is not a linear progression towards an inevitable winner-take-all scenario of total assimilation of the Bedouin population and their transformation into fellahin over time, as other observers assume. The archival sources, the research literature, as well as 59 in-depth interviews conducted between the years 2013–2015 with Bedouin and Fellahin inhabitants in various Arab towns and villages in the Galilee suggest a much more complex and dynamic story.

Acknowledgments

Writing this book about the Bedouin has not been, by any means, a lone or singular enterprise: There is not sufficient space in an acknowledgement to thank individually the countless people who have provided advice and support in this endeavor. However, I would like to take this opportunity to give special thanks to some friends and colleagues whose encouragement was of particular value.

In Israel, I am grateful to Haifa University's Department of Middle Eastern and Islamic Studies; particularly I would like to express my deep gratitude to Dr. Ido Shahar, chief advisor for my dissertation, without whose intensive involvement and ongoing support throughout the writing stages of my research, I'm not sure I would have had the strength to complete this complex project. Special thanks are also in order to Prof. Mahmoud Yazbak, my second co-advisor, whose guidance in ensuring that the research would meet high academic standards was an essential element in completion of my doctorate.

Likewise, in the UK, I am grateful for the hospitality I was extended by Oxford University's St Antony's College as a visiting fellow in 2018–2019, a period that enabled me to expand my doctoral research toward publication of this book, enriched by the lectures, conferences, and workshops that I attended. Special thanks are due to Prof. Walter Armbrust and Prof. Eugene Rogan of the Middle East Center (MEC).

The project would have made little headway without the patience and advice of many librarians and archivists. Their institutions are listed in the bibliography, but I am especially grateful to archivist Debbie Usher at St Antony's College, Oxford.

In retrospect, I am struck by how much this project has been worked on conducted "aloud": in conversations, seminar presentations, and conference papers. I am extremely grateful to the many conveners at Oxford University, Hebrew University, and Haifa University who gave me an opportunity to speak at their gatherings, enabling me to formulate my findings coherently at crucial junctures.

I want to express my thanks and deep gratitude to my wife Halima, and my children Sahar, Razi, Sheerin, and Aya for their patience, tolerance, and encouragement as I pursued this project, from the initial idea as a research topic, through its writing and to its conclusion. Their support was essential in fulfilling a dream.

I would like to thank all those with whom I conducted in depth interviews, to all the Bedouin and Fellahin living in the Galilee towns and villages. Without them, this book would not have been published.

Thanks are due also to Anthony Grahame, Editorial Director at Sussex Academic Press.

Oxford, AUGUST 2019

List of Maps, Figures, Graphs and Tables

Maps
1.1	The origin of the Bedouin and their migration to Palestine.	33
1.2	Settlement of Bedouin tribes near Fellahin villages and towns in the Galilee in the late 19th century.	47
2.1	Bedouin families who moved to Fellahin villages and towns in the Galilee under British rule, 1918–1948.	67

Figures
1.1	Wadi al-Saki'a Neighborhood in Shafa-Amer, 1910.	49
5.1	Wadi Al-Saki'a Neighborhood in Shafa-Amer, 2020.	148

Graphs
2.1	Estimates of the Bedouin population in the Galilee under British rule.	83
5.1	Comparison of Bedouin estimates between the years 1969–1982.	143
5.2	A multi-year graph showing Bedouin IDF enlistees in the Galilee and the Naqab/Negev between the years 1998–2016.	158
5.3	A comparative graph of the number of Bedouin volunteers in the IDF from Bedouin localities and from Fellahin villages and towns in the Galilee between the years 2011–2016.	160

Tables
2.1	Estimated distribution of Bedouin residing in Bedouin tribes in the Galilee, 1922.	72/73
2.2	Estimated distribution of Bedouin residing as permanent inhabitants and as Nomads in the Galilee near Fellahin villages and towns, 1945.	76
4.1	Demographic distribution of Bedouin tribes in the Galilee in 1962.	118/119

4.2	Distribution of Bedouin in Shafa-Amer, 1963.	126
4.3	Distribution of Bedouin in Fellahin villages and towns in the Galilee, 1969.	128/129
4.4	Distribution of Bedouin in Bedouin villages in the Galilee, 1969	130
4.5	Distribution of Bedouin residing nomadically in the Galilee, 1969.	131
5.1	Bedouin families who moved or transferred to existing Fellahin villages and towns, 1970s.	135
5.2	Bedouin in Fellahin villages and towns in the Galilee, 1982.	138/139
5.3	Bedouin in Bedouin villages in the Galilee, 1982.	141
5.4	Bedouin living nomadically in the Galilee, 1982.	142
5.5	Bedouin in Fellahin towns in the Galilee, 2020.	149
5.6	Bedouin in Fellahin villages in the Galilee, 2020.	150/151

List of Abbreviations

CBSPC	(Israel) Central Bureau of Statistics, Population Census
CO	(British) Colonial Office – London
CZA	Central Zionist Archives – Jerusalem
HHA	Haganah Historical Archives – Tel Aviv
IDF	Israel Defence Forces
ILA	Israel Lands Authority
IP	Israeli Pound [*Israeli Lira*]
JAI	Jewish Agency for Israel – Jerusalem
JNF	Jewish National Fund
JPRCA	Jezreel Plain Regional Council Archives
LP	Palestine Pound (*Filastini Lira/Junyah*)
MECA	Middle East Centre Archive, St Antony's College – Oxford
MK	Member of Knesset
NAL	National Archives – London
OSA	Ottoman State Archives – Istanbul
PI	Physical Identification
PJCA	Palestine Jewish Colonization Association
RPA	Rosh Pina Archives
SAI	State Archives of Israel – Jerusalem
UN	United Nations
VMA	Valley of Maayanot Archives – the Beisan Valley

From Desert
to Town

Introduction

A View from the Field

This study examines the settlement and integration process of the Bedouin population into Arab Fellahin (Arabic for "peasants")[1] villages and towns in the Galilee between the years 1700–2020, from a historical, social, and cultural perspective.[2] It seeks to illuminate through a host of historical, sociological, and anthropological inputs, what prompted Bedouin to settle and integrate into Fellahin villages and towns in the Galilee. The term "integration" is employed in this work as it suggests engagement, the Bedouin themselves being an active entity in the process where in Bedouin throughout the period under study were *initiators*, not passive subjects – this despite the presence of government plans, i.e., initiatives in the background in some cases *imposed* on the Bedouin population (also addressed in the book).

The book's main argument is that the process of Bedouin settlement in Galilee Fellahin villages and towns was an outcome of both external and internal factors. On the one hand, the centralized Ottoman, British, and Israeli policy, combined with other political-economic developments of the 18th, 19th, and 20th centuries, played a crucial role in the Bedouin move to settle. On the other hand, Bedouin settlement stemmed from internal social dynamics within and between tribes and the Fellahin villagers. These dynamics demonstrate that Bedouin social identity is flexible and fluid, rather than rigid and well-defined. Particularly notable in this regard are the social relations between Bedouin and Fellahin,[3] and the book demonstrates that the boundaries between these two social groups are blurred and permeable.

According to the main argument, there is ongoing social, economic, and political interaction between Bedouin and Fellahin. Moreover, over time, this relationship has been based on a social interest that serves the two communities, such as exogamous marriage (marriage outside the tribe framework) or the advantages of commercial-trading ties for economic gain that at times are essential to the welfare of both communities.

Furthermore, this work argues that the reciprocity between Bedouin and Fellahin should not be viewed as "the desert against the sown" or as a "war" between the desert and the sown (i.e., the existence of two conflicting subcultures in the Arab region);[4] specifically, that ultimately the town population is destined to defeat the desert population, as reflected in Ibn Khaldun's conception of the dichotomous relations between Bedouin nomads and settlers.[5] Ibn Khaldun classified the Arab population into two categories: the Bedouin (*al-Badu*), and the sedentary people (*al-hadari*: rural-*Fellahin* and urban dwellers).[6] He claimed that the differing lifestyles of the two groups, deriving from their distinct ecological conditions, is the key factor distinguishing the groups from one another. He adopted a paradigm of ecological determinism, whereby ecological existence shapes not only the way of life, but also shapes culture and personality structure or mindset (i.e., determining personal change such as weakening of tribal loyalty, where this element becomes less necessary and less relevant in towns and villages).[7]

It is true that Ibn Khaldun described the interrelationships between Bedouin and Fellahin living in a specific geographical unit, Maghreb, during the 14th century. Yet his paradigm still exists among contemporary scholars, as will be shown below, and is part of the impetus for my writing this book. Instead, this book argues that there is a close interplay between grazing and cultivation that fosters much more complex relationships characterized by permeable (I prefer the term "liquidity", used henceforth) boundaries in social, cultural, economic, and political realms between these two social groups.[8]

In its integration of historical documents with ethnographic data, this work serves as a bridge between "top-down" and "bottom-up" scientific knowledge. In doing so, the findings are relevant to a wider audience than anthropologists, including readers who are interested in how governments treat marginalized populations, and not just those readers with a particular interest in Bedouin, not to mention solely Bedouin in the Galilee. Moreover, the book will doubtless engender keen interest among the Bedouin and Fellahin themselves, who are the subjects of this study.

Why another book on Bedouin settlement?

The question of Bedouin settlement in Fellahin towns and villages in the Galilee and the relationships between them has not yet been studied systematically – either from a diacritical perspective (describing the historical, social, cultural, economic and political processes that led there to development of this phenomenon), nor from an ethnographic or sociological perspective (the situation of Bedouin who settled in Fellahin villages and towns in the Galilee and their identity).

Historical studies on the Bedouin in Palestine during the Ottoman Empire are rich in intellectual challenges and multidisciplinary experiences, which can be classified into three genres: "Western/European travelers' narratives"; narratives by historians, and narratives by geographic researchers, all three of which tended to rely on a narrow interpretation of communal life, casting the Bedouin and Fellahin as two opposing groups disinclined to mixing or building a shared communal life.

The most problematic is the first genre: Western travelers and diaries of Europeans, especially travellers during the 19th century, including accounts by John Lewis Burckhardt, Henry Baker Tristram, James L. Buckingham, Edward Robinson, and others, such as British Consul for Jerusalem and Palestine James Finn.[9] Despite the relatively brevity of these travelers' visits, these accounts, collectively, are a rich source of information on the population in the Middle East, including Palestine, at the time. The accounts, however, present descriptions of the Bedouin population and the relationships between them and the urban and village inhabitants in somewhat essentialized terms, relying on stereotypical and largely uncomplimentary descriptions of the Bedouin population. These accounts often presented the Bedouin as thieves and bandits, lying in wait for the Fellahin and their commercial convoys and pilgrims' route to Mecca.[10]

On his 1812 expedition, Burckhardt described Bedouin attacks on Fellahin towns (Tiberias, Safad, Nazareth, and Beisan), and even demand of protection money (*khawa*, or "brotherhood" payments) from villagers and townspeople.[11] I would point out that like other travelers and Orientalist-oriented writers, Burckhardt refers to the concept "*khawa*" as being a brother/sister of the tribe. In other words, according to his accounts, Bedouin would demand *khawa* in the form of various goods of material value (money, legumes, and clothing) from all those residing in their vicinity – Fellahin, from weaker Bedouin sub-groups, or strangers accosted on the road (like the Western travelers) as they passed through Bedouin territory. In return, these remitters would become the Bedouin's responsibility and be under the protection of these local Bedouin against robberies, marauding, looting, or vandalism by others.[12]

Another mid-19th century observer was the British Consul James Finn, who lived in Palestine between 1845 and 1863, described the "wars" between Bedouin and Fellahin that began in Jerusalem and Nablus and spread throughout Palestine.[13] Henry Tristram, who visited Palestine in 1863, wrote of the "great tension" between Bedouin and Fellahin, citing for example, Bedouin such as Aqil Agha imposing a heavy annual tax on the village of Isfiya in return for his protection.[14] At the same time, Banu Hassan, Banu Adwan, and Banu Saqer imposed *khawa* payments from Fellahin villages in Marj Ibn Amer (the Jezreel Valley) and the Beisan Valley.[15]

These descriptions by Western reflect a Eurocentric and almost eliding of incidents that they observed or were told about that lack a central axis. Such accounts are not only fragmentary impressions; they reflect the observer's prejudices. Note that until the 1980s, scholars tended to consider these travelers' accounts to be reliable and accurate, without a trace of questioning. Edward Said was the first to draw attention to their biases in his book *Orientalism* (1978),[16] which took to task the observers' skewed perspective that painted peoples of the East as primitive and weak,[17] serving as justification for their conquest by the "civilized" [enlightened] West.[18] According to Said, the new Orientalist cast the orient as an "imitation" of the West.[19] Said's charges are echoed in Bernard Lewis's 1964 tome *The Middle East and the West* wherein Lewis wrote that the Levant can only improve itself when its nationalism "is prepared to come to terms with the West".[20]

A parallel line of criticism, by American anthropologist Talal Asad, challenges and opposes the concept of "cultural translation" that manifests in British social anthropology.[21] Asad argued that the objective of "cultural translation is to define by overt or covert signs. The ethnographers should not approach the research field as group leaders or tourists to interpret what the 'native' says, or to embellish illogical things".[22] Asad continued: "Cultural translation is inevitably enmeshed in conditions of power-professional, national, international. And among these conditions is the authority of ethnographers to uncover the implicit meanings of subordinate societies".[23]

Another avenue of criticism was developed by anthropologists Khaled Furani and Dan Rabinowitz in their article on ethnography in Palestine[24] wherein they described the literature authored by Western travelers as "biblical anthropology", in thrall to an ancient biblical symbolism, directed toward proving that the Holy Land does not belong to the Muslims, thereby justifying its re-conquest. In this sense, their argument went, these travelers and their narratives paved the way for the early Zionists. According to them:

> Proto-ethnographic work in Palestine involved European writers animating their own patrimony by following the footsteps of emblematic biblical figures. This conveniently supported a European claim to shape Palestine's administrative reality and to morally incorporate it in a European universe […], which is mentally and politically external to

the lands of Islam. One consequence of this "biblical anthropology" was validation of the nascent Zionist claim of a "historic" return to a "promised" land.[25]

They also claimed that most of these travelers' sojourns in Palestine were far too short to grasp the economic, social, and cultural situation. Unsurprisingly, these accounts have been subjected to pointed criticism by contemporary scholars, not least for their hostility.[26]

Also, most of their descriptions were devoted to adventure stories with a strong affinity for *culturism*, a discourse that focuses mainly on minority groups' quaintness and attributes in their social and political life that are piquant.[27] As such, in the subtext they forge a racist discourse that goes farther than merely accusing the natives of cultural backwardness as measured by a Western yardstick. It almost goes without saying that this genre has very little to contribute to understanding relationships and interactions between the Bedouin and the other populations in Palestine.

The second genre consists of works by Historians of the mid-to-late 20th century, who followed in the footsteps of these Western travelers. While these researchers substantiate their analysis and even present very definitive conclusions about the Bedouin population in Palestine, their work is rife with judgmental bias.[28] While I do not deny the fact that the information they gathered can be used (in the absence of other sources), it should be used with a certain degree of caution. The quantitative input and information they gathered about tribes or place names is valuable; less so their qualitative analysis of field findings and interpretations of attitudes, strategies, and interactions among these communities.

Four examples of such historical scholars – Uriel Heyd, Moshe Sharon, Moshe Ma'oz, and Adil Manna'[29] – and their studies on the Bedouin population in Palestine during the Ottoman period – illustrate this problem: Heyd based his research on a collection of Sultanic decrees from the famous Muhimme Defterleri collection in Ottoman archives. These decrees often discuss Bedouin insurrection and insubordination, including frequent references to wars that erupted between Ottoman forces stationed in the region and the Bedouin.[30] The Ottoman government viewed the Bedouin as a threat and a nuisance, and often inflicted cruel punishment upon them that was not meted out on troublesome villagers.[31]

In his study on the Bedouin in Palestine in the 16th and 17th centuries, Moshe Sharon endorsed Heyd's conclusions. Basing his argument on Arabic chronicles and descriptions provided by European travelers, Sharon seasons his accounts with terror: raids on trade caravans and pilgrims, and highwaymen demanding ransom.[32] Thus, was Sharon's attitude toward the relationships between inhabitants of the desert and the sown as enemies locked in mortal combat forged.

In his 1968 work, Moshe Ma'oz claimed that a key preoccupation of the Ottoman regime was fighting the Bedouin tribes. He defines this struggle in historical terms as "... an ancient theme in ... Middle Eastern life".[33] For example, in the subsection of his book that discusses Bedouin turbulence and aggression, he wrote:

> After a short period of peace and order under the Egyptians [1831–1840], the Syrian provinces became again a vulnerable target [for] Bedouin aggression and turbulence; as in the pre-reform era, the main victim was the peasant [Fellahin]. Bedouin tribes, driven in spring from the desert to find pasture for their flocks, would periodically raid villages and lay them waste [...]. Places like Homs and Hama in Syria, Bethlehem, Jericho, and Gaza in Palestine, were almost constantly surrounded by nomads and sometimes even besieged by them. One major target of Bedouin assault were the roads. Almost no road in Syria or Palestine was free from this menace: Travelers and caravans were, as in the past, constantly subject to Bedouin attack and pillage.[34]

Heyd's, Sharon's and Ma'oz's works all reproduce and enhance well-known stereotypes of the Bedouin; tropes that until today many scholars accept without question, incorporating these into their own studies as well-documented historical fact. These same weaknesses are evident in Adil Manna's study of an essay on the Farrukh (a Bedouin tribe), the governors of Jerusalem, and their relations with the Bedouin, that stresses the weakness of central government and its inability to restrain "rebellious" Bedouin, while the researcher viewed positively the Ottoman government's curtailment of Bedouin activity in the first half of the 16th century as a relative improvement (that subsequently petered out toward the end of the century).[35] Manna' even devoted a second study to the Jerusalem district, this time to the volatile relations between the Farrukhs, the Bedouin, and the Fellahin.[36] Ties between Bedouin and governors were always depicted as being at the expense of the settled population; here, Manna' goes to lengths to describe how the local provincial elite (such as the governor, Muhammad Ibn Farrukh) betrayed their duty to protect the populace and allied themselves instead with "ruthless nomads".[37]

Collectively, all of these studies paint a negative picture, placing an incorrect focus on structural violence as a defining factor in relations between Bedouin and Fellahin in Palestine. The Bedouin are portrayed as wild and barbaric: terrorizing the urban and village populations, commercial convoys, and pilgrims throughout the Ottoman Empire. These descriptions fit into the genre of Orientalist, ethnocentric, and eclectic accounts; unsurprisingly, they have attracted harsh criticism over the years. Dror Ze'evi, for example, viewed the Bedouin as an integral part of the Ottoman Empire's politics, culture, and economy.[38] They were as much a part of society in the districts of Palestine as were villagers or town-dwellers, he argued, adding that Bedouin served as soldiers and commanders in the armed forces of all local governors in the 17th century. A case in point of such a role filled by Bedouin sheikhs is Ibn Farrukh, who controlled the northern regions of Transjordan for several decades. Another example is the sheikhs from the Trabay family, who were governors of Lajjun district (16 km northwest of Jenin, Megiddo area).[39]

The third genre of literature on interrelations between the Bedouin and the Fellahin is by geographical researchers, authored mainly in the second half of the 20th century. These include Arnon Medzini; Yosef Ben David; Amnon Barkai and Yosef Ben David; Avshalom Shmueli; Gil Kaufman; and Gideon Golani.[40] These academics studied the Bedouin population in Palestine during the Ottoman Empire, under British rule,[41] and in the modern State of Israel. Their descriptions of the Bedouin population are presented mainly in geographical terms: settlements; immigration; and the transition from a nomadic existence, via a semi-nomadic way of life, to sedentarizaion in Bedouin villages.

These researchers suggested that, in general, Bedouin life followed a linear process with a beginning, a middle, and an end, i.e., from nomads to semi-nomads to permanent settlers in a defined setting. The outcome, they argued, is the inevitable end of a distinct Bedouin culture. As Avshalom Shmueli declared in *The End of the Nomads* (1980):

> The expected development of the Beer Sheba sub-district in the coming decades [...] requires that planning be done not only in housing and in economic projects. The authorities must pay attention to cultural and social integration of Bedouin within the population of the Beer Sheba sub-district, and integrate them into the economy of the entire region.[42]

Note that these researchers focused mainly on Bedouin settlement in Bedouin villages, during the Mandate era and after the establishment of the State of Israel in 1948. They rarely referred to Bedouin settlement and integration in existing Arab towns and villages in the Galilee. This elision may be for one or more of several reasons (a) Focus: this was not the subject of their study as stated; (b) Absence of subtext: a lack of characterization and an inability to identify the subtleties and distinctions characterizing the two populations, Bedouin and Fellahin, living together in Arab towns and villages in the Galilee; and (c) Preconceptions: such mixed settlements were not consistent with the dominant perception of two rival, diametrically opposed communities.

The current book combines abstract and coherent epistemology to propose a far more complex relationship that portrayed in the existing literature. On one hand, each sub-grouping – Bedouin, and Fellahin – adopts and integrates-acculturates aspects of the other's culture, at times creating shared patterns and similarities. On the other hand, and alongside the first, each subgroup also aspires to remain separate, to preserve aspects of their unique culture, even striving for cultural and social distance between the two groupings in order to ensure this. Thus, for example, in certain ways and under certain circumstances, the distances and differences between the populations in Bedouin-Fellahin mixed villages actually become sharpened through the proximity of the two groups.

This book seeks to overturn the Orientalist assumptions of 19th-century Western travelers, and 20th-century historians and geographical researchers, by presenting ethnographic studies that highlight coherence, interaction, and co-existence between Bedouin and Fellahin. To date, no diachronic research has been conducted encompassing the social, economic, political, and cultural processes characterizing the Bedouin who settled in existing Arab towns and villages in the Galilee. The fact that this study is the first of its kind underscores its importance. The material presented herein contradicts the assumption that Bedouin and Fellahin are historical rivals, and instead articulates a history of cooperation forming at the beginning of the 21th century.

Historically, there have been integrative relations between the Bedouin and Fellahin. The anthropological study of Daniel Bates (and other anthropologists as described in detail later in the book), which describes the relations between nomad and Fellahin populations in Syria, provides a good example.[43] Bates proposed that ecological conditions contributed to the symbiosis between Bedouin and Fellahin. One example thereof is in the integration of the land uses of the Bedouin and Fellahin: Bedouin sell livestock products, such as milk, cheese, butter, meat, and skins, to the Fellahin, and buy agricultural products from them in exchange. The Fellahin work the land; after harvesting, the Bedouin bring their herds into the fields, contributing to land fertilization ahead of the forthcoming planting season.[44]

Definitions vs. Depictions in the Existing Literature

Although this is a book, not a dissertation, the review of the existing literature above is essential as a point of departure for various reasons. While I employ shared definitions and concepts with prior scholars, the theoretical framework upon which the work at hand is based is largely my *response* or *reaction* to the depictions in the existing literature.

In light of the above, the first priority should be definition of the research population terminology: What is meant by the terms *Fallah* ["farmer"] and *kafr* ["village"] that one finds in existing studies on Arab Fellahin villages in Israel? Secondly, how do we define the terms "Bedouin" and "tribe?"

Definition of the terms *Fallah* and *kafr*

The term *Fallah* in Arabic connotes a farmer or agricultural worker in the Middle East and North Africa, derived from those who work the soil/farm (as the act of ploughing and sowing) to yield a crop.[45] The farmer in the Middle East usually worked two fields: Their first plot was plain soil, where in winter the Fallah grew wheat and barley, and in summer sorghum, sesame, watermelons, legumes, and so forth; their second field was mountainous soil, where the Fallah tended orchards (olives, figs, pomegranates, grapes, etc.).[46] Land is at the heart of the Fallah's life. The livelihoods of approximately 65% of the Arab village inhabitants in Palestine one year before the end of the British Mandate (1947) rested on agricultural work.[47]

Yet, according to Henry Rosenfeld, in his study in Turan in the 1950s, all of the villagers were considered and defined in the Galilee as Fellahin, although not all were necessarily farmers.[48] They were divided into several categories of employment: agriculture (farming their lands), ploughmen (engaged in farming for one-fifth of the harvest), agricultural labourers (field hands), and shepherds (some who owned the flock, others hired to tend a flock), camel drivers (transporting goods from villages to towns), merchants, small craftsmen, and teachers.[49] However, Rosenfeld called the future of Fellahin villages into question, as Fellahin had become proletarians marked by a shift from agricultural work that tied them to the soil, to hired labour in the village and beyond. Thus, Rosenfeld argued, most Fellahin had lost their agricultural identity. I take issue with this assertion, as there is a social structure with deep-seated, ancient, symbolic clan-based cultural memory that survives this process. Therefore, it is incumbent upon us to examine from a diacritical perspective the relations between Fellahin and ruling parties in the Middle East: the impact of the Ottomans, the British, and the Israeli authorities on the Fellahin's urbanization and identity, as well (but this subject is beyond the scope of this work).

Negative Image of Middle East Fellahin in the Pre-Modern Era

There is no doubt that the Fellahin population of the Middle East throughout history was shaped by a feudal regime. Ibn Khaldun described the pattern of Fellahin settlement in the 14th century: They live "on isolated farms and in villages in mountainous areas",[50] whose livelihood rested on agriculture for whom, according to Ibn Khaldun, grain crops were more suitable than for nomads. We can surmise that Ibn Khaldun's outlook on Fellahin stemmed from his grouping of Fellahin along with Berbers and non-Arab peoples, as less robust stock that need and seek "comfort and luxury in their living conditions and customs".[51]

Even after Ibn Khaldun, historical and Islamic literature continued to describe the Fellahin using negative imagery. This was evidenced in the writings of elites as well as Western travellers, both describing Fellahin as ignorant, submissive, and miserable. For example, during the reign of the Mamelukes (1250–1517) when Egypt established its rule over Palestine; Egyptian historian Ibn Iyas (son of a Mameluk father) described the meek submission of Fellahin to governors of the towns and villages, who forced the Fellahin to store their crops in the local chieftains' storehouses, then during shortages of basic commodities in the marketplace such as flour, sold them back their products at double the price.[52] Historian Abd al-Fatah Ashur wrote in 1976:

> Fellahin are great black [sic. dark-complected] inhabitants, some of them in the Mameluk period typified by negligence and contempt until the expression 'Fallah' during this period became synonymous with a feeble and desperate man. This situation increased even further because of the culture of taxes and oppression by government officials and clerks who took inordinate sums of money from them [the Fellahin].[53]

Another account by Al-Maqrizi (1364–1442), testified to sharp increases in grain prices in Egypt, *Al-Sham* [the Levant], and Iraq.[54] When Fellahin appealed to the Mameluk governor to reduce taxes, he told his military forces to beat and arrest them.[55]

Harassment and rigidity void of any compassion continued, even increasing, under Ottoman rule. Historian Abd al-Rahman bin Hassan Al-Jabarti (1753–1822), described injustices to Egyptian villagers, especially in the 18th century, as a consequence of new Ottoman decrees [*firmans*] that further oppressed village dwellers such as "right-of-way" fees, beyond existing ones.[56] There were fines for the death of farm animals (donkeys and horses) and for presence of plant diseases and pests such as mice, imposing a severe economic burden that caused a sharp rise in prices of livestock.[57] Occasionally there were cases of entire villages being burned to the ground by a local governor for refusal (or inability) to pay taxes to the Ottoman governor [*wali*]. A prime example in the records of such events was the burning of Lebanese villages in the Beqaa Valley (Wadi al-Biqa') in 1747 by the Druze tax collector [*multiz*] Amir Melhem al-Shuhabi.[58] This state of affairs prompted the *wali* of Damascus, As'ad Pasha al-Azem,[59] to go personally to investigate the delay in payment of taxes.[60]

Until the early 19th century in Egypt, and until the middle of the 20th century in the rest of the Arab countries, the land regime was based on *iltizam*, or leasing out the gathering of taxes based on recruiting senior military personnel, heads of important families, Bedouin sheikhs, clerics, and others. Each tax collector [*multiz*] was assigned one or more villages from which he was expected to levy taxes on behalf of the Ottoman regime, and a private plot of land for his own use at a fixed rate paid to the state. These *pashas* usually received their income from the villagers.[61]

Thus, the *Fallah* was at the bottom of the economic ladder, forced to live under harsh conditions: "he was, in essence, enslaved to his *pasha* and even forbidden to leave his village without permission, even for a limited time".[62] Burckhardt described the Fellahin's arduous living conditions in villages in Syria and Palestine – especially the villages in the Hauran Mountains – where the men slept in the living room [*madafa*], and families subsisted mainly on legumes, eating meat only on holidays and at weddings.[63] One needs to keep in mind that the sources of these descriptions of Fellahin as the wretched of the earth come from elites, and Western travellers; in later studies, this image of submission and unhappiness was refuted.

Changes in the Conditions and Status of the Fellahin in the Modern Era

Between the years 1812–1814, Muhammad Ali Pasha abolished the *iltizam* system in Egypt, and in the 1830s, tax farming ceased in the rest of the Ottoman Empire.[64] As part of land reforms between 1839–1876, called *Tanzimat*,[65] many changes were implemented that negatively affected the lives of the farmers. In 1858, a Land Code was enacted; in

1861, the Tabu Code followed that established a Land Registry of ownership. However, under the clauses of these laws, the state repossessed many lands: *Mulk, Miri,* or *Amiri* land (for an example, see Appendix B) and *Waqf, Matruke,* and *Mawat* land.[66] Following the reform, taxes were collected directly from the villager's farmers.[67] In practice, the *Tanzimat* led to dispossession of most of the Fellahin (as well as the Bedouin) in the Middle East, who thus lost ownership of the land they had worked, becoming, in essence, tenant farmers. This occurred because when government officials came to make precise measurements in order to record ownership of the land, they met primarily with *mukhtars* and urban elites [*ayan*], who registered most of the land in their own names.[68] For example, in Syria, large tracts of land were registered in the names of well-placed families such as the Al-Azem, Al-Abadi, Al-Jaza'ari, Al-Ayubi, and Al-Kutali families, and others.[69]

As fragmentary as the writing may be, all of the aforementioned testifies to the plight of the Middle East Fellahin population during the 18th and 19th centuries and even into the first half of the 20th century. However, the power relations between Fellahin and landowners were not as one-sided as previously assumed by past scholars. Gabriel Baer pioneered understanding of what he termed "agrarian relations" and the relationship between the ruler, land-owning elites, and the Fellahin. He viewed these agrarian relations as more complex than those described in the writings of elites up to the 19th century. Baer collected testimonies on this topic in the course of his research on Egyptian peasant uprisings in the 18th, 19th, and the first half of the 20th century.[70] He also examined the balance of power between Fellahin and landowners, and found that contrary to the conventional image of the submissive Fallah, there were many rebellions, some of which succeeded. For example, the 1820–1 rebellion in the Egyptian village Al-Selmiya (in the Qana district) broke out against government officials in response to imposition of heavy taxes. In 1823–5, another revolt broke out because Ismail Pasha forced the Fellahin to work in his new, large estates at wages lower than the norm. In 1919, Fellahin rebelled against requirements that they join units operating against the British, while the Ottomans commandeered their livestock for this purpose. Inhabitants of Asyut, a village in Upper Egypt, fought against large landowners such as Mahmoud Suleiman. To a certain extent, this phenomenon was elevated from the local to the national level when Sa'id Zaglul of the *Al-Wafed* party described a revolt that broke out in 1951 that had been set in motion by increases in the rental price of land that led to social and economic instability, as a popular "uprising".[71] Baer summed up misconceptions of the passive Fallah's image thusly:

It can be concluded that in the past two hundred years, there have been quite a few peasant revolts in Egypt against recruitment, taxation, expropriation of land and livestock, lowering wages and raising rents – including rebellions that reached a magnitude that only a significant military effort could suppress. It turns out that generalizations of the 'surrender of Egyptian Fallah' are based solely on this or that impression whose significance doesn't extend past the moment when it was created and are completely subjective.[72]

Baer's appraisal suggests that in fact, the Fellahin persisted in their rebellion against tremendous odds and refused to accept their disgraceful conditions. In addition, the government found it difficult to silence these rebellions. Alongside uprisings in Egypt and later as well, rebellions took place in Syria and Palestine. The greatest revolt of all took place in 1834, in response to drafting the Fellahin into the army of Muhammad Ali Pasha and against commandeering of livestock and grain for the Egyptian army in Syria and Palestine.[73]

Thus, in fact, in the pre-modern era, the negative and submissive image of Fellahin was largely without foundation. While Fellahin in villages across the Middle East and North Africa were portrayed as living under threat and humiliation and exploitation, in a stroke of secondary victimization, they were discounted in period accounts written by "their betters" as, in essence, having been deserving of and responsible for their circumstances due to their purported passivity. As for the status of Fellahin in the modern era, in the subtext, the research literature reveals that there were powerful processes afoot under the aegis of "progress" – the Land Code (1858) and *Wilayats* Code (1864) that the Ottomans introduced to modernize their vast empire with a unified administrative hierarchy in all domains – including land management, that when coupled with greed and local corruption, were particularly detrimental to the farmers' way of life, and were even disempowering to the rank-and-file Fellahin's already-inferior status in the Middle East under the local power structure.

Studies on Arab villages in Israel

Among the first ethnographic studies on Arab villages in Israel was the work of Israeli anthropologist Henry Rosenfeld, who specializes in the Arab village's political economy. In 1964, Rosenfeld conducted research in Turan in the Galilee.[74] He focused on the economic and political changes that occurred there,[75] noting that economically, when the State of Israel was established in 1948, agricultural labour as an occupation and livelihood was largely replaced by trade and marketing. Many inhabitants began working in industrial plants in Jewish towns,[76] while a portion of the Fellahin continued to engage in agriculture, raising crops for market as well as selling surpluses from their harvests as in the past, for instance, part of the harvest from their orchards and surpluses of lentils, watermelons, and melons from their own fields. Alongside this, they sometimes raised specific vegetables such as tomatoes, cucumbers, parsley, lettuce, mint, and radishes specifically for market.[77] Rosenfeld's research reflects how agricultural outputs shifted to profit-making (cash crops) from subsidence agriculture for home and hearth, seeking a livelihood even farther afield; farmers opened vegetable stands and greengroceries in Arab towns and villages in the Galilee to maximize profits. One side effects of this process: the diversified independent sources of income also liberated those selling such farm produce from dependence upon the head of the family, who traditionally solely controlling the extended family's capital, thus undermining the existing social order. This led to disintegration and fragmentation of extended clans in the village, Rosenfeld argued.[78]

In 1965, another ethnographic study of the Arab village in Israel, published by Avner Cohen, focused on Kafr Qasem, a village south of the Arab Triangle on the central coastal plain, that hugs the Green Line.[79] In his book,[80] Cohen did not reveal the identity of his informant, but rather used a pseudonym: *Bint al-Hudud*, literally "border daughter" in Arabic. Cohen analyzed diacritically the political changes that Kafr Qasem underwent, especially in clan structure. During the Ottoman period, members of each *hamula* [clan] in the village held-owned land in common (called *musha*) that was rotated among clan members. During British rule, this method was replaced by vertical stratification of large landowners, which led to inequality among the inhabitants. According to Cohen, when Israel was established in 1948, a large part of Fellahin land was "lost".[81] This prompted a change in the prevailing employment model, as villagers were compelled to seek a livelihood elsewhere, as wage labourers in the Jewish sector of the Israeli economy. For instance, villagers in the "*Little Triangle*" (*Al-Muthaluth*, in Arabic)[82] began working in nearby Jewish towns such as Hadera, Netanya, and so forth, and in Tel Aviv.[83] In terms of standard of living, this shift improved the economic situation of poor villagers. Cohen also cited in his research the effect of participation of Arab communities in Israeli municipal and national elections, party politics that sparked a "revival" in clan-based allegiances in Arab villages that were particularly marked in the Knesset elections of 1959.[84]

While Cohen shed light on growing integration of rural Fellahin in labour market in Israel, his research is more descriptive than analytic. Moreover, he did not discuss the effect of Israel's post-war Military Rule (1948–1966) (imposed in Arab-populated areas following the 1948 war, and which was only slowly dismantled over a period of almost two decades) that curtailed the free movement of Arab citizens (curfews, special permits to travel outside their villages, etc.); and how Military Rule shaped the construction of Arab villages in Israel. Cohen's research was sharply criticized by American anthropologist Talal Asad, who viewed Cohen's research as mediocre in quality in terms of his conclusions.[85] Asad charged that Cohen unduly simplified the historical picture up until the 1948 War [*Nakba*] and later, was "very coy" in his description referring to the fact that Cohen ignored the context of military governance,[86] Zionist hegemony, and the marginalized inferior status and relative powerlessness of the Arabs in Israel, presenting developments in villages as the result of "modernization processes that meet a traditional society". Asad rejects there was any shift in the status of the village clan because of participation in elections; on the contrary, Asad asserted that clan structure changed as an outcome of Zionist ideology.[87] In other words, Asad viewed Cohen's study as having a clear ideological bent and as deeply flawed by modernist and Zionist assumptions.

Asad's criticism of Cohen's work also cites Gil Eyal's 1993 article on the Arab village in Israel.[88] Eyal recognized the period of Military Rule (1948–1966) in Israel, labelling it a process of "objectification" that the Arab village underwent at the hands of Jewish society in Israel.[89] Objectification of the Arab village enabled the Zionists to adopt a self-serving view of the relationship between tradition and modernity wherein "the Arab village is presented as a solitary island of tradition in ... a turbulent ocean of progresses".[90]

This Jewish-Israeli orientation that emerged following the establishment of Israel in 1948 was addressed in the work of anthropologist Dan Rabinowitz in his 1997 study of Nazareth, a city with a mixed population of Arabs and Jews.[91] Rabinowitz's work noted an echo chamber effect in collective discourse of Jewish society vis-à-vis the Arab village in Israel, which in turn shaped a hegemonic discourse of military conquest, supremacy, rigid laws, institutions, and power relationships, epitomized in the socio-political name chosen for the Jewish district of Nazareth in the late 1950s: *Nazareth Illit* (Upper Nazareth).[92] The objective of establishing this Jewish presence in the heart of an area densely populated by Arab citizens was to block territorial contiguity of Arab towns and villages in the Galilee – Kafr Kana, Mashhad, Reina, Ein Mahel, Nazareth, Yafa or Yafat al-Nasira – even going so far as to declare this Jewish settlement (*Nazareth Illit*) a separate jurisdiction in 1974.

In his 1998 book *Anthropology and Palestinians*, Rabinowitz continues his criticism of other researchers who investigated Palestinian villages,[93] even criticizing Henry Rosenfeld and Avner Cohen. Rabinowitz claimed that Turan as a village – the subject of Rosenfeld's study – does not reflect or represent a classic Arab village, as its lands were *not* expropriated by the Jewish state in the 1950s, rendering it "ideal" as representing the traditional Palestinian village pre-Israel, but one of little relevance for understanding realities in the Arab sector.[94] In addition, the increased importance of clan in the 1950s, found by Rosenfeld and Cohen, had much to do with timing: Their research was conducted at the height of clans successfully becoming a key element in local municipal and national elections.[95]

Rabinowitz's criticism goes beyond timing and ideological cravats: He criticized Rosenfeld's and Cohen's analytical framework of social analysis that they applied, which was overly influenced by British functional anthropology, primarily structural functionalism that led to sweeping generalizations and shaky axioms, as well as questionable linkages about the nature of things and cause and effect, and the dynamics of other unrelated phenomena. Rabinowitz supported American-Palestinian anthropologist Lila Abu-Lughod's more complex approach as presented in her 1986 study of the Bedouin in Egypt,[96] which holds that there is far more heterogeneity in individuals' inner and emotional worlds that defies pat classifications.[97] In a similar vein, the structure of the *hamula*, as well as the village, is not uniform or a constant, and should not be analyzed functionally. Rabinowitz, therefore, challenged the research of these scholars, regarding them as having adopted an inappropriate functionalist approach to their subject. On the other hand, Rabinowitz does not clearly present alternatives for conducting research on Palestinian inhabitants of Israel.

Recall that the political context of an Arab minority in a Jewish state is of *marginal* significance in the study at hand, although there is no doubt that to a certain extent, it influenced the integration of Bedouin into Fellahin towns and villages in the Galilee as a reaction to government policies in the 1950s and 1960s: efforts to overturn the demographic composition of the Galilee and the Naqab/Negev with their overwhelmingly indigenous Arab populations, alongside expropriation of land held by Bedouin and Fellahin.

This policy was a mixture of spatial, social, and ethnic planning. In his 1997 study of Majd al-Krum during the years 1985 and mid-1995, Oren Yiftachel shed light on this combination of objectives.[98] Yiftachel believed that control of a minority population and forced ethnic mixing constituted a recipe for ongoing conflict between the dominant Jewish majority and the minority it was seeking to control and mould, clout that Yiftachel believed was destined to wane over time.[99] In examining this assumption, he found that in the first three decades following Israel's establishment, Majd al-Krum (according to estimates of its local council, mostly corroborated by Israel Lands Authority documents) lost 13,865 dunams/13.86 sq. km. to expropriation, which constituted approximately 69% of the village land, subsequently allocated for development of Jewish settlement (*Yihud*, in Hebrew) in this area.[100] This land expropriation policy caused conflict and even sparked protests by village inhabitants: For instance, participation of Arab village inhabitants in the 30 March 1976 mass protest that became known as Land Day (*Yawm al-'Ard*, in Arabic);[101] a large demonstration in 1977 in Majd al-Krum protesting demolition of a house built without a building permit; protest in 1983 of the establishment of a new Jewish settlement, and demands by the villagers to expand Majd al-Krum's municipal boundaries; 1985 protests of the route of the Acre-Safad road and issuance of demolition orders for houses built within a forbidden construction space.[102] Yiftachel's predictions about the ramification of expropriation of land from Arab inhabitants proved correct: It led local populations such as the inhabitants of Majd al-Krum to challenge this policy, protests that led authorities to roll back spatial planning policy.[103] Thus, the overall perspective in studies that purported to profile the Arab village, and focus of research on primarily economic changes, is far too narrow, and even through this limited prism, was superficial and highly biased. Suffice it to say that Bedouin who moved to Arab villages remain invisible in the research literature.

While the work at hand cannot rectify all of the flaws in existing knowledge in the scholarly literature of the Arab village, it does seek to shed light on a phenomenon that escaped previous scholars almost entirely: a comprehensive description and analysis of mixed Bedouin-Fellahin villages in the Galilee. Unlike previous works' focus on the economic sphere (further marred by a skewed self-congratulatory narrative of modernity), the canvas of the work at hand is much broader – addressing social, economic, political, and even cultural aspects – and therefore is far more complex. Yet before embarking on this task in earnest, it is imperative to clarify – define and explain – the term "Bedouin" and its inherent relationship to the concept of "tribe".

Definition of the terms "Bedouin" and "Tribe"[104]

The term *Bedouin* (*badawi* in Arabic) is derived from the word *badia*, which means "desert", thus it derived as a designation for "desert dwellers". In the past, Bedouin (this work has opted to use the same term as a singular and plural proper noun in English) traditionally lived in a tribal framework. A tribe consists of a grouping that constitutes a social, cultural, economic, and political organization[105] whose members generally resided in the same geographical unit that they have chosen for themselves (or have come to dwell in consequent to tribal rivalries or other external pressures).

Throughout history, the Bedouin population has experienced a process of dynamic and unremitting changes in their way of life. Historian Abd Al-Rahman Ibn Khaldun in the 14th century described nomadic Bedouin in his book *Muqaddimah* ["introduction"] as a "natural group".[106] In addition, the relationships between members of a specific tribe are based on tribal allegiance or loyalty to kinship, "*al-asabiyah al-qabaliyah*", literally, "a sense of solidarity" between tribe members. Originating in the root *'asab* ["nerve"]*'asabiyah* denotes a strong sense of "us", or the self-evident solidarity and intimacy that most cultures associate with the nuclear family, but in this case extended to a wider kinship group. In other words, according to Ibn Khaldun, the tribe is a social group that conforms to ecological conditions wherein it is located in order to prevail. Ibn Khaldun's ecological paradigm is, however, problematic, as it is deterministic, which is characterized by linearity; and is fixed on unidirectionality. In the subtext, Ibn Khaldun assumes that "Bedouin identity" and "urban identity" are dichotomous and essentially incompatible. As he put it:

> We find that urban culture is a goal for the Bedouin; he [the Bedouin] strives to reach it by his own strength [*sic* – attain it on his own], which is the fate of all urban-bound Bedouin. [By contrast] the urbanite does not aspire to live in a desert, [he does so] only in extreme cases that force him to do so.[107]

This paradigm does not discuss daily interactions and practices that are performed (including ceremonies) in tribes themselves, and does not even mention individual actions or heterogeneity within tribes. Rather, it describes the tribe as one cohesive group.[108] Accordingly, the definition of "tribe" as a cohesive cultural entity continued exist long after Ibn Khaldun. in his book *Kinship and Marriage in Early Arabia* (1903), Robertson W. Smith described in part the complexity of tribes (such as inter-tribe quarrels: Ous vs. Khazarj, Baker vs. Ta'alb, Abas vs. Debian) at the advent of Islam.[109] Each tribe was considered a segment related to blood ties. For instance, when a member of a certain tribe was murdered, the victim's tribe members immediately joined together and declared, "Our [in the plural] blood has been spilled". Tribal members call themselves *ahel* or *qom*, i.e., "community",[110] as in a cohesive segment. Smith took this attribute and applied it to describe and explain the workings of tribes throughout the Arab countries in general, viewing them as identical in their cultural, social, and political characteristics. Smith's book remains too vague and rife with generalizations to explain the complexity of the tribe, and therefore was criticized by later scholars.[111] Smith's observations reveal overdependence on segmentary theory. It is functionalist and problematic in trying to understand the tribal structure, assuming each tribe has internal segments that maintain the existing order and contribute to sustaining the tribe's existence, wherein every member of the tribe receives protection and support from the rest of his or her lineage. This theory, however, fails to note, theoretically or empirically, the political, social, and economic dynamics within tribal society. Such conclusions were subsequently "confirmed" by anthropologists who worked in colonial overseas capacities in the 19th and first half of 20th century.

Accordingly, the founders of anthropology as a science *assumed* not only that the tribe is the basic building block of the social, economic, and cultural unit, but they moreover assumed that members of a given tribe were of common ancestral origin. The tribe became a model for tagging and dissecting other nomadic tribes in the Middle East and Africa. A pioneer and proponent of this theory was anthropologist Evans Pritchard.[112] In the 1940s, Pritchard described the Nuer tribe in the Upper Nile in Sudan, saying that lineage organization (in a closed, homogeneous unit in tribal territories) determined or dictated the inhabitants' social, economic, and political behaviour, and emanated from the absence of a strong central government, commenting:

> When a man [in the tribe] feels that he has suffered an injury, there is no authority in order to whom he can make a complaint and from whom he can obtain redress, so he at once challenges the man who has wronged him to a duel, and the challenge must be accepted.[113]

In other words, the only chance for a tribe member to obtain justice, to receive compensation for damage caused him or her, or to protect him- or herself from other factions, was by joining forces with his/her tribe, thus internal tribal organization was functional. Pritchard defined tribe members as "collectivists", i.e., anglers, hunters, and gatherers who worked in tandem, and even eat together. Accordingly, the organization of the tribe and their behaviour was based on a fusion within the segmental structure, based on mutual commitment to all other members of the tribe.[114] Another similar but more recent study (1990) based on the same segmentary theory was conducted by anthropologist Emrys Peters on Bedouin tribes of Cyrenaica in Libya.[115] Peters divided the big tribe (tribal headquarter) down into small tribes (essentially identical segments), each tribe on a genealogical kinship to one shared ancestor. However, the novelty of Peters' approach-prognosis (compared to Evans Pritchard) is that while the ecology is changing, segmentation does not,[116] i.e., if a tribe moves from one place to another, such as from the desert to the town, its members remain a single segment unit.

Following these studies characterizing the tribe, recently conducted studies reflect new approaches, and undermine the old theory of tribal definition. They view this theory as too general and the tribe as far from being a segmental society. A pioneer in this approach was anthropologist Dale F. Eickelman, who conducted research on the Banu Bataw tribe in Morocco, published in 1998.[117] Eickelman raises two fundamental questions: The first: What is the definition of a tribe? And the second: Is the concept of segment theory relevant to understanding the tribal system? His answer to the first question was that "tribe" can be understood according to four criteria: Firstly, the definition of individual tribe members of selfhood as a tribe: In general, they are descendants of a common ancestor, and he is a man. Secondly, states use the term "tribe" for administrative purposes: The state deals with tribesmen as an administrative unit (not individuals) – i.e., as a category/collective entity – in enforcing the law on them or exacting performance of civil duties from them. Thirdly, the functions of tribe internally, in practice: These are the social values and behavioural norms of the tribe members. Fourthly, anthropological perceptions of tribe: "The anthropological interpretation on the tribe".[118]

In answering the second question, Eickelman completely rejects use of segmentary theory to analyze interactions and practices within the tribe. As he wrote in *The Middle East and Central Asia: An Anthropological Approach*:

> These are some of the principal objections to segmentary lineage theory. As an ideology of social relations among many tribal groups in the Middle East, the nation of segmentation has considerable importance. As a sociological model, it is inadequate. I have dealt with it at length only because it has mistakenly led many anthropologists to explain

virtually every problem in tribal social relationships in terms of the lineage system.[119]

Paul Dresch demonstrated the same, based on two cultural factors: "honour" [*sharaf*] and "respect" [*aihtiram*] among Bedouin of the Hashid and Bakil tribes in Yemen.[120] Incidentally, he disagreed completely with segmental theory, arguing that there is a structural hierarchy with practical responsibility for fulfilling the social and cultural concepts within the tribe. Thus, for example, the maintenance of *sharaf* hinges on safeguarding *'ard*,[121] and each individual has a different role in taking responsibility for these concepts, including in practice.[122]

Another criticism of segmentary theory was levelled by anthropologist Stephen Caton in his study of the Berber tribes in Morocco[123] wherein Caton challenges Pritchard's and Peters's approaches, which in his view perceive the clan as a "bloc" against another tribe. Caton proposed (as did Eickelman) that there is usage of specific cultural components such as power, beliefs, and language as a means of mediating and resolving both tribal and intertribal tribal conflicts.[124] Moreover, lineage segmentation of tribe is hardly uniform, as can be seen from the conclusions of Talal Asad in his observations of Kababish tribes in northern Sudan.[125] Asad reported that the tribal composition was based on two linkages: The first, direct offspring [*nassel*] – patrilineal descendant (a blood relative in the direct line of descent, i.e., the children, grandchildren, great-grandchildren, etc.); the second, social relations [*qrabuh*], which encompasses other, more distant relations. Offspring is defined by the father's blood kinships, while social relations does not require this. The latter rests on custom or the habit of defining certain families from other tribes living in the same mixed tribe as a kinship group.[126] Asad's findings clearly reject a uniform picture and confirm heterogeneity within the tribe.

Many studies totally reject the segmentary theory,[127] and have even taken to task those researchers who have but taken issue with this or that aspect of the theory of segments. New approaches explain Bedouin and tribal processes from a totally new and fresh theoretical and conceptual standpoint. Scott Atran, for example, claims that Eickelman conflated two terms[128] – description, and interpretation – and that these two approaches have an epistemological order that is diametrically opposite to what Eickelman presented.[129] According to Atran:

> Eickelman might reasonably have been expected to proceed with an analysis of the tribe in terms of underlying social and material relationships; Instead, he appeals to the implicit notion of 'practical' ideology,

rather than to formally explicit ideology, as a basis for understanding the tribe, in particular, and Middle Eastern society, in general.[130]

Therefore, Atran suggested using "explicit ideology", which can offer interpretation outside the tribe.[131] In other words, the possibility of writing as reliable a commentary as is humanly possible (without emotions interfering as a result of cultural constructs of this or that tribe) hinges on the writer going outside the boundaries of the tribe to reach his or her conclusions.

Atran's critique of Eickelman's research was but a prelude to Donald Cole's 2003 article, which opens with a question: "Where Have the Bedouin Gone?"[132] Cole's answer is that during Ottoman and British rule, the Bedouin usually lived within tribal framework, and the tribe was their social, cultural, economic, and political framework. Their lifestyle – their economy and very identity as an integral part of their particular tribe – was for the most part based on ecology. But this changed when Ottoman land laws created a new ecology marked by the ascendancy of urban elites [*effendis*] controlling large estates, and who dispossessed Bedouin and many Fellahin from their lands and even curtailed the Bedouin's pastureland; by industrialization (the oil industry in Libya and the Gulf states and opening of factories in the 1950s); and erosion of traditional norms and values under the impact of modernization characterized by education, health, and social mobility for employment, all of which constituted a real and grave threat to the lifestyle of the Bedouin population of the Middle East. These threats caused a large portion of the Bedouin population to sedentarize, either in existing towns and villages, or government-promoted permanent Bedouin settlements. Thus, they became citizens of countries with identity cards and the right to vote. Incidentally, while Cole viewed segmentary theory as irrelevant, as it reflected a rather narrow dimension,[133] he ultimately concluded that the fact that *lifestyle* changes does not necessarily mean that cultural and social *identity* is lost or assimilated. For example, Saudi Arabian Bedouin who abandoned camels and replaced them with trucks in transporting fuel and water to their grazing land; and Syrian Bedouin in Syria who are sheep and meat traders (middlemen). While loyalty to the tribe has shifted to loyalty to the nation-states, this has not necessarily changed *self-ascription*. Francoise Metral summed this up in one sentence in 2000: "Lifestyles change, but identities remain".[134]

This is the departure point of my research, set forth in this book. Cole's and Metral's conclusions are indeed correct and relevant to the Bedouin population in Israel. In part, they were expressed in anthropologist Emanuel Marx's study in the 1970s on economic changes among Israeli Bedouin living in two different geographical locations (the Naqab/Negev and the Galilee).[135] Marx supports a "cultural ecology" approach that is similar to Ibn Khaldun's ecological theory. This old-new theory suggests that environmental or ecological conditions are what shape the cultural and behavioural patterns of individuals in a given culture. This school of thought, largely fathered by American anthropologist Julian Steward in his seminal 1977 piece on the "concept and method of cultural ecology"[136] has since been honed and improved over time. Particularly worthy of mention are the changes made to this theory by American anthropologist Marvin Harris in his study of the reason for sanctification of the cow in India,[137] which Harris termed "cultural materialism".[138]

To return to Marx: The Israeli anthropologist notes that on the one hand, Middle Eastern Bedouin have increasingly integrated into the economic and civil life surrounding them due to ecological necessity, including lack of water sources and grazing lands.[139] At the same time, in his study of Israeli Bedouin, he found that they seek to preserve the unique character of their lives, thus maintaining control over increasing proximity to the orbit of surrounding Israeli society while maximizing the material utility of such ties. Marx viewed Bedouin living in towns as a reflection of the significant change in lifestyle that comes with caveats: While such a move involves loss of assets and reduction or even abandonment of agrarian life entirely, he believed that there are no substantive cultural changes, thus he defines their condition as "semi-urbanization".[140] These Bedouin migrate in large groups of lineages, cluster in "tribal enclaves" in urban neighbourhoods,[141] and tend to preserve social ties with their father's and mother's tribes for marriage of their offspring. Marx's conclusions attest to the fact that ecology plays a significant role in Bedouin society, particularly evident in economic terms. Nonetheless, the degree of cultural separation that Bedouin preserve is marked, and this is apparently, in part, the product of identity politics. These urban clusters are designated by Bedouin in terms of status as "the Fellahin Bedouin" in Arabic, preserving cultural components of tribe membership with kin geographically distanced from them. In other words, these are people who physically left the tribe, but continue to belong to the tribe in the town, as well.

While Marx's research provided a welcome foundation for a study that focuses on "the town Bedouin" (he called it "the tribalism in the town"),[142] it differs significantly from my work on a number of levels. First of all, Marx focused on economic aspects of Naqab/Negev Bedouin and their relationship with the surrounding society, including Jewish-

Israeli society. His work did not examine Bedouin settlers from a historic perspective; nor does it examine the socio-economic and cultural interactions between town dwellers (Bedouin and Fellahin), although it does address the differences and similarities between them that are the result of structural and emergent processes. Nonetheless, there is a common denominator between the two studies, namely that there are no "binary oppositions" between Bedouin and other populations.[143]

In this context, a more focused study of the Bedouin population living alongside the indigenous Arab population of towns was conducted by anthropologist Gideon Kressel in 1975,[144] wherein Kressel described the dynamics in Bedouin communities in the Juarish neighbourhood of Ramle. Kressel's work draws on two opposing philosophical approaches: "ecological-demographic determinism", and "cultural determinism". According to the first approach, the social order is determined by environmental conditions (sources of livelihood: extent of exhaustion of means of exploitation, manner of allocation, etc.). According to the second approach, the social order is determined by culture (moral codes, art, opinions, etc.).[145] Kressel argued that the social structure can be elucidated by embracing and meshing both these theories, based on assumptions that the sociological effects of ecology and culture factors shape the social structure and therethrough, the conditions of matter and cultural patterns effects on one another. Thus, Kressel's main contribution was the inclusive theoretical framework that he employed, which found room to incorporate in its empirical findings seemingly incompatible perspectives: Through the prism of "ecological-demographic determinism", Kressel concluded that ecological forces that determined the social structure in Juarish communities are sometimes clear-cut, sometimes lead in different directions, and sometimes the trajectories are contradictory or collide. By contrast, "cultural determinism" is far less forgiving and far less equivocal in posture, holding that the nature of the social order is primarily the product of cultural patterns. For instance, endogamous marriages are common among communities in the Juarish neighbourhood (community members and women usually marry in in-group settings and according to their region of origin). Kressel explained that various factors are at work here: division of inheritance, the necessity of strengthening the intra-tribal alliance (a political explanation), and preservation of the purity of origin.[146]

In addition to the work of Marx and Kressel on Bedouin population in Israel, there are additional studies on Bedouin of which I have not, failed to take note: Some address mainly intra-tribal social aspects such as customs, blood feuds, and conflict resolution.[147] Others address geographical aspects, describing the process of sedentarizaion of Bedouin in Bedouin communities or in villages.[148]

Thus, both historical and ethnographic studies of Middle Eastern Fellahin, Arab villages, and Bedouin in general and in Israel in particular, in part serve as a foundation for the research at hand from an epistemological perspective in understanding social, economic, political, and cultural aspects thereof. However, as noted previously, these previous studies did not examine aspects of social and cultural integration. Furthermore, they did not analyze the interrelations between communities within Arab neighbourhoods, and my objective is to fill this gap toward shedding light on the social, cultural, and political dynamics in Arab communities in the Galilee.

In closing, it would be helpful to set forth the theoretical framework of the work at hand for the reader: It champions a cultural structure, agency, and transformation approach,[149] that views the phenomenon of semi-urbanized Bedouin and their relationship with their Fellahin neighbours as a continuous process, with flexible and even liquid boundaries between the two groupings – Bedouin and Fellahin – in almost all aspects of life, from the political and economic to the social and cultural. Also relevant in my mind, and adopted in my theoretical framework, is the theory of identity politics,[150] which emerged in the post-modern era to challenge the melting pot concept. This new structural approach champions and legitimizes the presence of various cultural identity groups in society who maintain their respective cultural and political distinctiveness, and emphasize their uniqueness to leverage their vested political and economic interests.

Framework and Research Boundaries

The literary review and theoretical framework above – with its insights and its shortcomings – helped forge this book's empirical focus, and are reflected in the findings: That in these shared spaces there exists a complex web of social, economic, political, and daily relations and interactions that have created a synergy between Bedouin and Fellahin living in these mixed towns and villages. At the same time, the two groupings continue to preserve and at times create parallel social and cultural differences that signify the otherness between them. Within the realm of theoretical frameworks, these processes can be framed and understood as a process of construction, agencies of change, flexibility, liquid borders, identity politics, and even ever-shifting boundaries between Fellahin and Bedouin, all presented in depth in the chapters that follow.

But before embarking on a detailed discussion of these findings, it would seem prudent to set the stage so to speak, and clarify for the reader in spatial terms what is meant by "in the Galilee" in both this work's title and in the boundaries of the research: The Galilee is circumscribed on the north by the Lebanese border, which is a political border: the international border between Israel and Lebanon. To the east, the Galilee encompasses the Hula Valley, the Sea of Galilee, and the Jordan Valley. To the southeast lies the Marj Ibn Amer plain (Jezreel Valley, or *emek yizrael* in Hebrew) and the Beisan Plain (rebranded by Israeli authorities as "Beit She'an Valley" or "the Valley of *Maayanot* [springs])". To the west, the Galilee extends to the Mediterranean coast, enclosed on the south by Haifa and the Carmel Range (this study includes two localities in the "southern Carmel" as well). It should be noted that the *Little Triangle* area (*Al-Muthaluth*, in Arabic) was *not* included in my study. Although the following chapters focus on a particular place and time, they do not ignore the larger picture of the role of deserts and nomads *across* the region's political boundaries. As aforementioned in this Introduction, my focus is not on *all* of the inhabitants of the Galilee, and not even all of its Bedouin inhabitants, but rather solely mixed towns and villages of Arab populations.[151] Yet that having been said, it does broaden the canvas at the outset to trace and describe historical aspects of the origin of all Bedouin in the Galilee.

According to 2020 data (the last census) from Israel's Central Bureau of Statistics, Population Census (CBSPC), the Galilee Bedouin numbered 63,632.[152] They live in 20 permanent Bedouin settlements (17 of them recognized by Israel authorities). This figure does not, however, include the Bedouin who live in Fellahin towns and villages in the Galilee, since as far as the authorities are concerned, this population is considered part of the rural Fellahin population. Thus, even the data in the work at hand breaks new ground, as it is based on statistical data gathered item by item from the jurisdictions and local councils wherein the research was conducted (records of tax payments and local elections in particular are available in councils), together with in-depth interviews with these "invisible" Bedouin residing in Arab towns and villages in the Galilee.

The population of this study is hardly inconsequential: It was found that the Bedouin population missed-misclassified by the CBSPC stood in 2020 at 44,042,[153] located in 36 mixed Fellahin towns and villages in the Galilee: Thirty villages – Eilabun, Al-B'ena, Nahaf, Al-Jadida, Al-Makr, Al-Maghar, Al-Rama, Iblin, Abu Snan, Isfiya, Daliyat Al-Carmel, Sha'ab, Tarshiha, Deir Hanna, Bu'enie-Nujeidat, Kafr Maser, Uzair, Iksal, Reina, Turan, Jish, Daburiya, Kafr Kana, Kisra, Kabul, Kafr Manda, Sheikh Danun, Ein Mahel, Yafa, Manshiya Zabda – and six towns: Shafa-Amer, Nazareth, Haifa, Sakhnin, Acre, and Tamra. In other words, the Bedouin to date unseen by most anthropologists and misplaced by demographers and statisticians; and absent from the research literature and even official statistical data, constitute about 40.9% of the total Bedouin population in the Galilee. Combined, the urban Bedouin population in the Galilee (including the rest of the Bedouin population in singularly Bedouin communities – 63,632 inhabitants) stands at 107,674 Bedouin in all forms of residence, including nomadic Bedouin in "unrecognized villages",[154] labelled by Israeli officialdom "the Bedouin Diaspora".[155]

One can use a number of demographic indices to weigh the importance of Bedouin inhabitants in Israel. The number of Bedouin in Ramle and Lod (Lydda) is estimated at a mere 16,500. (It is reasonable to assume that there is also a Bedouin population in Jerusalem, but they are not counted for some reason). The total Bedouin population in Israel – 344,174 – constitute about 17.5% of the total Arab population in the country (all told, about 1,956,200), and 3.7% of the total population of Israel (approximately 9,291,592).[156] Whatever the index, a margin of error to the magnitude of 44,000 Bedouin unaccounted for is more than significant.

Structure of the Book

The first chapter provides an historical overview on the beginning of settlement and integration of the Bedouin population into Fellahin villages and towns in the Galilee, from the 18th century until the end of Ottoman rule in 1918. The second chapter describes and examines the integration of Bedouin into Fellahin villages and towns under British rule (from 1918 until 1948). The third chapter analyzes the impact of the 1948 war on the Bedouin, and examines the influx of Bedouin to Fellahin villages and towns in the Galilee and their fate as a consequence of the war. The fourth chapter reviews the ongoing integration of the Bedouin population from the end of the 1948 war until full abolition in 1966 of the Military Rule imposed upon the Arab communities in the aftermath of the 1948 war. The fifth chapter is devoted to discussion of governmental processes and events that contributed and even led to settlement of Bedouin population in existing Fellahin villages and towns in the Galilee in the late 20th century. The sixth and final chapter provides a summary of the findings and whatever conclusions one can draw therefrom.

CHAPTER

1

Historical Background: The Bedouin in Palestine, 1700–1918

This chapter presents an overview of the historical background of Bedouin in the Galilee in general, and their settlement in Arab Fellahin villages and towns in the Galilee in particular, and the dialectic dynamic of interaction and coexistence that existed between Bedouin and Fellahin. Although hard to substantiate in records, in fact, as early as the 18th century and even before that,[1] Bedouin and Fellahin maintained extensive "flexible" interrelations that led Bedouin to became Fellahin, and Fellahin to became Bedouin. Their presence over time provided invaluable input into the research, in tracing the distribution of Bedouin and their patterns of settlement, which have changed over various periods against the backdrop of ongoing economic interactions and practices with Fellahin community. There are parallels in Daniel Bates' research on nomadic and agricultures population in Syria, wherein the author argues that ecology drives a symbiotic relationship between Bedouin and Fellahin.[2] Bates noted that land use is interplayed between Bedouin and Fellahin; Bedouin sell dairy products such as milk, cheese, butter, meat, and animals skins to Fellahin; Fellahin cultivate their land and after their crops are harvested, Bedouin shepherds graze their flocks in Fellahin fields, their livestock helping to fertilize the soil for the next growing season.[3] Although my findings do not support the ecological paradigm in Bates's findings, the dynamics are similar: Practices and interactions existed between two categories – Bedouin and Fellahin – in the Galilee, as well between Bedouin and Fellahin.

Thus, the chapter traces prevailing circumstances under which Bedouin began to settle in villages and towns in the Galilee, describing and analyzing the distribution of Bedouin settlement in rural and urban localities. A good example is the growth of large Bedouin tribes (such as Trabay and Al-Ziadnah) in the Galilee region in the 18th century, who gained control over parts of the country at various times in the past, but ended up settled in Arab towns and villages in the Galilee. Also discussed are the policies of Egyptian and Ottoman rulers during the 19th century to settle and concentrate the Bedouin. Note that the Ottoman government initiated several agrarian reforms consequent to "Modernization Discourse" that borrowed from European colonialism, which impacted on settlement processes among some Bedouin tribes within Arab towns and villages in the Galilee; of particular interest are the *Tanzimat* reforms in the second half of the 19th century and onward that drove continued settlement of Bedouin population in Arab Fellahin towns and villages in the Galilee until the end of Ottoman rule in the second decade of the 20th century. Lastly, to flesh out this process, the chapter homes in from the general to the specific, pinpointing the identities of Bedouin families settled permanently in Fellahin villages and towns at the end of Ottoman rule, and after World War I.

Migration of Bedouin Tribes to Palestine and Early Settlement by Some amongst Fellahin Villages and Towns in the Galilee

Throughout history, there has been a cyclical movement of Bedouin tribes in and out of Palestine: emerging from the desert and moving on to agriculture land, then receding back into the desert. That is, tribes habitually switched back and forth between a nomadic lifestyle and semi-sedentarizaion, then back to nomadic living.[4] At the beginning of the Christian era, several Arabic-speaking tribes lived in the Palestine region, such as the Nabataeans, Thamud, and Banu Salih.[5] From the 3rd century CE to the 6th century, the Ghassanids came from Yemen, and Manadhirah tribes came from southern Iraq and eastern Arabia. They settled in Houran, Balqa in northern Jordan, western Syrian and the Palestine region.[6]

One outstanding case thereof was the migration of large Bedouin tribes to the *Al-Sham* region – that is, including the Galilee, that began with conquest of the Fertile Crescent by Muslims from the end of 7th century. It was a migration of peoples in micro, as some of Banu Judham settled in the area of Tiberias, al-Lajjun, al-Yamun, and Acre; Banu Tay settled in the Haifa area; Banu Lukham settled in Ramle, Houran, and the Golan Heights; Banu Amela settled in the Tiberias area, and Banu Dhubyan settled in the Beisan Valley.[7] The second great migration occurred in the 9th century, when the two great tribes of Banu Hilal and Banu Salim migrated from Najd (the central Arabian Peninsula) to Iraq, later migrating into the Levant, and reaching North Africa in the 11th century.[8] This movement out of the Arabian Peninsula, termed the Arab Conquest, continued even more intensely with the third great migration that occurred during Ottoman rule (1516–1918), mainly at the end of the 16th century and the beginning of the 17th century, due to the wars between the Banu Shammar and Mawali tribes in Iraq, which led to the scattering of many tribe members into the Al-Sham region.[9]

Other migratory waves and settlement of Bedouin were sparked by famine, drought, epidemics, or occupation, which caused many Fellahin to lose their lands, rendering them nomads. From 1517 onward for the next 400 years, the Ottoman Empire ruled over a vast area in the Middle East and North Africa. Ottoman policy, while flexible, was not always consistent; it was not the same and stable in all empire-controlled areas. In addition, there were few plans to settle Bedouin in an effort to remove them from blowing/shifting desert land and to push them onto agricultural land. Moreover, the purpose thereof was to protect the commercial convoys, and especially the *Hajj* convoy.[10]

In their study of Bedouin settlement in the late Ottoman period,[11] Seth Frantzman and Ruth Kark explained the effect of ecology on settlement of Bedouin migrations, which began as early as the 7th century, when Muslims conquered the Middle East and North Africa, and continued until the 20th century. The majority of them were nomadic Bedouin, who settled mainly on coastal plains and in valleys due to appropriate ecological conditions, i.e., good water sources and pastures.[12]

However, the first Ottoman plan to settle a nomadic population into sedentary life was carried out in central and east Anatolia between 1691 and 1696.[13] Resat Kasaba described the recruitment and drafting of tribal groups into the Ottoman army in the 17th century, a campaign that enlisted tens of thousands.[14] The reasons for this settlement effort were to improve the visibility and security of the Ottoman Empire's borders with Austria and Russia by building new citadels and repairing neglected structures in the frontier zones.[15] In addition to the special troops stationed there, the frontier zones had been routinely crossed by peasants, peddlers, and nomads.[16] Indeed, it was in Balkans or in Anatolia, hundreds of nomadic tribes from various parts of Anatolia were settled as *derbends*[17] between Aleppo and Damascus in 1690s.[18] Bedouin generally considered themselves as belonging to Ottoman Empire. As Ze'evi described the Bedouin in this period: "Defending the realm", "an integrated economy and social system".[19] Nonetheless, the Empire regarded them as "civilizational exceptions", as described later in this chapter.

Moreover, from the mid-17th century and through the 18th century, the largest and most important migration of Bedouin took place in the Levant.[20] This migration was accompanied by tribes of Banu Shammar who came from the Shammar Mountains in the northwestern Arabian Peninsula, and Al-Anezzah tribes from Najd. The Euphrates River was a natural border between the two most powerful tribes of this period: Shammar, in eastern Mesopotamia, and Al-Anezzah in northern Syria and in the desert southwest of Damascus.[21]

This big migration was the result of the establishment of the first Saudi (Wahhabis) state in the Arabian Peninsula in the late 17th century. The historical process by which the Bedouin became semi-settlers can be learned from the descriptions of the Arab chronicler Hussein Ibn Ghannam, who descripted this move as mass migration which took place after the final conquest by Wahhabis to the Shammar Mountains – a stronghold of the Shammar tribes – toward the end of the 17th century.[22] This migration led to the two major tribes, Shammar and Al-Anezzah, migrating northward to Iraq. This migration prompted further migrations in the Fertile Crescent region, causing migration of other tribes in this area, such as weak tribes who migrated to the desert of Syria and the outskirts of the blowing land (see Map 1.1.), and were forced to become farmers. Norman Lewis described this intrusion and its consequences:

> Many of the tribal groups which suffered at the hands of the Anizeh [Al-Anezzah] and other incoming tribes in the seventeenth, eighteenth, and nineteenth centuries, and were pushed into agricultural regions on the edge of the desert, naturally tended by degrees to become agriculturalists. Such were some of the Kurds and Turcomans of the northern frontier, the Naim [Al-Na'im] and many Mowali [Mawali] sections of the Homs-Hama area, and the Fadl between Mount Hermon and the Sea of Galilee.[23]

This forced migration,[24] alongside other economic factors, caused the Bedouin tribes to move to the Galilee. On the other hand, in the Naqab, the cause of the Bedouin migration was Napoleon's conquest of Egypt in 1798, as described below.[25] Bedouin tribes settled mainly in three regions in Palestine: The Naqab, Beisan and Marj Ibn Amer valleys, and in the Galilee:

Naqab: Arrival of the great tribes from Egypt, e.g., Tarabin and Tiha (or Tiyaha)[26]

Clinton Bailey described in detail the movement of these tribes in the 18th and 19th centuries.[27] According to Bailey, these tribes arrived from Sinai to the Naqab (1798–1801) following Napoleon's invasion of

Egypt. In the early 19th century, they began to spread to northern Sinai in search of pasture for their flocks, similar to the Al-Tarabin, who, supported by the Ramadin, lived in the northeastern Naqab. The arrival of these two great tribes to the Naqab led to displacement of other tribes northward, such as Al-Howeitat tribe.[28]

In addition, a number of wars took place among Bedouin tribes themselves, which caused migration of Bedouin from one place to another. The Abu Sarhan war (1813–1816), between the Hakuk and Qdirat, who belonged to the headquarters of Al-Tiha, together with the Tarabin, fought all of the neighboring northern tribes: Suarqha, Al-Jbarat, and Al-Atawneh. This caused the displacement of the Banu Atiya in 1830 to Wadi Araba, by members of Al-Tiha tribe. Resistance by some tribes, such as Al-Jbarat and Al-Atawneh, to the conquest of Ibrahim Pasha (1831–1840), caused them to disperse east of Beer Sheva. The Odeh and Amer war, between two Tiha leaders (Al-Huzayil and Al-Atawneh), took place during two periods (1842–1853, 1855–1864). The Zar'a war, between the Tiha and Tarabin, also took place in two periods (1875–1879, 1882–1887). Moreover, the Azazmah and Tarabin War took place in 1877–1890).[29] All of these wars led Bedouin tribes to disperse over a large area and to settle in the northern Naqab, Hebron, and Bethlehem.

The Beisan and Marj Ibn Amer Valleys: The Bedouin arrival from Transjordan

Bedouin originating in the eastern side of the Jordan River settled mainly in eastern Palestine, including the Beisan Valley, the entire southern Marj Ibn Amer, and Tiberias Lake. They entered mainly into empty areas or into rural areas where population density was low,[30] such as headquarters of Banu Saqer, Banu Sakher, Banu Khalid, Al-Bashatwa, Al-Ghazzawiyya, Al-Hanadi, and other tribes.[31]

The Galilee: Bedouin arrival from Hauran, the Syrian Desert and the Golan Heights

Bedouin who came from Transjordan and Syria settled mainly in northern Palestine, including the Galilee, Hula, Beisan, Marj Ibn Amer, and Zebulun Valleys (Al-Ramil tribes);[32] and tribes such as the Numeirat, Sabarja, Al-Na'im, Al-Sayyid, Heib, Shamalana, Samkia, and Al-Subayh.[33]

Map 1.1 (opposite) shows the origins of the Bedouin tribes and their migration routes until some of them arrived in Palestine between the

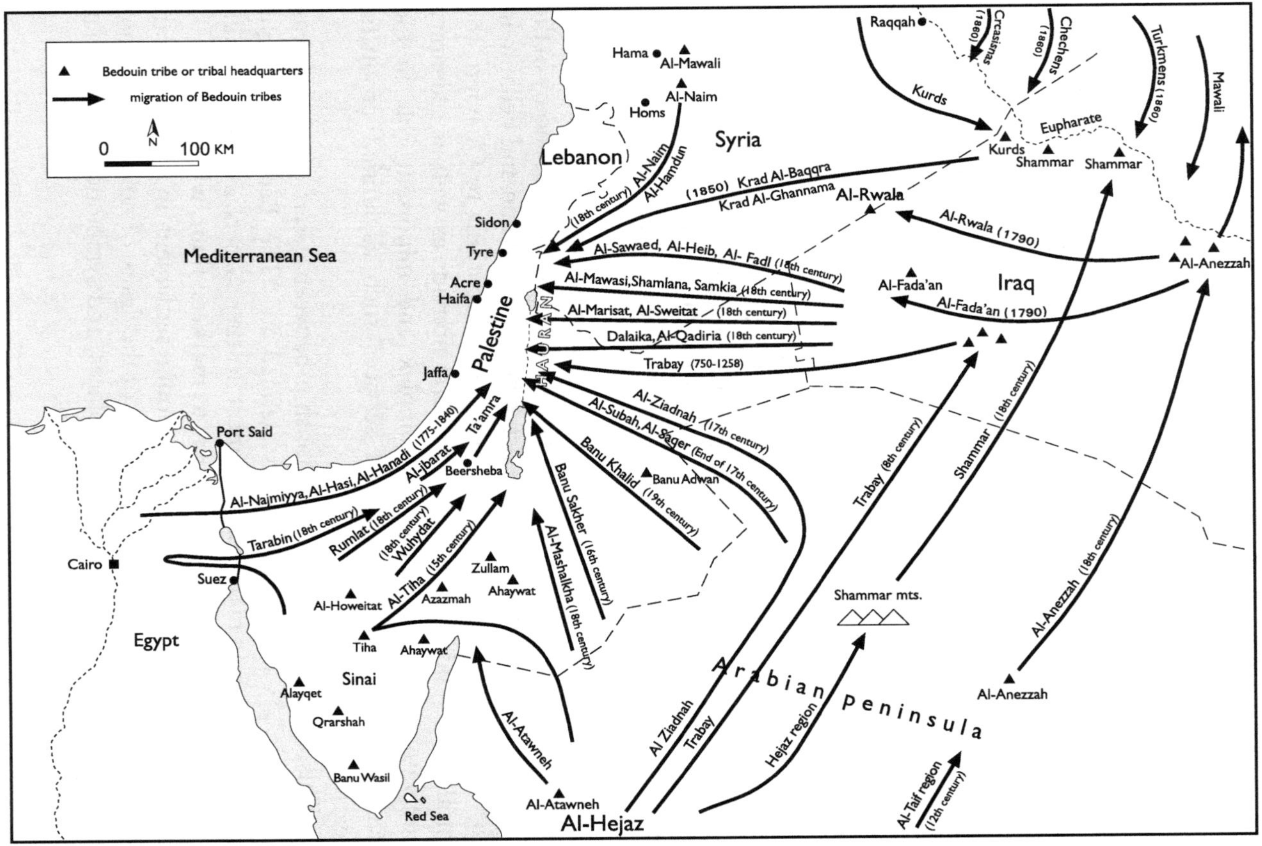
Bedouin tribe or tribal headquarters
migration of Bedouin tribes
N
0 100 KM
Mediterranean Sea
Lebanon
Syria
Iraq
Palestine
HAURAN
Egypt
Sinai
Arabian peninsula
Al-Hejaz
Red Sea
Hama
Al-Mawali
Al-Naim
Homs
Sidon
Tyre
Acre
Haifa
Jaffa
Port Said
Cairo
Suez
Beersheba
Raqqah
Kurds
Crcasisnas (1860)
Chechens (1860)
Turkmens (1860)
Mawali
Eupharate
Shammar
Shammar
Al-Rwala
Al-Anezzah
Al-Fada'an
Al-Rwala (1790)
Al-Fada'an (1790)
Al-Naim
Al-Hamdun
(18th century)
(1850) Krad Al-Baqqra
Krad Al-Ghannama
Al-Sawaed, Al-Heib, Al- Fadl (18th century)
Al-Mawasi,Shamlana, Samkia (18th century)
Al-Marisat, Al-Sweitat (18th century)
Dalaika, Al-Qadiria (18th century)
Trabay (750-1258)
Al-Ziadnah (17th century)
Al-Subah, Al-Sager (End of 17th century)
Banu Khalid (19th century)
Banu Adwan
Banu Sakher (16th century)
Al-Mashalkha (18th century)
Ta'amra
Al-jbarat
Al-Najmiyya, Al-Hasi, Al-Hanadi (1775-1840)
Tarabin (18th century)
Rumlat (18th century)
Wuhydat (18th century)
Al-Tiha (15th century)
Zullam
Ahaywat
Azazmah
Al-Howeitat
Tiha
Ahaywat
Alayqet
Qrarshah
Banu Wasil
Al-Atawneh
Al-Atawneh
Al Ziadnah
Trabay
Hejaz region
Shammar mts.
Trabay (8th century)
Shammar (18th century)
Al-Anezzah (18th century)
Al-Anezzah
Al-Taif region (12th century)

17th and 19th centuries. Note that this map does not show the out-immigration from Palestine.

As aforementioned, this settlement did not clash with Ottoman interests. On the contrary, Ottoman policy during the 18th century was to settle the nomadic population. It was in fact a spontaneous settlement, which was not counter to Ottoman interests, as it contributed to the empire's economy, preserving the local population, and thereby increasing agricultural production.[35] In other words, the significance of this settlement did not stem from concern for the interests of the Bedouin themselves, but rather out of broader considerations serving primarily Ottoman hegemony. This phenomenon becomes clearer with the penetration of the Ottoman administration into the outlying areas of the empire.

At this point, note that administratively, Palestine was divided into two provinces – Sidon, and Damascus – until it conquered by Ibrahim Pasha (1831–1840).[36] The coastal plain of Haifa, including Jenin and Gaza, belonged to *iyalet* Sidon [Sidon province];[37] while the mountainous and hilly regions – the Golan Heights, Tiberias, the mountains of Safad and the Galilee, Nablus, Jerusalem, and Hebron belonged to *iyalet* Damascus. The main function of the Ottoman provincial governors (*walis*) of Damascus and Sidon was collecting taxes from inhabitants to ensure their safety.[38]

Settlement of Bedouin in Palestine, together with rural Fellahin inhabitants, greatly contributed to strengthening the Ottoman economy in the 18th century. Commercial ties existed between Bedouin and Fellahin in the Fertile Crescent, including Palestine.[39] According to Quataert, the rural countryside was home to pastoral nomads as well as sedentary cultivators. Nomads played a complex and important role in the economy, providing goods and services such as animal products, textiles, and transportation.[40]

This explains how the "relationship between desert and sown was symbiotic",[41] as Bruce Masters defined it: "The Bedouin brought products to urban markets: milk, meat, leather carpets, and wool, while the Fellahin brought grain products to markets: flour, wheat, etc.".[42]

Therefore, the beginning of Bedouin settlement in existing Arab Fellahin towns and villages is a result of the desire of nomadic Bedouin settlers, who tend to settle in stable places, and symbiotic relations that were forged between two populations.

Bedouin Settlement in Fellahin Villages and Towns in the Galilee during the 18th century: The Case of Trabay and Al-Ziadnah

From the second half of the 17th century, local notables called *ayan* began arising throughout the Ottoman Empire.[43] These ayan became owners of large estates and politically controlled swaths of the Fertile Crescent during the 18th century.[44] Inalcik and Quataert termed this period "the Age of the *Ayans*, 1699–1812".[45] This growth was a direct result of weakness of the central government in Istanbul, which began to rely upon the local elite and middle class to carry out its will.

These elite and their retinues collected very high taxes from the Fellahin, who made up between 20% and 25% of output. At the other extreme, Ottoman sharecropping of the 18th century and later took up as much as 50% of unirrigated zones,[46] and sometimes two thirds of Fallah's crop, such as Egypt's and Iraq's villagers, who surrendered up two thirds of their product to the village *multizim*, or tax farmers.[47] In Syria, as in the central provinces, tendencies toward local autonomy, a response to looser control, became increasingly apparent in the late 18th century. Whereas before the 1770s, the governors of Aleppo and Damascus contended with local elites to maintain a balance of power, after 1770 the coastal town of Acre emerged to challenge them as the third center of power in Syria, based on a lion's share of the taxed farms and the largest military retinues of the province.[48]

This greatly affected the Fellahin fieldwork, and in many cases led them to flee from their villages and even abandon them entirely.[49] In the districts [*sanjaks*], officials were local, mostly town dwellers. Some received *khawa* payments, and in some cases, they constituted a link between the local inhabitants and the Ottoman governors. In many cases, they abused the Fellahin, some of whom (in Palestine) fled and chose to settle in the district of a Bedouin amir from Trabay tribe, a locale that gave them personal and financial security.[50] For instance, an official decree [*firman*], issued by the Ottoman Sultan on 1 October 1615 and sent to the Damascus province governor [*wali*] and to the *kadi* of Al-Lajjun, noted:

> Ahmad Ibn Tarbiyeh [Trabay] is the district Chief of al-Lajjun, God save him and lengthen his life. He told us, [that] there are many Fellahin who came to settle in his village [...], they came from surrounding villages [...], and have been lived in al-Lajjun, more [than] twenty years [...], and who refuse to return to their former villages, because of the humiliating and degrading treatment they would have received there.[51]

Trabay tribe, belonging to the major tribal headquarters of Banu Harith, is descended from Banu Tay tribe from Yemen. This tribe came to Palestine from the Syrian desert during Abbasid Caliphate rule.[52] This was the largest Bedouin tribe at the time, which decided to settle and establish its control over territories rich in water and sloping meadows. Banu Harith included 18 sub-tribes, which settled throughout Palestine during the 17th century.[53]

Note that at the beginning of the 17th century, the Galilee was under the control of the Druze amir Fakhr Al-Din Al-Ma'ani, who was appointed by Ottoman Empire authorities in 1624.[54] A few years later, the Ottoman regime viewed this ruler's strength as a threatened to its interests. Therefore, it employed a "divide and conquer" policy against him. Accordingly, they rewarded Amir Ahmad Ibn Trabay control first of Safad district, then Jenin. It also issued local amirs, such as Muhammad Ibn Farrukh, permission to control other parts of Palestine.[55]

The result of this policy was the outbreak of several battles among local amirs, the largest of which was Al-Auja River (today, Yarkon river, north Tel Aviv) in 1622.[56] Amir Fakhr Al-Din al-Ma'ani, and Amir Qasem Ibn Ali al-Shuhabi (a Lebanese Druze), together with about 1,500 soldiers, came to fight Amir Ahmed Ibn Trabay.[57] The main cause of this battle was Druze amirs having burned many villages in the Galilee and Mount Carmel. They conquered almost all of the Galilee and Marj Ibn Amer. Finally, in the Al-Auja River battle, Amir Ahmad Ibn Trabay, aided by Ottoman Empire forces, succeeded in defeating Fakhr Al-Din's forces. Thus, control of Amir Ahmad Ibn Trabay was restored to the Galilee.[58]

Toward the 18th century, the Ottomans faced a threat to empire interests in the form of amirs of Trabay tribe. Assisted by Druze amirs (Al-Ma'ani), a phalanx of empire forces retook the Galilee from Trabay control. Consequently, some Trabay fled to Syria and Lebanon, while others chose to live in existing Fellahin villages such as Sakhnin, Tulkarm, Jenin, Gaza, Deir al-Balah, and El-Arish.[59]

Muhammad Khalil Trabiyeh, also known as "Abu Al-Amin", of Sakhnin, said in an interview about his family's origins, that it was descended from Trabay tribe.[60] Its roots date back to the period of Abd al-Mu'ati Trabay (son of Amir Ahmad Ibn Trabay), who settled in the forest south of Sakhnin, today called the *Al-Ghabah* ["forest"] neighborhood, as Muhammad Khalil Trabay testified:

> My family [Trabiyeh] founder in Sakhnin . . . was Abd al-Mu'ati, who began farming together with his sons. At first, he lived in a tent, and

later he built a stone house. Today, the Trabiyeh family numbers about 2,500 souls who reside in Sakhnin, and almost all of them work in industry and commerce in Karmiel.

In the early and mid-18th century, other tribes arrived in northern Palestine, such as Banu Saqer, Al-Ghazzawiyya, Al-Bashatwa, and Banu-Khalid, who settled in Beisan and Marj Ibn Amer.[61] Al-Ziadnah tribe entered the Galilee and replaced Trabay tribe, which demonstrated weakness in controlling the Galilee. Al-Ziadnah was considered a strong and great Bedouin tribe in the 18th century. Its origin is from Al-Hejaz, whose lineage is attributed to offspring of Zaid Ibn Husayn Ibn Ali Ibn Abi Talib (of the Prophet Muhammad's family).[62] Al-Ziadnah settled first in the Tiberias area, from whence they imposed their authority over the entire Galilee, and pushed southward into Al-Subayh and Banu Saqer tribes.

The most important period of Al-Ziadnah reign was that of Zahir Al-Umar (1689–1775), who ruled the Galilee from the 1830s until the mid-1870s; and was considered a centralized regime.[63] This period, in which security prevailed (such as in Tiberias, Nazareth, and Acre), contributed to the region's stabilization and a flourishing import–export trade. In 1747, Zahir Al-Umar delayed for two years the annual tax payments to Wali Suleiman Pasha Al-'Azam in Damascus, similar to the behavior of other amirs. This delay forced the *wali* to leave Damascus with a large military force to collect tax payments. He surrounded Tiberias for three months until leaving it to go on hajj. In fact, the *wali* failed and left Zahir Al-Umar as de facto ruler of the Galilee.[64]

Zahir Al-Umar's behavior indicates that he did not live a nomadic lifestyle, but rather a rural one, residing in permanent communities in the Galilee. In the first half of the 18th century, the settlement of this family began. During this period, some sons of Zahir Al-Umar controlled the Galilee villages as feudal rulers over Tiberias, Safad, Araba, Deir Hanna, Tamra, Shafa-Amer, Nazareth, and Kafr Manda.[65]

Zahir Al-Umar's younger sons had conflicts over control of certain areas, such as the prolonged rebellions of Uthman, Ali, and Said. On the other hand, their older brother Salibi (see Appendix A) was a relatively quiet man who had spent 30 years in Tiberias and did not participate in rebellions with his brothers against his father. Ahmed, a son of Al-Umar ruled for several years in Deir-Hanna. He then took control of Irbid and Ajloun together with Al-Subayh tribe, and later settled in Jordan.[66]

Descendants of Al-Ziadnah tribe, some of whom still live until today in various villages in the Galilee:

- Abbas dynasty, son of Zahir Al-Umar, former governor of Nazareth, now resides in Nazareth (see Appendix A).
- Ali dynasty, son of Zahir Al-Umar, former governor of al-Damun, lived in Nazareth until 1948,[67] after which they moved to Kafr Manda and Tamra.[68]
- Said dynasty, son of Zahir Al-Umar, former governor of Deir Hanna, purchased land and settled in Deir-Hanna (see Appendix B).

I interviewed Ziad Abu Sa'ud Al-Zahir Al-Zidani, who lives today in Nazareth,[69] and he told me that his family's origin, Al-Ziadnah, was Fellahin. He claimed that Zahir Al-Umar lived throughout his life in towns and villages such as Tiberias, Shafa-Amer, and Nazareth, and in fact he was a farmer. While in other interviews, members of the Zahir Al-Umar family, who reside in Kafr Manda and Deir Hanna, claimed that they were descended from Al-Ziadnah tribe, "pure and noble" Bedouin, rather than Fellahin. According to them, Zahir Al-Umar lived most of his life in towns and villages, but he continued to travel among towns and villages in the Galilee and maintained contact with nomadic members of his tribe, Al-Ziadnah.[70]

In this discourse, I would like to point out that it is not my intention to judge or decide on this issue, but rather to demonstrate reciprocity and to indicate liquidity and flexibility in the transitions between one lifestyle and the next. Moreover, there is an effect of "identity politics", i.e., if a member of Al-Ziadnah tribe believes that he is a *Fallah*, then he is, and if a member of the same tribe believes himself to be Bedouin, the so he defines himself, and thus the population in his social sphere defines him accordingly. Anthropologically, this process is defined as "enculturation" based on a "cultural routine" or a process via which an individual learns about his/her own culture (such as language, linking symbols to their meanings, and expressed in verbal and non-verbal language).[71] Sociologically, this process is defined as "socialization" or the process by which an individual internalizes and implements the norms and ideologies of her/his society.[72] Main agents of socialization are family, peer group, school, and mass media. This entire process can be summed up in one word – *habitus* – meaning the entire set of beliefs, values, educations, behaviors, and the environment in which we live, which is reflected or seen in daily life.[73] In this sense, if the Bedouin continue view themselves as Bedouin, structuring practices and representations of Bedouin symbols, then they remain Bedouin even if they continue to live in Fellahin towns and villages; and the same applies to Fellahin.

These examples illustrate Bedouin having settled in Fellahin towns and villages, and integrated into the structure thereof long before modernization. Note that on the one hand, that most Fellahin villages and towns in Palestine in the 17th and 18th centuries were located on mountains and hills, from the Galilee Mountains in the north to the Hebron Mountains in the south.[74] On the other hand, permanent Bedouin settlement in Bedouin villages occurred mainly in valleys and coastal plains, since in these areas they (such as tribes in Beisan Valley, Marj Ibn Amer, and others) could continue to graze their herds.

Therefore, in 17th, and 18th century migration of the Bedouin population to sedentarizaion in existing towns and villages, it can be seen that ecology was not an influential factor, as it had been before. Bedouin begin to settle in villages not out of ecological necessity, but under local and bureaucratic circumstances, as became pronounced in the 19th century. In addition, a pattern of scattered and dispersed settlement of Bedouin in villages of Fellahin indicates, perhaps, weakening of the tribe's segmentary ideology.

I can also state that during the 18th century, and even before, under Ottoman Empire rule, there was economic interaction, mainly between the Bedouin and Fellahin population: Bedouin tribes came to trade in urban markets, selling dairy and meat products such as camels, sheep, goats, sheep wool, skins, milk, butter, cheese, honey, tobacco, and plant-based coloring compounds to urban and rural Fellahin.[75] In turn, they bought from Fellahin such goods as textiles, weapons, jewelry, coffee, sugar, sweets, and more.[76] All this came under the description "close interplay" as "polar complementaries, not polar opposites",[77] which these communities have maintained in practical dependence, economic interactions and exchange between them. Roger Owen called this interplay "the economic practices engaged in between Bedouin and Fellahin".[78]

Ottoman and Egyptian Concentration Policy in the First Half of the 19th century and its Impact on the Bedouin Population in the Galilee

The Egyptian regime in Palestine and Syria lasted for nine years (1831–1840), under which important administrative changes occurred. In 1831, Ibrahim Pasha abolished Ottoman provincial division and established a new system.[79] He appointed a general governor over the entire Al-Sham (including Palestine); his source of rule was Damascus; and all local rulers in towns were subordinate to him. Ibrahim Pasha's centralization led to weakening of local rulers' power (some of whom had been appointed by the Ottomans) and led to an increase in status of local governors appointed by the centralized government of Egypt.

These new local governors, such as Aqil Agha, under Ibrahim Pasha's guidance, began in November 1831 to deploy guard troops from regular and irregular cavalry in the Galilee, such as Bedouin from Al-Hawara and Al-Hanadi tribes that were of Egyptian origin.[80] These troops ranged from 50 to 130 cavalry patrolling areas prone to trouble. In addition, garrisons were stationed on roads and near settlements, such as Sheikh Abreik garrison station between Nazareth and Tiberias, and Jisr al-Majami garrison station between Tiberias and Beisan.[81]

Enforcement of the regime and order increased inhabitants' general security; and increased European tourism to Palestine.[82] However, regular, efficient, and organized government began to burden inhabitants: Most Bedouin were unable to migrate and were obliged to pay taxes, especially farmers who were drafted into the army, and were thus forced to abandon their villages. This situation led to outbreak of a Fellahin rebellion in 1834.[83]

Following these revolts, large Egyptian forces were sent to towns to establish order. Harsh punitive measures taken by Ibrahim Pasha against Bedouin tribes that joined this rebellion were directed specifically against Al-jbarat and Al-Howeitat tribes, located south of Al-Asi River (today Nahal Shikma) as well as Al-Ta'amra tribe.[84] Other tribes also joined this revolt from the Galilee, such as Al-Hawara, under Aqil Agha's command. These latter tribes began to function in this period under Ottoman rulers' service and acted against Egyptian forces until expulsion thereof from the region.[85]

In 1840, the Ottoman regime, assisted by British forces and aided by an internal Arab uprising, returned to Al-Sham after expelling the Egyptian army. The return of Ottoman rule differed significantly from what had prevailed in the region before Egyptian rule, reflected mainly in the Ottoman trend toward concentration, one of whose causes was the military reform of Sultan Mahmoud II (who ruled the empire between the years 1808–1839). This reform began before the Egyptian conquest in 1831, and its results were abolition of janissaries in 1826 and their replacement by the regular army Nizam-I Djedid, which was subordinate to central government independent of local amirs or sheikhs such as Ahmad Trabay, Zahir Al-Umar, and Aqil Agha.[86]

Presence of this new regular army in provinces somewhat reduced Bedouin mobility,[87] and in some cases, whether intentional or not, even led to settlement of this Bedouin population in permanent places. Bedouin tribes that had been nomadic and semi-nomadic, such as near

Aleppo, Damascus, and Hauran, were forced to settle in these nearby towns, and possibly elsewhere. This occurred during the reign of Namik Pasha, commander of Ser-asker and the governor of Damascus (1844–1849).[88]

Note that this is not the direct or the only factor that pushed Bedouin settlement. Other practical factors contributed significantly thereto: implementation of direct tax collection by the central government; and Sultan Mahmoud II expropriating the Timar lands (lands owned by Sipahis, or Knights of the Sultan) and turning them into state lands.[89] At the same time, *iltizam* rights were reduced. The aim of these new reforms, which began during Mahmoud IIs reign, and continued even after Egyptian occupation, was to institutionalize a new administrative system, based on Western European methods, while ignoring the tribal Bedouin population.

The *Tanzimat* and their Impact on the Bedouin Population in the Galilee

The Ottoman Empire, especially from the end of the Egyptian occupation (1840) onwards, began to adopt "modernization discourse" borrowed from European colonialism, or "Ottoman Orientalism",[90] which acquired a hegemonic status in shaping government policy from the time of the Egyptian occupation onwards, leading to the implementation of important administrative reforms, land ownership patterns, and economic patterns. This discourse strongly influenced the settlement of the Bedouin.

Between 1839 and 1876, the Ottoman regime instituted a series of comprehensive reforms called *Tanzimat*, whose purpose was to effectively and rationally reorganize government institutions and practices across the empire.[91] These reforms touched upon all aspects of life and were accompanied by new legislation aimed at bringing order and reorganization to the empire. Hence, the regime enacted new Land Laws Registration in 1858, which regulated registration of land ownership in exchange for annual taxes and military conscription; the Trade and Punishment Laws of 1860–1863; *Wilayats/Eyalets* Law (State Law) in 1864; Law of Administration of *Wilayats* (State Administration Law) in 1871; and the *Mecelle*-Civil Code 1869–1876.[92]

The arrangements established by provincial regime laws between 1864 and 1867 divided the Ottoman Empire territory anew into provinces (*wilayats* or *eyalets*, governed by *walis*); districts (*sanjaks*, governed by *sanjaks-beys/mutesarrifs*); sub-districts (*kazas*, governed by *kadis*); communes (*nahias*, governed by *kaymakams/mudirs*); and villages (*qarias*, governed by *mukhtars*).[93]

Palestine was divided into two provinces: *Wilayat* Beirut that included the Galilee and the entire coastal region (between Acre and Haifa); and *Wilayat* Damascus that included all of the mountainous areas bordering the Jordan River and Tiberias, and Ma'an and al-Karak district.[94] According to the *Wilayats* Law of 1864, a subdivision was implemented in Palestine: Acre district belonged to *Wilayat* Beirut, and included the sub-districts of Acre, Haifa, Safad, Nazareth, and Tiberias; Nablus district, belonged to *Wilayat* Beirut, and included the sub-districts of Nablus, Jenin, and Tulkarm; and Jerusalem District (which was independent and directly related to the regime in Istanbul) included the sub-districts of Jerusalem, Jaffa, Gaza, Hebron, and Beer Sheva.[95]

In addition, three types of security forces were established during *Tanzimat*: First, the Al-Darak Force (border guard, a gendarmerie), located in Damascus and Beirut, which was called upon when necessary to help impose public order everywhere. Second, a "control force" whose task was to administer criminal records and to assist *mukhtars* in imposing order and collecting taxes. Third, a "National Police Force Check", whose function was to check visas and track foreigners. In 1882, these forces totaled about 2,520 police officers in the Syrian and Beirut municipalities.[96] As a result, security prevailed in Palestine at the end of the 19th century.

Tanzimat reforms and their specific implementation in the form of a series of laws and regulations such as the *Wilayats* Code (1864) and Land Code Reform (1858), and Law of Administration of *Wilayats* (State Administration Law) in 1871, and the *Mecelle* – Civil Code 1869–1876 (Civil regulations, such as marriage law, renting and selling houses and so). Accordingly, it seems that this regulation considers the process of sedentarizing the nomadic Bedouin. Yet unfortunately, this process was influenced by European imperial-colonial discourse, which viewed the Bedouin as spending the empire's money, not loyal to the regime, as quarrelsome, unproductive, and non-beneficial to the state.[97] Moreover, these reforms reflected imperialist plans that served primarily Ottoman aspirations of becoming a new civilization in imitation of the West, to prolong its survival. Therefore, the regime was in an ambivalent state between whether to become a modern civilization, or to maintain the Islamic religious tradition (expressed mainly in establishment of the Islamic caliphate, including *Sharia* law according to the Hanafi School).

In any case, this new "civilization" did not consider the tribal communities under the *Tanzimat* reforms, an arrangement based on plans for Bedouin settlement. The Ottoman Empire did precisely the opposite, considering these communities "neglected", "tribal", "savage",[98] "living in an extra-state space and in a constant state of conflict driven by Bedouin savagery and blood revenge".[99] Obviously, the Empire regarded them as "civilizational exceptions",[100] and as excluded as lying outside the purview of Ottoman administrative civilization discourse.[101] This attitude of the Ottoman elite and center toward tribal communities, as part of the periphery, was strongly negative. As Serif Mardin noted, "the clash between nomads and urban dwellers generated the Ottoman cultivated man's stereotype that civilization was a contest between urbanization and nomadism".[102]

This discourse has relevance for **Culturism**,[103] as in an anthropological and epistemological sense, it focuses mainly on minority groups and attributes various phenomena from their socio-political experience to their culture.[104] Moreover, it is also an Orientalist and racist discourse that denies being so. Therefore, these descriptions are far from being classifiable into the category of "cultural lag"; nor do these descriptions make a significant contribution to understanding the relationship and interaction between Bedouin and other categories in Palestine during Ottoman rule.

From this perspective, Ottoman authorities dealt with the Bedouin population according to tribal laws in its governance of Bedouin affairs, as part of its focus on Bedouin autonomy. They established "tribal courts" among the Bedouin, such as Beer Sheva.[105] These courts engaged in conflict resolution between tribes "by the language that the other side understand". That is, by use of military force, militant and rigid.

While scholarship contains well-known examples of military intervention in "resolving" inter-tribal conflicts, many of them are influenced by the noble savage stereotype.[106] The authoritative Arif Al-Arif provided a more detailed account of Bedouin conflicts and fighting,[107] while situating it largely within the same narrative. He devoted a long section to Bedouin "civil wars", mainly between the years 1875 and 1890. Nonetheless, Al-Arif did not note that the level and frequency of fighting prompted Jerusalem governor, Rauf Pasha to try to persuade Bedouin sheikhs to make peace. Upon their refusal, he decided to use military force.[108] Thus, the Ottomans tried to move beyond "merely" disciplining or educating (*te'adib*) the Bedouin.[109] The absurdity therein was the Bedouin agents active in this period of Ottoman administration and politics, such as Arif Al-Arif and other local sheikhs.

At the same time, alongside the *tanzimat* reforms and militant countermeasures taken by the Ottoman Empire against the Bedouin population, there are examples of local circumstances that pushed Bedouin to settle in Fellahin towns and villages during the 19th century.

The first example thereof is agricultural cultivation in the Naqab and coastal towns. Agricultural cultivation by Bedouin in the Naqab continued to grow; there was a concomitant increase in barley exports to Britain via Gaza port.[110] Major trade centers for the Naqab Bedouin were coastal towns (Gaza and Jaffa), mountain towns (Hebron and Jerusalem), and particularly Lod and Ramleh, which are on the road leading from the coastal towns to Jerusalem.[111] It is possible that what influenced the increase in agricultural activity was not militancy, but rather an Ottoman land code enacted in 1858. This law reduced grazing areas as a consequence of confiscation of land that had been uncultivated for three years, and thus became state lands [*miri*], compelling Bedouin to streamline their farming and cultivate and produce more on smaller grazing areas.[112] Central trade centers in the major towns thus made their mark on deepening the process of Bedouin "departing" (becoming Fellahin). A second example was increase in the share of agricultural crops among Bedouin tribes in the Beisan and Hula Valleys.[113] In 1915, two Turkish travelers, Muhammad Rafiq al-Tamimi and Muhammad Bahjat, described the Bedouin tribes in Marj Ibn Amer and Beisan Valleys as barley and wheat growers who planted about 10 kg of wheat, and at the end of the season harvested over 100 kg of wheat crop. In addition, these tribes sold about 30% of this crop in Beisan, while the rest were sent for wholesale in nearby towns such as Haifa, Nazareth, Jenin, Tiberias, and Nablus.[114] These economic capital practices contributed to economic relations between Bedouin and Fellahin. Bedouin purchased essential goods such as coffee and clothing and sold dairy products and meat to the town inhabitants.[115]

To illustrate this claim in Palestine, documents from Ottoman Archives in Istanbul describe ownership of Al-Hanadi tribe of land in Al-Dalhamiya, (a Fellahin) village in Tiberias district.[116] In 1874, some of this tribe (about 60 individuals) decided to purchase 12,000 dunams in this village, and even settle there. In 1887, these tribesmen formally registered the land. However, (according to Ottoman Tabu Office) in 1907 some members of them (about 30 individuals) sold part of it to effendis Sa'id Fahum and Alfred Musa Sursock. However, the Ottoman authorities did not recognize this sale, claiming that "the person who was registered on the registration form of 1887 is Muhammad Abbas; therefore, the land ownership passes to the deceased's sons only".[117]

This appeared to reflect a policy of encouraging Bedouin settlement in Fellahin agricultural villages. Nonetheless, this encouragement apparently stemmed from concern of "the interest of foreigners in land purchases in Palestine", as written in these documents, and not from serious intentions to settle Bedouin in permanent locales.

A third example is social reasons: The Bedouin urbanization process continued during the period of control of Bedouin Governor Aqil Agha in the Galilee.[118] In 1847, Aqil was appointed by the governor of Acre as commander of a "Bedouin force" of 50 soldiers who were in charge of maintaining order and security in the Galilee. Aqil's residence was established in Iblin. This period was characterized by good relations between Bedouin tribes and the town and village population in the Galilee.[119] Aqil settled religious disputes that arose between various communities, such as conflicts that arose in 1845 between Muslims and Christians in Nazareth.[120] These social relations contributed to Bedouin living proximate to towns and villages, and over time, they moved to nearby Fellahin towns and villages.

A fourth example reflects Ottoman interests and internal considerations: As part of the implementation of the Ottoman modernization process, Sultan Abdul Hamid II initiated projects aimed at the settlement of the nomadic Bedouin population, and even encouraged the strengthening of the Bedouin's attachment to the land and its regular cultivation.[121] This project was carried out alongside the expansion of Bedouin agriculture in the Naqab and the Galilee.[122] Between 1871 and 1922, the central government in Istanbul established ten mixed Bedouin and Fellahin villages in the Galilee (see Map 1.2), where nomadic Bedouins from the surrounding areas moved to live.[123] Thus, for example, some members of the Al-Sayyid and Al-Qdirat tribes lived in a different village; parts of the Al-Ghazzawiyya and Al-Bashatwa tribes settled in the village of Al-Ghazzawiyya; and the tribes of Al-Bawati and Al-Saqer dwelt in the village of Al-Khunayzir. It is probable that some of the Fellahin inhabitants in these villages are of Bedouin descent, but there is no doubt that with the establishment of these villages, inhabitants who had hitherto maintained a Bedouin lifestyle for all intents and purposes, settled there. This transfer was not necessarily spontaneous, but was rather directed from above by the authorities.

Relations between the tribes and the Ottoman government representatives were quite complex. The lands in these areas belonged mostly to the sultan's [*khas*'s] estate, and were cultivated by the tribes residing in the mixed villages. Overseeing the management of the land's cultivation was a *muder* who sat in the town. In exchange for cultivating the land, as is customary with regard to the leasing of the sultan's lands, the Bedouin paid the *khums* tax (a fifth of their crop) imposed on their lands as per the annual crop estimate calculated by the government officials under the auspices of the gendarmerie.[124]

The aforementioned examples are of the manifestations of the Ottoman Empire's "exclusion" and "neglect" policy at the end of its rule, as reflected in *tanzimat* reforms, toward tribal populations in general and in the Galilee in particular, which encouraged and strengthened the status of urban dignitaries. They moreover weakened the status of tribal sheikhs and greatly facilitated purchase of land by Jewish organizations (the KKL – Keren Kayemeth Leisrael, the JNF – Jewish National Fund, and the PJCA – Palestine Jewish Colonization Association) from these effendis,[125] as most lands were registered in effendis' names and those of land dealers from the late 19th century until the collapse of the Ottoman Empire in 1918.

Map 1.2, opposite, shows the locations of settlement of nomadic and semi-nomadic Bedouin tribes in the Galilee in the late 19th century,[126] and as can be seen, many of them settled near Fellahin villages and towns; this stage preceded the transition and settlement of the tribes within the towns and villages.

In general, initial Bedouin settlement in Fellahin towns and villages was characterized by construction of tents and barracks located in outlying neighborhoods. They built houses of stone and concrete, similar to the local villagers, only after their economic and social consolidation in the region. The reasons for this settlement were not uniform: some was economic, some social, and some political.

Large Bedouin Tribes that Settled in Existing Fellahin Towns and Villages During the 19th and Early 20th Centuries

Al-Madi tribe in Ijzim. Lineage names: Ali Masoud, Ali Salih, Ali Amro, Ali Sa'ad al-Addin, Ali Aziz, Ali Marad, Ali Khadr, Ali Yasin, Ali Nayif, and their children. Originated from tribal headquarters Al-Wuhaydat from Naqab, which wandered north at the end of the 18th century.[127]

Al-Hanadi tribe in Al-Dalhamiya, south of Tiberias. Originally from Egypt, arrived in Palestine during Ibrahim Pasha Conquests (1831–1840). First settled in Gaza, and in the second half of the 19th century moved to Dalhamiya.[128]

Al-Hasi tribe in Iblin is descended from Aqil Agha Al-Hasi. Originated from the tribe's headquarters: Al-Hanadi, as mentioned above. This tribe came from Egypt in 1814 and settled first in Gaza (where Aqil was born in 1820).[129] Later, in 1845, the tribe moved to settle in Al-Dalhamiya.[130] In addition, Sheikh Aqil was not there permanently: He accompanied the Lynch research expedition during its study of the Jordan River and the Dead Sea in 1848.[131] Descendants of Al-Hasi tribe still live in Iblin. The graves of Aqil Al-Hasi and his brother,

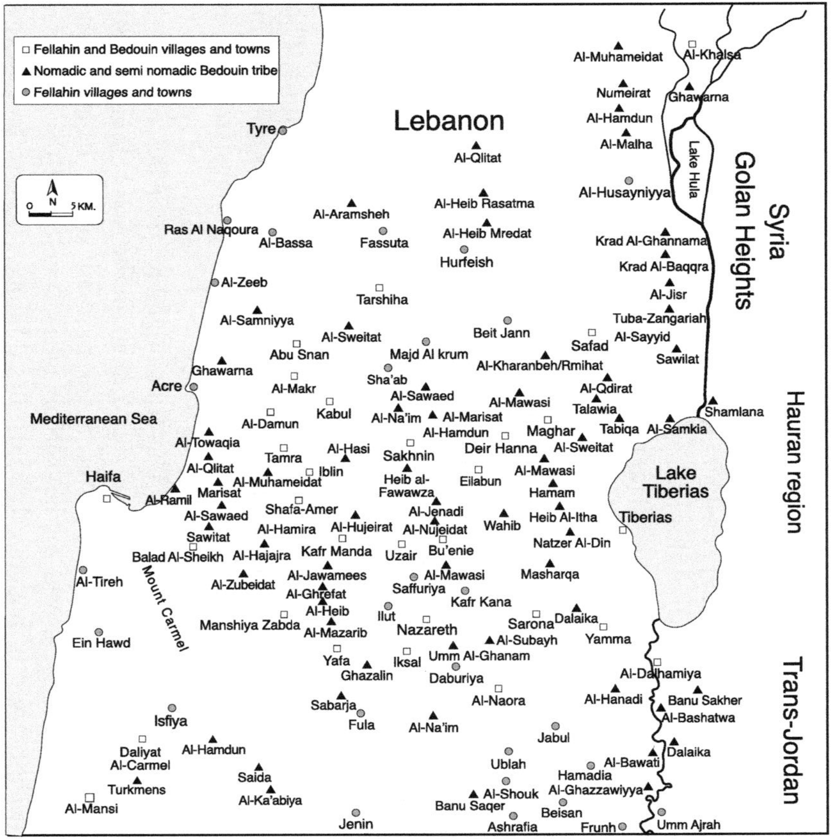
Fellahin and Bedouin villages and towns
Nomadic and semi nomadic Bedouin tribe
Fellahin villages and towns
N
0
5 KM.
Lebanon
Syria
Golan Heights
Hauran region
Trans-Jordan
Mediterranean Sea
Lake Hula
Lake Tiberias
Mount Carmel
Tyre
Ras Al Naqoura
Al-Bassa
Al-Zeeb
Acre
Haifa
Al-Muhameidat
Al-Khalsa
Numeirat
Ghawarna
Al-Hamdun
Al-Malha
Al-Qlitat
Al-Husayniyya
Al-Heib Rasatma
Al-Aramsheh
Fassuta
Al-Heib Mredat
Hurfeish
Krad Al-Ghannama
Krad Al-Baqqra
Al-Jisr
Tarshiha
Al-Samniyya
Tuba-Zangariah
Al-Sweitat
Beit Jann
Safad
Al-Sayyid
Sawilat
Abu Snan
Majd Al krum
Al-Kharanbeh/Rmihat
Ghawarna
Sha'ab
Al-Qdirat
Al-Makr
Al-Sawaed
Al-Mawasi
Talawia
Shamlana
Kabul
Al-Na'im
Al-Marisat
Al-Damun
Al-Hamdun
Maghar
Tabiqa
Al-Samkia
Al-Towaqia
Al-Hasi
Sakhnin
Deir Hanna
Al-Sweitat
Tamra
Al-Qlitat
Iblin
Al-Mawasi
Al-Muhameidat
Heib al-Fawawza
Eilabun
Hamam
Marisat
Al-Ramil
Shafa-Amer
Al-Jenadi
Al-Sawaed
Wahib
Heib Al-Itha
Tiberias
Al-Hamira
Al-Hujeirat
Al-Nujeidat
Sawitat
Natzer Al-Din
Balad Al-Sheikh
Al-Hajajra
Kafr Manda
Uzair
Bu'enie
Al-Tireh
Al-Jawamees
Al-Mawasi
Masharqa
Al-Zubeidat
Saffuriya
Al-Ghrefat
Kafr Kana
Al-Heib
Ilut
Dalaika
Manshiya Zabda
Sarona
Ein Hawd
Al-Mazarib
Nazareth
Al-Subayh
Yamma
Umm Al-Ghanam
Yafa
Iksal
Ghazalin
Daburiya
Al-Dalhamiya
Al-Naora
Al-Hanadi
Banu Sakher
Sabarja
Al-Bashatwa
Isfiya
Fula
Al-Na'im
Jabul
Daliyat Al-Carmel
Al-Hamdun
Dalaika
Ublah
Al-Bawati
Saida
Hamadia
Turkmens
Al-Shouk
Al-Ghazzawiyya
Al-Ka'abiya
Banu Saqer
Beisan
Al-Mansi
Jenin
Ashrafia
Frunh
Umm Ajrah

Saleh, are located in Iblin, and serve as evidence of settlement of this tribe.[132]

Al-Najmiyya tribe in Iblin also arrived in Palestine during the Ibrahim Pasha Conquests (1831–1840). Some of its members (Issa Agha al-Najmi, Akil's deputy commander in Acre) entered an alliance with Aqil Al-Hasi tribe, which settled in Iblin village at the end of the 19th century.[133]

Al-Dalaika (or Dalayikah) tribe in Tiberias. This tribe lived alongside other Bedouin tribes west of Al-Kaddish, between Poria and Tiberias.[134] Schumacher (1887) estimated this tribe in this locality at 695 inhabitants.[135] Lineage names: Al-Issa (sheikh of this lineage, Muhammad Al-Khatib), Al-Shahdat (sheikh of this lineage, Hassan Al-Shahada), Ali Muhammad (sheikh of this lineage, Muhammad Al-Ibrahim).[136]

Mawasi tribe in Eilabun. This tribe originates from the Al-Kadhimiya region of Iraq. Tribal headquarters was in the Khirbet Sabana area, east of Eilabun village in Tiberias district.[137] The sheikh of this lineage was Muhammad al-Ajaj. Some members chose to live in Yaquq village near tribal headquarters, north of Tiberias.[138] During Ottoman rule, some tribe members participated in battles alongside Zahir al-Umar al-Zidani. The tribe lineages: Shawahdeh, Issat, Zahran, Awabda, Battatah, and Daheisa.[139] At the end of the 19th century, part of Mawasi tribe established its tents closer to Eilabun. It was only during the British Mandate that stone houses began to be built in this village.[140]

Al-Ghazalin tribe settled in Iksal at the end of the 19th century. This tribe originates from descendants of Zubaid and Qahtani tribes, from Hejaz. They migrated to Iraq and Syria, eventually settling in Palestine.[141]

Zubeidat tribe in Sakhnin. This tribe originates from descendants of al-Zubaid tribe, which originated in Yemen. In the first half of the 18th century, it moved to Iraq. Later, in the first half of the 19th century, some members moved to the Tab'un hills (founders of the Zubeidat neighborhood in Bussmat Tab'un). In addition, a second part of this tribe lived in the northern neighborhood of Sakhnin.[142]

Masharqa tribe in Sarona. This tribe originates from descendants of Banu Sakhr tribes.[143] Some members of this tribe came from Syrian in the second half of the 19th century, and settled in tents in Sarona, southwest of Tiberias.[144]

Al-Hawara tribe in Nazareth, Iblin, and Shafa-Amer. Descended from Al-Hawara tribes from Egypt (from Al-Sa'id, Al-Buhaira, and Al-Fayoum).[145] Some of them left Egypt and accompanied Ibrahim Pasha's conquests to Al-Sham (1831–1840).[146] Their important sheikh was Muhammad Amran Amin, uncle of Ahmad Bey, supreme

Commander of Ibrahim Pasha's Army.[147] Al-Hawara tribe firstly settled in Abu Shusha, Qusqus, Tab'un, and Jeida. When a Lebanese land dealer, Sursock, sold lands of these villages to the Jewish Agency for Israel (JAI) in 1924, these inhabitants moved to Nazareth, Iblin, and Shafa-Amer.[148]

Figure 1.1 (above) depicts a southwestern neighborhood (Wadi al-Saki'a) of Shafa-Amer in 1910. In this year, the town was recognized as a city and jurisdiction headed by Dahoud Suleiman, first mayor of Shafa-Amer. Its jurisdiction included responsibility for 22 villages: Al-Birwa, Sha'ab, Kabul, Ruweis, Al-Damun, Tamra, Al-Dar, Iblin, Al-Mejdal, Jadro, Azar, Al-Baida, Al-Harithiya, Al-Sheikh Bureik, Umm al-Amad, Bethlehem of Galilee, Tab'un, Tel al-Shamam, Jeida, Al-Mansi, Alwrqani, Abu Shusha) and five Bedouin tribes (Arab Turkmens, Arab al-Tawatha, Arab al-Shkirat, Arab al-Urdon, and Arab Baniha in Mount Carmel).[149,150]

During Ottoman rule, dichotomous or linear relations between Bedouin and Fellahin do not characterize Bedouin settlement in Fellahin villages in the Galilee. However, there are cases wherein Fellahin adopted a Bedouin lifestyle, such as Egyptian villagers, who penetrated Naqab in the first third of the 19th century and became Bedouin in order to earn a livelihood. Other cases are known in Galilee of Fellahin who became Bedouin due to various circumstances, as described below.

Fellahin clan/*Hamula* who become Bedouin

Al-Sa'diyya clan/*Hamula* settled near the Bedouin village tribe of Zubeidat, which later was called Bussmat Tab'un (a Bedouin) village. Origin of this clan is from Saffuriya, a Fellahin village near Nazareth.[151] The main reason for moving to a Bedouin village was escape against the backdrop of blood revenge. In 1928, this clan began building its homes on land (about 300 dunams) that they had previously purchased from Druze effendis from Shafa-Amer.[152]

Al-N'arani clan settled beside the Bedouin village tribe of Zubeidat (similar to Al-Sa'diyya). The origin of this clan is from Meithalun, a Fellahin village near Jenin,[153] whose primary origin was a Bedouin from Al-Anezzah tribe, who came from the Arabian Peninsula. Members of this clan reached Zubeidat in the mid-19th century.

Masarwa clan settled near the Bedouin village of Al-Hajajra. The origin of this clan, members of which reached Al-Hajajra during the Ibrahim Pasha Conquests (1831–1840), was in Egypt.[154]

What these clans have in common is in nearly all cases, the same income: They made a living from raising sheep and goats, and mainly maintained a Bedouin lifestyle alongside Bedouin.[155] Known as semi-Bedouin, they view themselves as Bedouin: They live in separate neighborhoods but overlap Bedouin neighborhoods in the communities in which they live. With the help of Bedouin, the Fellahin were influenced to change their accent to Bedouin, and their houses do not differ much from those of their Bedouin neighbors. Bedouin who consider themselves "genuine" do not readily agree to marry their daughters to these clans. In an interview with Yazid Zubeidat, a Bedouin inhabitant of Bussmat Tab'un, he said:

> We have good bidirectional relationships with *Hamulat* al-Sa'diyya. [We] participate with them in weddings and funeral ceremonies, and they often visit us. [Question: are you willing for your sister or daughter marry someone from Sa'diyya?] I prefer my sister or daughter marry someone from my family [...] and if not, then I will not oppose her.[156]

We can interpret from Yazid's words that he prefers endogamous marriage, apparently out of concern for family honour [*sharaf*]. In other words, a marriage of a Bedouin young woman to a man outside the family (especially to Fellah) is considered a violation of the Bedouin family/tribe's honour. Secondly, he views superiority and perhaps "purity" of the Bedouin family as a value to be preserved. In fact, while Yazid manifests a mirror image of settlement of Fellahin families in

Bedouin villages, as well the opposite – Bedouin settlement in Fellahin villages – the Fellahin are not as invested proud their origins as are the Bedouin.

At the end of Ottoman rule, the Bedouin tribes in the Galilee numbered about 47. Of these, only four had more than 600 members.[157] Accordingly, the Bedouin population in the Galilee can be estimated at approximately 30,000. In addition, the total Bedouin population in Palestine is estimated at between 70,000 and 90,000.[158] In other words, the Bedouin population in the Galilee constituted about 42% of the total Bedouin population in Palestine.

In addition to this estimate, this study indicates an estimate of the Galilee Fellahin population during this period – the second half of the 19th century – in order to assess the size of the Bedouin population that joined these Fellahin villages. For this purpose, an edition of the Ottoman *Salanameh* (Ottoman Administrative Yearbook) of 1871 was used to estimate the population of rural Arabs (without distinction between Fellahin and Bedouin) in the Galilee.[159] Although this estimate is neither accurate nor reliable, it nonetheless gives some sense of the size of this population. Apparently, some of the rural population was not included in this yearbook, due to their concerns about their enlistment in the army and tax payments to the Ottoman Empire. Thus, the estimate includes households' numbers as recorded in Ottoman government documents, and the names of Bedouin families that settled in some Fellahin villages in the Galilee (during and after the 19th century).

Accordingly, Fellahin villages in the Galilee in 1871 numbered 141.[160] Another estimate, by Abd al-Aziz Muhammad Awad in 1885 (14 years after the *Salanameh* estimate) was 138 villages belonging to the Acre, Haifa, Safad, Nazareth, and Tiberias districts.[161] If we add thereto statistical data collected from literary material, and interviews conducted with individuals belonging to the same tribes, it is possible to estimate the Bedouin population residing in Fellahin towns and villages in the Galilee at the end of the 19th century and the beginning of the 20th century at 2,500,[162] which constituted about 17% of the total rural Arab population in the Galilee. It is possible to estimate the Fellahin population residing in the Bedouin localities Tab'un and Hajajra, during this period, at about 175.[163]

As we shall see below, the Bedouin population residing in Fellahin towns and villages continued to grow in the 20th century as well. This chapter presented statistical data that showed a gradual transition from provincial governments, which existed until the *tanzimat* period, to establishment of a new administrative system characterized by a centralized government and a police force responsible for enforcing public order. This was result of the implementation of laws and governmental reforms, both Egyptian and Ottoman.

While not all of these factors came into play in the Bedouin population, they did have some influence and led to a significant change in the process of Bedouin settlement and integration into existing Fellahin towns and villages, examples of which are the Madi tribe who settled in Ijzim; al-Hanadi tribe in Al-Dalhamiya, Al-Hasi tribe and Al-Najmiyya tribe in Iblin; Al-Dalaika tribe in Tiberias; Mawasi tribe in Eilabun; Al-Ghazalin tribe in Iksal; Zubeidat tribe in Sakhnin; Masharqa tribe in Sarona; and Al-Hawara tribe in Nazareth, Iblin and Shafa-Amer. In addition, this chapter presents Fellahin settlement in Bedouin villages, such as Al-Sa'diyya and al-N'arani in Zubeidat, and Masarwa in Hajajra.

In addition, the chapter illustrates that there is indeed social, cultural, economic, and political fluidity, and that there are permeable boundaries between these two social groups. For example, Bedouin become Fellahin; and in some cases, Fellahin become Bedouin. However, there are dimensions of conflicting identities and preservation of social, cultural, economic, and political components of each community separately. The distinctions between Bedouin and Fellahin are therefore fluid, dynamic, context-dependent, and woven into the politics of identities and social change processes, as they continued to manifest themselves even during the British Mandate period.

It should be emphasized that at the end of Ottoman rule, most Bedouin in the Galilee had settled sedentarily. They purchased land and registered it in their names or in those of village mukhtars. They demarcated their land and began to cultivate it. In addition to Bedouin living in Fellahin towns and villages, there were also Bedouin tribes living in Bedouin localities/villages. For instance, tribes of Krad al-Baqqra and Krad al-Ghannama in the Hula Valley; Al-Heib tribe in Tuba-al-Zangariah village; and Turkmen tribes on southern Mount Carmel. These are, in fact, examples of sedentarizaion. This forced them (such as Bedouin living in Fellahin villages and towns) to remain in Palestine during World War I (1914–1918),[164] so that the war did not affect the Bedouin population in Palestine.

CHAPTER

2

Galilee Bedouin under British Rule, 1918–1948[1]

This chapter focuses on continued settlement and integration of Bedouin into Fellahin towns and villages in the Galilee under British control. It elucidates how British government pressures spontaneously acted as drivers that led to creation of a common identity: Fellahin-Bedouin under Arab nationality. The actions of the British also created a partnership of interests that would result in a struggle, with common Arab goals. The chapter also discusses other factors such as governmental and other external pressures, and internal Bedouin circumstances, which fed the trend toward Bedouin settlement in Fellahin villages and towns. These all occurred under a prevailing paternalistic trope that "the British understand and handle nomads better than anyone else based on a range of assumptions, prejudices and calculations".[2] This migratory trend continued without a backlash, while the British, for their part, deigned to extend their administrative organization to the desert. But while desert dynamics between rival tribes cut across national boundaries, they were fed by complex, local struggles for authority between Bedouin tribes, urban politics, and imperial officials (such as officers Claude Jarvis, Frederick Peake, and John Glubb), so that the growth of British desert administration and its machinery varied considerably.[3] Accordingly, the British administration's policy toward Bedouin in the Middle East was "a more progressive policy" toward nomadic pastoralism.[4]

As noted in the previous chapter, Bedouin tribes that moved to Fellahin towns and villages during the period of British rule, also exemplify cyclical movement and permeable boundaries between the two communities, Bedouin and Fellahin. Lastly, the research provides an opportunity to reexamine British statistical estimates (1922, 1931, and 1946) of the Arab population in the Galilee, including Bedouin, and their accuracy when compared to archival documentation, research literature, and interviews with Bedouin inhabitants that the author painstakingly gathered. This not only enables us to estimate and quantify the Bedouin population living in Fellahin villages and towns in the Galilee, but also to investigate the reasons for the significant decline in number of semi-nomadic Bedouin.

The concept "external pressures" refers to wars and processes afoot independent of the Bedouin themselves, which drove settlement and integration of Bedouin into Fellahin towns and villages. For instance, the impact of the secret and public agreements signed during World War I (1914–1918),[5] such as the McMahon–Hussein Correspondence (1915–1916),[6] the Sykes–Picot Agreement (1916), the San Remo Conference (1920)[7] and the Cairo Agreement (1921) that redrew the map of the Middle East and its players. On other words, the processes that contributed to strengthening ties between Bedouin and Fellahin occurred during and after World War I, including disintegration of the Ottoman Empire, international agreements, direct colonial domination by European powers, and the rise of national movements.

Bedouin Participation in Rebellions in Palestine during the British Mandate Period

These political processes, which took place outside Palestine's borders, had a significant impact on how Bedouin politically, militarily, and nationally influenced history, part of which took the form of rebellions in the 1920s, 1930s, and 1940s in Palestine. These rebellions were called "events" in the official Jewish-Zionist narrative, and later the Jewish terminological discourse adopted this terminology.[8]

These rebellions, referred to in older Arab narratives of the 1920s as guerrilla war,[9] included car bombs and destruction of water pipes and electricity infrastructure of the enemy; murders of British and traitors, burning government offices, demolition of bridges, and more.[10] These were also called "events" in the Palestinian narrative.[11] In the new Arab narrative, however, these events are called "uprisings" (intifada) or "revolutionary initiatives" laying the groundwork for the Arab Rebellion of 1936–1939.[12] It is important to mention that most of the revolts that took place among Bedouin and Fellahin had the common purpose of promoting a greater Arabic state in the Middle East, as promised by the British according to the McMahon–Hussein Correspondence of 1915–1916.

The first major Arab revolt broke out in 1916, officially led by Hussein bin Ali, Sharif of Mecca. This first large uprising preceded the British mandate and took place in the middle of World War I (1914–1918). Some Bedouin in Palestine participated therein (such as Banu

Sakher, Banu Hauran, Rwala, and Howeitat in Transjordan; and Ghawarna, Al-Jabarat, Tiha, Tarabin, and Azazmah, to "liberate the lands of Al-Sham". Therein, Bedouin and Fellahin fighters fought alongside the British against the Ottoman Empire toward a common purpose:[13] an Arab nation. The sheikhs who participated in these rebellions were Nur Sh'alan, sheikh of Rwala tribes; Auda Abu Tayeh, sheikh of Al-Howeitat tribe, and amir Mahmoud al-Fa'ur, sheikh of Al-Fadl tribes in the Galilee and Golan Heights.[14]

George Antonius summed up the Bedouin tribes' agreement to this cooperation as follows: "The Bedouin swore to be brothers in this war under command of Faisal [king of Syria] in order to liberate the lands of the Arabs, a more important value than kinship and life itself".[15]

———❖———

As mentioned in the previous chapter, Bedouin continued to settle into existing Fellahin towns and villages yet maintained their ties to their tribal home. On 19 February 1920, when a French army unit arrived to conquer Al-Khalsa village (today Kiryat Shmona), the village opposed this occupation, and together, Fellahin and Bedouin fired on the French forces. They also sought help from Bedouin Amir Sheikh Al-Fadl, who sat in the Golan Heights, and he accepted their request. Thusly, the inhabitants of Al-Khalsa – Fellahin and Bedouin – along with rescue force sent by Amir Mahmoud Al-Fa'ur, managed to fend off the French and inflict heavy damage on them.[16]

The Arab Rebellion (1936–1939) was the second major event that took place during British Mandate rule. Local research literature and fighter Subhi Yasin indicate that about 10,000 Palestinian fighters participated therein, organized into sub-bands [*fasa'il*, sing. *Fasil*],[17] classified as follows: 3,000 villagers, Fellahin and Bedouin (called "mountain men"); 6,000 irregular fighters, employing the "bouncing" method to repelling the enemy (Yasin called these rescuers "men of help/*najdh*"); and another 1,000 from the towns. Other researchers, such as Kimmerling, Migdal, and Marlowe, estimated the number of participants in this revolt to be about 15,000 Arabs (urban and rural) throughout in Palestine. They organized in guerrilla units in the mountains, with the aim of striking at British institutions and Jewish settlements.[18]

Here it is important to note joint actions – Bedouin and Fellahin – against Mandatory institutions and Jewish settlement. In 1938, about 1,800 Palestinian fighters took part in attacks on British establishments and infrastructure in Palestine. They succeeded in damaging telephone lines, railways, roads, and the Kirkuk-Haifa oil pipeline.[19] In addition, about 450 fighters attacked Jewish settlements, wherein some 1,300 sniper shootings were carried out.[20]

This cooperation during the Arab Rebellion is important to this study. Subhi Yasin, was a *Fallah* fighter in this uprising, and in describing it, often cited references to Bedouin-Fellahin cooperation. In one of his accounts, he testifies as follows:

> On the morning of 4 October 1938, large British forces from Nazareth and Acre arrived in Kafr Manda, Iblin, and Kaukab Abu Al-Hija, aiming to capture rebels in these villages, who were accused of being involved in the Abu Garad battle on 1 October 1938, led by Sheikh Mahmoud Al-Salam [Fallah Commander of Shafa-Amer region]. When British forces arrived in Kaukab Abu Al-Hija, the rebels called for help/najdh from Al-Hujeirat villagers [Bedouin] to fight against the British. These villagers agreed to help, and after three hours of fighting, the result was a victory for the rebels. The results of this battle were, on the one hand, that the rebels managed to kill dozens of British soldiers; on the other hand, Muhammad Diab [a Bedouin] was killed, and Abdullah Saleh Sari and Hussein Al-Qasem were wounded, all of them brave Arabs from al-Hujeirat village.[21]

We can understand from Yasin's words not only about Bedouin-Fellahin cooperation, but also about the basis for this connection and how the relationships were shaped. As aforementioned, Bedouin settled in and joined villages (such as Kafr Manda, Iblin, and Kaukab Abu Al-Hija) before continuing to maintain contact with the members of their nomadic tribes, who were not far from them. In times of distress or risk, the Bedouin in Fellahin villages or towns, were aided by these instrumental connections with their fellow nomadic Bedouin. In addition, Bedouin commanders were among the rebel leadership (such as Saleh Mahmoud Al-Hujeirat and Hussein Mahmoud from Al-Helf tribe; Muhammad Suleiman Hujeirat, Ibrahim Al-Nimr Hujeirat, and Khalid Al-Sa'ud from Al-Khawaled tribe; Muhammad Al-Ibrahim from Al-Heib tribe, Hussein Zubeidat from Al-Zubeidat tribe, and others), who sought assistance from Bedouin tribes.[22]

In this Arab Rebellion, both permanent and nomadic Bedouin, and urban Fellahin, together helped provide food, money, and active mobilization against British forces. They also served as cells for hiding and for launching attacks when necessary.[23]

Therefore, we can summarize participation of Bedouin in all of these rebellions as that of activists having joined together and acted against

British and Zionist targets, operating under a common identity of "Palestinian Arab nationalism". As described, cooperation and interaction were maintained in nearly all systems in which Bedouin participated: Bedouin were soldiers and commanders, and in some cases Bedouin tribes on the home front were mobilized to employ the "bouncing" method to aid Fellahin villages when the latter were trapped or surrounded by French forces, such as at Al-Khalsa.

Thus, Palestinian Arab nationalists managed to unite and form a common front, both militant and instrumental, that included most Arabs who did not take an active part in these uprisings. This nationalism drove more unification than ever before in Bedouin < > Fellahin relations. This affected Bedouin settlement in Arab Fellahin towns and villages in the Galilee, as will be illustrated below.

Additional Processes that Affected Settlement and Integration of Bedouin into Fellahin Towns and Villages in the Galilee during the British Mandate

The process of permanent Bedouin settlement in the Galilee intensified during the British Mandate, 1918–1948, due to a number of factors: development of common Arab national consciousness and a shared sense of national identity, as described above; a continuing and accelerated process of land acquisition by Jewish organizations (that created a scarcity of vacant land); mandatory governmental pressures; and social processes among the Bedouin, all of which drove rapprochement between the two communities: Bedouin and Fellahin.

The land issue

At the end of Ottoman rule, land began to become a very important issue. During the Mandate, most territorial purchases were from prominent Lebanese landowners such as the Sursock and Khoury families. At the same time, Bedouin pasturelands were reduced as a result of purchases of lands by Jews for establishing colonies and institutions in Palestine. The following are a few cases that illustrate this phenomenon in the Galilee:

> The Jewish Agency purchased Al-Subayh tribe territory, which covers an area of 3,000 dunams north [of] Mount Tabor, in 1944. This transaction is [a] continuation of [the] land purchase process by the Jewish

Agency from 1927. At that time, about 2,175 dunams [were] purchased on which Kh/Kadoorie School was built later in 1933.[24]

Moreover, transfer of ownership lands of Sarona village (western Tiberias) to Jews was aided by British. Reading the correspondence between Sarona tribe to the Arab Higher Committee, it can be understood that the Jews dispossessed the Sarona of their lands, even though the villagers admitted in one of the letters that Jews owned land (letter dated 18 May 1947).[25] This purchase caused great distress among the Bedouin, even forcing them to move to other locales, such as the tribes Maslama and Khalidi having moved to Al-Naora and Nazareth, as described below.

Al-Dalaika tribe, which lived west of Tiberias, was forced to leave its location as well, due to sale of land to Jews. This purchase was made by PICA at the beginning of the 20th century, and as a result, some 80 Al-Dalaika families moved into tents and mountain ranges west of Tiberias and until 1939, some of them settled in Sarona. Following the Arab Revolt (1936–1939), these families from Sarona again were forced move to Ubeidiya village, south of Tiberias in the Jordan Valley.[26]

Mandatory authorities changed registration ownership of the lands, which entailed issuing certificates of ownership to individuals, in contrast to the practiced up until then, wherein the land was in sheikhs' names only. These purchases of land by Jews expanded during the Mandate, affecting Bedouin mobility, and leading them to adopt a more settled lifestyle and even sedentarizaion in Bedouin communities, with some moving to nearby Fellahin towns and villages.

Mandatory government pressures

At the beginning of the Mandate in 1920, British officials noticed that some Bedouin tribes were scattered over large territories in the Galilee.[27] As per their Bedouin conception, they had right to graze and/or cultivate agricultural areas in between the existing settlement patter (tribal territories, or *dirah*), of an approximate size of 5–13 km long and 3–5 km wide,[28] which was an embarrassment to British authorities' rigid bureaucracy. This bureaucracy came to serve, primarily, strengthening mandatory rule, did not considerate Bedouin needs, and indirectly caused and led to settlement and integration of Bedouin into Fellahin towns and villages in the Galilee.

An interwar-period debate between the British imperial government and the desert administrators/British officers in the Middle East, Claude Jarvis (Governor of Sinai, 1923–1936), Frederick Peake (Trans-Jordan,

1921–1939), and John Glubb (southern Iraq and Trans-Jordan, 1939–1956) was based on techniques of coercion, prejudices, and using relevant local resources and local personnel.[29] British officers did not know to distinguish between nomads, farmers, villagers, or tribes, believing that these modes of life constituted distinct social "types", which were not acceptable to British rule, thus, they drafted special administrative measures accordingly.[30] This applies to what Eugene Rogan said in "Neither Pro-Zionist nor Pro-Arab, but Pro-Empire: A Re-assessment of British Policy in the Palestine Mandate".[31] In other words, the British Empire cared only for its own interests: to be a powerful, occupying power vis-a-vis other European countries.

Accordingly, the British adopted new strategies and even enacted new laws (bureaucratic rules/ordinances) that served their interests and toward other goals, regardless of those of the local inhabitants such as Bedouin. The absurdity of these strategies lay in some of them forcing Bedouin to settle in permanent places, i.e., Bedouin or Fellahin villages.

Bureaucratic rules/ordinances that illustrate the above

First ordinance – Border Pass Agreement between United Kingdom and France, 2 February 1926.[32] In 1916, the secret Sykes–Picot agreement signed between the United Kingdom and France redrew international borders in the Middle East. As a continuation thereof, on 2 February 1926, an agreement was signed between the United Kingdom and France concerning border crossings, which required a certificate to cross.[33] This agreement obliged every tribe, whether nomadic or semi-nomadic, desiring to move to another territory, to obtain approval of the district commissioner of that area (for example see Appendix C). In correspondence between Commissioner of the Galilee district in Nazareth, Charles Tunstall ("C.T.") Evans, and High Commissioner of Palestine in Jerusalem, Harold MacMichael on 27 March 1943, the former stated his concern about Bedouin border crossings in the Beisan Valley area:

> During a visit paid by the assistant district Commissioner of Southern Galilee to Irbid, Trans-Jordan, on 24 March, the question of border passes for members of the Bedouin tribes that camp on each side of the Jordan [river] was discussed. There are four tribes affected, so far as Galilee District is concerned, namely the Sager [Saqer], Ghazzawiyya, Bawati, and Bashatwa. At present when a member of any of these tribes living on one side wishes to pass to the other side of the [Jordan] river, he is supposed to be in possession of a passport and have it visa'ed for

entry into the other territory. [...] such an arrangement already exists along the frontier of Palestine bordering the Lebanon and Syria.[34]

In other words, this ordinance actually restricted Bedouin movement, thereby forcing some of them to settlement in permanent locales.

Second ordinance – Expropriation Land Ordinance, 1926.[35] Expropriation of land for British public purposes, such as construction of an airport in 1934 in Haifa and King David-Lloyd George airport in Marj Ibn Amer in 1937 (today, Ramat David Airbase);[36] construction of new roads in the Galilee; establishment of schools (such as expropriation of 3,000 dunams from Al-Subayh tribe and given to PJCA, for to establishing Kh/Kadoorie Agricultural School next to Mount Tabor, in 1933).[37]

Third ordinance – Forest Ordinance, 1926.[38] The purpose thereof was to reserve a "closed forest area" for protecting endangered trees or for any other British purposes, causing Bedouin to lose their mobility, for instance, by afforestation of uncultivated land within the boundaries of the two adjacent German communities of Waldheim and Bethlehem, both in Haifa Sub-District, in 1944.[39] The land in question is 4,146 dunams (of 9,225 taxable and arable dunams of construction-zoned land) in Waldheim and 2,382 dunams (of 7,526 taxable and arable construction-zoned) in Bethlehem.[40] This forced most of the Bedouin tribes living in this area, especially semi-nomadic tribes such as, Sawaed, Al-Hajajra, Al-Saida, Al-Mazarib, Al-Ghrefat, Al-Jawamees, Al-Heib, and others, out of these wooded areas.[41]

Fourth ordinance – Collective Punishments Ordinances, 1926–1936,[42] provided for the levying of fines and other penalties on the inhabitants of villages and tribal areas (listed in the schedule). Accordingly, when any area or portion thereof, in the High Commissioner's opinion, is in a 'dangerous and disturbed' condition, he may, order the police to arrest 'invaders' in this territory. According to the schedule list,[43] most of the entries are of Bedouin tribes, so this ordinance was enacted against Bedouin suspected of "invading" state lands. The punishment for violation of these laws was decreed collective, i.e., applying to all members of the tribe.[44] However, this law became individual punishment in the 1940s, when the "Bedouin Control Ordinance" was enacted in 1942.[45] The purpose of the Collective Punishments Ordinances was to enable Bedouin settlement, which served Mandatory policy of maintaining stability and quiet in Palestine. This was expressed in correspondence between Galilee District Commissioner in Nazareth Charles Tunstall Evans in his complaint on 3 September 1943 to High Commissioner of Palestine in Jerusalem

Harold MacMichael, about the movement phenomenon of Al-Subayh and Al-Mazarib tribes from one place to another in Marj Ibn Amer (see Appendix D). The High Commissioner's response on 21 September 1943 to Galilee District Commissioner (see Appendix E):

> You will appreciate that the Bedouin Control Ordinance [1942] is intended to be applied only to nomadic or semi-nomadic tribes and only in cases of real necessity, but not ad-hoc in every case where there is only a small community of tent dwellers. In these circumstances, I ask you to be good enough to confirm that you are satisfied that the tribes mentioned in your letter do in fact fall within the category of nomads or semi-nomads for whom the Bedouin Control Ordinance is designed. Moreover, that it would not be sufficient to make them obligated to the Collective Punishments Ordinance under which several of them are scheduled already.[46]

It can be concluded from the High Commissioner's words that he encouraged Bedouin to settle into permanent locales.

Fifth ordinance – Land Settlement Ordinances, 1928–1930.[47] These ordinances, begun by survey in 1928, produced village maps with blocs to facilitate the taxation of rural property. These maps then served as a basis upon which registration blocs were parceled and surveyed. Consequent to these regulations, many Bedouin were dispossessed of their lands, as some of them were present in grazing areas during the survey, not in the encampment area (*dirah*).[48] Moreover, some of the land was registered in names of effendis and mukhtars.[49]

Sixth ordinance – Bedouin Control Ordinance of 1942 (see Appendix F),[50] and individual punishment (instead of the collective punishment used at the beginning of the Mandate, see "Fourth ordinance" above) of lawbreakers. This ordinance's purpose was to confer upon District Commissioners general control over nomadic tribal communities in Palestine, including the power to investigate and punish offences committed by members thereof (see Appendix F). Evidence thereof can find in the correspondence between District Commissioner of the Galilee district in Nazareth Charles Tunstall Evans and High Commissioner of Palestine in Jerusalem, Alan Gordon Cunningham, on 7 February 1947, wherein the former notified the latter of Bedouin movement from one place to another in Tiberias region, and sought to implement the Bedouin Control Ordinance on these tribes:

> It will be possible to take action under Section 4 [general power, control, and investigation] of the ordinance to exercise general control

of their movements, as and when desirable. The tribes are Arab Wahib, Dalaika, Masharqa, Nujeidat, Samkia, and Khawaled (sub-tribe of Trans-Jordan tribe). I accordingly request that the High Commissioner exercise his power under Section 3 [Application of ordinance to certain nomadic tribes] of the ordinance as amended, to declare that the provisions of the ordinance apply to the tribes mentioned.[51]

While the purpose of this complaint was to prevent Bedouin movement from one place to another, there were likely other goals, such as ensuring Jewish settlement in Palestine. Nonetheless, the Bedouin movement restrictions contributed to their settlement.

All of these bureaucratic rules curtailed Bedouin's mobility and increased their settling sedentarily. In fact, these agencies of change[52] affected and forced these tribes to move to nearby Bedouin or Fellahin villages.[53] Incidentally, the order of Bedouin Control Ordinance was repealed by Israel on 6 February 1963, in a Knesset vote.[54]

Internal/local circumstantial pressures

The geographical proximity between the two categories, Bedouin and Fellahin, and the economic interaction between them also influenced some Bedouin to purchase land and settle in Fellahin towns and villages. Moreover, the town served as a center providing extensive services to the periphery inhabitants, and thus attracted the Bedouin population.

Local circumstantial cases that illustrate the above

Firstly, physical-geographical proximity of a town or village and the economic interaction between Bedouin and Fellahin, i.e., the Bedouin economic need to market products derived from livestock, such as meat, wool, and dairy products, in exchange for goods essential to the Bedouin, such as food products (mainly legumes), animal fodder, fabric, tent canvas, saddles, and more.

From the beginning of the Mandate, Bedouin youth sought occasional employment by wealthy Fellahin. For example, Bedouin from Sawaed tribe who lived in a permanent locale in Al-Hamira (southern Shafa-Amer) worked in Shafa-Amer Fellahin Christians' orchards.[55] Moreover, a few Bedouin from various tribes worked as cattle herders among affluent families in nearby villages, such as, Bedouin youth from Sweitat tribe who worked as cattle herders in Abu Snan, and later they lived in this village.

Thus, geographic proximity, coupled with constant and dynamic economic reciprocity, caused some of tribal population to settle nearby and within towns and villages to which they had often previously arrived.[56]

Secondly, the town is an attraction that provides extensive public services:

HEALTH: In urgent cases, some Bedouin arrived to towns to treat medical cases. Sanitation: A town's veterinary service provided animal care. In some towns, such as Beisan, animal care was free and included medication.[57] A public notice sent by sub-district officer of Beisan Abdullah Khair, on 13 February 1937 asked all livestock breeders in his area, to bring their livestock for veterinary care, recently opened in Beisan:

> This clinic will be open Mondays and Thursdays every week, working hours will be 7:20 a.m. to 2 p.m. The animals will be treated free of charge, as well as necessary medication being provided to the animal owner for free.[58]

TAX PAYMENTS: Permanent Bedouin inhabitants came to towns to pay taxes. Types of taxes were house and land tax, rural property tax,[59] urban property tax (1.70 Palestine Pound (LP) for each structure),[60] animal tax,[61] and tithes (10% of annual crop).[62]

Filing complaints in courts to punish lawbreakers. For example, a complaint filed on 21 September 1946, at agriculture ministry in Beisan sub-district against Bedouin from Arab Al-Saqer (Shahada Al-Hasian) tribe, who lived in Al-Ashrafia, for bringing his sheep to Al-Jawsaq Spring, thus causing contamination of drinking water,[63] precluding other inhabitants from using this spring at the same time. The law enforcement authorities handled the offense severely, and on 1 October 1946 (10 days later), this Bedouin was summoned to the "municipal tribunal" in Beisan and fined five LPs for his offense.[64]

Thirdly, requests for assistance from the state's legal authorities: The degree of connection between Bedouin and their dependence upon legal authorities varied from place to place, depending upon their proximity and willingness to move to sedentarizaion in towns and villages. For example, Bedouin, who lived in Fellahin villages or in tribal headquarters around Beisan, were in constant contact with town offices. This connection surrounded mainly regulation of distribution of water, such as dates of watering livestock and agricultural growth, including requests for assistance in repairing and cleaning springs and streams that led to fields that were cultivated by some Bedouin who lived sedentarily.

These factors – continued land acquisition by Jewish organizations, Mandatory governmental pressures; or circumstantial and/or other – led Bedouin in the Galilee during the Mandate to begin to occupy land as a primary source of livelihood and housing needs. As aforementioned, most of them purchased small plots from Fellahin farmers, especially near built-up areas. These purchases were intended for construction of stone houses for residential purposes, nearby Fellahin's houses.

Some Names of Bedouin Families that Integrated into Fellahin Towns and Villages during the British Rule, 1918–1948

Nujeidat tribe settlement in Bu'enie: this tribe belongs to the Al-Howeitat tribes from Najd region.[65] In the first half of the 19th century, the head of this tribe was Muhammad Subayh Alwan Nujeidat, who joined Ibrahim Pasha's conquests in Al-Sham, and who decided to settle in Subayh lands, north of Sahl Al-Battuf. I would point out that this tribe first had settled on the slopes of Mount Tabor, although it continued wandering north to Sahl Al-Battuf seeking resources – pasture and water – according to the seasons, until it reached a final settlement near Bu'enie village.[66] The reasons for this settlement were the spring in this area, and the grazing territories that were good for sheep in the wide, fertile valley. The connection between these tribes occurred when the chief of Nujeidat tribe formed an alliance with Subayh tribe (Al-Subayh tribe consists of five tribes: Maqtrin, Jadida, Sneedat, Tiherat, and Shibli).[67] The territory of al-Subayh tribe extended from tribal headquarters (*dirah*) on Mount Tabor to the Bu'enie village area. In addition to the aforementioned alliance, another alliance with Fellahin was forged in 1928 between the Sheikh of Nujeidat tribe, Issa Khalid Ishtiywi who married Haja Suleiman, the daughter of the mukhtar of Bu'enie. This caused the rest of his Bedouin family, from Subayh tribe, to move to this village in chain migration fashion, where they purchased about 300 dunams belonging to Suleiman's family in the 1930s and 1940s (see Map 2.1, page 67).[68]

Shawahdeh tribe settlement in Eilabun in the 1930s. Some of this tribe decided to leave the tribal headquarters Al-Mawasi that were located on Al-Hami Mount, east of Eilabun, and moved to the western slope of Eilabun and settled in tents, the reason therefor being the spring in this area.[69] Later, they gradually began to purchase lands from Fellahin villagers (such as Matar, Sursock, and Zurik) in Eilabun. The method of purchase was and "exchange deal", wherein about 10 goats were exchanged for a dunam of land, the exchange rate at that time. At the same time, another part of the Al-Mawasi headquarters decided to move to Tamra and Shafa-Amer.[70]

Settlement of **Marisat** tribe in 1925, which moved from the tribe's headquarters in the dunes [*Qaba'il al-Ramil*] between Acre and Haifa, inland to Iblin.[71]

Settlement of **Sawilat** tribe in Balad al-Sheikh. The origin of this tribe is the Hula Valley.[72] In the 1930s, about six families from this tribe decided to settle in Balad al-Sheikh village, about nine families from this tribe moved to al-Manawat village, and another part of this tribe decided to live in Maros village in the Hula Valley.[73] The reasons for this transition were economic: the search for water and grazing land.

Settlement of **Heib Al-Fawawza** tribe in Eilabun. This name (Al-Fawawza) is related to the father's family name, As'ad al-Fawaz of Heib tribe headquarters. This tribe was nomadic in Sahl Al-Battuf (southwest of Eilabun). In the 1930s, this tribe decided to relocate to southern outskirts of Eilabun, about 100 meters away from Sahl Al-Battuf.[74]

Settlement of **Sweitat** tribe in Eilabun and Deir Hanna. In the 1930s, part of Sweitat tribe who located in *Khirbet Sabana* territory east of Eilabun, moved to al-Hami Mount near Eilabun. Other part moved to Deir Hanna village during the 1948 war.[75]

Settlement of **Al-Ghazalin** tribe in Yafa. In 1942, this tribe's mukhtar, Hussein al-Uthaman, was camping together with his tribe, eastern of Iksal village, he purchased 25 dunams from Yafa resident Salem al-Mas'ad.[76] Later, al-Uthaman and some of his tribe moved to the southern neighborhood of Yafa. After the 1948 war and during the 1970s, the rest of this tribe moved to Yafa via chain migrations.[77]

Settlement of **Sawaed Abu Shahab** tribe in Shafa-Amer. Some of this tribe arrived in 1944 from tribal headquarters in an encampment near Al-Husayniyya village north of Safad, moved to Shafa-Amer. Later, during the 1948 war, another part of this tribal headquarters moved to Sha'ab and Tamra.[78]

Settlement of **Sawaed** tribe in Maghar. This tribe arrived from Wadi Salameh north of Maghar in the 1940s, and settled in this village.[79] The reasons for the transition were economic.

Settlement of **Rmihat** tribe in Maghar. The tribe arrived in this village in the 1940s from Al-Ghuwair region, north of Tiberias Lake. Their sheikh was Abdallah Muhammad Al-Jum'ah, who came with his four brothers: Ramih, Jum'ah, Hamad, and Samir. The reason for their arrival was water sources (Mamilla and al-Mansoura springs).[80]

Settlement of some of **Sweitat** tribe in Abu Snan. The tribe was encamped in Jadin village, and in the 1940s, some members began working at a ranch owned by wealthy Druze villagers as a cattle hands and as farmhands sowing tobacco, wheat, and vegetables. At the beginning of this settlement, they built tents at their place of work. After the 1948 war, they purchased lands from Druze and built stone houses.[81]

Settlement of another part of **Sweitat** tribe in Balad al-Sheikh. This part was encamped in the dunes [Qaba'il al-Ramil] between Acre and Haifa, and in the 1940s, some members of this tribe moved to Balad al-Sheikh village.[82]

Settlement of **Qlitat** tribe in Balad al-Sheikh. This tribe was nomadic in the Al-Bassa area (12 km north of Acre) in the 18th century, and camped in the dunes [Qaba'il al-Ramil]. Later, at the beginning of the British mandate, tribal sheikh Nayef Abu Dallah, decided to move to Balad al-Sheikh village near Haifa.[83]

Settlement of **Ghawarna** tribes in Al-Khalsa and Acre. These tribes were semi-nomadic villagers, who lived along the Jordan and Hula Valleys. Around 1876, when swamps began to be drained by authorities in these valleys, a large portion of Ghawarna made sure to register their ownership of land [tabu].[84] Some, who did not have ownership or registration of land, moved to Al-Khalsa village; and another moved its encampment to Qaba'il al-Ramil between Acre and Haifa. Later, in the 1940s, they moved to Acre and dwelt there.

Settlement of **Turkmens** tribes in villages on Mount Carmel.[85] The source of these tribes is Turkmenistan region. They are Muslims, speaking Arabic with a Bedouin dialect, who came to Marj Ibn Amer during Saladin's wars against the crusaders in the 12th century.[86] Horse competitions and watermelon crops were their occupations, which is why they settled in Marj Ibn Amer.[87] During Ottoman rule, especially at the beginning of the 20th century, seven Turkmens nomadic tribes (Banu Suaidan, Banu Alkama, Banu Gerra, Banu Baniha, Al-Shkirat, Al-Tawatha, and Al-Nagnagia) began settling in permanent places on the Mount Carmel ridge.[88] They established a new villages (on the ruins of abandoned villages), mixing with Fellahin farmers along the southern hills of Mount Carmel in Al-Mansi, Lydd al-Awadin, al-Ghubayya al-Fawqa, al-Tahta, and Abu Shusha.[89]

Settlement of **Maslama** tribe in Al-Naora. This lineage belonging to Al-Na'im tribes headquarter from the Golan Heights and Syria.[90] Members of this tribe were shepherds in summer at Marj Ibn Amer region, and in winter, they returned to tribe headquarter in Golan Heights (*Dirah*). In the 1920s, they bought farmland in Al-Naora and settled there. On the eve of the 1948 war, there were about 15 inhabitants.[91]

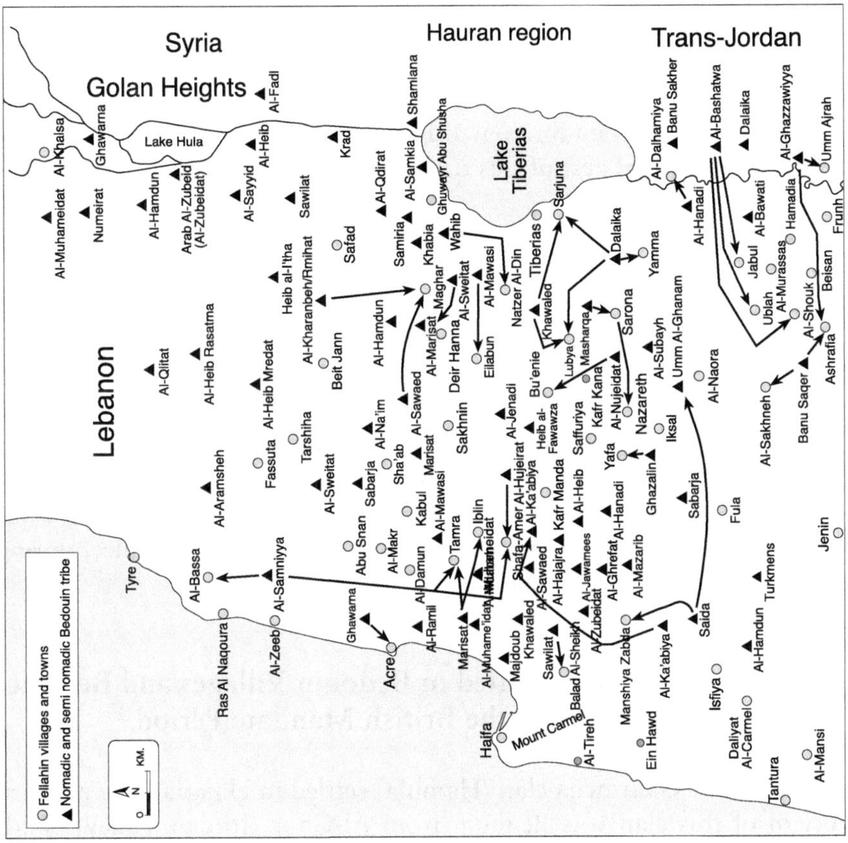
Syria
Golan Heights
Hauran region
Trans-Jordan
Lebanon
Lake Hula
Lake Tiberias
Mount Carmel
Fellahin villages and towns
Nomadic and semi nomadic Bedouin tribe
N
KM.
Al-Khalsa
Ghawarna
Al-Fadl
Al-Heib
Krad
Shamlana
Al-Muhameidat
Numeirat
Al-Hamdun
Arab Al-Zubeid (Al-Zubeidat)
Al-Sayyid
Sawilat
Al-Qdirat
Al-Samkia
Ghuwayr Abu Shusha
Samiria
Khabia
Wahib
Safad
Heib al-I'tha
Al-Kharanbeh/Rmihat
Maghar
Al-Sweitat
Al-Mawasi
Natzer Al-Din
Tiberias
Sarjuna
Dalaika
Yamma
Al-Dalhamiya
Banu Sakher
Al-Hanadi
Al-Bashatwa
Dalaika
Al-Bawati
Al-Ghazzawiyya
Umm Ajrah
Hamadia
Frunh
Jabul
Ublah
Al-Murassas
Beisan
Al-Shouk
Ashrafia
Banu Saqer
Al-Sakhneh
Al-Qlitat
Al-Heib Rasatma
Al-Heib Mredat
Beit Jann
Al-Hamdun
Al-Marisat
Deir Hanna
Eilabun
Khawaled
Lubya
Masharqa
Sarona
Al-Subayh
Umm Al-Ghanam
Al-Naora
Bu'enie
Kafr Kana
Al-Nujeidat
Nazareth
Iksal
Tarshiha
Al-Na'im
Al-Sawaed
Sakhnin
Al-Jenadi
Heib al-Fawawza
Saffuriya
Yafa
Ghazalin
Sabarja
Fula
Jenin
Al-Aramsheh
Fassuta
Al-Sweitat
Sabarja
Sha'ab
Marisat
Kabul
Al-Mawasi
Al-Hujeirat
Al-Ka'abiya
Kafr Manda
Al-Heib
Al-Hanadi
Tyre
Al-Bassa
Al-Samniyya
Abu Snan
Al-Makr
Al-Damun
Tamra
Iblin
Shafa-Amer
Al-Sawaed
Al-Hajajra
Al-Jawamees
Al-Ghrefat
Al-Mazarib
Saida
Turkmens
Ras Al Naqoura
Al-Zeeb
Ghawarna
Acre
Al-Ramil
Marisat
Al-Muhameidat
Majdoub
Khawaled
Sawilat
Balad Al-Sheikh
Al-Zubeidat
Manshiya Zabda
Al-Ka'abiya
Al-Hamdun
Isfiya
Haifa
Al-Tireh
Ein Hawd
Daliyat Al-Carmel
Tantura
Al-Mansi

Settlement of **Samniyya** tribe in Shafa-Amer and Tarshiha. This tribe included two lineages: al-Atatra, and al-Manasara. This tribe's sheikh during the Mandate was Asmar al-Mahmoud.[92] During the 1948 war, the tribe moved to Shafa-Amer, and a few of them moved to Tarshiha village.

Settlement of **Al-Hanadi** tribe, which wandered in the hills surrounding Shafa-Amer. At the beginning of the Mandate, this tribe moved from the Shafa-Amer hills to the Khan al-Tajjar area (merchants' market) north of Mount Tabor in search of pasture. There, they clashed with members of al-Subayh tribe, and consequently moved to camp in Qaba'il al-Ramil between Acre and Haifa, where they lived until the end of the Mandate, when Ibrahim al-Hindawi purchased a house in Shafa-Amer's center. The rest of this tribe moved to Shafa-Amer in the 1950s in a chain migration.[93]

Settlement some of **Al/El-Hujeirat** tribe in Shafa-Amer and Uzair. Their tribal headquarters in the 19th century was in Sahl Al-Battuf, and their sheikh in this period was Abid al-Ramli.[94] In the 1948 war, some members of this tribe moved to Shafa-Amer and Uzair (see Map 2.1, page 67).[95] Alongside the migration of Bedouin to Fellahin towns and villages, a rural-Fellahin population moved to existing Bedouin communities. In addition, in rare cases, a mixed Bedouin-Fellahin village was established, such as Manshiya Zabda in the 1940s.

Map 2.1 also shows the movement of some nomadic and semi-nomadic Bedouin to Fellahin towns and villages in the Galilee, during British Mandate rule in Palestine, 1918–1948.[96]

Fellahin Clans Who Settled in Bedouin Villages and Became Bedouin during the British Mandate Period[97]

Ghourani or **Ghawarna** clan (Hamula) settled in Hajajra. The primary origin of this clan was Bedouin from Al-Ghor (Jordan Valley). With Ibrahim Pasha's conquest (1831–1840) of Al-Sham, the tribe moved to Saffuriya (a Fellahin village), began cultivating land, and became Fellahin/farmers. From there they moved to their lands nearby Hajajra village. Note that the boundaries of Saffuriya village extended up to the German Templar village of Bethlehem of Galilee, near Hajajra. The reason for this settlement was economic: Agricultural work prompted them to live in nearby Hajajra.

Sulaimani clan (also called Al-Darwish) established Manshiya Zabda in 1945. In 1910, this clan came from Ilut (Fellahin village) to cultivate their land. Note that the boundaries of Ilut village extended far from their village of origin. At that time, the reason for this transition was mainly economic. The head of this family, Muhammad Hassan Darwish, came to cultivate his land along with his sons, Hassan, Sabri, Hussein, and Saleh. At first, they built barracks near their fields and began to live there temporarily. They also began to establish social and economic ties with Bedouin living in their vicinity, especially with Saida tribe, which arrived later in the 1940s, and which was camped on Mount Carmel in *Jira* near Al-Mansi village (see Map 2.1). The reason for transfer of members of this tribe was sale of land to the Jewish Agency, which compelled them to move to other places (some moved to Manshiya Zabda, and others moved to Bedouin villages such as Umm al-Ghanam, near Shibli; and Daburiya).[98]

Abdel al-Halim clan came from Ilut in 1945 and settled in Manshiya Zabda. The reason for their transition was conflict with the extended family of Abu Ras.[99] Consequent thereto, this clan fled its original village (Ilut) and looked for a safe place to live. Nahalal police Sergeant Yitzhak Shvili, who the Arabs called Abu Khader, gave sanctuary to members of this family,[100] whose founder, Abdel al-Halim, along with his four sons: Ahmad, Faleh, Kamel, and Mufilh, built tents near Nahalal police precinct. Soon, they converted the tents to barracks and spontaneous settlement developed, and called Manshiya Zabda. Shortly after the establishment of Israel in 1948, more clans from Ilut, such as al-Baba clan, joined Manshiya Zabda. At the same time, Bedouin families from the Saida tribe joined. Later on, villagers allowed building concrete houses in the 1950s. Manshiya Zabda was known as a Bedouin village, as most of its inhabitants are of Bedouin origin.

Bedouin in the Galilee on the Eve of the 1948 War: Statistical Data and Settlement Distribution

The British Mandate officially (1920–1948) divided Palestine administratively into three provinces: Northern, Jerusalem, and Southern. Moreover, each province was divided into districts. The Northern Province was divided into nine districts: Tulkarm, Nablus, Jenin, Beisan, Nazareth, Tiberias, Safad, Acre, and Haifa. This province included the Galilee, which had six districts: Beisan, Nazareth, Tiberias, Safad, Acre, and Haifa, including about 260 villages.[101]

During this period, three censuses were taken intended to count the entire population of Palestine, including the Bedouin population (the British called them censuses; in retrospect, these estimates gave "quantity orders" of populations, particular the Bedouin population), which was difficult to count due to its nomadic lifestyle. Additionally, these estimates considered natural increase.

Thus, in this sub-section, I present the three British Mandate censuses (1922, 1931, and 1946) in regard to population of districts and their sub-districts, which included Bedouin, and which will indicate causes of the Bedouin population decline in Palestine. In addition, in the end, I will present a new estimate based on archives, research literature, and interviews with Bedouin, in order to estimate the Bedouin population that lived in Fellahin towns and villages in the Galilee and compare it to rest of the Bedouin population, both nomadic and permanent.

First census conducted by British Mandate in Palestine, 1922[102]

According to this census, the population in Palestine numbered 757,182, including 83,794 Jews; 73,024 Christians; 590,890 Muslims; and 9,474 inhabitants belonging to other ethnic groups.[103] This estimate counted the Arab population in the Galilee as 58,325,[104] subdivided into districts as follows:

Nazareth District: Total: 22,681 (urban: 7,424 and rural: 15,257). The Muslim population of Nazareth was estimated at 2,486. **Beisan District**: Total: 10,679 (urban: 1,941 and rural: 8,738). Muslim population in Beisan was estimated at 1,687. **Tiberias District**: Total: 20,721 (urban: 6,950 and rural: 13,771). The Muslim population in Tiberias was estimated at 2,096. **Haifa District**: Total: 56,457 (urban: 26,922 and rural: 29,535). The Muslim population in Haifa was estimated at 9,377. **Acre District**: Total: 35,535 (urban: 6,420 and rural: 29,115). The Muslim population in Acre was estimated at 4,883. **Safad District**: Total: 22,790 (urban: 8,761 and rural: 14,029). The Muslim population in Safad was estimated at 5,431.[105]

In this estimate, the Bedouin were estimated at about 71,000 inhabitants, which constituted about 12% of the total Muslim population of Palestine.[106] The number of Bedouin in the Galilee was estimated at 16,969 (see Table 2.1 below), which constituted 23% of the total Bedouin population of Palestine, and about 29% of the Fellahin population in the Galilee, and 2.2% of the total population of Palestine. This estimate is based on data taken from reports by government officials.

Note that this low estimate of the number of Bedouin in the Galilee does not show a high level of reliability of this census, due to several reasons, one of which was absence of a comprehensive survey of all Bedouin tribes living in the Galilee at the time. Bedouin were concerned that the census was for preparing to collect taxes and draft them into the army, as Ottomans did before them. Therefore, some of them avoided

British census officials. Table 2.1.pages 72, 73) presents tribes' names and the number of inhabitants (men and women over 18 years old) of nomadic Bedouin according to their geographic proximity in Galilee towns and villages during the British Mandate.

Second census conducted by the British Mandate in Palestine, 1931[107]

The total population of Palestine in 1931 was 1,035,821, of which 759,712 were Muslims; 174,610 were Jews; 91,398 were Christians; and another 10,101 were members of other ethnic groups.[108] The estimate presented the Arab population of the Galilee as 84,855.[109] It was divided into districts and sub-districts as follows:

Nazareth District: Total: 28,592 (urban: 8,756 and rural: 19,836). The Muslim population in Nazareth was estimated at 3,226. **Beisan District**: Total: 15,123 (urban: 3,101 and rural: 12,022). The Muslim population was estimated at 2,699. **Tiberias District**: Total: 26,975 (urban: 8,601 and rural: 18,374). The Muslim population was estimated at 2,645. **Haifa District**: Total: 95,472 (urban: 53,227 and rural: 42,245). The Muslim population in Haifa was estimated at 20,324. **Acre District**: Total: 45,142 (urban: 7,897 and rural: 37,245). The Muslim population in Acre was estimated at 6,076. **Safad District**: Total: 39,713 (urban: 9,441 and rural: 30,272). The Muslim population in Safad was estimated at 6,465.[110]

In this estimate, the Bedouin numbered in Palestine: 66,553.[111] In addition, this estimate partially counted the nomadic Bedouin population in various sub-districts of the Galilee: about 11,510 (Safad and its sub-district: 2,800; Tiberias and its sub-district: 2,444; Acre and its sub-district: 1,271; Beisan and its sub-district: 4,995).[112] According to Yaacov Shimoni, the Bedouin population of the Galilee numbered about 13,000 in that year.[113]

Accordingly, the nomadic Bedouin in the Galilee constituted about 17% of the total Bedouin population in Palestine, about 13% of the total Arab population in the Galilee, and about 1.1% of the total population in Palestine. It can assume, therefore, that there has been a certain decline in the number of nomadic Bedouin in the Galilee.[114] This indicates that Bedouin have become permanent inhabitants (therefore, the two censuses "not counting" Bedouin). The statistics of the two above estimates (despite these estimates' weakness) indicate that there was a decline in the number of nomadic Bedouin, a decrease of approximately 5,459 nomadic Bedouin during a period of nine years. (In 1922, the nomadic population numbered 16,969; if we compare to 1931, the

Table 2.1. Estimated distribution of Bedouin residing in Bedouin tribes in the Galilee, 1922

Beisan District Tribe name	Number	Tiberias District Tribe name	Number	Safad District Tribe name	Number
Banu Saqer	1,521	Al-Kharanbeh/Rmihat Masharqa	144	Azizat	98
Al-Ghazzawiyya	932		100	Krad al-Ghannama	265
Al-Bashatwa	950	Al-Samkia	193	Krad al-Baqqra	245
Al-Bawatiya	348	Wahib	61	Al-Hamdun	148
Al-Zinati	519	Netzer Din	279	Hamam	76
Jisr al-Majami	298	Nuqib	287	Heib Al-Itha	370
		Tazawia	623	Kaosh	157
		Sumara	204	Mawasi	66
		Talawia	332	Al-Muhameidat	55
		Tabiqa	245	Heib Rasatma	133
		Manara	121	Al-Sayyid	57
		Mawasi	145	Zangariah	526
		Seragnah	91	Shamlana	278
		Al-Kaddish	64	Umm Sa'id	93
				Sawaed	59
				Sweitat	83
				Numeirat	64
				Al-Qdirat	194
				Al-Malha	440
				Al-Jisr	59
				Al-Nujeidat	125
Total	4,568		2,889		3,591

(*Continued on Next Page*)

Table 2.1. Estimated distribution of Bedouin residing in Bedouin tribes in the Galilee, 1922 (continued)

Acre District		Nazareth District		Haifa District	
Tribe name	Number	Tribe name	Number	Tribe name	Number
Al-Aramsheh	199	Al-Jawamees	117	Al-Shkirat	403
Al-Heib	74	Al-Mazarib	125	Al-Saida	--
Al-Ramil	121	Al-Heib	86	Sweitat	119
Al-Ghawarna	243	Al-Subayh	59	Al-Qlitat	118
Al-Howeitat	8	Al-Sabarja	653	Al-Sammiyya	139
Al-Sweitat	128	Al-Ghazalin	59	Al-Towaqia	93
Al-Qlitat	11	Al-Hujeirat	103	Al-Na'im	17
Al-Towaqia	93			Beni Semran	45
Al-Hmeirat	12			Al-Tawatha	301
Al-Sammiyya	139			Al-Hujeirat	18
Al-Sawaed	349			Turkmens	1,037
Al-Mawasi	17			Al-Nafi'at	336
Al-Tawalha	5			Al-Zubeidat	363
Al-Hamdun	4			Al-Hamdun	22
Al-Hujeirat	200				
Al-Jenadi	14				
Al-Marisat	74				
Al-Na'im	17				
Total	**1,708**		**1,202**		**3,011**

Bedouin population numbered 11,510). These data indicate that the decline points to an intensive sedentarizaion process, both in Bedouin communities and in Fellahin towns and villages in the Galilee. I should emphasize that during this period, there was no negative migration. On the contrary, Bedouin tribes continued to immigrate to the Galilee, mainly from the Syrian region, due to the economic prosperity in Palestine under the British Mandate.[115]

Therefore, what appeared as a reduction in Bedouin numbers in the Galilee was actually due to sedentarization. Moreover, given high natural increase, sedentarizaion became more intensive.[116] In other words, despite the increased immigration and high natural increase (which should have reflected a high rate of nomadism), there was a decline in nomadic Bedouin numbers due to settlement of these Bedouin in existing Fellahin towns and villages and/or in existing Bedouin communities/villages, which continued in the third British estimate of 1946.

According to **third census conducted by the British Mandate in Palestine in 1946**, the population numbered 1,845,560 (including 1,076,780 Muslims, 608,230 Jews, 145,060 Christians, and 15,490 inhabitants belonging to other ethnic groups).[117]

The Northern Province was divided administratively and demographically (which included Bedouin population) into six districts:

Nazareth district (including Fula, today, Afula): Total: 49,910 (urban: 15,540, rural: 31,900, and other rural from Fula: 2,470). The Muslim population in Nazareth was estimated at 6,290. **Beisan district**: Total: 24,950 (urban: 5,540 and rural: 19,410) The Muslim population in of Beisan was estimated at 5,080. **Tiberias district**: Total: 41,470 (urban: 11,810 and rural: 29,660). The Muslim population in Tiberias was estimated at 4,990. **Haifa district** (included Shafa-Amer and Hadera): Total: 253,450 (urban: 145,430 rural 96,690; Shafa-Amer: 3,740; Hadera: 7,590). The Muslim population in this district was estimated at approximately 41,000. **Acre district**: Total: 73,600 (urban: 13,560 and rural: 60,040). The Muslim population in Acre was estimated at 10,930. **Safad district**: Total: 56,970 (urban: 12,610 and rural: 44,360). The Muslim populaion in Safad was estimated at 9,780.[118]

Another estimate, called the "Village Statistics 1945", was carried out a year earlier, by the British Mandatory government between the years 1945–1946,[119] conducted especially for estimating the rural population in Palestine. This estimate was based on data from the 1931 census, but was unreliable for several reasons: a rough estimate of the natural increase attributed to the Arab population between the years

1922–1944 is 2.53% per year; absence of a survey of all of the nomadic Bedouin tribes inhabiting all of the districts in the Galilee during that period; absence of data on permanent Bedouin living in or near Fellahin towns and villages in the Galilee, who may have been counted as inhabitants of Fellahin villages and towns.

This estimate indicates that the number of Bedouin in the Galilee was about 9,760 (nomads and permanent inhabitants, not including Bedouin who live in Fellahin towns and villages) of which only 2,530 were nomadic Bedouin (Al-Subayh tribe: 1,320, Acre Sub-district: 560; Al-Shamlana tribe: 650 in Safad Sub-district). From these statistical data, it can be seen that the estimate relates more to permanent Bedouin than to nomadic Bedouin. Despite the problem with this estimate, the data indicate a sharp decline number of Bedouin from to previous estimates.

It can also be assumed that geographical proximity was a decisive factor in the transition of nomadic populations to Fellahin towns and villages. In fact, most of Bedouin inhabitants listed in the table below had previously lived close to Fellahin villages and towns, which made it easier to move to them. This was reflected in the decline in the nomadic Bedouin population, and the increase in the number of inhabitants in towns and villages. For example, in 1922, Acre had 4,883 inhabitants. In 1931, this number rose to 6,076, and in 1946 the number reached 10,930. At the same time, the number of rural inhabitants of this district in 1922 was 20,042, and in 1931, it was 25,829. In 1945, it reached 37,400.[120] On the other hand, in 1922, the number of Bedouin inhabitants of Acre was 1,523. In 1931, this number dropped to 650, and in 1946, it was 560 Bedouin. This was the case in most other Arab towns and villages in the Galilee. Table 2.2 (overleaf) shows the total number of Bedouin, estimated at 9,760, according to the 1945 survey of villages, from which a Bedouin lifestyle due to their having transitioned from nomadic to sedentary can be clearly deduced (the table presents names of Bedouin-only localities and the number of their inhabitants in the Galilee at the end of the British Mandate according to the British Villages Survey of 1945).

Noted that these three British Mandate censuses do not relate all to Bedouins living in Fellahin towns and villages. Therefore, a new estimate is required in order to map in statistical form the passage of nomadic Bedouin population into Fellahin villages and towns, which is one of the purposes of this study, to characterize mixed towns and villages in the Galilee. In other words, a distinction must be drawn, both nominally and numerically, between three kinds of Bedouin populations (nomadic/pastoral; permanent inhabitants in Bedouin villages; and Bedouin who moved to Fellahin villages and towns).

Table 2.2. Estimated distribution of Bedouin residing as permanent inhabitants and as Nomads in the Galilee near Fellahin villages and towns, 1945

Beisan District Tribe name	Population	Tiberias District Tribe name	Population	Safad District Tribe name	Population
Al-Ghazzawiyya	1,020	No data	No data	Shamlana	650
Al-Bashatwa	1,560			Al-Buwaida	510
				Krad al-Ghannama	350
				Krad al-Baqqra	360
				Tuba-Zangariah	590
				Nomadic Bedouin	820
Total	**2,850**		**--**		**3,280**

Acre District Tribe name	Population	Nazareth District Tribe name	Population	Haifa District Tribe name	Population
Nomadic Bedouin	560	Al-Subayh	1,320	Fuqara	310
				Ghawarna	620
				Al-Nafi'at	820
Total	**560**		**1,320**		**1,750**

This new estimate is based mainly on: A. Archives: State Archives of Israel (SAI),[121] Central Zionist Archives (CZA),[122] Valley of Maayanot Archives [Emek Hamaayanot] (VMA) near Beit-Shean (Beisan),[123] and Haganah Historical Archives (HHA).[124] B. Various books, mainly the encyclopedia of Mustafa al-Dabbagh,[125] Oppenheim,[126] Walid al-Khalidi,[127] and others. C. In-depth interviews with nomadic Bedouin, and Bedouin who live both in Bedouin villages and in Fellahin towns and villages in the Galilee. During the British Mandate, many Bedouin moved into Fellahin towns and villages. It is now possible to present statistics of the Bedouin population who camped alongside Fellahin villages and towns at the end of British Mandate period:

Firstly, **Haifa district**: The presence of semi-nomadic Bedouin in Haifa district and Mount Carmel: Haifa District contained about 52 villages, 11 Bedouin tribes, and 62 Jewish settlements.[128] According to the data, which I collected from the Central Zionist Archives (CZA) and from the encyclopedia of Mustafa al-Dabbagh and Walid Al-Khalidi, the total number of Bedouin in Haifa and its environs can be estimated at approximately 4,749,[129] divided as follows:

Bedouin families in Haifa: 274 inhabitants, divided as follows: Al-Madi, 40; Turkmen, 96; Azuid, 90; Al-Na'im, 20.[130]

Bedouin families who lived in Fellahin villages in Haifa district totaled 1,507, divided as follows:

Abu Shusha: 720 (475 Fellahin, and 245 Bedouin).[131] The Bedouin families' names were Al-Shkirat, and Al-Saida.[132] Ijzim:[133] 2,970 (2,572 Fellahin, and 398 Bedouin).[134] The Bedouin families' names were Al-Madi, who came from Al-Wuhaydat tribal headquarters in Naqab and wandered north at the end of the 18th century, as aforementioned. Balad Al-Sheikh: 4,120 (3,875 Fellahin, and 245 Bedouin).[135] Names Bedouin families' camping near this village: Al-Sawilat tribe (120); Samniyya (42); Al-Towaqia (55); Al-Qlitat (2 houses, 8 inhabitants); and Sweitat (five houses, 120 inhabitants).[136] Al-Sindiyana: 1,250 (1,026 Fellahin, and 224 Bedouin).[137] Bedouin families' names in this village: Al-Hamdun (74); Al-Wahib (30); Ali Nazal (from Al-Na'im tribal headquarters, 15); Al-Meqbel (60); Al-Jubwabra (25); and Al-Swalma (20).[138] Turkmen villages on Mount Carmel and in the northern Marj Ibn Amer included seven large tribes (Banu Suaidan, Banu Al-Kama, Banu Gerra, Banu Thabiya, Al-Shkirat, Al-Tawatha, and Al-Nagnagia) totaling 1,130 inhabitants,[139] some of whom (about 250 are Bedouin) lived in mixed villages with Fellahin: Al-Mansi, Lydd al-Awadin, al-Ghubayya al-Fawqa, and al-Tahta.[140] Tab'un: 370 (225 Fellahin, and 145 Bedouin).[141] Bedouin families' names in this village: N'arani (15); Al-Zubeidat (100); Samniyya (15); and Ghrefat (15).[142]

Semi-nomadic Bedouin tribes and permanent inhabitants living in Haifa district and Mount Carmel on the eve of the 1948 war totaled 2,968 Bedouin inhabitants, divided as follows: Abu Kulib (or Kulibat) family (10 inhabitants) of two houses located in Balad Al-Sheikh village valley.[143]

Bedouin tribes in Haifa sub-district, located on southern Mount Carmel comprised 2,370, distributed as follows: Arab al-Fuqara – 310;[144] Arab al-Ghawarna near Jisr al-Zarqa village – 620.[145] Al-Rarmil tribes, camped in the sands between Haifa and Acre, numbered 588 inhabitants,[146] some of whom lived near Haifa. They included the following tribes: Arab Al-Araqiya occupied about 70 houses; Arab Al-Sawaed, about 100 houses; Arab Al-Samniyya, about three houses; Arab Al-Wazaoza, about four houses; Arab Sweitat, six tents; Arab Al-Ghrefat (Abu-Tzahiyun family, Ali Mahmoud family), about four tents; Arab Al-Hajajra, about three houses; Arab Al-Hanbuzi, about four houses; Arab Al-Abidiyya about four houses; Arab Al-Numeirat, about three houses.[147]

Summary: The total number of Bedouin inhabitants in Haifa district and its sub-districts is estimated at 4,749. The number of semi-nomadic Bedouin and permanent inhabitants is estimated at 2,968. The remaining 1,781 Bedouin inhabitants lived in the city of Haifa and in the Fellahin villages around it.

Acre district: Bedouin presence in Acre district was approximately 2,730, divided as follows:

Bedouin families living in Acre: 160 (Majdoub, Al-Ghawarna).

Al-Rarmil tribes were located east and north of Acre, which were estimated, on the eve of the war, at about 650, divided into the following tribes: Arab Al-Majdoub (70), Arab Al-Ghawarna (80), Arab Al-Sawaed (168), Arab Al-Towaqia (40), Arab Marisat (120), Arab Al-Qlitat (122), and Arab Al-Samniyya (50).[148]

Semi-nomadic Bedouin in Acre sub-district: Arab Al-Aramsheh, about 199 inhabitants.[149]

Bedouin who lived in Fellahin villages in Acre sub-district: estimated on the eve of the 1948 war at 1,721, divided into the following villages: Al-Jadida and al-Makr: 280 (140 Fellahin, and 70 Bedouin).[150] Bedouin families' names in this village: Sweitat (45) and Fadeli (25 – from the tribal headquarters Al-Fadl,[151] who camped in the Golan Heights).[152] Tarshiha: 3,830 (3,709 Fellahin, and 121 Bedouin).[153] Bedouin families' names in this village: Al-Na'im (77) and Sweitat (44).[154] Abu Snan: 820 (790 Fellahin, and 30 Bedouin).[155] Bedouin families' names in this village: Sweitat (30).[156] Al-Damun: 1,310 (1,145 Fellahin, and 165 Bedouin).[157] Bedouin families' names in this village: Al-Ziadnah

(165).[158] Tamra: 1,380 (840 Fellahin, and 540 Bedouin).[159] Bedouin families' names in this village: Al-Ziadnah (80), Al-Marisat (340), and Mawasi (280).[160] Sakhnin: 2,600 (1,850 Fellahin, and 750 Bedouin).[161] Bedouin families' names in this village: Zubeidat (400), Trabiyeh (the original tribe name: Trabay) (350).[162] Deir Hanna: 750 Muslim inhabitants (725 Fellahin, and 25 Bedouin).[163] Bedouin families' names in this village: Al-Ziadnah (13) and Sweitat (12).[164] Majd al-Krum: 1,400 (1,380 Fellahin, and 20 Bedouin).[165] Bedouin families' names in this village: Sawaed (20).[166]

Summary: The total number of Bedouin inhabitants who lived in Acre and its sub-districts was estimated at 2,730 inhabitants. Semi-nomadic Bedouin and permanent inhabitants was estimated at 849. The rest were 1,881 Bedouin who lived in Acre and in the Fellahin villages around it.

Shafa-Amer sub-district: Bedouin presence in Shafa-Amer sub-district: The total number of inhabitants: 3,630 (Fellahin and Bedouin).[167] In addition, the total number of Bedouin in Shafa-Amer and its sub-districts was approximately 2,715 inhabitants, divided as follows:

Bedouin families living in Shafa-Amer: 330.[168] Bedouin families' names in this village: Al-Ziadnah, Al-Hawara, Sawaed, Al-Marisat, and Al-Samniyya.

Shafa-Amer sub-district contained 1,820 semi-nomadic Bedouin inhabitants, divided as follows: Zubeidat (410), Arab al-Safsaf (450), Arab Al-Helf (280), Arab Al-Amariya (410), Arab Al-Khawaled (80), and Arab Al-Sawaed (190).[169]

Bedouin who lived in Fellahin villages in Shafa-Amer sub-district on the eve of the 1948 war were estimated at about 565 inhabitants, divided among the following villages: Iblin: 1,660 (1,110 Fellahin, and 550 Bedouin).[170] Bedouin families' names in this village: Al-Hasi (15) (the family of the governor of the Galilee, Aqil Agha, in the second half of the 19th century), Sweitat, Marisat, Mawasi, Al-Sawaed, and Al-Amariya.[171]

Kaukab Abu Al-Hija: 490,[172] including (15) Bedouin from Hujeirat tribe.[173]

Summary: The total number of Bedouin inhabitants of Shafa-Amer and its sub-districts was estimated at 2,715 of whom nomadic, semi-nomadic, and permanent Bedouin inhabitants was estimated at 1,820. The remaining (895) Bedouin inhabitants lived in Shafa-Amer and in the Fellahin villages around it.

Safad district: The Bedouin presence in Safad district and sub-district: The total number of inhabitants in this area on the eve of the war was 5,123, divided as follows:

Bedouin families living in Safad: 120 (Al-Sayyid tribe, originated from the tribal headquarters of Al-Na'im in Syria).[174]

Nomadic, semi-nomadic, and permanent Bedouin inhabitants were estimated on the eve of the 1948 war to be 4,503, divided among the following tribes: Tuba-Zangariah (840), Krad al-Ghannama (350), Krad al-Baqqra (360), Al-Wahib (370), Al-Hamdun (590), Shamlana (650), Kaosh (820) from Al-Fadl tribal headquarter, Al-Muhameidat (55), Al-Numeirat (25), Wadi Al-Hamam (70), Umm Sa'id (93), and Khayam al-Walid (280).[175]

Bedouin who lived in Fellahin villages (i.e., mixed Fellahin and Bedouin villages) in Safad sub-district were estimated at 500, divided as follows: Jubb Yusuf: 170 (100 Fellahin, and 70 Bedouin from Al-Sayyid tribe, some of whom also lived in Safad).[176] Al-Malha: 890 (700 Fellahin, and 190 Bedouin, from Al-Zubeidat tribe).[177] Al-Khalsa: 1,840 (1,600 Fellahin, and 240 Bedouin of Al-Ghawarna tribe, originating from the Hula Valley area).[178]

Summary: The total number of Bedouin inhabitants of Safad and its sub-districts was estimated at 5,123, of whom the number of nomadic, semi nomadic, and permanent Bedouin inhabitants was estimated at 4,503. The remaining (620) Bedouin lived in Safad and in Fellahin villages around it.

Tiberias district: The Bedouin presence in Tiberias district and sub-districts: There were estimated to be 26 Fellahin villages in this sub-district, 17 Bedouin tribes, and 24 Jewish settlements.[179] The estimated number of Bedouin on the eve of the 1948 war was 3,496 inhabitants, divided as follows:

Bedouin who lived in Tiberias: 25, from Al-Dalaika and Al-Abidiyya tribes.[180]

Nomadic, semi-nomadic, and permanent Bedouin inhabitants who lived in Tiberias sub-district were estimated at 3,211 inhabitants, and divided among the following tribes: Al-Qdirat (390), Al-Mawasi (100), Al-Wahib (147), Al-Samkia (380), Al-Manara (490), Al-Talawia (523), Masharqa (100), Al-Kaddish (60), Al-Kharanbeh/Rmihat (157), Seragnah (173), Nassir Al-Din (179), Nuqib (267), and Tabiqa (245).[181]

Bedouin who lived in Fellahin villages in Tiberias sub-district were estimated at 260 inhabitants, divided as follows: Maghar: 400 (380 Fellahin, and 20 Bedouin from Al-Kharanbeh/Rmihat tribe).[182] Eilabun: 550 (375 Fellahin, and 175 Bedouin from Marisat, Shawahdeh, Sweitat, and Heib al-Fawawza tribes).[183] Sarona: This village existed until February 1938, and its population was 131, including the Bedouin Masharqa family.[184] With the establishment of the Jewish settlement "Sharona" on the Sarona village lands, all of the villagers moved to

Yamma village, including the Bedouin family, where they lived in temporary tents, and after five years, built barracks.[185] Al-Dalhamiya: 390 inhabitants (345 Fellahin, and 45 Bedouin from Al-Hanadi tribe).[186]

Summary: The total number of Bedouin inhabitants of Tiberias and its sub-districts was estimated at 3,496, of whom the number of nomadic, semi-nomadic, and permanent Bedouin inhabitants was estimated at 3,211 inhabitants. The remaining (285) Bedouin inhabitants lived in Tiberias and in Fellahin villages around it.

Nazareth and Marj Ibn Amer: The Bedouin presence in Nazareth and Marj Ibn Amer was estimated at 3,922, divided as follows:

Nazareth: Muslims: 5,600.[187] Bedouin families who lived in Nazareth were Al-Subayh and Al-Zahir (dynasty of Zahir al-Umar al-Zidani from the 18th century, estimated at 110).[188]

Semi-nomadic and permanent Bedouin inhabitants in Nazareth sub-district were approximately 2,270, divided into tribes as follows: Arab Al-Subayh (1,320), Arab Al-Sabarja (nearby Reina) (75), Al-Mazarib (130), Al-Ghrefat (120), Al-Heib (60), Al-Hajajra (110), Al-Ka'abiya (185), Al-Hujeirat (120), and Al-Ghazalin (20).[189]

There were other nomadic Bedouin tribes in Marj Ibn Amer, totaling 930 members, divided as follows: Al-Tawatha tribe (680), Al-Na'im (250).[190]

Bedouin who lived in Fellahin villages in Nazareth sub-district, an estimated 612 inhabitants, divided among the following villages: Iksal: 1,110 (including 20 Bedouin from Ghazalin tribe).[191] Al-Naora: 340 (including 20 Bedouin from Obeidat and Khalidi tribes).[192] Uzair: 150 (including 15 Bedouin from Hujeirat tribe).[193] Rumana (nearby Uzair): 590 (including 72 Bedouin from Heib and Hujeirat tribes).[194] Manshiya Zabda: 35 (including 5 Bedouin from Saida tribe).[195] Yafa: 1,070 (including 215 Bedouin from Ghazalin, Hamdun, and Na'im tribes).[196] Bu'enie-Nujeidat: 540 (including 125 Bedouin from Nujeidat tribe).[197] Kafr Manda: 1,260 (including 140 Bedouin from Ziadnah tribe).[198]

Summary: The total number of Bedouin inhabitants of Nazareth and its sub-district was estimated at 3,922, of whom the number of nomadic, semi-nomadic and permanent Bedouin was estimated at 3,200. The remaining 722 Bedouin inhabitants lived in Nazareth and in Fellahin villages around it.

Beisan district: Bedouin presence in Beisan district and its sub-districts was estimated at 3,617,[199] divided among three large tribes:

Banu Saqer: 1,037. They lived southwest of Beisan. The sheikh of this tribal headquarters was Fadel Al-Ursan.[200] Some of this tribe was considered nomadic (about 517); the rest (520) lived in the following

Fellahin villages: Umm 'Ajara: 260 (70 Bedouin); Al-Hamra: 730 (130 Bedouin); Al-Khunayzir: 260 (40 Bedouin); Al-Sakhina: 530 (60 Bedouin); Al-Safa: 650 (150 Bedouin); Al-Arida: 150 (30 Bedouin); Al-Fatur: 110 (40 Bedouin).[201]

Al-Ghazzawiyya: 1,020, who lived in the Jordan Valley. The Sheikh of this tribal headquarters was Bashir Al-Hasan Al-Ghazzawiy.[202] Some of this tribe settled in Fellahin villages: Masil Al-Jizl: 100 (45 Bedouin); and Wadi Al-Bira 70 (35 Bedouin).[203]

Al-Bashatwa: 1,560, divided into 15 sub-tribes, located northeast of Beisan.[204] Some of this tribe settled in Fellahin villages: Tell Al-Shouk: 120 (40 Bedouin); Al-Ashrafia: 230 (70 Bedouin); Umm 'Ajra: 260 (75 Bedouin); Qumya: 440 (175 Bedouin).[205]

Summary: The total number of Bedouin inhabitants of Beisan and its sub-districts was estimated at 3,617, of whom the number of nomadic, semi-nomadic and permanent Bedouin inhabitants was estimated at 2,917. The remaining 700 Bedouin lived in Beisan and in Fellahin villages around it.

The statistics can be summed up as follows: The number of the Bedouin residing in the Galilee on the eve of the 1948 war was estimated at 26,352. They broke down as follows:

- ☐ 12,120 – Bedouin living in permanent locales
- ☐ 2,530 – Nomadic Bedouin
- ☐ 11,702 – Bedouin living in Fellahin towns and villages (including the calculation of natural increase, which was considered higher among the Bedouin than the rest of the population, about 70% on average).[206]

Compared to other estimates in this period, the Bedouin population in other estimates was lower than my estimate. That estimated by the "Information service" of the *Haganah* was 21,460 inhabitants;[207] according to Mustafa Al-Dabbagh and Oppenheim it was close to 20,000 inhabitants (note that this estimate of my study is based in part on them).[208] However, these estimates did not consider the Bedouin who lived in Fellahin towns and villages. Therefore, this study completes this quantitative schema.

It can be argued that according to these figures, there was a significant decline in the population of nomadic Bedouin. This is due to the ongoing and massive process of Bedouin settlement in Fellahin towns and villages. Moreover, during the Mandate, there was no significant out-migration of Bedouin from Palestine;[209] on the contrary, there was positive migration into Palestine due to economic prosperity, resulting

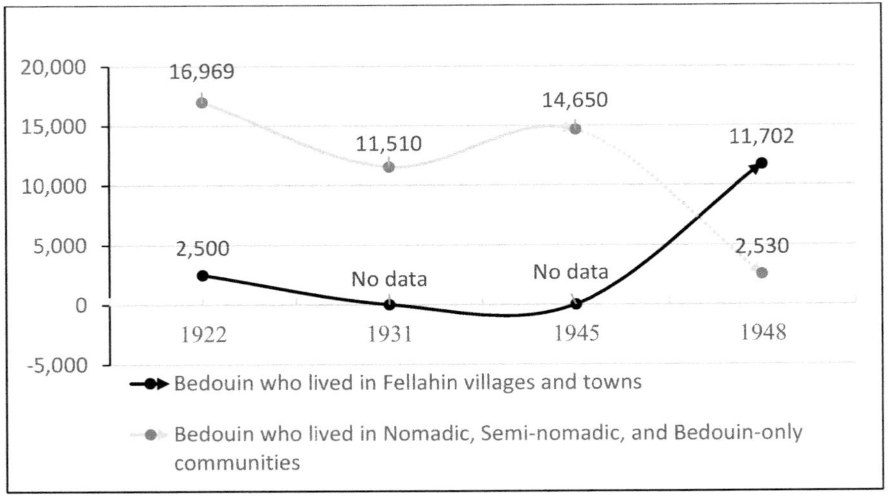

Graph 2.1 Estimates of the Bedouin population in the Galilee under British rule.

a decline in the rate of nomadic Bedouin in the Galilee, as they preferred to settle in secure locations.[210]

In order to illustrate the movement of the nomadic Bedouin population, we can compare it with Bedouin who lived in Fellahin towns and villages in the Galilee under British rule(11,702), and to the nomadic Bedouin population on the eve of the 1948 war, which totaled 2,530 Bedouin who lived in Bedouin localities, or 12,120 inhabitants (see Graph 2.1, page 83).[211]

The graph shows, on the one hand, decline of nomadic and semi-nomadic Bedouin (from 16,969 in 1922 to 14,650 on the eve of the 1948 war). On the other hand, it shows an increase in the number of Bedouin who lived in Fellahin towns and villages (from 2,500 at the beginning of the 20th century to 11,702 on the eve of 1948 war). This proves the massive process of Bedouin settlement in Fellahin villages and towns. The 1948 war generated considerable demographic changes among the Arab population in general and among the Bedouin population in the Galilee in particular, as will be described below.

In the final analysis, integration of Bedouin into towns and villages during British Mandatory rule on the one hand caused a significant decline in the number of nomadic Bedouin. On the other hand, it caused a significant increase in the number of inhabitants of the Fellahin towns and villages in the Galilee (from 58,325 in 1922 to 84,855 in 1931, and to over 265,000 in 1946).[212] Accordingly, on the eve of 1948 war, Bedouin who settled in Fellahin villages and towns were estimated at 11,702, constituting 54.52% of the total Bedouin population, and approximately 4.41% of the total Fellahin Arab population in the Galilee.

In addition, this chapter tracked bi-directional movement of Bedouin to Fellahin towns and villages, and in reverse, passage of Fellahin to Bedouin communities. This theme typifies the structural-procedural approach, whose major characteristics are fluid and permeable boundaries between the two categories – Bedouin and Fellahin – and preservation of identity of each category separately. However, the 1948 war significantly changed the demographic balance in Palestine and the balance of the Bedouin population specifically.

CHAPTER
3
Impact of the 1948 War on the Bedouin

This chapter presents the impact of the 1948 war on the fate of the Bedouin population in Galilee and its implications for subsequent Bedouin settlement in Fellahin towns and villages. The clash between Palestinians and Jews was inevitable after World War I, the war that gave birth to the Balfour Declaration on 2 November 1917, by Great Britain, supporting the establishment of a "National Home" for the Jewish People in Palestine.

Arab opposition to the United Nations' Partition Plan for Palestine, which was adopted by the UN General Assembly on 29 November 1947 (Resolution 181) and which served as the legal basis for establishment of a Jewish state within part of Palestine,[1] led to a five-and-a-half month "civil war" between the Jewish and the Arab communities in Palestine, that ended on 14 May 1948.[2] Israel's declaring independence on that date sparked a larger war between the Jews and invading Arab armies of the Middle East. The war came to an end on 20 July 1949 with the signing of an armistice agreement between Israel and Syria (following similar armistices with Egypt, Lebanon, and Jordan in previous months).[3]

In the Arab narrative generally, the 1948 war is called "the first Palestinian war";[4] and in the Palestinian narrative, it is called *Al-Nakba*, or "the [Palestinian] catastrophe".[5] In the Israeli narrative, this war has several names: "the Arab–Israeli war", "the 1948 independence war", or simply "the War of Independence".[6] Some scholars employ a more neutral term: the "1948 war".[7]

This war caught the Palestinians unprepared, as they were still suffering and in disarray from the ramifications of the Arab Rebellion of 1936–1939, which led not only to quelling of the revolt of local Arabs against British authority and the presence of the Jews, but also was marked by the defeat of moderate Palestinian factions led by the Husseini family in Jerusalem, in an internal power struggle for hegemony over Arab political-military leadership in Palestine.[8] Most of those who were not assassinated (such as the Husseinis) fled. Between October 1938 and April 1939, British forces liquidated the strongholds in cities (including mixed cities: Arabs and Jews), in Arab villages, and in the hiding places (such mountains) of the Palestinian armed units, the militant leadership of Palestine (under Haj Amin al-Husseini) fled to Lebanon, and others fled to Iraq.[9] The unprepared and vulnerable state of Arab military forces for the 1948 war and the role thereof in the Arabs' defeat is discussed by Subhi Yasin, a Fellah fighter from Shafa-Amer:

> In the beginning [of the 1920s events], there was a war of gangs [i.e., locally formed Arab Palestinian militias] with full coordination between the military factions, but now after the Arab Liberation Army' entered [the war zone in Palestine from neighboring territory], the situation has changed [...]. Jews have three combat units under one military command. [Against this unified Jewish force] seven Arab armies [invaded Palestine] under one symbolic leadership. The armies are Egyptian, Saudi, Syrian, Jordanian, Iraqi, Lebanese, together with the [local] Palestinian fighters.[10]

Yasin's remarks reflect not only the lack of Arab leadership, but also the lack of coordination between all these armies in the field, which played a major role in the victory of the Jews at the end of this war, which established Israel as a polity. During the fighting, many Palestinians fled the war zone or were forcibly expelled, while others were wounded and killed. Among those who fled or were expelled were Bedouin and Fellahin who crossed into neighboring Arab countries such as Lebanon, Jordan, and Syria.[11]

This chapter focuses on the situation of Bedouin during this war, who were divided into three main camps: those who joined the Jewish military organizations, those who joined the militant Palestinian national movement, and those who did not take an active part in this war, the latter whom constituted the majority, and who affected the Bedouins' fate during the war and thereafter. As in previous chapters, comparative statistics on the Bedouin population before and after the 1948 war and their movements are documented.

In this chapter. I argue that the 1948 war did not affect the ongoing historical process of settlement and integration of Bedouin population into Fellahin towns and villages in the Galilee. In fact, during the war (despite flight or expulsion of Bedouin to neighboring Arab countries in the Middle East), Bedouin settled and integrated into Fellahin villages and towns. Yet on one hand, events caused an increase in the proportion of the Bedouin population living in such towns and villages; on the other hand, there was a sharp decline in semi-nomadic Bedouin. In addition, the chapter testifies to the existence of structural process or dynamics afoot wherein under the pressures of wartime conditions, Fellahin allowed Bedouin refugees to settle in their towns and villages. In other cases, uprooted Fellahin clans become Bedouin. Chain migration alongside implementation of government settlement programs greatly accelerated the integration of Bedouin into towns and villages of Fellahin, which continued even after the war.

In contrast to the 1936–1939 Arab Rebellion, most of the Bedouin who lived in Palestine during the 1948 war did not take part in militant activities. As noted, on the eve of the 1948 war, the Bedouin were divided into three camps: those who sided with the Jews; those who sided with the Palestinian national movement, and those who chose to remain passive or neutral. The first camp was organized along tribal lines and individual groups as part of the Jewish community's pre-state *Palmach* and *Haganah* organizations. Others chose to attach themselves to local Palestinian national movement militia-like "gangs" or join "salvation forces" from abroad who fought against Zionists in Palestine.[12] The majority belonged to the "Arab Liberation Army", most of whom fled Palestine after the war along with retreating invasion forces. The third camp were Bedouin tribes who decided to remain neutral – remaining passively on the sidelines – most of whom remained in Israel after the war. This division would lead to fissures during and after the war among the Bedouin population in Israel and their leaders, and in their attitudes toward the Jewish state.

First camp: Bedouin enlisted as tribal groups and as individuals into the Palmach and *Haganah* Jewish units. These ties were in many cases an outgrowth of social ties forged earlier between Bedouin and Jewish settlers, which evolved into a military alliance. Early evidence of these social connections dates back to 1925 when Lord Balfour visited Al-Ja'una (today Rosh Pina).[13] Palestinian inhabitants of this area were invited, some of whom did not heed the Mufti of Safad, who called on Arab inhabitants to boycott the event. Nonetheless, the Sheikh of (Al-Heib) Tuba-Zangariah tribe attended the reception. Hussein Ali (Abu Yusuf) said:

> Honorable *Vizier*, we heard that you [heard] slander this country and [that] bad relations exist between Jews and Arabs. Our request: Bring many Jews to Palestine, because as long as there were no Jews here, lice ate us; and now we eat bread.[14]

In the 1930s, ties between Bedouin and Jewish settlers grew even stronger against the backdrop of land purchases. During the Arab Rebellion of 1936–1939, Sheikh of Tuba-Zangariah, Hussein Ali, sold about 500 dunams of his tribal land to the Jewish National Fund (earmarked for Jewish settlement), upon which Kibbutz Kfar Hanassi was later built.[15]

Another testimony to growing ties between Bedouin and Jewish settlers can be found among Bedouin in the Beer Sheva region in the 1940s: In 1943, Odeh Abu M'ammar, Sheikh of Mas'udin tribe in Naqab, began to serve as a guard in Jewish settlements. Later, he was involved in acquiring stolen British weapons and smuggling them to the *Haganah*. Odeh's uncle, Sheikh Salameh, Sheikh of the Azazmah tribe, was also involved throughout the 1940s in promoting real estate transactions on behalf of the Jewish National Fund.[16] Since the 1940s, there have been many other cases of Bedouin aiding Jews in the purchase of land. The Sheikh of the Umm Az-Zinat tribe on Mount Carmel, Muhammad Zinati, was also involved in selling land to Jewish organizations, meeting with the seller to close transactions with Jewish land dealers Yehoshua Hankin, Zvi Wolf, Mussa Goldenberg, and others. In 1946, Muhammad Zinati was shot and killed while he was in a barbershop by a member of the Arab underground resistance movement "Black Hand".[17]

Shortly before the war, these ties grew closer and became a military alliance. The same tribe of Al-Heib in Tuba established a military unit called "Pal-heib" (Heib Company) under the command of Yitzhak Henkin,[18] which operated in coordination with the *Hagana* and the *Palmach*.[19] This collaboration was based on a blood pact between Bedouin of Tuba-Zangariah and the Jewish settlements in the Hula valley in 1948 war. Saul Dagan and Avner Kozviner wrote a pamphlet titled *Pal-heib* about this joining of forces. Mola Cohen, commander of the *Yiftach* brigade (one of the *Palmach*'s three brigades in the 1948 war), testified about those relations in this account:

> The cooperation between *Palmach* and Al-Heib tribe began when Yigal Allon met Abu Yusuf, Sheikh of Al-Heib, after a failed attempt by Arabs to take over the Nabi Yusha police fort, and after preparations for *Yiftach*'s operation to conquer the Galilee [...]. At this meeting, they decided that tribesmen would form a military unit, which would be subordinate to the Yiftach Brigade.[20]

In the Rosh Pina Archives, I found additional evidence of the military alliance between Bedouin and the *Palmach* brigade, describing the capture of the "Customs House" on 18 May 1948 from the Syrian army:

> When darkness unfolded, a company belonging to the *Yiftach* brigade moved over the Jordan River, its soldiers armed with light weapons and loaded bags of explosives. At the same time, Yigal Allon, commander of the *Yiftach* Brigade, was in a tent of Al-Heib tribe.[21]

This Bedouin unit numbered about 200 soldiers, commanded by the sheikh of the tribe, Abu Yusuf. These soldiers participated in *Yiftach*'s operation in northern Upper Galilee,[22] and Operation *Matateh* ["broom"] to occupy and "cleanse" eastern Upper Galilee.[23] In April 1948, they participated in the conquest of areas north of Tiberias and the Hula Valley with *Palmach* assistance.[24] In May 1948, operations at command headquarters of the *Yiftach* brigade sent the following telegram to General Staff in Tel Aviv:

> Bedouin unit under our command [...]. This unit raided a village near Rosh Pina, whose inhabitants began to return to it. Thus, it drove them away. The unit set fire toward the village and took a lot of booty. Moreover, our forces returned safely.[25]

Uri Milstein and Dov Doron noted in their book *Sayeret Shaked* ["Shaked Reconnaissance Unit"] that the Bedouin unit *Pal-heib* carried out "dirty tasks", i.e., expulsion of Arabs from their homes, missions that they carried out with extreme cruelty and destruction of their villages. Milstein and Doron said that such missions characterized the use of minority units in the 1948 war, i.e., utilization of Bedouin units that *Haganah* leaders learned from the British, who operated thusly in their colonies in Africa and Asia, setting local members of differing national or religious groups at one another's throats.[26]

The *Pal-heib* unit served as a platform and logistic infrastructure for attracting additional Bedouin fighters to join the IDF after Israel's establishment in 1948. In addition to Pal-heib, there were individuals who linked their fate with the Jews during the 1940s and even played a significant role in defending the Jewish community of Palestine [Hebrew: The *Yishuv*].

Abd al-Majid Salim Obeidat (Amos Yarkoni), from Al-Mazarib tribe northern Marj Ibn Amer, is the most outstanding example of such an individual. He formed friendships with Jews in Nahalal, including Moshe Dayan.[27] Abd al-Majid was born in 1920 in Obeidat sub-tribal encampments east of Al-Naora (Fellahin) village. About two years later,

Abd al-Majid's sub-tribal unit (Obeidat) returned to the tribal headquarters of Al-Mazarib near Nahalal.[28] Abd al-Majid was purported to be an individual of extraordinary courage, wisdom, and daring. During the Arab Rebellion (1936–1939), he joined Arab gangs and took part in the sabotage of the Kirkuk-Haifa oil pipeline. However, an internal conflict broke out among the gang members, and some accused Abd al-Majid and another two tribesmen (Mathkal and Hussein Mazarib) of treason and unwillingness to eliminate dissidents. The three were imprisoned in an empty cistern east of the village of Kabul, awaiting trial. At night, Abd al-Majid climbed onto his friend's shoulders to exit the cistern. After assisting the other two to climb out, the three fled to the Mazarib tribe's encampment. A few days later, Abd al-Majid met Moshe Dayan, at the time a young commander in the *Haganah*, who provided Abd al-Majid with protection against gang members (in case of danger, he could take refuge in Nahalal). In 1947, Abd al-Majid worked in the Haifa Refineries as a courier. On 17 December 1948, he enlisted in the IDF's Unit 300 for Minorities, and in 1953 completed officer training; in 1955, he established the Sayeret Shaked commando unit, and later became its commander.[29]

When the 1948 war broke out, Bedouin who joined the Zionist camp fought alongside the Jews, some even providing important information about gangs and the armies of Arab countries, especially Syria and Lebanon. They also collected a large quantity of weapons that the Bedouin had in the Galilee and passed them on to Jewish fighters such as Giyora Zaid and Oded Yanai (Abu Nur).

Second camp: Bedouin joined the Palestinian Arab national movement. This symbiosis formed during World War I, when many Bedouin joined the national army of Sharif Hussein bin Ali and his son Faisal, king of Syria, some of whom fought the British and French Mandate regimes, and on the other hand, and others fought Zionist settlement in Palestine. Throughout the events of the 1920s and during the Great Arab Revolt (1936–1939), they became partners to the emerging united national Arab-Palestinian movement. Therefore, they cooperated fully with the Palestinian national movement as described in the previous chapter.

In his study on Bedouin-Jewish relationships during the British Mandate in Palestine,[30] Muhammad Sawaed described Bedouin groups who took a relatively small part in the Arab struggle against Jewish settlement in the north of Palestine, especially in two major events: the Arab Revolt (1936–1939); and events until the end of 1948 war.[31] At that time, gangs were willingly accepted by Palestinian Arab nationalists, and became national heroes in their eyes after the war.[32]

The buds of these events began in neighborhood conflict between Jews and Arabs, whose ignition point was in Haifa, and spread to other towns and villages in Palestine.[33] During and after the 1948 war, most of these Bedouin were expelled or fled – out of fear for their lives – to Jordan, Syria, and Lebanon. They included members of the tribes: Turkmens (Mount Carmel), Al-Dalaika (southwest Tiberias), Al-Mawasi (western Tiberias), Al-Saqer (southwest Beisan), Al-Ghazzawiyya and Al-Bashatwa (northern Beisan), Al-Qdirat (northwest Tiberias), Al-Ghawarna (Hula Valley), Arab Al-Heib Al-Rasatma (northern Safad), and many others.[34] The following are some battles in which Bedouin participated with the "Arab liberation army", and took an active part in the 1948 war:

Arab Al-Subayh: This battle began on 3 January 1948, between a group of about 20 rebels led by Sheikh Al-Subayh Mahmoud al-Uthman, against Jews from Beit Keshet. Eight Jews were killed.[35]

Following this battle, the Jews sought aid from *Haganah* forces, which soon arrived. Al-Subayh also called for help from close Fellahin villages and towns: Shajara, Kafr Kana, and Nazareth, under command of Abd Al-Latif Fahum. This battle began on 4 January 1948, in which 20 Jews were killed and 20 others wounded; on the Arab side, two were injured.[36] Arif Al-Arif described this event as willingly accepted by Palestinian Arab nationalists, and said that the Fellahin became national heroes in their eyes.[37] However, this success did not last long. On 8 June 1948, an IDF force attacked tribe, and a battle ensued in which the sheikh and four of his men killed.[38]

Following Al-Subayh Battle, a battle developed nearby, in Ein Mahel (Fellahin village), in cooperation with tribe members from Kafr Kana and Nazareth, and Bedouin from Al-Subayh. However, the IDF force was stronger in both personnel and military skill, and at the end of the battle, the IDF force succeeded in conquering Al-Subayh and other villages in the Nazareth area.[39]

Al-Mansi Battle: On 4 April 1948, an Arab "rescue force" including infantry, four armored vehicles, and five cannons, entered Turkmen villages on Mount Carmel. Fawzi Al-Qawuqji, commander-in-chief of the Arab nationalist military forces, arrived on Mount Carmel to protect Arab villages. The force was stationed mainly in Al-Mansi, and aided by local rebels of this village. On 11 April, a *Haganah* force began encircling Al-Mansi in order to occupy it. The Arabs began shooting toward the Jewish settlement Mishmar Haemek. A fierce battle ensued, during which 25 Jews and 21 Arabs were killed.[40] Later, the Arab "rescue force" withdrew, and two days later, the village was captured by *Haganah*. All of the inhabitants were put on buses and deported to Jenin.[41]

Nassir Al-Din Battle: On 12 April, a company of the Golani Brigade attacked this village (western Tiberias).[42] The villagers went outside to protect themselves, and they asked for assistance from Bedouin inhabitants who lived near Arab Dalaika and Arab Al-Mawasi, and their help was not long in coming. The battle took place between two forces, during which the village was conquered, and 14 Bedouin were killed.[43] Morris claimed that 22 Arabs were killed in this battle (including Bedouin),[44] and the rest fled to Tiberias and surrounding villages.[45]

After the occupation, the IDF continued its conquest of Tiberias and the surrounding countryside. Morris described this as follows:

> The Golani Brigade cleared the southern shore of the Galilee Sea [...]. Sumakh battle, which was on 29 April, was short and cost relatively few casualties [...]. The militia fighters and remaining inhabitants [in Tiberias region] fled to Jordan and Syria.[46]

Tel el-Husn Battle:[47] this battle began on 1 May 1948, when a *Haganah* force of about 300 soldiers conquered the mound, a tactical operation for conquest of Beisan. This force began shelling and bombarding Beisan and the surrounding villages. Arab forces, led by Tawfiq al-Tahtamouni, numbered about 100 Palestinians and about 75 Jordanian soldiers. They tried to defend Beisan with Bedouin military assistance forces from Banu Saqer tribe, who came from the western side of the town.[48] Morris described these battles as follows:

> On 11 May, Golani forces conquered two neighboring villages of Beisan, Frunh and Al-Ashrafia, [whose] their inhabitants fled to Jordan. Golani fighters blew up the houses of these villages. At next night, they took control of Tel el-Husn, and from there they shelled the town with mortars. One of two local militia commanders, Ismail al-Faruqi, fled together with his fighters to Jordan [...]. After Beisan's conquest, Bedouin tribes who lived near it moved to Jordan.[49]

After this conquest, Golani forces came to conquer southern Beisan, where headquarters of Al-Saqer tribe had settled.[50] These Bedouin, led by Sheikh Fadel al-Ursan tried to repel this conquest, but could not.[51] They fought, and some were killed, and others fled or were expelled to Jordan.[52]

Third camp: Tribes that decided on neutrality. During the 1948 war, many Bedouin did not fight or oppose occupation, and did not fit into one of the two opposing camps (Zionist military or Palestinian Arab national movement). This affected how Israel treated them after its establishment.

Thus, the Bedouin situation in the Galilee during the 1948 war was not uniform: One part of this population joined Jewish military organizations and fought alongside them. Another part formed local gangs, and came to aid the Palestinian Arab national movement. A third part decided not to intervene or participate in the emerging conflict between Arabs and Jews. Therefore, relations between Bedouin and Fellahin became even more intense and constituted grounds for Bedouin settlement and their integration into Fellahin towns and villages in the late 1948 war.

Impact of 1948 War on Bedouin Population's Fate in the Galilee

This war between Arabs and Jews in Palestine strongly affected the population in general and the Bedouin population specifically after Israel's establishment state in 1948. The following sub-sections will describe Bedouin expulsion and/or their fleeing Israel. Moreover, it presents data on internal refugees who moved to settle in other localities.

I argue that the war and its ramifications did not constitute an obstacle to continued settlement and integration of the Bedouin population into Fellahin towns and villages. On the contrary, following the war, many Bedouin fled or were expelled to existing Fellahin villages and towns. Thus, this section presents data on Bedouin who became refugees outside Israel, those who became refugees in Fellahin towns and villages inside Israel, and will present the number of Bedouin who settled as permanent inhabitants, and those who remained nomads.

The Fate of Bedouin in Haifa, its sub-districts, and Mount Carmel during the 1948 war

All of these Bedouin numbered 4,749 before the war. After the war, this number decreased.

Haifa: Bedouins numbered 274 on the eve of the war.[53] During the war, most of them fled, mainly to Lebanon;[54] few remained in Haifa. Other Bedouin refugees from surrounding villages moved to Haifa: Abu Kulib, Turkmens, and Al-Subayh, for a total of 210 Bedouin inhabitants of Haifa.[55] This means that during the war, about 75 fled the country.

Bedouin families' fate who lived in Fellahin villages in Haifa sub-districts, which totaled about 1,507 inhabitants, described as follows:

Abu Shusha: This village numbered about 720 inhabitants (Fellahin and Bedouin).[56] Of these, 245 were Bedouin from Al-Shkirat and Al-Saida, which came from the Naqab.[57] On 10 April 1948, the *Haganah* attacked this village. Palestinian rebels defended the village and managed to expel the attackers.[58] Several fell in this battle, some of them Bedouin.[59]

Three days later, Mount Carmel (including Al-Mansi and Alruha) was captured by IDF alongside withdrawal of Commander Fawzi Al-Qawuqji, who fled to Jenin and after that to Jordan.[60]

Ijzim: This village numbered about 2,970 inhabitants (Fellahin and Bedouin).[61] Bedouin families' names were Madi (398) and included Yasin, Khadir, Amru Saleh, Sa'id al-Din, Al-Zuyd, Alduaima, Al-Zabadna, and Tarafsha.[62] The Fellahin families' names were Abu Zard (they came from Egypt, with Ibrahim Pasha's conquests), Al-Baghdadi (also from Egypt), Albalata, Khaddish, and Abu Asad. The last mukhtar of this village was Tawfiq Aref Al-Madi.[63]

On 22 July 1948, when Arab 'rescue forces' left the village, the IDF arrived and conquered it, and the inhabitants were expelled by bus to Jenin, and later became refugees in Jordan, Syria, and Iraq.[64]

Balad al-Sheikh: This village numbered about 4,120 inhabitants (Fellahin and Bedouin).[65] Bedouin (245) who lived near this village: Al-Sawilat (120), Samniyya (42), Al-Towaqia (55), Al-Qlitat (8), and Sweitat (20).[66] On 24 April 1948, the *Haganah* conquered the village,[67] all of whose inhabitants were expelled and fled to Acre, and from there to Lebanon. About 104 refugees found sanctuary in Isfiya and Shafa-Amer villages.[68]

Al-Sindiyana: This village numbered about 1,250 inhabitants (Fellahin and Bedouin).[69] Bedouin (244) who lived in this village: Ali Nazal, Muqbel, Al-Jawabra, Al-Hamdun, and Al-Sawalma. The Fellahin families are Al-Muthani and Abu Libdeh. The mukhtar's name, Tawfiq al-Haj Hussein Al-Muqbel, was of Bedouin origin.[70] In June 1948, a *Haganah* force arrived and expelled all of the villagers.[71] Of the 224 Bedouin inhabitants, 141 fled and became refugees in Tamra and Shafa-Amer, and the remaining 45 moved to Haifa: Ali Nazal (20) and Muqbel (25).[72]

Turkmen's villages on Mount Carmel: The villages involved in the war: Al-Mansi, Lyyd al-Awadin, al-Ghubayya al-Tahta, and al-Fawqa. On 4 April 1948, the Arab "rescue force" entered these villages (including infantry, 4 armored vehicles. and 5 guns),[73] commanded by Fawzi al-Qawuqji, and assisted by local rebels, and began shooting toward the Jewish settlement Mishmar Haemek. Two days later, the Arab force withdrew, and most of the inhabitants were expelled to

Jordan and Syria.[74] One Turkmen family, Bezia (five inhabitants), moved to Nazareth.[75]

Tab'un: This village numbered about 370 inhabitants (Fellahin and Bedouin).[76] Bedouin (145) who lived in this village: N'arani (15), Zubeidat (100), Samniyya (15), and Ghrefat (15).[77] During the war, except for Zubeidat tribe that remained, the Bedouin fled to Fellahin villages: Samniyya fled to Shafa-Amer, N'arani (10) fled to Nazareth and Yafat al-Nasira (30) refugees. In addition, Ghrefat tribe moved to Zarzir,[78] for a total of 55 Bedouin who moved to Fellahin villages.

The fates of nomadic and permanent Bedouin who lived in Haifa sub-district and on Mount Carmel. On the eve of the war, they were estimated at 2,968, described as follows:

Haifa sub-district and southern Mount Carmel: estimated at 2,370, divided as follows: Arab al-Fuqara (310), Arab al-Ghawarna (620) near Jisr al-Zarqa.[79] During the war, a *Haganah* force entered and expelled about 588 Bedouin (except Ghawarna, who moved to Jisr al-Zarqa and settled there) first to Jenin, and later to Transjordan.[80] So 2,380 inhabitants remained, while some, such as Ghawarna (650), moved to Jisr al-Zarqa.[81]

Al-Ramil tribes (588):[82] These tribes dwelt on sand dunes between Haifa and Acre. Their fate was:

Arab Sweitat: estimated at 104,[83] almost of whom moved to Fellahin villages: Isfiya (16), Abu Snan (3), Tamra (25), Shafa-Amer (15), and Tarshiha (45) as refugees,[84] totaling 104 Bedouin who moved to Fellahin villages.

Arab Al-Qlitat: estimated eight inhabitants who lived near Balad al-Sheikh. During the war, they moved to Isfiya. First, they set up tents on the western side of the village, and later built houses.[85]

Arab Abu Kulib (or Kulibat): estimated about 10 inhabitants who lived near Balad al-Sheikh. During the war, they moved to Daliyat al-Carmel, and six months later all of the tribe members moved to Haifa.[86] **Arab Al-Araqiya:** estimated about 70 households, during the war, they fled to Jordan. **Arab Al-Sawaed:** estimated about 100 households, during the war about 175 fled to Shafa-Amer.[87] **Arab Al-Samniyya:** estimated about three households, during the war they fled to Shafa-Amer. **Arab Al-Wazaoza:** estimated about four households, during the war they fled to Lebanon. **Arab Al-Hanbuzi:** estimated about four households, during the war they fled to Tamra.[88] **Arab Al-Abidiyya:** estimated about four households, during the war they fled to Jordan. Arab **Al-Numeirat:** estimated about three households, during the war they fled to Jordan. **Al-Ghawarna:** estimated about 50 households, during the war they fled to Jordan. **Arab Al-Ghrefat** (Abu-Tzahyon family) estimated about 4 tents, during the war they fled to Tab'un, and six months later they moved to north of Marj Ibn Amer (which later became part of Zarzir village). **Arab Al-Hajajra**: estimated about three households, during the war they fled to Wadi al-Malak River (which later became part of Al-Ka'abiya-Helf, a Bedouin village).[89]

That is total of 235 Bedouin refugees that moved to Fellahin villages in Haifa District.

Summary: On the eve of the war, Bedouin in Haifa and in its sub-districts were estimated at 4,749 inhabitants. Nomadic Bedouin or those who lived in temporary localities numbered 2,968. Bedouin who lived in urban areas, i.e., in Haifa and in Fellahin villages: about 1,781 inhabitants. After the war, Bedouin who remained in Haifa area were estimated at 2,768, broken down as follows: (a.) Approximately 1,664 who remained/moved to Fellahin villages and/or Haifa; (b.) about 1,104 remained in their locations, some moving to Bedouin communities/villages in the Galilee. Less than half of this population (about 1,981) was expelled or fled to neighboring Arab countries. The remaining Bedouin settled in Bedouin settlements (mainly in their own tribal headquarters, which the state later recognized as Bedouin villages).

The Fate of Bedouin in Acre and its sub-districts during the 1948 war

Bedouin inhabitants who lived in nomadic, temporary localities, Fellahin villages, and in Acre were estimated on the eve of the war at 2,730. Their fates were as follows:

Acre: 160 Bedouin inhabitants lived in this district (Arab Al-Ramil, Majdoub, and Ghawarna). These inhabitants remained in place and were joined by about 85 refugees from Ghawarna tribe who settled in northern Acre. They were estimated at 245 Bedouin after the war.

Nomadic and permanent Bedouin residents' fates who lived in Acre sub-district:

Nomadic Bedouin and permanent inhabitants of **Arab Al-Rarmil** camped southeast of Acre: On eve of the war, they were estimated at 650,[90] divided into the following tribes: Arab al-Majdoub (70), Al-Ghawarna (80), Al-Sawaed (168), Al-Towaqia (40), Al-Marisat (120), Al-Qlitat (122), and Al-Samniyya (50).[91] These tribes' fates after the war: some fled to Fellahin villages: Tamra, Iblin, and to Acre. A larger portion of them fled to Syria and Lebanon.[92]

Following are parts of tribes who moved during the war to Fellahin villages in the Galilee:

Al-Majdoub: some (35) moved to Abu Snan,[93] and the rest fled to Syria, where they became refugees.[94] **Al-Ghawarna:** this tribe was comprised of three families, Al-Qais, Al-Janhawi, and Ali Ahmad, whose last tribal mukhtar was Tawfiq Muhammad Al-Qais.[95] During the war, some (15) moved to Acre,[96] and the rest fled to Lebanon.[97] **Al-Sawaed:** some (25) moved to Tamra and (15) Iblin, and the rest fled to Syria.[98] **Al-Towaqia:** only two of them moved to Shafa-Amer; the rest fled to Lebanon.[99] **Al-Marisat:** they relocated to northern Kaukab Abu Al-Hija village; some (25) fled to Syria,[100] the rest remained in the tribal headquarters (later, the tribe would be recognized as a Bedouin village, Al-Marisat).[101] **Al-Qlitat:** located near Tarbikha. Some (12) moved to Isfiya;[102] most fled to Lebanon.[103] **Al-Samniyya:** located in northern Acre. Some (20) moved to Shafa-Amer; the rest fled to Lebanon.[104] That is a total of 1,112 Bedouin who moved to Fellahin villages in Acre Sub-district.

Bedouin villages in Acre Sub-District: **Arab Al-Aramsheh**, estimated at 199 inhabitants.[105] This village remained in the same location.

Fates of Bedouin families that lived in Fellahin villages in Acre Sub-district, estimated at 1,721 on the eve of the war, divided into the following villages:

Al-Jadida – Al-Makr: This village numbered about 280,[106] including the Bedouin Sweitat family, which was estimated at 70 inhabitants,[107] who did not take part in the war. They remained in place and were joined by other Bedouin refugees such as, Al-Fadl (today, Fadly) and Sweitat (30) from the Golan Heights.[108] That is a total of 100 Bedouin remaining in Al-Jadida-Al-Makr after the war.

Tarshiha: This village numbered about 5,360 (Fellahin and Bedouin).[109] Bedouin (121) who lived near this village are members of the Al-Na'im (77) and Sweitat (44) families.[110] During the war, they (50 Al-Na'im, 20 Sweitat) entered Tarshiha. Kitan Al-Na'im said, "Thanks to our relationships with a Druze, Nimer, from Kisra, who helped us to stay and not to be expelled from the country".[111] That is total of 191 Bedouin remaining in Tarshiha after the war.

Abu Snan: This village numbered about 820 (Fellahin and Bedouin),[112] including Bedouin (30) from Sweitat tribe. During the war, members of this tribe, together with all the villagers, were rounded up by the IDF, in the center of the village for two weeks, and after the war, they returned to their homes, purchased land from the Druze, and built stone and concrete houses.[113] That is a total of 150 Bedouin of who remained in Abu Snan after the war (including refugees from the neighboring Bedouin tribes of Arab Al-Rarmil).

Al-Damun: This village numbered about 1,310 (Fellahin and

Bedouin),[114] including Bedouin (165) of the Al-Ziadnah family.[115] During the war, Al-Damun was destroyed and most of its inhabitants fled to nearby Tamra (including some 70 refugees from the Al-Ziadnah family), and others were deported by the IDF to Lebanon.[116] That is a total of 70 Bedouin refugees from the Al-Ziadnah family who moved to Tamra village.

Tamra: This village numbered about 1,380 (Fellahin and Bedouin),[117] including Bedouin (540) of the Al-Ziadnah (80), Al-Marisat (340), and Mawasi (280) families.[118] During the war, some of them (120 from Marisat) fought the occupation army, and these fled to Lebanon and later to Syria.[119] That totals 750 Bedouin refugees from Arab Al-Ramil who moved to Tamra.

Sakhnin: This village numbered about 2,310 inhabitants (Fellahin and Bedouin),[120] including Bedouin (750) of the Trabay (350) and Zubeidat (400) families.[121] During the war, the Bedouin remained in Sakhnin.[122] The number of Sakhnin's inhabitants rose from 2,310 on the eve of the war to 3,477 on 31 November 1949,[123] consequent to the number of refugees who came to Sakhnin during the war, including Bedouin. There were a total of 1,275 Bedouin in Sakhnin. In other words, there was no flight from or absorption of Bedouin into Sakhnin.

Deir Hanna: This village numbered about 750 (Fellahin and Bedouin),[124] including the Bedouin families (25) Ziadna (15), whose name changed to Shibli, due to fear of Jews taking revenge) and Sweitat (10). During the war, they remained in place, joined by 100 refugees, 75 from the same tribe who lived before in Khirbet Sabana, east of Eilabun; and 25 from Marisat tribe who lived in Arab Al-Rarmil (southern Acre), who moved to the eastern side of Deir Hanna,[125] for total of 150 Bedouin inhabitants in Deir Hanna, including refugees.

Majd al-Krum: This village numbered about 280 (Fellahin and Bedouin),[126] including Bedouin (20) from the Sawaed family. During the war, they moved to their tribal headquarters in Wadi Salameh.[127] In other words, there were no Bedouin left in Majd al-Krum after the war.

<u>Summary</u>: On the eve of the war, Bedouin in Acre and its sub-district were estimated at 2,730, divided as follows: Bedouin inhabitants who lived in Acre and in Fellahin villages estimated at 1,881; nomadic Bedouin and inhabitants of Bedouin localities are estimated at 849 inhabitants. After the war, the total number of all the Bedouin in Acre and its sub-district declined slightly to 2,635 inhabitants, divided as follows: 2,436 remained/moved to Fellahin and/or Acre villages; and 199 remained in place, i.e., Arab al-Aramsheh.

Fate of Bedouin in Shafa-Amer Sub-district during the 1948 War

The inhabitants of Shafa-Amer sub-district on the eve of the war numbered 3,630 (Fellahin and Bedouin).[128] Bedouin who lived in nomadic, temporary localities, Fellahin villages, and in this area, were estimated on the eve of the war at 2,715. Their fate was:

Shafa-Amer: 330 Bedouin inhabitants (Ziadnah, Hawara, Sawaed, Marisat, and Samniyya) remained in place.[129] There was one case of Sawaed tribe (lineage: Abu Shahab 20 inhabitants), which escaped and returned to Shafa-Amer. They lived in the Abu Shahab neighborhood, fled to tribal headquarters in al-Husayniyya, and stayed there until the end of the war, after which they returned to Abu Shahab neighborhood.[130] This case of escape to tribal headquarters and return to the town was rare, illustrating the personal security felt within the tribe's headquarters.

In addition, under influence of the war, some members (40) of the Al-Hujeirat tribe, who lived close to Kaukab Abu Al-Hija, moved to the Othman neighborhood in Shafa-Amer, while other refugees of Muhameidat (7) and Mawasi (20) tribes fled from the Golan Heights to Shafa-Amer.[131]

What is interesting is that all refugees settled in outskirts of Fellahin villages or towns, which largely characterized the entire population of Bedouin refugees who settled into Fellahin villages or towns in the Galilee during the 1948 war. Abu Mahmoud Abu Shahab, son of the founder of Abu Shahab neighborhood in Shafa-Amer, said:

> The inhabitants of Shafa-Amer [Fellahin] welcomed us well; they gave us food, drink, and everything [...]. However, they did not want us to live in their neighborhoods [...]. They told us: Find a place close to town, and we will help you.[132]

In addition to the aid provided by Fellahin to Bedouin refugees, Abu Shahab's remarks attest to preservation identity of each community separately. In other words, Fellahin refugees from Fellahin towns and villages, in most cases, settled in Fellahin neighborhoods in towns and villages that had become sanctuaries. In contrast, Bedouin refugees from tribal territories were not allowed settle in Fellahin town or village centers, but were allowed to live in outer neighborhoods. A total of 2,397 Bedouin were in Shafa-Amer after the war was (including many refugees who came from the Arab Al-Ramil region of Acre).

Shafa-Amer sub-district: Nomadic and permanent Bedouin, on the eve of the war, were estimated at 1,820 inhabitants,[133] divided as follows: Arab Zubeidat (410), Arab al-Safsaf (450), Arab al-Helf (280), Arab al-Amariya (410), Arab al-Khawaled (80), and Sawaed al-Hamira (190),[134] all of whom remained in place. Later, the State of Israel recognized these as Bedouin villages.[135]

Marisat tribe, who settled in 1948 at the tribe headquarters of *Sanib'a* in Kaukab Abu Al-Hija hills, fought against the IDF when it came to conquer their area. Several Bedouin were killed, and about 1,820 remained.[136] About 1,170 moved to Shafa-Amer, and the rest – about 650 – moved to Bedouin communities.

The fate of Bedouin families that lived in Fellahin villages in Shafa-Amer sub-district, whose number was estimated at 565 on the eve of the war, divided into the following villages:

Iblin: This village numbered about 1,660 (Fellahin and Bedouin).[137] Bedouin families (550): Al-Hasi (45), Al-Najmiyya (35), Hawara (25), Sweitat (70), Marisat (85), Mawasi (110), Sawaed (120), and Samniyya (60).[138] During the war, they stayed in Iblin. another 20 refugees from Mawasi (Shuhiti) tribe, who lived near Ibtin Bedouin village, joined them. Some other members (15) of Mawasi tribe, who lived in Arab Al-Rarmil, fled to the northern neighborhood of Iblin.[139] That is a total of 670 Bedouin who lived in this village after the war.

Kaukab Abu Al-Hija: This village numbered about 490 (Fellahin and Bedouin),[140] including one Bedouin family, Al-Hujeirat (55).[141] In 1948, members of this family fought against the IDF when it came to conquer their village. As a result, 11 were killed or fled to Syria, and the rest moved to nearby Al-Hujeirat tribe (later Bir al-Maksur, a Bedouin village).[142] Moreover, about 20 inhabitants moved to Othman neighborhood in Shafa-Amer.[143] There are no Bedouin left in Kaukab Abu Al-Hija.

Summary: On the eve of the war, Bedouin were estimated in Shafa-Amer sub-district at 2,715, of which nomadic and permanent Bedouin inhabitants were 1,820. The rest, about 955, lived in Shafa-Amer and in Fellahin villages. After the war, the number of Bedouin remaining in Shafa-Amer area rose to 4,237 inhabitants, divided as follows: 3,572 remained in/moved to Shafa-Amer or Fellahin villages; and 655 Bedouin remained in place (e.g., Ibtin, Khawaled, Arab al-Helf, and Arab Sawaed al-Hamira), and the state would recognize these settlements as Bedouin settlements.

The fate of Bedouin in Safad and its sub-district during the 1948 war

The inhabitants of Safad and its sub-district at eve of the war numbered 5,123 (Fellahin and Bedouin). Their fate was as follows:

Safad: 120 members of Al-Sayyid tribe, which originated from tribal headquarters at Al-Na'im in Syria.[144] During the war, they fled to tribal headquarters in Syria.[145] After the war, all Bedouin former inhabitants of Safad fled to Syria.

Bedouin inhabitants who lived in nomadic, temporary localities, or Fellahin villages in this sub-district were estimated on the eve of the war to be 4,503, divided into the following tribes: Tuba-Zangariah (840), Krad al-Ghannama (350), Krad Al-Baqqra (360), Al-Heib (370), Al-Hamdun (590), Al-Shamlana (650), Kaosh (820), Al-Numeirat (25), Al-Hamam (70), Al-Sayyid (93), and Khayam al-Walid (280).[146] The fate of these tribes during the war was as follows:

> On 28 April, a *Palmach* force captured the British police fortress in Al-Ja'una and the British military camp nearby.[147] On 3–4 May, a first *Palmach* brigade captured the villages around Safad, and expelled Bedouin tribes.[148] The *Palmach* brigade testified: These Bedouin placed explosive devices and fired at *Palmach* forces passing through the main axis connecting Tiberias and Rosh Pina. Tents burned down and most of the houses were blown up. This was an act of destroying points of attachment to invading forces from east.[149]

The results of this conquest were the loss of a few Bedouin in battles, and cattle herds taken from some of them. Another portion fled to Syria, and the rest fled to tribal headquarters in Tuba-Zangariah.[150]

The case of Krad al-Khait tribe in Hula Valley

This tribal headquarters consisted of two tribes: Krad al-Baqqra (360) who raised livestock/cattle, and Krad al-Ghannama (350) who raised sheep and goats.[151] Until the eve of the 1948 war, these tribes together were estimated at 710 inhabitants.[152] These tribes did not participate in the 1948 war.[153] On 31 March 1951, all tribe members were transferred to Sha'ab village by Israel authorities.[154] However, in summer 1951, some of the 460 inhabitants (most of them from al-Baqqra) returned to their former residence in the Hula Valley. During the 1956 war (the Sinai Campaign. Hebrew: *Mivtza Kadesh*),[155] this last group was deported to Syria. In contrast, the first group, 326 inhabitants, remained in Sha'ab.[156]

According to Hillel Cohen, at the beginning of 1953, each family of these inhabitants received 30 dunams (25 for grazing, and 5 for orchards).[157] On the other hand, Mahmoud Azayzah, a Bedouin from Krad al-Baqqra tribe who was witness to this case, claimed in an in-depth interview:

> We were indeed offered financial compensation in exchange for giving up land in Jalbina, south of Hula Valley, but my tribe refused. We stayed living in a temporary location in Sha'ab until 1968, on which the authority prepared lands for building, and only then, could we exercise our entitlement to purchase construction plots. Each plot of land was about 750 square meters, and its price was about 22,000 Israel pounds (IP).[158]

In an ongoing process in 1951, 1953, 1955, and 1989, some Bedouin who remained in Sha'ab and who lived in temporary locations (shacks) left the village for economic and political reasons, and dispersed to various villages in the Galilee such as Tuba, Abu Snan, and Shafa-Amer. At the end of this transition process, in 1989, the two Krad tribes numbered some 1,600 inhabitants in all Fellahin villages in the Galilee.[159] That is a total of 350 Bedouin inhabitants who remained in Wadi al-Hamam, in Wadi Salameh (Sawaed), and in Tuba-Zangariah (later, the state would recognize Wadi al-Hamam, Wadi Salameh, and Tuba-Zangariah as Bedouin settlements).

The fates of nomadic Bedouin tribes in the Hula Valley (Safad sub-district)

Some of the Bedouin who lived in the southwestern foothills of Golan Heights, such as Shamlana, Al-Muhameidat (belonging to Al-Fadl tribe), Dalaika, and Al-Fadl,[160] grazed their livestock between Hula Valley and Safad, as many scholars point out.[161] Moreover, some of them even moved to Fellahin villages during and after the 1948 war, hence their importance for this research.

On the eve of the war, 820 nomadic Bedouin lived in the Hula Valley: Arab Al-Fadl (nomadic, from Lebanon's Beqaa Valley in the north to the Hula Valley and the Golan Heights in the south), Sawaed (Wadi Salameh), Al-Muhameidat, Hamam (Wadi al-Hamam), Sawilat, Numeirat, and Mawasi.[162]

During the war, most of these tribes were expelled to Syria and Lebanon,[163] and some of them fled to Fellahin villages in the Galilee: About 77 inhabitants from Sawilat tribe fled to Yarka (Druze village) and remained there until 1973. From there, they moved to Abu Snan and Al-Makr.[164] About 10 members from Al-Fadl tribe fled to Al-Makr;[165] seven members of Al-Muhameidat tribe fled to Shafa-Amer;[166] 20 Mawasi fled to Shafa-Amer;[167] some Hamam who settled in Wadi al-Hamam fled to Syria. About 25 members (8 households) of Numeirat tribe fled to Sha'ab, and all the rest fled to Syria.[168] While this tribe returned to their former settlement (in the Hula Valley) in 1951, similar to Krad tribe, in 1956, they were expelled to Syria, from where 15 returned to Sha'ab.[169] Accordingly, 62 Bedouin inhabitants moved to Fellahin villages in the Galilee.

The fate of Bedouin who lived in Fellahin villages of Safad sub-district

On eve of the war, they were estimated at 500, as follows:

Jubb Yusuf: This village numbered about 170 (100 Fellahin and 70 Bedouin from Arab al-Sayyid). During the war, the tribe fled to Syria.[170]

Al-Malha: This village numbered about 890 (700 Fellahin and 190 Bedouin from Al-Zubeid tribe).[171] During the war, Al-Malha was destroyed, and all its inhabitants deported to Syria and Lebanon.[172]

Al-Khalsa: This village numbered 1,840 (1,600 Fellahin and 240 Bedouin from Ghawarna tribe).[173] During the war, Al-Khalsa was destroyed, and all its inhabitants deported to Syria and Lebanon.[174]

Sha'ab: This village numbered 1,740 Fellahin.[175] During the war, 360 Bedouin from Krad al-Baqqra tribe, and another 25 from Numeirat tribe moved to Sha'ab,[176] for a total of 385 Bedouin transferred to Sha'ab during the war.

Summary: On the eve of the war, Bedouin who lived in Safad and its sub-district were estimated at 5,123. Those nomadic and permanent Bedouin inhabitants numbered 4,503 inhabitants. The remaining 620 Bedouin lived in Safad and in its sub-district of Fellahin villages.

After war, most of the inhabitants, including Bedouin, fled, or were expelled. The total number of Bedouin remaining in Safad district declined to approximately 735, divided as follows: about 385 remained or moved to Fellahin villages; about 350 remained in place, and later (the 1960s), the state recognized Wadi al-Hamam, Wadi Salameh, and Tuba-Zangariah as Bedouin settlements.

Note that most Bedouin inhabitants of Safad sub-district (mainly nomadic Bedouin) fled of their own volition to Syria and Lebanon during the civil war (between November 1947 and mid-May 1948), some due to fear from uncertainty of the war, while others were expelled by *Hagana* and *Palmach* forces, who burned their tents and bombed most of their homes, as occurred in Arab al-Shamlana and Arab al-Zangariah, according to Morris.[177] Arab inhabitants of Safad abandoned their neighborhoods in the face of massive open and deliberate mortar fire by *Haganah* and *Palmach* commanders toward Arab neighborhoods of Safad in early May 1948. After the occupation, Jews began to take control and rob Arabs' property.[178]

The fate of Bedouin in Tiberias district and its sub-districts during the 1948 war

The inhabitants of Tiberias and its sub-districts on the eve of the war were estimated at 3,496 (Fellahin and Bedouin). Their fate in the war was as follows:

Tiberias: The Dalaika family (25), who during the war, fled to Jordan.[179] All other Bedouin fled to Syria.

Tiberias sub-districts: estimated at 3,211 Bedouin, divided among the following tribes: Al-Qdirat (390), Al-Mawasi (100), Al-Wahib (147), Al-Samkia (380), Al-Manara (490), Al-Talawia (523), Masharqa (100), Al-Kaddish (60), Al-Kharanbeh/Rmihat (157), Seragnah (173), Nassir Al-Din (179), Nuqib (267), and Tabiqa (245).[180] During the war; 1,696 moved to the Fellahin villages of Shafa-Amer, Eilabun, Maghar, and Nazareth; the rest fled to Syria and Jordan.

Fate of Bedouin that lived in Fellahin villages in Tiberias sub-districts

They were estimated on the eve of the war to 260 inhabitants, as follows:

Maghar: This village numbered about 400 (380 Fellahin and 20 Bedouin from Kharanbeh tribe).[181] During the war, the Bedouin remained there, joined by 20 Kharanbeh who were camped west of Tiberias district, and another 20 Al-Heib from Wadi Salameh Bedouin village; as well as another large family of about 20 Al-Na'im who lived near Hittin village (western Tiberias), consequent to Nassir Al-Din Battle in which they fought with Al-Dalaika tribe against the *Hagana* forces.[182] Accordingly, it was assumed that the Bedouin inhabitants of Maghar after the war numbered 80.

Eilabun: This village numbered 550 (375 Fellahin and 175 Bedouin from Marisat, Shawahdeh, Sweitat, and Heib al-Fawawza tribes),[183] whose fate in the 1948 war was as follows: Marisat: almost all fled to Syria, due to having fought in the war against the IDF. Those who did not fight (30) remained in Eilabun.[184] Shawahdeh: almost none of this tribe fought the IDF. Therefore, it remained in place, in the eastern neighborhood of Eilabun. The tribe numbered 30 inhabitants and was joined by 15 members from Mawasi tribal headquarters from west of Tiberias area.[185] Sweitat: This tribe numbered 15 inhabitants, who during the war moved from Eilabun to tribal headquarters in Deir Hanna.[186] Heib al-Fawawza: This tribe numbered 45 inhabitants, who during the war fled from Hittin to tribal headquarters on the southern outskirts of Eilabun.[187] Accordingly, the Bedouin inhabitants of Eilabun after the war had declined to 135.

Sarona: This village existed until February 1938. Its population was 131, including 20 Bedouin of the Masharqa family.[188] With establishment of the Jewish settlement "Sharona" in 1938 on Sarona's lands, all of the villagers (including the Bedouin family) moved from Yama (or Yemma),[189] where at first, they lived in temporary tents, and five years later, they built shacks. In the 1948 war, this Bedouin family moved to Al-Fakhura neighborhood in Nazareth,[190] for a total of 20 refugees of Masharqa family who moved to Nazareth.

Al-Dalhamiya: In 1945, this village numbered about 390 (345 Fellahin and 45 Bedouin from al-Hanadi tribe).[191] During the war, all of the villagers fled to Jordan and Syria, and the village was destroyed.[192]

Summary: the total number of Bedouin inhabitants of Tiberias and its sub-districts was estimated at 3,496. Nomadic and permanent Bedouin: 3,211. The remaining 285 Bedouin lived in Tiberias and in neighboring Fellahin villages. After the war, most of the villagers, including Bedouin, fled or were expelled. The total number of Bedouin remaining in Tiberias area declined to 1,696 as follows: About 810 inhabitants remained/moved to Fellahin villages. About 886 Bedouin became refugees in Bedouin communities/villages: Arab Al-Shibli, Zubeidat, and Wadi al-Hamam. Most Bedouin inhabitants of Tiberias fled to Lebanon and Syria.

The Fate of Bedouin in Nazareth and Marj Ibn Amer during the 1948 war

The inhabitants of Nazareth and Marj Ibn Amer at eve of the war were estimated at 3,922 (Fellahin and Bedouin). Their fate in the war was as follows:

Nazareth: About 110 Bedouin from the tribes Al-Subayh and Al-Zahir (belonging to Zahir al-Umar al-Zidani from the 18th century) remained in Nazareth.[193]

In addition, additional Bedouin refugees came to Nazareth, including two brothers, Mahmoud, and Mansur Wahash (now called "Manasra family") of Al-Subayh tribe;[194] and another family, Al-Khalidi (15 refugees) came from Qumiya village (east of Marj Ibn Amer).[195] In addition, the N'arani family (10 refugees) from Tab'un in Haifa District, moved to Nazareth (taken into account in Haifa estimate),[196] for a total of 820 Bedouin in Nazareth (including refugees from Nazareth sub-districts).

Bedouin inhabitants who lived in nomadic and temporary localities in Nazareth sub-districts were estimated on the eve of the war at 2,270, divided into tribes as follows: Arab Al-Subayh (1,320), Arab Al-Sabarja (nearby Reina village) (75), Al-Mazarib (130), Al-Ghrefat (120), Al-Heib (60), Al-Hajajra (110), Al-Ka'abiya (185), Al-Hujeirat (120), and Arab Al-Ghazalin (20),[197] most of whom remained in place. Some moved to Nazareth, and others transferred as refugees to surrounding villages, and about a year later returned, as Israel recognized them as Bedouin villages, as will be expanded upon later. Also, on the eve of the 1948 war, Arab Al-Subayh numbered 1,320. On 8 November 1948, they dropped to 402; and on 31 December 1949, there was another decline to 398 inhabitants.[198] These figures are the result of this tribe's resistance to occupation, which caused most of them to flee, mainly to Jordan.[199]

Bedouin who lived in Marj Ibn Amer numbered 930, divided as follows: Al-Tawatha tribe (680) and Al-Na'im (250). During the war, they moved to Nazareth.[200]

Fate of Bedouin that lived in Fellahin villages in Nazareth sub-districts

They were estimated on the eve of the war to be 612 inhabitants:

Iksal: 1,110 (including 20 Bedouin from Ghazalin tribe),[201] who did not participate in the war and remained in place.[202] **Al-Naora**: 340 (including 20 Bedouin: 10 from Obeidat tribe, and 10 from Khalidi tribe),[203] who did not participate in the war and remained in place.[204] **Uzair**: 150 (including 15 Bedouin from Hujeirat tribe),[205] who did not participate in the war and remained in place.[206] **Rumana**: 590 (72 Bedouin from Heib and Hujeirat tribes),[207] who did not participate in the war and remained in place.[208] **Manshiya Zabda**: 35 (including 35 Bedouin from Saida tribe),[209] who did not participate in the war and remained in place.[210] **Yafa**: 1,070 (including 215 Bedouin from Ghazalin, Hamdun, and Na'im tribes,[211] who did not participate in the war and remained in place.[212] **Bu'enie Nujeidat**: 540, including 125 Bedouin from Nujeidat tribe,[213] who did not participate in the war and remained in place.[214] **Kafr Manda**: 1,260, including 140 Bedouin from Ziadnah tribe,[215] who did not participate in the war and remained in place.[216] Moreover, they were joined by another 100 Bedouin refugees from Al-Jenadi and Khalil.[217] **Reina**: 1,290 inhabitants,[218] including two Bedouin brothers, Hussein and Ahmad Ali Mansur (now called "Manasra family"), as well as refugees who came to Kafr Manda from Al-Subayh tribe during the war.[219] **Turan**: 1,350 inhabitants,[220] including two Bedouin brothers, (Mahmoud and Ahmad Ali Mansur, now called "Manasra family"), refugees who came to Kafr Manda from Al-Subayh tribe during the war.[221] That makes a total of 616 Bedouin inhabitants and refugees living in Fellahin villages in the sub-districts of Nazareth.

Summary: The total number of Bedouin inhabitants who lived in Nazareth and Marj Ibn Amer was estimated at 3,922. Nomadic and permanent Bedouin numbered about 3,200. The remaining 722 lived in Nazareth and in neighboring Fellahin villages. After the war, most of the villagers fled/were expelled, including Bedouin. The total number of Bedouin remaining in Nazareth area thus declined from 3,922 to 3,112, divided as follows: 862 remained/moved to Fellahin villages. About 2,250 Bedouin remained in place. Later the state would recognize them as the Bedouin settlements Beit Zarzir/Zarzir, Bir al-Maksur, Shibli (including umm al-Ghanam), Ka'abiya-Helf Tabash-Hajajra, and Bussmat Tab'un).

The Fate of Bedouin in Beisan district and its Sub-districts during the 1948 War

Bedouin in Beisan numbered 3,617 on the eve of the war.[222] Their fate during the war was as follows:

Banu Saqer: 1,037, located in southwestern Beisan. The tribal headquarters of all these tribes was Fadel al-Ursan.[223] About 517 members of this tribe were considered nomadic Bedouin; the remaining 520 lived in Fellahin villages.[224] During the war, all of them fled to Jordan.[225]

Al-Ghazzawiyya: 1,020,[226] located in the Jordan Valley between Beisan and Tiberias. The tribal headquarters of all of these tribes was Amir Bashir al-Hasan al-Ghazzawi. During the war, all fled to Jordan save some who settled in nearby Fellahin villages: Masil al-Jizl (100 inhabitants) and Wadi Al-Bira (70), totaling 170.[227]

Al-Bashatwa: 1,560, located in northeast Beisan,[228] some of whom settled in the nearby Fellahin villages Tell Al-Shouk, population 120 (40 Bedouin); Al-Ashrafia, population 230 (70 Bedouin); Umm 'Ajra, population 260 (75 Bedouin); and Qumya, population 440 (175 Bedouin).[229] During the war, all members of those tribes fled to Jordan.[230]

Noted that some of these tribes resisted and fought against the Jewish occupation during the war. Those who fought were instructed to act against Jews from their military headquarters in Beisan, separating Fakhr al-Din and the Farouki district officer. These Bedouin participated in the great Battle of Tell el-Husn,[231] as aforementioned. With fall of Beisan at the end of the war, all of the Bedouin fled to Jordan and especially to Syria.

Some the following Bedouin families' flight from Beisan sub-district to Nazareth

Mjali family: 15 refugees (belonging to Zubeidat tribe), located in Beisan Valley and belonging to tribal headquarters of Banu Saqer.[232] During the war, they moved to Nazareth's eastern neighborhood.[233]

Banu Rabiah: 25 refugees, who were located in Beisan Valley.[234] During the war, they moved to Nazareth's eastern neighborhood.[235] That is total of 40 Bedouin who moved from Beisan to Nazareth.

Summary: Total number of Bedouin in Beisan and its sub-districts was estimated at 3,617, including 2,917 nomadic and permanent Bedouin. The remaining 700 Bedouin lived in Beisan and in neighboring Fellahin villages. During the war, 3,577 were expelled to Jordan, and 40 fled to Nazareth.

Cases of Government Policy of Transferring Bedouin During the 1948 War

During the war, the IDF deliberately initiated several transfers of Bedouin inhabitants. Bedouin refugees were transferred consequent to the decision of the Committee for Transfer Arabs Office of Minorities, or its common name, Transfer Committee. At its meeting of 15 December 1948,[236] the committee decided to disperse Bedouin refugees in Fellahin villages in the Galilee. The goal thereof, in the words of Elisha Schultz, a military governor of Nazareth, was "ripping the chain". In other words, preventing "[creation of] Arab national territories within the Jewish state".[237]

During this period, about half of the territories of Arab villages in Palestine were transferred to the state in a variety of ways.[238] Most efforts were directed at transfer of refugees' lands – those outside the borders of the state and those whose communities were destroyed – to the state to build Jewish settlements (such as Upper Nazareth [today Nof haGalil] and Karmiel) or to build various development projects (such as the National Water Carrier) after the establishment of Israel.[239]

Some cases of deliberate transfers of Bedouin tribes in Nazareth and Marj Ibn Amer by the authorities

Transfer of Bedouin tribes from Nazareth sub-district to Ilut village (Fellahin village). This decision was based on the decision of the Transfer Committee of 15 December 1948, carried out by military forces. In accordance thereto, 517 Bedouin from the Lower Galilee (western Nazareth) were transferred to Ilut. The IDF obliged all the Bedouin inhabitants (men, women, and children) to transfer. Tribe names: Al-Mazarib (169), Al-Ghrefat (123), Al-Jawamees (107), Al-Heib (50), Al-Saida (68), and Al-Ghazalin (70).[240]

In 1949, about a year after the war, all Bedouin tribes returned to their pre-war locations[241] owing to good relations that they had with Jews (before and during the war, such as enlistment of Bedouin into IDF units).[242] As noted, these tribes returned to their former Bedouin settlements, with the exception of Al-Ghazalin tribe, members of which wandered westward to Ilut and settled near Mazarib tribe.[243] Until the 1970s or so, most members of Mazarib tribe underwent "chain migrations" to Yafa or Nazareth.[244] In 1974, all of these Bedouin tribes were recognized as Bedouin villages.[245]

Transfer of Bedouin tribes from Nazareth sub-district to Ein Mahel (Fellahin village). According to the same Transfer Committee decision, 541 Bedouin from Mount Tabor area (Saida tribe) were transferred to Arab Al-Subayh and Umm al-Ghanam, and concentrated in Ein Mahel.[246] However, at the end of the war, these tribes returned to their locations (as in the previous case). Three brothers from Arab Al-Subayh of the Mansur (now called Manasra) family chose to stay and settled near Ein Mahel.[247]

Transfer of Al-Khalidi family (15 refugees) from Qumiya village (east of Marj Ibn Amer) to Nazareth.[248]

Notably, there have been other cases of Bedouin transfers to Fellahin villages, such as Al-Sweitat tribe who lived in northern Abu Snan, who were transferred to the center of Abu Snan, and a few weeks later, returned to northern Abu Snan.[249] Another transfer of Sawaed tribe, who lived in southern Sha'ab, were transferred to Sha'ab, and a few weeks later they returned to southern Sha'ab.[250]

Beyond Israel's "land redemption" policy, transferring Bedouin to Fellahin villages or to Bedouin settlements has had many ramifications, mainly on the settling of Bedouin inhabitants in Bedouin localities or in Fellahin towns and villages. This policy would be gaining momentum again, especially in the 1960s, as will be described later. For most part, Bedouin who remained in Fellahin villages and towns in the Galilee were refugees.[251] Most of the Bedouin refugees who came to villages settled on outskirts of the village and outside built-up areas.[252] At first, especially during the first two or three years of their absorption, they built tents and shacks of various materials, usually tin, on plots of threshing floor and on farmland on the edge of the built-up area of the village, consequent to their having lost their herds and land to graze them on.[253] Moreover, Military Rule acted to implement a plan to deal with the refugee population, such as renting homes for them in village centers (this was especially true of Fellahin) or moving them into homes of those who had fled the country during the war.[254]

A Comparative Statistical Summary of the Bedouin Population in Fellahin Towns and Villages in the Galilee Before and After the 1948 War

The Bedouin in the Galilee on the eve of the war numbered 26,352 inhabitants. As described in the previous chapter, they were divided into two categories: the nomadic Bedouin population, and permanent residents, who on the eve of the war were estimated at 14,650. The Bedouin population residing in Fellahin towns and villages was estimated at 11,702 inhabitants.

After the war, this population declined to 17,504 inhabitants, a decrease of about 33%. Of these, the number of nomadic and permanent Bedouin residing in the Galilee declined to 4,456. On the other hand, the number of Bedouin living in Fellahin towns and villages rose to 13,048.

In other words, during the war the Galilee saw an increase of 1,346 inhabitants (16%) among Bedouin who lived in Fellahin towns and villages, the outcome of which was the entry of Bedouin refugees despite the great flight and expulsion that took place among Bedouin population.

Note that during the war, large numbers of Bedouin escaped mixed villages and took up residence outside the UN Resolution borders (e.g., in Al-Mansi, Ijzim, Al-Sindiyana, Al-Damun, Tiberias, and nearly all of the villages in Beisan district).[255] This decrease amounts to approximately 8,848 inhabitants (see below).

Thus, statistics can summarize as follows: Total number of Bedouin remaining in Palestine after the 1948 war is estimated at 17,504 inhabitants, divided as follows:[256]

- 3,000 – Bedouin inhabitants who lived in Bedouin localities/villages
- 1,456 – nomadic Bedouin
- 13,048 – Bedouin inhabitants of Arab Fellahin towns and villages

Moreover, the statistics on the Bedouin refugee category are as follows:

- 8,848 who crossed Palestine's borders after having escaped or having been expelled
- 1,350 internal refugees or "displaced inhabitants" who have since integrated into localities/villages, whether of their own volition or were transferred by the IDF.
- 1,346 who moved to existing in Fellahin towns and villages in the Galilee, having migrated of their own volition or were transferred by the IDF.[257]

Compared to other estimates for the same period, the above estimate is larger than that of this study (4,456, both nomadic and permanent). For example, researchers such as Medzini and Sawaed estimated this population at fewer than 6,500 in 1949.[258] According to Ghazi Falah, at the end of 1948, this population numbered about 5,000.[259] There is no doubt that these estimates did not include the Bedouin population who lived in Fellahin towns and villages.

After the 1948 war, Bedouin tribes that remained nomadic and semi-nomadic were concentrated in five main locales: the hills between Tab'un and Shafa-Amer; Sahl Al-Battuf; Sakhnin Valley; Mount Tabor area; and the hills between Bir al-Maksur and Kaukab Abu Al-Hija.[260] Most of these tribes remained in their locations until the early 1960s, when the state promoted plans to transfer Bedouin from areas classified as "essential to the country", in order to "clear" the land for Jewish settlement. However, as early as the 1948 war, this policy was implemented in practice.

An exception in this context is cases wherein Fellahin fled and found sanctuary in Bedouin localities. This is because during the war, they chose a hiding place that provided personal security, and not necessarily economic security. Thus, they adopted the Bedouin lifestyle, similar to cases during Ottoman rule, e.g., the Mahmoud clan/hamula (25 inhabitants), whose origin was Saffuriya, and who settled in Heib al-Frush-Rumana village (nearby Uzair) during the war.[261] This case illustrates fluidity between two categories (Bedouin and Fellahin), especially in cases of security risks that threaten lives of one category. This also illustrates nonlinear directionality in the transformation of one lifestyle.

To conclude, during 1948 war, the Bedouin in Palestine were divided into three main camps: those who joined/allied themselves with the Zionists (*Palmach* and *Haganah*) and fought with them; those who organized and joined Palestinian national movement "rescue forces", who fought the Zionists, and mainly belonged to the "Arab liberation army"; and those who did not take an active part in the war.

This war, on the one hand, led to strengthening ties between Bedouin and Fellahin populations, in light of the Palestinian national alliance that formed between them. On the other hand, the war also segregated and separated Bedouin and Fellahin, which to an extent shaped the Bedouin refugee population. The latter entered Fellahin towns and villages and settled in temporary tents and outlying neighborhoods, where local Fellahin gave them food, drink, and even helped them to settle in and welcomed them.

This chapter detailed and analyzed, historically and sociologically, the fate of Bedouin tribes, which was largely residing in mixed villages (Bedouin and Fellahin) that had been abandoned during the war. In addition, the chapter presented statistical data for each category: permanent and nomadic Bedouin inhabitants, from which their fate can be learned.

As aforementioned, after the war, the number of Bedouin in the Galilee dropped from 26,352 to 17,504 inhabitants (a decrease of about 33%). Of this number, the nomadic Bedouin population and the permanent residents of the Galilee dropped from 14,650 to 4,456 inhabitants. In contrast, the number of the Bedouin who lived in Fellahin towns and villages rose from 11,702 to 13,048. This latter increase is explained as the consequence of entry of Bedouin refugees into Fellahin villages and towns and their integration therein, despite the transfer or exile of Bedouin who lived in these mixed villages.

Thus, it turns out that the 1948 war and the Nakba did not constitute a significant factor in processes of continued settlement and integration of Bedouin into Fellahin towns and villages in the Galilee. While the war accelerated Bedouin this process, it also brought on a sharp decline in the number of nomadic Bedouin residing in Bedouin localities, a process that would continue after the war that was characterized by chain migrations and along with government programs, greatly accelerated the process of Bedouin integration into Fellahin villages in the Galilee.

CHAPTER

4

Israeli Military Rule, 1948–1966: Chain Migrations and Government Plans

This chapter presents and describes the continuation of the Bedouin settlement process in Fellahin towns and villages in the Galilee. This process not only did not cease after the 1948 war, but rather intensified and accelerated as per Military Rule policy that was introduced in Israel's first decade.

In general, Israeli Military Rule's (1948–1966) effect on Bedouin settlement in the Naqab and northern Israel was considerable. According to Falah, in his article on the development of "Planned Bedouin Settlement" in Israel 1964–1982,[1] the prohibition of free movement and mobility of the Palestinian population (*siyeg* in the Negev plan) and policy of expropriation of lands from Bedouin,[2] contributed significantly to their transition to sedentarizaion.[3] During and after the Military Rule, Israel implemented three government programs (mainly during the 1960s), whose ultimate goal was to evacuate the Bedouin from areas defined as "essential lands for the state" and settle them in populated Fellahin towns and villages.[4]

As noted, this government policy "as agency" contributed largely to continued integration of Bedouin into Fellahin towns and villages, and reduced the differences between the Bedouin and Fellahin lifestyles. Moreover, the spontaneous migration of Bedouin and/or their dispersal to mixed Fellahin villages and towns also contributed to ties between these two communities.

In addition, this chapter lists in detail Bedouin families who joined Fellahin towns and villages, as well as reviewing and analyzing the three government programs that contributed significantly to settlement and integration of Bedouin into Fellahin villages and towns in the Galilee. Furthermore, the chapter present statistical data for the end of the 1960s.

Chain Migrations of Bedouin During the 1950s

After the 1948 war, Bedouin families began to move in chain processes and join their anchor families, who had previously lived in Fellahin towns and villages. Usually, these settled geographically close to their Bedouin tribes. The reasons for these transitions were varied: social (family reunification), geographical, and economic proximity.

The following Bedouin families who moved to Fellahin towns and villages in the Galilee in the 1950s and 1960s and the reason for their transitions:

Al-Ghazalin tribe in 1950: About 20 inhabitants moved from Zarzir region to Yafa (southwest of Nazareth). Reason: family unification.[5] **Al-Sawaed** (15) and **Al-Samniyya** (10) tribes in 1953 moved from Tab'un Forest (Al-Hamira hills) to Shafa-Amer. Reason: family unification.[6] **Al-Sweitat** tribe in 1951 (15 inhabitants), who lived in tents at tribe headquarters in Jadin, moved to Abu Snan. Reason: family unification.[7] **Al-Hujeirat** tribe in 1951 (10 inhabitants) moved from tribal headquarters in Al-Thahra (about 6 km east of Shafa-Amer) into Shafa-Amer (later establishing their own neighborhood, Osman).[8] Reason: family unification. **Al-Sweitat** tribe in 1952 (15 inhabitants) from al-Zinar area (northern Sakhnin) moved to Tarshiha. The reason for this transition was as per a government plan, as will be explained later in this chapter).[9] **Al-Sawaed** tribe in 1955 (30 inhabitants) who lived in Tab'un Forest (Al-Hamira hills), moved to Wadi al-Saki'a neighborhood in Shafa-Amer.[10] The reason for this transition was not only geographic proximity, but also the connection with the UN representative, who came weekly to distribute food to Bedouins living in tents. Moreover, after the war, foodstuffs were provided them by voluntary relief organizations, such as the Belgium-based Jewish Society for Human Services.[11] Then, in December 1948, the UN replaced Relief for Palestinian Refugees (UNRPR), which coordinated between various organizations and UN agencies, including Red Cross, whose activity continued during the period of Military Rule.[12]

Banu Rabiah tribe in 1955 (25 inhabitants) from the eastern neighborhood of Iksal, where they lived in temporary tents, moved to the neighborhood of Bir Abu al-Jish (later called Al-Fakhura neighborhood) in Nazareth. This family purchased vacant land and built concrete houses.[13] **Al-Zubeidat** tribe in 1955 (6 inhabitants) exchanged land with the state authorities and moved from their tribal headquarters in Tab'un to the southern neighborhood of Daburiya near Mount Tabor.[14] Reason: intra-tribal conflict. **Maslama** tribe in 1960 (20 inhabitants) moved from Al-Naora to Al-Fakhura neighborhood in Nazareth due to state authorities encouraging land exchange.[15] **Al-Hanadi** tribe (Hussein, Hassan, and Ibrahim Alwani) in 1960 (15 inhabitants) transferred from Arab Al-Ramil (near Ibtin) to the Al-Basiliya, Wastani, and Sarkis in neighborhoods in Shafa-Amer, where they purchased land from wealthy Shafa-Amer families and built stone houses.[16] Reason: pressure from state authorities.

Settlement and integration of these Bedouin families within Fellahin towns and villages shows on the one hand, the flexible and non-dichotomous relationship between Bedouin and Fellahin, and on the other hand, despite good neighborly relations, their preservation of identities of each community separately. Thus, Bedouin families' chain migration, as well as government programs (as we shall see below), contributed to continued settlement of Bedouin families into Fellahin villages and towns in the Galilee.

Government Plans in the Early 1960s for Bedouin Settlement in the Galilee

Statism, which began after the establishment of Israel state, led to the conversion or transfer of institutions of government that existed during the *Yishuv* (pre-state) period to responsibility and supervision by the nascent state.[17] In order to implement this principle, it was necessary to "militarize" the society, i.e., blur the boundaries between the army and civilian society. Uri Ben-Eliezer noted that this militaristic ideology was the driving force behind the formation of a "nation in military uniform" and became the center of Israeli Jewish collective consciousness.[18] This concept was based on assumption that the war had not yet ended, but rather continues.

On 11 June 1958, Yosef Weitz, head of the JNF Northern District Lands Division, sent Deputy Chief of staff Tzvi Tzur a letter attesting to cooperation between the IDF and the JNF:

> At a meeting held on 29 December 1957, with Major General Amit [Meir Amit, head of IDF Central Command], a proposal was discussed and agreed upon, that the IDF would expropriate Training Area 9 [near Sakhnin] to nationalize and privatize the eastern plot land of this area to establish two agricultural [Jewish] settlements. In addition, the JNF was commissioned to conduct a land survey that will be used to plan the settlement and payment of compensation to Arabs for their lands [...]. I would like to order cooperation between our people through Mr.

Nachman Alexandrovsky [Director of the JNF Department of Mapping and Measurement] and the army in direction of the above goal.[19]

This is a good example from which we can learn about the close relationship between the JNF and the IDF working toward a common goal, as expressed in Trade and Industry Minister Pinhas Sapir's letter to Yosef Weitz: "I will do all in my power to fulfill settlement of gentile enclaves in the Galilee".[20]

Accordingly, plans were formulated with the aim of implementing these projects, known collectively as *geulat ha-karka* ["redemption of the Land"],[21] whose purpose was to concentrate Bedouin in certain settlements and to evacuate most of their lands in order to Judaize the Galilee.[22] In December 1964, Knesset Member (MK) Tawfiq Toubi of the Israeli Communist Party, said in the Knesset plenum:

> Such actions [government policy in the Galilee] have many names. Once it was called "concentration of the Bedouin", though these inhabitants long ago settled on their lands; they purchased it decades ago, which means that if they are Bedouin, it is permissible to shake them off as you would dust from a rug [...]. Once again, it's called 'keeping state land' [...]. The Eshkol government calls these actions 'development of the Galilee'. Today, the Ben-Gurion government calls it 'Judaizing the Galile'. This is a continuation of a dispossession operation that encompasses more than 420,000 dunams of cultivatable land [...], and this policy lies behind the acts of dispossession are related in Sawaed village [near Shafa-Amer], and Sweitat tribe and other tribes. A stupid policy, it advances neither development nor security, but means the dispossession and deprivation of rights of the Arabs.[23]

Without getting into the ambivalence of terminology formulation, the state, through its legal organs such as the Israel Lands Administration (ILA, established in 1960), began to supervise construction of residential housing. For this purpose, it decided to conduct a survey to locate areas for Bedouin construction in the Galilee; theretoward, it formulated a plan to concentrate Bedouin construction.[24] In 1961, a census found that Bedouin in the Northern District numbered 25 tribes, including 1,767 families and 9,267 inhabitants.[25] This estimate did not include the Bedouin who lived in settlements and as nomads, nor did it include Bedouin who lived in Fellahin towns and villages (such an estimate will be presented at the end of this chapter). According to ILA estimate, Bedouin land ownership was very limited and constituted about 10% of areas actually held by them.[26]

According to a 1962 ILA survey, some 6,000 buildings in the Galilee (inhabited by Bedouin or Fellahin) – most of them built after Israel's establishment but without building permits[27] – were deemed "illegal"; about a third of these were Bedouin. At the same time (early 1960s), the ILA brought 3,659 lawsuits for "illegal" (without a building permit) construction in 64 Arab towns in the north.[28] In addition, the ILA reported that more than 50% of the buildings constructed outside authorized construction areas were located "on state land", i.e., land overseen by the ILA.[29] This "illegal" construction prompted the ILA committee to recommend the following measures as "essential steps" for Israel:

Firstly, within approved construction areas: A. The state will not enforce judgments relating to buildings erected on private land. B. Negotiations will be conducted with owners of buildings built on state land, to exchange land or sell lots. Secondly, regarding expanding construction and planning of construction: A. examining the possibility of expanding construction areas. B. The ILA will allocate and plan construction plots in all Arab communities in the Galilee. Thirdly, execution of judgments for demolition: A. Judgments relating to buildings constructed outside approved construction areas will be executed. B. A "firm hand" must be used on any building built without a permit. Fourthly, planning for housing projects: drafting new master plans for construction by Bedouin in Arab towns and villages in the Galilee. Accordingly, the state, through the ILA, drafted three master plans for Bedouin settlement in the Galilee (as described below).

Government Plans for Bedouin Settlement in the Galilee in the Early 1960s

As of 1962, three government plans for Bedouin settlement in the Galilee had been drafted as per the ILA's recommendations.[30] These contributed significantly to settlement and integration of Bedouin into Fellahin towns and villages. The plans were:

First Plan: to transfer Bedouin tribes that lived in areas defined as "vital to the state" to existing Fellahin villages,[31] by providing a "basket of incentives and economic benefits" to the Bedouin. The ILA allocated 3,373 lots for transfer of Bedouin thereto.[32]

According to the above, the ILA defined Bedouin tribes as "a problem for the state", and mapped areas inhabited by Bedouin. It also presented an accurate estimate of the Bedouin population that was supposed to

Table 4.1. Demographic distribution of Bedouin tribes in the Galilee in 1962

No.	Tribe name	Location	Family number	Resident number
1	Zubeidat	West of Tab'un	147	756
	Al-Sa'diyya	Tab'un forest	84	414
	Al-Helf	Tab'un forest	29	187
	Total		**360**	**1,357**
2	Al-Amariya	Ibtin	15	91
	Al-Khawaled	1km north of Ibtin	32	196
	Tab'un	1.5 km east of Ibtin	19	92
	Total		**66**	**379**
3	Al-Sawaed	Shafa-Amer	60	317
	Al-Samniyya	Shafa-Amer	25	140
	Al-Ghazalin	Yafa	3	19
	Total		**88**	**476**
4	Hujeirat al-Thahra	East of Shafa-Amer	74	324
	Hujeirat Bir al-Maksur	East of Shafa-Amer	224	1,290
	Ka'abiya	South of Shafa-Amer	78	488
	Total		**376**	**2,102**
5	Al-Sawaed	Mount Kamaneh	193	1,102
	Al-Sawaed	Mount Mal (eastern Karmiel)	--	--
	Total		193	1,102

(Continued on Next Page)

Table 4.1. Demographic distribution of Bedouin tribes in the Galilee in 1962 (*continued*)

No.	Tribe name	Location	Family number	Resident number
6	Al-Mazarib	Zarzir	58	340
	Al-Jawamees	Zarzir	28	161
	Al-Saida	Manshiya Zabda	30	147
	Al-Ghrefat	Zarzir	37	205
	Al-Heib	Zarzir	28	178
	Al-Hajajra	Near Ka'abiya-Helf Tabash	26	222
	Total		**207**	**1,253**
7	Arab Al-Subayh	Shibli/near Mount Tabor	128	669
	Al-Saida	Umm al-Ghanam/near Mount Tabor	48	247
	Total		**176**	**916**
8	Wadi Al-Hamam	North of Tiberias	135	630
	Nujeidat	Bu'enie-Nujeidat	72	457
	Total		**207**	**1,087**
9	Al-Na'im (Al-Zinar)	North of Karmiel	26	176
	Total		**26**	**176**
10	Heib Al- Battuf	Sahl Al-Battuf	67	419
	Total		**67**	**419**
	Totality		**1,767**	**9,267**

populate these areas: 9,267 inhabitants located in 10 different areas in the Galilee (see Table 4.1, previous page), including tribes' name and families' numbers. In other words, 10 areas in the Galilee were inhabited by Bedouin tribes (nomadic and semi-nomadic) must be transferred to existing Fellahin towns and villages or to Bedouin villages.

Later, the ILA marked areas where Bedouin are located on a map, as well as, the Arab Fellahin towns and villages to which the Bedouin could be transferred.[33] In a 12 November 1963 debate in the Knesset plenum on "preventing illegal construction in the Galilee", Knesset Member Baruch Uziel asked Deputy Interior Minister Shlomo Ben-Meir: Does the government intend to immediately take decisive and constructive measures to put an end to this situation [illegal construction by the Bedouin that "undermine landscape of the country"]?[34] To which Ben-Meir replied:

> In response to the severity of the problem of illegal construction, the Interior Ministry has come up with constructive and effective solutions [...]. The Interior Ministry allocated 38,000 IP [Israel Pounds] from its development budget, for this purpose, to 14 local councils. Detailed outline plans and plans prepared for Bedouin communities will enable the Bedouin population of the Galilee to move to planned settlements [...], [we're doing] special radio broadcasts and lectures to inhabitants of the villages, and distributing pamphlets and posters in villages to explain the benefits of this planned construction.[35]

According to Deputy Interior Minister Shlomo Ben-Meir, the state indeed prepared plans to demolish houses defined as illegal, and to evict Bedouin living on land wanted by the state. One of these plans was to evacuate Bedouin from Training "Area 9", near Sakhnin, and transfer them to existing villages.

Transfer of Training Area 9 Bedouin near Sakhnin to nearby Fellahin villages

Until Israel's establishment in 1948, "Area 9" was used for British army training, and most of the inhabitants of this area (Bedouin) lived in tents and huts. During the army's training periods, Bedouin were temporarily transferred to locales near Fellahin villages, far from this training area.[36] Note here, that the mountainous lands of Bedouin tribes (*dirah*) and Fellahin villages such as Deir Hanna, Ba'ana, Maghar, Majd al-Krum, Araba, Sajur, Sakhnin, Nahaf, Sha'ab, and Al-Rama lie inside this area of 63,129,091 dunams.[37]

With Israel's establishment, many Bedouin continued to build permanent houses and barracks, most of which were built on their land (in Area 9). According to the ILA, in this area, 196 houses were "built on state land", compared to 207 houses built on private land belonging to Bedouin. In these houses, 1,200 inhabitants lived, of which 683 lived on "state land" and 517 on private land.[38] In 1961, four Bedouin tribes of 1,200 inhabitants lived in this area: Arab Al Na'im (20 families); Arab Al-Marisat (20 families); Arab Al-Hamdun (20 families); and Arab Al-Sawaed (170 families).[39]

In a Knesset plenum session held on 2 December 1964, MK Tawfiq Toubi raised the issue of expulsion of Arab al-Sawaed and Arab Al-Na'im from Area 9:

> The demolition of residents' houses belonging to Arab Al-Sawaed and Al-Na'im, located in central Galilee in what is now known as Training Area 9, which began on 21 June 1964, has continued in several operations over the last few months, based on the claim that their construction is illegal. However, the authorities did not conceal their intention to expel inhabitants, nearly 250 families, some 2,000 inhabitants, who will be expelled from their land and transferred to another territory, and forced to accept government programs that violate their rights.[40]

Toubi's words reported what was happening on the ground. The state, through the ILA, offered Bedouin (according to the plan above) to move to villages located near these tribes, and in return, each tribesmen would choose one: either a free plot for residential purposes in one of the existing villages [Bedouin or Fellahin villages]; or financial assistance for transfer to a new place of residence; or a one-time sum for building a house in one of the nearby villages; or a loan under favorable terms from the Housing and Construction Ministry, to build a house in a nearby village.[41]

Accordingly, most of the tribes mentioned chose one of the options offered to them and moved to nearby villages. This relocation of Bedouin in Area 9 was a pilot for the state that was implemented elsewhere in the Galilee, as will be described below.

Families that relocated from Area 9 to Fellahin villages as per the state proposal (the first plan)

Al-Na'im tribe in 1964, about 200 members who lived in *Al-Zinar* area (northern Sha'ab), moved to Abu Snan, carried out by authorities in order to evacuate Bedouin from this area as part of Judaization of the Galilee. The state, through the ILA, gave monetary compensation for this relocation: For each dunam, they received 3,000 IP; for each built house, they received 300 IP; and for each well, they received 300 IP.[42]

Another part of Al-Na'im tribe between the years 1964–1972 from *Al-Zinar* area moved gradually to Tarshiha.[43] At first, about 20 members, the Kuftan family, emigrated in 1964. Afterwards, about 15 members, the Rzamak family, emigrated; and finally, about 10 members, the Sarhan family, emigrated in 1972. In these cases, too, the transfer process was accompanied by financial compensation.[44]

Sawaed tribe in 1965, some 90 members (about 20 households) from tribe headquarters in *Kamaneh Mount*, moved to the western side of Al-Rama.[45]

In 1965, about 15 members of **Sawaed** tribe moved from tribe headquarters in *Kamaneh Mount* to the eastern side of Nahaf.[46]

In 1965, about seven members of **Al-Heib** tribe moved from the Sakhnin Mountains to the northeastern side of Al-Rama.[47]

In 1965, 10 members of **Al-Hamdun** tribe moved from Arab Al-Ramil area (east of Acre) to the western neighborhood of Abu Snan.[48]

In 1965, 30 members of **Marisat** tribe moved from Z'atara (northern Kaukab Abu Al-Hija) to Iblin.[49] The same year, another 15 **Marisat** immigrated from Tamra to Iblin.[50]

In 1965, another 10 members of **Sawaed** from tribe headquarters in *Kamaneh Mount* moved to Shafa-Amer.[51]

Families that relocated to Fellahin villages from other places in the Galilee as per the state's proposal (the first plan)

In 1960, 15 members of **Al-Na'im** (*Hamamdeh*) tribe moved from Hajajra (Bedouin village), to the Marah al-Ghuzlan neighborhood of southern Yafa.[52] This family belonged to Al-Na'im headquarters in Syria (see Map 1.1) and came at the end of the 19th century and camped nearby Lubya village, west of Tiberias.[53] In 1948, they moved to Hajajra, and from there, in 1960, to Yafa.[54] In 1967, about 11 *Hamamdeh* households (24 members) moved from Yafa to Nazareth. The reasons for these transitions were kinships, and mostly governmental.[55]

In 1963, 20 members of **Al-Heib** (*Falahat*) tribe moved from the area of Kibbutz Kfar Hahoresh (in Arabic: *Al-Qaqour*) to the Umm Qubi and Al-Fakhura neighborhoods in Nazareth. The reason for the transition was mainly governmental.[56]

Quzli tribe: On the eve of the 1948 war, this family lived near Tirat (or Al-Tireh) Al-Carmel, and during the war, it fled to Karaman Farm. In 1962, 15 members from Karaman Farm of Taher Karaman near Damun Prison on Mount Carmel (Abu Ahmad Quzli and Mazid Quzli and their families, about 15 persons) moved to the western neighborhood of Isfiya, where other Bedouin tribes (Sweitat and Qlitat) were located.[57] The reason for the transition was mainly governmental.[58]

Masharqa: In 1962, 12 members, from Yama (or Yamma) moved to Kafr Kama (a Circassian village), where they rented five houses, and in 1973, two brothers, Yunis and Ali Ahmad Masharqa, together with their wives and children (about 17 persons) purchased land in Al-Fakhura neighborhood in Nazareth and moved there. The reason for this transition was mainly governmental.[59]

Al-Khalidi: In 1965, 22 members from Al-Naora moved to Al-Fakhura neighborhood in Nazareth. The reason for this transition was mainly governmental.[60]

Al-Muhameidat family: In 1965, 12 members from the Shafa-Amer Mountains moved to Shafa-Amer, where they purchased vacant land and built stone houses there. The reason for this transition was mainly governmental.[61]

Mawasi tribe: In 1967, 15 members from the area of Checkpost Quarry in Haifa, moved to Iblin, where they purchased lands from the Fellahin Sakran family, and settled in the western neighborhood. In 1973, two more families (Mawasi Qasem and Ali) came from Tarshiha and settled nearby the first family. The reason for this transition was mainly governmental.[62]

Al-Na'im tribe: In 1969, 25 members from Al-Dahi in Marj Ibn Amer moved to the Al-Fakhura neighborhood in Nazareth.[63] This transition was carried out at the request of ILA, which promised this tribe alternative land, according to an outline plan for construction of permanent houses in a new area. In fact, this promise was not fulfilled, and these Bedouin live in houses without building permits as of this writing. Part of this tribe purchased land in the 1980s in neighboring Yafa and moved there. The reason for this transition was mainly governmental.[64]

As such, for most part, the government program was implemented and completed. Most Bedouin inhabitants of these areas in the Galilee – approximately 8,900 inhabitants (of 9,267, as stated), from 10 different areas of the Galilee – settled in accordance with the plan. This is in addition to some 350 who remained in their locations, which the state defines as nomadic or diasporic unrecognized Bedouin settlements. These include some 30 from Al-Na'im tribe who remained in the Al-Zinar area; and some of 40 from Sawaed tribe who remained in

"Area 9"; some 20 of Hujeirat tribe in the Al-Thahra area; some 90 of Hujeirat tribe remain east of Shafa-Amer; some 20 of Hujeirat tribe in the Al Battuf Valley; and some 150 of the Al-Na'im Abu Garad tribe remained in "Area 9".

However, inhabitants of these unrecognized Bedouin settlements (350 inhabitants) felt very frustrated. In an interview with Nimr Al-Na'im, chair of Na'im Abu Garad tribe (a Bedouin dispersal near Sakhnin), he said, "We did not agree to the evacuation plan, because the state authorities demolished our houses in 1963, but we continued our justified struggle to recognize our settlement".[65]

Al-Na'im's remarks reflect harsh resentment among the inhabitants, due to the state's refusal to recognize their village. In other words, this population, which refused to settle in local Fellahin towns or villages, felt frustration mixed with loathing of law enforcement authorities, out of fear that at any given moment, their houses might be destroyed. These fears were likely to find an outlet in protests and riots on Land Day, 30 March 1976.

Second plan: Annexing existing tribes to existing Fellahin towns and villages

This plan's objective was to annex, both statutorily and geographically, Bedouin who lived in Bedouin encampments/locations close to Fellahin towns or villages, and recognize them as belonging to the same villages or towns from a jurisdictional standpoint. This plan also promoted transfer of Bedouin who lived nomadically or "diasporically" to these neighborhoods, as they were located in proximity thereto. From the protocol of the Government Planning and Building Committee meeting in 1963 regarding the Bedouin population in the Shafa-Amer area, according to which the ILA representative stated:

> In order to curb the wild construction in this [Galilee] area, the ILA has planned four Bedouin settlements near their main tribes, as well as planning plots for construction in Shafa-Amer, for Bedouin who would like to move there. Shafa-Amer will be an area for tribes of Sawaed, Al-Samniyya, and Ras Ali. The ILA grants Bedouin plots for building purposes, with all expenses including access roads and water supply at the ILA's expense. [In addition, we will extend] financial assistance to transfer residence to the planned location. Construction plans are covered by a Housing and Construction Ministry loan so that they can build permanent homes.[66]

According to the ILA, Bedouins were distributed in the southern region of Shafa-Amer as of 1963. This distribution included 13 tribes (together with the Fellahin village Ras Ali) (see Table 4.2, overleaf).

The data above (in Table 4.2) that lists Bedouin families in tribes in the southern Shafa-Amer area total 467 households (approximately 2,468 inhabitants, including 66 Fellahin inhabitants from Ras Ali, which owned 845 buildings). About 473 buildings were deemed private and legal, and another 372 were found to be on ILA land. The ILA at that time acted in accordance with the annexation plan for Bedouin neighborhoods located near Fellahin towns or villages.

In an interview with Muhsin Sawaed, a Bedouin resident of Sawaed Al-Hamira neighborhood (south of Shafa-Amer), told me of his satisfaction with the annexation plan: "This plan allows us to build houses, and also provides us services such as access roads, water, and sewage lines and more [...]".[67]

In another an interview, with Anis Karawi, a Fellah inhabitant of Shafa-Amer, he expressed his views on the annexation plan: "I don't remember anyone in Shafa-Amer who opposed this annexation of the Bedouin neighborhood of Al-Hamira to Shafa-Amer. The reason for this is that this did not harm the town; on the contrary, this annexation increased the town's annual budget".[68]

We hear from these interviews that inhabitants did feel neither bitter nor frustrated by the state plan to annex their neighborhood to Fellahin town. This is in contrast to first plan, wherein those who refused to move felt very frustrated.

Third plan

Intended to recognize some existing Bedouin settlements as sedentary with municipal authorities.[69] This would enable Bedouin who had been living elsewhere in the Galilee to settle in existing or new Bedouin settlements, which would be established specifically for this purpose. In 1963, the government decided to establish four such Bedouin communities: Bussmat Tab'un (recognized finally in 1966), Wadi Al-Hamam (recognized finally in 1968), Ibtin (recognized finally in 1970), and Bir al-Maksur (recognized finally in 1972). The idea behind establishing these Bedouin settlements was to accommodate nomadic Bedouin in order to make way for Jewish settlements.

In fact, the aforementioned four settlements existed as Bedouin villages, which the state planned to declare as such, as separate municipal entities. Note that these localities were not established according to the original timetables. It was only in the late 1960s and early 1970s that

Table 4.2. Distribution of Bedouin in Shafa-Amer, 1963

Family name	Number of tribe members	Number of buildings	private buildings on private land	private buildings on ILA land
Zubeidat	527	185	42	143
Al-Zubeidat tribe (in Tab'un forest)	66	26	26	0
Helf	234	75	49	26
Al-Sa'diyya	174	88	61	27
Al-Amariya	240	86	26	60
Al-Khawaled	79	35	12	23
Quzli	7	4	1	3
Al-Hujeirat	361	92	72	20
Ka'abiya	440	138	102	36
Al-Sawaed	183	58	44	14
Al-Marisat	51	9	0	9
Samniyya	40	25	16	9
Ras Ali (a Fellahin village in a Bedouin area)	66	24	22	2
Total	**2,468**	**845**	**473**	**372**

they began construction (I will not elaborate thereon, as this study does not discuss Bedouin living in Bedouin localities).[70]

❖

So, what was the Bedouin response to the three government plans? On the one hand, Bedouin acknowledged these plans' advantages, such as moving to a sedentarizaion, economic assistance for building houses, and receiving utilities such as access roads, schools, electricity, health services, and more. On the other hand, they identified the plans' shortcomings: dispossession of territories, tax collection, and damage to their lifestyle. Therefore, Bedouin understood that these plans were not intended to serve Bedouin' interests, but rather to clear land for Jewish communities. Arnon Medzini pointed out these plans' drawbacks:

> No grazing areas are designated alongside Bedouin settlements. A plot handed over to the Bedouin, was leased for a period of 49 years, not delivered free and clear. Houses were built at high density, which is not compatible with the Bedouin lifestyle. This transition obliged Bedouin to give up their flocks. These government plans did not address the lifestyle of the Bedouin and its tribal structure.[71]

De facto, these three government plans were operative, and from the mid-1960s, many Bedouin chose one of them and began to move to the locales offered. It can be said that during Military Rule (1948–1966), the state wished to prevent Bedouin from taking over Galilee lands, and thereby prevent continuation of their nomadic way of life. In order to achieve this overall goal, the state acted according to the first plan, namely, transferring Bedouin tribes who lived on "essential lands for the state" to existing Fellahin towns or villages in exchange for a "basket incentives and economic benefits" as temptation, as the ILA had prepared land for construction in existing Fellahin villages or towns for Judaizing the Galilee.

The next stage, implementation of the second plan, was annexation of Bedouin encampments to existing Fellahin villages and towns. Nonetheless, in the policy of those years of "divide and conquer",[72] the state had a contradictory goal of preventing settlement of Bedouin in Fellahin villages and towns, the solution to which lay in the third plan: recognition of existing tribes as purely Bedouin settlements, or establishment of separate Bedouin settlements. Therefore, the state decided to conduct a survey to designate construction areas in the Galilee,

Table 4.3. Distribution of Bedouin in Fellahin villages and towns in the Galilee, 1969

Tribe name	Fellahin Town and Village name	Number
Madi, Al-Shkirat, Qmirat, Al-Na'im (Nazal), Turkmen, Azuid, Hamdun	Haifa	425
Majdoub, Al-Ghawarna	Acre	375
Ziadnah, Hawara, Sawaed, Marisat, Al-Samniyya, Muhameidat	Shafa-Amer	4,468
Al-Zahir, Hawara, N'arani, Heib, Na'im, Rabiah, Turkman, Masharqa, Ghazalin, Khalidi, Subayh-Manasra	Nazareth	1,750
Zubeidat, Tarbiyeh (Trabay)	Sakhnin	2,870
Ziadnah, Marisat, Mawasi, Muhameidat, Hamdun, Sawaed	Tamra	960
Al-Hasi, Al-Najmiyya, Hawara, Sweitat, Marisat, Mawasi, Sawaed, Al-Samniyya	Iblin	920
Sweitat, Al-Fadl, Hamdun, Al-Ghawarna	Al-Jadida-Al-Makr	235
Na'im, Sweitat, Al-Samniyya, Heib	Tarshiha	345
Sweitat, Sawilat, Hamdun	Abu Snan	650
Ziadnah, Sweitat, Marisat	Deir Hanna	230
Kharanbeh, Sawaed	Maghar	615
Marisat, Mawasi, Shawahdeh, Sweitat, Heib-al-Fawawza	Eilabun	710
Krad Al-Baqqra, Numeirat	Sha'ab	525
Ghazalin, Hamdun, N'aim	Yafa of Nazareth	1,120

(Continued on Next Page)

Table 4.3. Distribution of Bedouin in Fellahin villages and towns in the Galilee, 1969 (*continued*)

Tribe name	Fellahin Town and Village name	Number
Nujeidat	Bu'enie-Nujeidat	1,890
Ghazalin	Iksal	32
Maslama, Khalidi	Al-Naora	20
Ziadnah	Kafr Manda	2,750
Hujeirat	Uzair	145
Subayh	Ein Mahel	52
Zubeidat, Subayh	Daburiya	33
Heib, Hujeirat	Rumana	165
Subayh-Manasra	Reina	120
Subayh-Manasra	Turan	54
Saida	Manshiya Zabda	35
Sweitat, Qlitat, Quzli, Ka'abiya	Isfiya	425
Qlitat, Quzli	Daliyat Al-Carmel	18
Heib, Sawaed	Al-Rama	125
Total		**22,062**

Table 4.4. Distribution of Bedouin in Bedouin villages in the Galilee, 1969

Family name	Village name	Number
Al-Amariya, Al-Khawaled, Qmirat	Ibtin	720
Zubeidat, Saida, Al-Dalaika	Bussmat Tab'un	1,420
Ghrefat, Mazarib, Al-Jawamees, Heib, Iyadat	Beit Zarzir	2,650
Subayh	Shibli	2,100
Heib, Al-Ghawarna	Wadi Al-Hamam	1,200
Sawaed	Wadi Salameh	210
Mizel	Aramsheh	620
Ghadir, Sawalha, Ramilat, Hujeirat	Bir al-Maksur	1,620
Ka'abiya, Helf-Tabash	Ka'abiya	1,710
Hajajra	Hajajra	415
Helf	Helf Umm Rashed	525
Saida	Umm Al-Ghanam	605
Heib, Zangariah	Tuba-Zangariah	1,950
Heib	Heib Al-Frush	450
Hujeirat	Makman	670
Hujeirat	Dameida	180
Total		**17,045**

Table 4.5. Distribution of Bedouin residing nomadically in the Galilee, 1969

Tribe name	Nomadic/Diaspora location name	Number
Arab al-Khawaled	located in two concentrations along Zippori stream	70
Arab Abu Shtayyeh	North of Tab'un	110
Arab Na'im Abu Garad	South of Karmiel	115
Arab Al-Marisat	North of Iblin	120
Arab Al-Hamdun	North of Deir Hanna	35
Arab Heib (Falahat)	Between Uzair and Bu'enie-Nujeidat	45
Arab Al-Jindawi	South of Bir al-Maksur	125
Arab Sawaed Kamaneh	Kamaneh mount, 'Area 9'	1,250
Arab Al-Hujeirat	North of Bir al-Maksur	670
Arab Al-Heib	Ya'ra	60
Arab Al-Sawaed	Ramia (middle of Karmiel)	30
Total		**2,630**

according to which it would permit construction of dedicated Bedouin settlements.[73]

Ultimately, having no choice, Bedouin acceded to the three options that the state offered them: A. land for construction of Bedouin neighborhoods in existing Fellahin towns and villages; B. annexation of Bedouin encampments to existing Fellahin villages and towns; C. establishment of separate Bedouin settlements.[74] The 1960s was thus the peak of Bedouin integration into Fellahin villages and towns in the Galilee. However, the problematic nature of these plans would ultimately lead to protests in the mid-1970s and in October 2000, as described below. Thus, we can summarize statistically the settlement distribution of Bedouin population in the Galilee after the military rule of 1966 ended, according to documents in the Jezreel Plain Regional Council Archives (JPRCA),[75] and interviews with Bedouin, as follows:

- 22,062 Bedouin lived in Fellahin towns and villages (see Table 4.3, page 128/129).
- Some 17,045 Bedouin lived in Bedouin localities recognized as such by the authorities (see Table 4.4, page 130).
- Some 2,630 Bedouin lived as nomads in unrecognized Bedouin villages and considered by the authorities to be diasporic (see Table 4.5, page 131).

The above tables show a significant increase in the Bedouin population in Fellahin towns and villages, from 13,048 inhabitants after the 1948 war to 22,062 in 1969 (an increase of 41%). According to the tables above, Galilee Bedouin in 1969 were estimated at 41,737. Moreover, we can discern significant increase among Bedouin settlements and nomadic Bedouin communities, whose number increased from 4,456 at the end of 1948 to 19,675 in 1969 (an increase of 77%). This sheds light, on the one hand, on high natural increase in these populations, and on the other hand, the preference on the parts of nomadic (diaspora) Bedouin to move to Bedouin localities after the 1948 war, rather than settle in Fellahin villages and towns.[76] According to these figures, there was an increase of nomadic Bedouin (about 36%) over Bedouin who lived in Fellahin villages and towns. In addition, the chain migrations of Bedouin families, whether spontaneous or governmental, continued even after Military Rule ended. Toward the end of the 20th century, they gradually diminished.

CHAPTER
5

Governmental and Civilian Events, 1966–2020: Bedouin Settlement in Fellahin Villages and Towns

The economic and social upheaval that Bedouin experienced during the 1948 war and during the Military Rule period (1948–1966) caused them to give up much of their lifestyle. The transition from nomadic to agriculture and to paid employment compelled Bedouin to reduce size of their herds, thereby also giving up their seasonal migration routes. Results of this transition were abandoned encampments in agricultural areas lands they owned [*dirah*].

This chapter address the continued integration of Bedouin into Fellahin towns and villages in the Galilee, from the end of Military Rule 1966 until the beginning of the 21th century. It describes what happened quietly in the 1960s (according to the three government plans), characterized by transfer of Bedouin to existing Fellahin villages and towns or Bedouin settlements, and later prompted riots and protests on Land Day, 30 March 1976; and the events of October 2000.

In addition, the chapter presents statistical data on Bedouin settlement and families living in Fellahin towns and villages in the Galilee, in 1982 and in 2020. The chapter also describes government policy, toward Bedouin living in mixed settlements (Bedouin and Fellahin) from the end of 20th to the beginning of the 21th century, when this policy was characterized by separating Bedouin from Fellahin regarding purchase plots for construction of residences for career IDF personnel, as opposed to Fellahin, who do serve in the IDF. Finally, a statistical estimate of Galilee Bedouin who volunteer for IDF service is presented, illustrating integration of this population (Bedouin living in Fellahin villages and towns) into an Arab Palestinian identity, and less to an Israeli one.

Bedouin Integration into Fellahin Villages and Towns from the end of Military Rule (1966) to Land Day (1976)

Toward the end of military Rule in 1966, Judaization of the Galilee discourse, defined as a vital goal for the state from its inception, continued to echo even after repeal of military rule. The Judaization of the Galilee policy is also reflected in interviews with Bedouin inhabitants of Fellahin towns and villages in the Galilee. In an interview with Hassan Al-Na'im Abu Ali, a Bedouin from Abu Snan, he told me that in 1967, he and some 70 members of his family, who lived in Al-Zinar area (northern Sakhnin), moved to Abu Snan. In addition, in 1972, another 30 members of this tribe moved by chain migration to Abu Snan.[1] According to Al-Na'im, ILA officials came up with tempting proposals for Bedouin receiving monetary compensation in exchange for relocating, "for a more normal life: stone houses, water, roads etc".[2]

From Al-Na'im words, it can be concluded that it is doubtful whether he was even aware of the Judaization of the Galilee project, and the state was far from paying attention to Bedouin quality of life and welfare. However, "temptation policy" combined with the fear of house demolitions succeeded to a great extent. This policy's results were considerable, as many Bedouin moved to new places offered to them. According to Al-Na'im, every Thursday an ILA inspector visits the tribe area and photographs every house or hut built "illegally", especially if it was built on state land.[3] We can learn from Al-Na'im's account that despite interest among Bedouin in opposing dictates of state authorities, they felt compelled to accept any offer made by representatives of the authorities.

Following are Bedouin families who moved or transferred to existing Fellahin villages in the 1970s due to social or governmental pressure (see Table 5.1, opposite).

According to the table, 77 Bedouin inhabitants who moved or transferred to Fellahin villages in the 1970s. Note the state did not attach importance to the Bedouin transfer process, whether it was transferred to recognized Bedouin settlements or to Fellahin villages or towns. In addition, the state viewed the Bedouin population living in Fellahin villages and towns as Arab Fellahin (Palestinian), and not Bedouin loyal to the state and serving in the army. The state's attitude toward this category of Bedouin, who lived in Fellahin villages and towns, was particularly discriminatory, especially in its policy of continuing expropriation of their land. This discrimination encouraged and even pushed the Bedouin to connect ideologically to Fellahin inhabitants of towns and villages, as reflected in Land Day.

Table 5.1. Bedouin families who moved or transferred to existing Fellahin villages and towns, 1970s

Bedouin family name	The year	Number	Moved from Bedouin localities	To Fellahin Towns/Villages	Reason for transition
Qlitat	1970	5	Isfiya (a mixed villag)	Daliyat al-Carmel	Family conflict
Sawaed	1972	8	Kafr Jatt	Abu Snan	Governmental
Sawaed	1973	7	Arab Al-Rarmil	Acre	Governmental
Qasum	1972	22	Al-Zubeidat	Iblin and Sakhnin	Family conflict
Sawilat	1973	20	Arab Al-Rarmil	Abu Snan	Governmental
Ghazalin	1979	15	Zarzir	Yafa	Governmental
Total		77			

Land Day: Forging of a Joint Arab Fellahin-Bedouin-Palestinian Identity

Land Day began on 30 March 1976 in Sakhnin as a protest against the government decision to expropriate some 6,300 dunams from Sakhnin and turn it over to Karmiel.[4] The state, through its law enforcement arm, continued to implement Judaization of the Galilee and the Negev as essential to the Jewish state, manifested in expropriation of lands and transferring Bedouin tribes living in "essential areas" to existing Arab villages. This was a direct cause of Land Day.

Another equally important factor of Land Day, albeit a less visible one, was state policy of inequality between Arabs and Jews manifested in neglect, particularly economic, of Arab towns and villages. This was reflected in a significant gap in allocation of funding between Jewish settlements and Arabs towns and villages. Examples of these gaps: The government budget for 1962 to Eilat (population: 7,000): 1,552,550 IP, compared to Shafa-Amer (7,675 inhabitants): 203,707 IP. In the same period, the government budget for Binyamina (population 2,680): 446,030 IP, compared to Yafa (population 2,730): 42,000 IP. The government budget for to Kiryat Binyamin (population 5,150): 613,810 IP, compared to Tamra's budget (population 5,650): 168,460 IP.[5]

Another driver of Land Day was formation of a joint Arab leadership. The declaration of the general strike by the Arab leadership, was a formative event in Arab society in the State of Israel. Until 1976, the Arab population lacked a leadership that would fight for rights and needs of Arab citizens, and to stop land dispossession. Jacob Landau believed that Bedouin land expropriation policy created tensions between Bedouin and the state, and has contributed to politicization of Bedouin, reflected in their increasing involvement in party politics in Israel.[6]

Against the backdrop of continued land expropriation and neglect of the Arab minority, alongside establishment of an Arab political leadership in Israel, demonstrations were held on March 30, 1976, mainly in Sakhnin, Deir Hanna, and Araba.[7] Bedouin in Fellahin towns and villages in the Galilee, participated therein. A general curfew in Deir Hanna (a mixed Bedouin-Fellahin village). was imposed by approval of Prime Minister Yitzhak Rabin.[8]

At the same time, the government acted to suppress these demonstrations, to no avail. In doing so, Israel security forces killed six Arab demonstrators.[9] The headline of *Yediot Aharonot* on 31 March 1976 read "Back to 1948".[10] The reporter's intent was that the state should treat Arab citizens of Israel similarly to how it did during the 1948 war. This proves that 1960s land expropriation (which was carried out quietly except for MK Tawfiq Toubi's speech in the Knesset plenum) toward Judaization of the Galilee formed the basis and platform for Land Day.

Since 30 March 1976, Arabs have had a separate identity within Israeli Jewish society. Their aspiration is "To be different yet equal", i.e., they differ from the Jewish majority in terms of nationality, but demand equality in terms of rights. Accordingly, Yiftachel viewed Land Day as a turning point: "The Arabs have remained on the fringes of the Jewish citizenry in Israel, and have begun to turn to alternative political and identity paths: establishing an Arab-Palestinian identity in Israel".[11]

Land Day for the Bedouin refreshed and reshaped relationships between Bedouin and Fellahin living in mixed towns and villages. These ties grew stronger, especially in the political arena. For example, Israel's policy of land expropriation or demolitions of "illegal" houses, as defined by the authorities, paved the way for the Islamic Movement to enter Bedouin society. This began in 1983, when for the first time this party participated in municipal elections in Israel, winning 51 council seats in 15 local councils, as well as electing six council heads (Rahat, Umm al-Fahm, Kafr Qasem, Kafr Bara, Jaljulia, and Kabul).[12] This movement managed to draw votes from Bedouin in both the Galilee and the Naqab, due to its efforts to protect Bedouin lands (especially in the Naqab) and its opposition to land expropriation and house demolitions. Conflicts therearound led to outbreaks of violence between Arab and state authorities.[13]

Despite the reshaping of Palestinian national identity, the migration of Bedouin to Fellahin towns and villages in the Galilee continued even after the 1970s. This was in most cases due to government programs:[14] A. continuing transfer of Bedouin tribes inhabiting regions deemed "vital to the state" to existing Arab towns and villages; B. annexation of Bedouin tribes residing in neighborhoods in existing towns and villages, such as Al-Hamira, south of Shafa-Amer; C. recognition of existing nomadic Bedouin tribe's "diaspora" locales as part of these communities. As aforementioned, the aim of these transfers was to evacuate Bedouin from areas considered "vital to the state",[15] even though Bedouin owned some of these lands outright. However, the state, through the ILA, demanded of this category of Bedouin, to move to existing Bedouin settlements or to Fellahin villages in exchange for a seductive "basket of incentives and economic benefits" as aforementioned.

The following Bedouin families moved or transferred to existing Fellahin villages during the 1980s and 1990s, and the reasons therefor were social or governmental:

Table 5.2. Bedouin in Fellahin villages and towns in the Galilee, 1982

Tribe name	Town/Village name	Number
Madi, Al-Shkirat, Qmirat, Al-Na'im (Nazal), Turkmen, Azuid, Hamdun, Kulibat	Haifa	615
Majdoub, Al-Ghawarna	Acre	420
Ziadnah, Hawara, Sawaed, Marisat, Al-Samniyya, Muhameidat, Samkia, Krad	Shafa-Amer	6,250 (with Sawaed Al-Hamira)
Al-Zahir, Hawara, N'arani, Heb, Na'im, Rabiah, Turkman, Masharqa, Ghazalin, Khalidi, Subayh-Manasra	Nazareth	2,350
Zubeidat, Tarbiyeh (Trabay)	Sakhnin	3,350
Ziadnah, Marisat, Mawasi, Muhameidat, Hamdun, Sawaed	Tamra	1,450
Al-Hasi, Al-Najmiyya, Hawara, Sweitat, Marisat, Mawasi, Sawaed, Al-Samniyya	Iblin	1,320
Sweitat, Al-Fadl, Hamdun, Al-Ghawarna	Al-Jadida-Al-Makr	315
Na'im, Sweitat, Al-Samniyya, Heib	Tarshiha	610
Sweitat, Sawilat, Hamdun	Abu Snan	890
Ziadnah, Sweitat, Marisat	Deir Hanna	345
Kharanbeh, Sawaed	Maghar	870
Marisat, Mawasi, Shawahdeh, Sweitat, Heib-al-Fawawza	Eilabun	930
Krad Al-Baqqra, Numeirat	Sha'ab	620
Ghazalin, Hamdun, N'aim	Yafa of Nazareth	1,350

(Continued on Next Page)

Table 5.2. Bedouin in Fellahin villages and towns in the Galilee, 1982 (*continued*)

Tribe name	Town/Village name	Number
Nujeidat	Bu'enie-Nujeidat	2,250
Ghazalin	Iksal	20
Maslama, Khalidi	Al-Naora	35
Ziadnah	Kafr Manda	3,250
Hujeirat	Uzair	190
Subayh	Ein Mahel	67
Zubeidat, Subayh	Daburiya	55
Heib, Hujeirat	Rumana	210
Subayh-Manasra	Reina	195
Subayh-Manasra	Turan	65
Saida	Manshiya Zabda	55
Sweitat, Qlitat, Quzli, Ka'abiya	Isfiya	780
Qlitat, Quzli	Daliyat Al-Carmel	30
Heib, Sawaed	Al-Rama	200
Subayh	Kafr Kana	150
Sawaed	B'ena	80
Sawaed	Nahaf	15
Total		**29,332**

The **Sawaed** tribe in 1990 (90 inhabitants), one of the largest tribes in the Galilee during the British Mandate, gradually transferred into recognized Bedouin communities such as Wadi al-Hamam and Wadi Salameh; and Arab Fellahin towns and villages such as Shafa-Amer, Tamra, and Iblin. The reason for this transition was mainly governmental.[16] The **Sawaed** family in 1980 (30 inhabitants) transferred from Al-Hamira hill to Shafa-Amer. The reason for this transition was mainly governmental.[17] The **Sawaed** (Abu Dallah) family in 1981 (20 inhabitants) transferred from Ramia (center of Karmiel) to Ba'ana. This family made a territorial exchange (land swap): 11 dunams in Ramia in exchange for 7 dunams in Ba'ana. The reason for this transition was mainly governmental.[18] The **Khawaled** family in 1980 (10 inhabitants) transferred from Kafr al-Manawat (today a Jewish settlement, Shlomi) to the western neighborhood of Abu Snan. The reason for this transition was mainly governmental.[19] The **Al-Na'im** tribe in 1990 (23 inhabitants) from Dahi region transferred to the Al-Fakhura neighborhood in Nazareth. The reason for this transition was mainly governmental.[20]

There were also tribal groups that did not succeed against the authorities or could not purchase plots, and so were forced to join to their relatives in recognized Bedouin villages or neighboring Fellahin villages or towns, such as the families from the headquarters of the Sawaed, Sweitat, Al-Na'im, Hujeirat, and Ghazalin tribes.

According to JPRCA data, together with interviews with Bedouin in the Galilee, it is possible to compile a statistical settlement distribution of Bedouin adults in the Galilee as of 1982: A. 29,332 in Fellahin towns and villages (see Table 5.2 previous page); B. About 26,515 inhabitants in Bedouin-only localities,[21] a few of which were recognized as Bedouin villages by the authorities (see Table 5.3 opposit); C. 3,439 who still lived in unrecognized Bedouin villages and which the authorities consider diasporic (see Table 5.4 below).

From the tables, it is possible to estimate all Bedouin in the Galilee in 1982 at 59,286 inhabitants. To compare the Bedouin population between 1969 and 1982 (according to natural growth), see Graph 5.1, Comparison of Bedouin estimates between the years 1969–1982,[22] on page 143.

The graph clearly shows the increase in the population in the three categories (Bedouin in Fellahin towns and villages, Bedouin in Bedouin communities/villages, nomadic/diaspora Bedouin) from 1969 to 1982: from 22,062 to 29,332, or an increase of about 25%. While government plans to disperse this population into sedentary communities influenced the decline of nomadic Bedouin, they did not disappear during that period, as will be described below.

Table 5.3. Bedouin in Bedouin villages in the Galilee, 1982

Family name	Village name	Number
Al-Amariya, Al-Khawaled, Qmirat	Ibtin	1,250
Zubeidat, Saida, Al-Dalaika	Bussmat Tab'un	3,150
Ghrefat, Mazarib, Al-Jawamees, Heib, Iyadat	Beit Zarzir	3,220
Subayh, Saida	Shibli, Umm Al-Ghanam	2,950
Heib, Al-Ghawarna	Wadi Al-Hamam	1,390
Sawaed	Wadi Salameh	1,850
Mizel	Aramsheh	950
Ghadir, Sawalha, Ramilat, Hujeirat	Bir al-Maksur	2,850
Ka'abiya, Helf-Tabash, Hajajra	Ka'abiya, Helf-Tabash, Hajajra	2,420
Helf	Helf Umm Rashed	825
Heib, Zangariah	Tuba-Zangariah	3,150
Heib	Heib Al-Frush	1,200
Hujeirat	Makman	1,100
Hujeirat	Dameida	210
Total		**26,515**

Table 5.4. Bedouin living nomadically in the Galilee, 1982

Tribe name	Nomadic locale name	Number
Arab al-Khawaled	located in two concentrations along Zippori stream	110
Arab Abu Shtayyeh	North of Tab'un	145
Arab Na'im Abu Garad	South of Karmiel	202
Arab Al-Marisat	North of Iblin	155
Arab Al-Hamdun	North of Deir Hanna	64
Arab Heib (Falahat)	Between Uzair and Bu'enie-Nujeidat	72
Arab Al-Jindawi	South of Bir al-Maksur	146
Arab Sawaed Kamaneh	Kamaneh Mount, "Area 9"	1,885
Arab Al- Hujeirat	North of Bir al-Maksur	660
Total		**3,439**

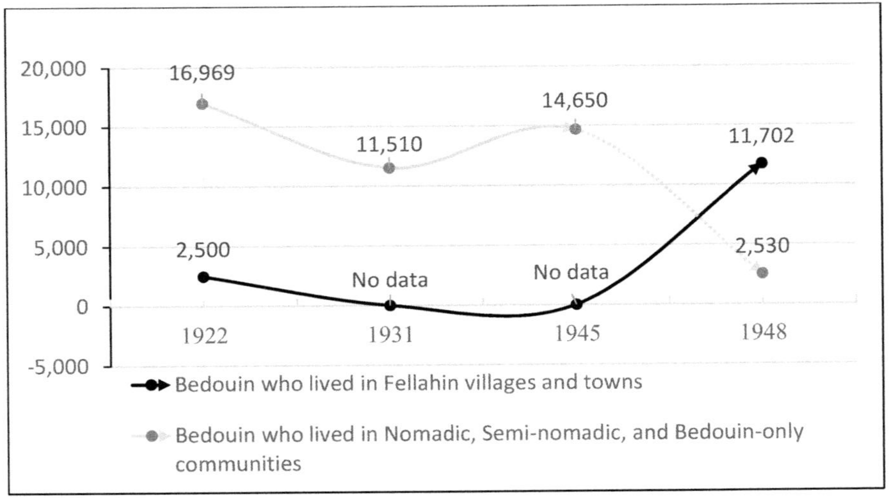

Graph 5.1 Comparison of Bedouin estimates between the years 1969–1982.

While Land Day marked a new age of cooperation between the Bedouin and their Fellahin counterparts in the Galilee, 24 years later, another major event took place: the October riots of 2000, which had far-reaching effects on these relationships.

October 2000: Its impact on the National, Political, and Social Unity of Bedouin and Fellahin

The October 2000 events have many names: Al-Aqsa Intifada, the October 2000 uprising, or the October riots. The common name used in Israel is Second Intifada, as opposed to the First Intifada in 1988. These events began at the end of September 2000, and they caused by the failure of the Middle East Peace Summit at Camp David in July 2000, between Israel and the Palestinians. The Summit ended without an agreement being reached, increasing tension between Israel and the Palestinians. On 28 September 2000, opposition leader Ariel Sharon visited Al-Aqsa Mosque on Jerusalem's Temple Mount/Haram al Sharif, sparking protests on the parts of Palestinians, where police clashed with demonstrators and dozens of civilians and police were injured. The next day, was a Friday (prayer day for Muslims), when the riots intensified and seven civilians were killed by police gunfire, prompting rioting in most Arab towns and villages nationwide. The death toll reached 13 Arab citizens who were shot by the police, and a stone throwing near Jisr al-Zarqa killed one Jewish civilian.[23]

Following these events, a state commission (known as the Or Commission after its chair, Justice Theodore Or) was established to investigate the clashes between security forces and Israeli Arab citizens.[24] In its conclusions (published in September 2003), the commission harshly criticized government ministers, police officers, and Arab leaders in Israel. The report stated unequivocally, "Arab citizens in Israel live in a reality in which they are discriminated against as Arabs".[25] Indeed, Arab citizens discriminated are against economically, socially, ethnically, and politically.

As'ad Ghanem and Sarah Ozacky argued that not only did severe harm and casualties resulted from these events, but also, the mutual trust between two the national communities – the Arab minority and Israeli establishment – was severely damaged, reflected in a notable rise in Israeli Arabs suing the state in connection with proof of land ownership and/or granting citizenship to Palestinian women married to Israeli Arabs, among others).[26]

In their comparative study of Arab identity in Israel, the researchers divided them into several groups: Arabs, Israelis, Palestinian-Arabs, Israeli-Arabs, Palestinian-Israeli, Palestinians in Israel, Palestinians.[27] Survey data in the years 1995–2001, about a year after the October events; showed a regression among Arabs themselves as Israelis, without regard to the Palestinian component. There was an increase in Arabs who define their identity as Palestinians, and less as Israelis. This indicates, on the one hand, a steep rise in the Palestinian identity component, and on the other hand, an increasing alienation from Israeli elements that have no suitable national or civilian response, as the researchers put it.[28]

These findings are also true of Bedouin society as a whole. In other words, the process of "Palestinization" that took place in the Bedouin in Bedouin-only locales in the Galilee was similar to that among the Bedouin living in Fellahin towns and villages. This was a result of the continued government policy that does not integrate Arabs into its institutions in a manner equal to that of Jews, in addition to land expropriation and non-issuance of building permits.

This policy has strongly affected national politics: Urban-Bedouin-Fellahin serves as a broad platform for political influence and ultimately leads to unification of the ranks of Arab society in Israel. For example, the day after the October 2000 events, MK Talab Al-Sana said, "The time has come for the Arab population to understand that the Bedouin problem in the Naqab is not only theirs, but that of all the Arabs in Israel".[29] Moreover, he demanded of the entire Bedouin population in Israel "To stand in silence for the memory of the 13 victims of the October events".[30]

MK Al-Sana's words contributed to raising Bedouin awareness in particular and that of Arab population in general, of Palestinian nation in the Israeli state. So that his words were consistent with those of the Higher Arab Monitoring Committee, he issued a leaflet accusing the state of "drowning in blood the just struggle of Israeli Arabs". He wrote:

> We say to the fascist beasts, we are the owners of this land, this is our homeland, and no one will forbid us from working and wandering in the country freely, and with our heads erect [...]. The essence of racist official policy toward Arabs has been revealed, a policy that borders on apartheid and treats us in our homeland as if we are foreigners and not equal citizens.[31]

This speech, contributed to the consolidation of Israel's entire Arab population, despite the conflicts that exist in some Bedouin neighborhoods in Fellahin towns and villages, where there is a difference in provision of municipal services to the Bedouin minority in towns and villages, compared with majority Fellah jurisdictions such as Shafa-Amer in 1998 (before the events of October 2000).[32]

An additional effect of the October 2000 events on the Bedouin population was a decline in the number of Bedouin enlisting in the IDF. Sa'id Quzli's study on the state's attitude toward Bedouin in the Naqab, presents statistical data on a significant decline in Bedouin volunteers between 2001 and 2002.[33] According to Quzli, during these years, many Bedouin would-be recruits had been removed from recruitment bureaus in Beer Sheva and Tiberias, as a result of their identification with the Fellahin Arab population. For example, in 2001 (after the October events), 136 Galilee Bedouin joined the IDF, compared to 241 in 1999; in the Naqab, there was a drastic decline: 59 recruits in 2001, compared to 139 in 1999. This decline jeopardized the Bedouin patrol battalion as a distinctly ethnic unit. In response to the decline, the Defense Ministry instituted a program to increase the number of Bedouin recruits. This plan includes affirmative action, loosened employment requirements, education, and vocational training during service and post-discharge.[34]

About two years after October 2000, events, in a lecture at Tel Aviv University, Or Commission member Shimon Shamir said:

> Two years after publication of the Or Commission's report, the situation as I see it, and as I tried to present it to you, does not bode well [...]. As a member of this commission, I stand before you in sorrow and disappointment. I have no other way to conclude my lecture except in the words of the commission chair, Justice Theodor Or one year ago: 'The writing is still on the wall'.[35]

We can therefore conclude that the October 2000 events constitute another milestone, as a continuation of Land Day 1976, in raising and strengthening the national consciousness of Israeli Arabs and in forging an Arab-Palestinian identity, which includes Bedouin as well.

During and following these national events, a common consciousness developed, called "Palestinization", a perception that includes interests common to the entire Arab population, including moderates among them, i.e., those who support "Israelization".[36] This Palestinization characterizes a new generation or "The Upright Generation", as Dan Rabinowitz and Khawla Abu Bakir called it:[37] a generation proud of its Palestinian identity and relating to Israeli citizenship as a technical matter, and therefore, viewing the State of Israel as not its state.[38] This process occurred as a reaction to state policy of discrimination and neglect of the Arab population. The government's discriminatory policy vis-à-vis Jews and Arabs regarding Jewish settlement in the Galilee, continues in the 2000s, under other names: "lone/single-household settlements", "establishing outposts", or "hilltop settlement" in areas "vital to the state".[39]

An article published in *Haaretz* newspaper on 16 March 1997, headlined "Zeldstein's tent" described the phenomenon of lone/single-household settlements, such as a tent and shed erected by a couple, Amnon Zeldstein and Dalia Spiegel, on Yodfat ridge in the Galilee.[40] This phenomenon was rejuvenated due to government support and pro-settlement entities that view it as a means of preventing invasion and seizure of territories by the Arabs (Bedouin). However, environmental advocates view it as a waste of resources and infringing on areas designated as nature reserves.

This lone/single-household form of settlement is a legitimate for Jews in locales formerly populated by Bedouin, and obtains its legitimacy from government agencies, and is emblematic of the next generation of Ariel Sharon in the Naqab and Meir Har Zion in Jerusalem. In 2003, Jews received approval to establish 54 lone/single-household settlements in the Naqab and another 31 in the Galilee, for which each settler received about 230,000 Shekels.[41]

This stage was implemented after implementation of Bedouin evacuation plans from areas defined as "essential lands for the state". As stated, the government's policy resulted in many Bedouin choosing to move to existing Arab towns or villages or Bedouin settlements, while encouraging, forcing, and seducing the Bedouin to cooperate. If so, it seems that the Bedouin population, including those living in Fellahin towns and villages, has undergone a similar process of "Palestinization".

Bedouin Estimate in 2020, Relative to other Galilee Populations

The Arab local authorities view Bedouin inhabitants living in Fellahin towns and villages as an integral part of their population. Note that in some of these jurisdictions there are Bedouin neighborhoods, which are annexed both geographically and municipally to those jurisdictions. To illustrate this point, see Figure 5.1,[42] overleaf, which shows Shafa-Amer from the south. On the near side of the road (inside the wadi) is the Bedouin neighborhood of Wadi Al-Saki'a. In addition, this figure can be compared to Figure 1.1 (page 49) in 1910, in order to demonstrate demographic increase.

Figure 5.1 Wadi Al-Saki'a neighborhood in Shafa-Amer, 2020.

Table 5.5. Bedouin in Fellahin Towns in the Galilee, 2020

Tribe name and the number of each family tribe	Fellahin Town name	Number
Madi (65), Qmirat (60), Al-Na'im (Nazal) (55), Turkmen (105), Hamdun (95), Kulibat (450), Khalidi (20), Subayh (130)	Haifa	980
Majdoub (30), Al-Ghawarna (80), Sawaed (25), Ghrefat (12) Ziadnah (940), Hawara (320), Sawaed (3,550), Marisat (25), Al-Samniyya (490), Muhameidat (125), Samkia (22), Krad (810), Al-Hanadi (1,050), Hujeirat (495), Azuid (405), Sawalmeh (385), Ka'abiya (300), Khawaled (285), Ghawarna (278), Jindawi (205), Khalidi (175), Majdoub (165), Jawamees (40), Saqer (34), Mawasi (26), Towaqia (12)	Acre Shafa-Amer	147 10,137 (with Sawaed Al-Hamira)
Ziadnah-Al-Zahir (550), Hawara (15), N'arani (1,730), Heib (225), Na'im (45), Rabiah (220), Turkman (60), Masharqa (62), Ghazalin (20), Khalidi (110), Subayh-Manasra (150), Mjali-belong to Zubeidat tribe (105),	Nazareth	3,292
Zubeidat (2,400), Tarbiyeh (Trabay) (2,550)	Sakhnin	4,950
Ziadnah (950), Marisat (510), Mawasi (100), Muhameidat (60), Hamdun (60), Sawaed (80), Abeed-Ka'abiya (110), Hanbuzi (105), Tarabilsi (85), Ghawarna (46), Hujeirat (27), Kharanbeh (14), Sweitat (10)	Tamra	2,157

Table 5.6. Bedouin in Fellahin Villages in the Galilee, 2020

Tribe name and the number of each family tribe	Fellahin Village name	Number
Al-Hasi (85), Al-Najmiyya (220), Hawara (200), Sweitat (35), Marisat (530), Mawasi (105), Sawaed (280), Al-Samniyya (24), Zubeidat-Qasum (350), Hujeirat-Awabda (195), Hamdun (21)	Iblin	2,045
Sweitat (40), Al-Fadl (12), Hamdun (11), Al-Ghawarna (45), Mawasi (28), Muhameidat (22), Hanbuzi (15), Hujeirat (12)	Al-Jadida	185
Al-Fadl (160), N'aim (95), Hamdun (30), Hujeirat (20), Sweitat (17), Muhameidat (12)	Al-Makr	334
Na'im (450), Sweitat (110), Al-Samniyya (155), Heib (80), Ziadnah (90)	Tarshiha	885
Na'im (950), Sweitat (210), Sawilat (12), Hamdun (22), Sawaed (50), Tarbiyeh (30), Khawaled (15)	Abu Snan	1,289
Mawasi (95), Sawaed (90), Marisat (75), Ziadnah (70), Sweitat (34), Aqila (45), Hamdun (30), Dalaika (22)	Deir Hanna	461
Na'im (620), Kharanbeh (550), Heib (175), Aqila (80), Sawaed (65)	Maghar	1,490
Heib-al-Fawawza (810), Mawasi (510), Shawahdeh (110), Nujeidat (80), Sweitat (45), Marisat (15)	Eilabun	1,570
Krad (800), Numeirat (50), Hamdun (35), Heib (20), Khalidi (15)	Sha'ab	920
N'arani (850), Ghazalin (760), N'aim (350), Hajajra (220), Hamdun (185), Mjali (20)	Yafa	2,385

(Continued on Next Page)

Table 5.6. Bedouin in Fellahin Villages in the Galilee, 2020 (continued)

Tribe name and the number of each family tribe	Fellahin Village name	Number
Nujeidat (2,850), Ziadnah (180)	Bu'enie-Nujeidat	3,030
Ghazalin (25)	Iksal	25
Ziadnah (4,400), Helf (75), Jindawi (25)	Kafr Manda	4,500
Hujeirat (270), Heib (15)	Uzair-Rumana	285
Subayh-Manasra (80)	Ein Mahel	80
Zubeidat (30), Subayh (29)	Daburiya	59
Subayh-Manasra (320)	Reina	320
Subayh-Manasra (90)	Turan	90
Saida (85)	Manshiya Zabda	85
Sweitat (850), Quzli (110), Qlitat (55), Ka'abiya (20)	Isfiya	1,035
Qlitat (22), Quzli (18)	Daliyat Al-Carmel	50
Sawaed (220), Heib (25), Mawasi (20)	Al-Rama	265
Kulibat (200), Al-Sammiyya (12), Hamdun (12)	Sheikh Danun	224
Saqer (75), Dalaika (45)	Kafr Maser	120
Subayhat (75), Subayh (25)	Kafr Kana	100
Sawaed (420)	B'ena	420
Sawaed (50)	Nahaf	50
Hamdun	Kabul	50
N'aim	Kisra	25
Hamdun	Jish	12
Total		**22,379**

It is difficult to estimate this population. To do so, I took a number of methodological steps to overcome this difficulty:

Firstly, I conducted interviews with Bedouin living in Fellahin towns and villages in the Galilee. In every town or village, I met Bedouin and Fellahin interviewees, and asked them to give me names of Bedouin families that live in their town or village, and their location of residence.

Secondly, I collected 2020 data from the voter registry for local jurisdictions, of all registered voters. Classification of the names, which are registered for the elections, was done by myself with the assistance of local councils' employees.

According to these interviews, together with the voter data, I estimated the Bedouin population living in Fellahin towns and villages in 2020 to be 44,042. The first group (21,663 inhabitants) resides in six towns: Shafa-Amer, Nazareth, Haifa, Sakhnin, Acre, and Tamra: (see Table 5.5, page 149). The second group (22,379 inhabitants) is spread across 30 Fellahin villages: Eilabun, Al-B'ena, Nahaf, Al-Jadida, Al-Makr, Al-Maghar, Al-Rama, Iblin, Abu Snan, Isfiya, Daliyat Al-Carmel, Sha'ab, Tarshiha, Deir Hanna, Bu'enie-Nujeidat, Kafr Maser, Uzair, Iksal, Reina, Turan, Jish, Daburiya, Kafr Kana, Kisra, Kabul, Kafr Manda, Sheikh Danun, Ein Mahel, Yafa, and Manshiya Zabda: (see Table 5.6, pages 150/151). This portion of the Bedouin population represents 9% of the total population of these towns and villages.[43]

Table 5.6 presents an estimate of the Bedouin population Fellahin villages in the Galilee in 2020. It appears that the total number of Bedouin living in 30 villages is 22,379.

Note that the total 2020 Bedouin population in the Galilee is estimated at 107,674 inhabitants.[44] Those who reside Bedouin-only settlements/villages, which numbered 63,632 (59.0% of the Bedouin in the Galilee) are divided thusly: 51,632 living in 15 recognized localities/villages; and another 12,000 who live in unrecognized localities such as Al-Na'im Abu Garad, Ramia, and Husayniyya (near Karmiel). A second group of 44,042 reside in Fellahin towns and villages.

Government Policy Toward Bedouin Living in Mixed Villages and Towns

Government policy toward Bedouin in Fellahin towns and villages is ambivalent to this day: In some respects, government officials have tried to preserve separation of Bedouin from the Fellahin population, and in other aspects, they treat the two populations as a single entity. According to the first, the state has done so officially: At least in its public statements, it recognized the Bedouin as a sector with its own unique needs. Evidence thereof is the government's declaration to establishment Bedouin municipal committees in 1961 in regional councils in the Galilee as a preliminary stage for establishment of local authorities such as Wadi Salameh, Ka'abiya-Helf Tabash-Hajajra, Zarzir, and Wadi Al-Hamam. As aforementioned, in 1963, the government decided to establish four new Bedouin villages: Bussmat Tab'un, Wadi al-Hamam, Bir al-Maksur, and Ibtin.[45]

Note that some of these committees continue to exist up to this writing, such as: Arab al-Aramsheh, an external committee in Mateh Asher Regional Council; Khawaled and Ibtin villages, members of Zevulun Regional Council; Wadi al-Hamam, members of Al-Batuf Regional Council; Manshiya Zabda, a member of Jezreel Valley Regional Council; Wadi Salameh, Dameida, Kamaneh, and Husayniyya, members of Misgav Regional Council.[46]

This recognition, as per government's policy, to recognize separate Bedouin committees and form Bedouin jurisdictions led, on the one hand, to Bedouin living in Bedouin-only communities enjoying a certain number of benefits, as will be described below. On the other hand, it prevented Bedouin living in Fellahin towns and villages from receiving these benefits, apparently because they are inhabitants of Arab Fellahin communities. These privileges, whether deliberate or not, manifest in three main aspects:

Construction lots

From the 1960s, as stated, the state, through the ILA, offered the nomadic Bedouin (defined by state as "diaspora") an arrangement according to which they would receive plots free in exchange for which Bedouin would relocate to new places that the state offered them.[47] However, since early 1980s, the ILA has hardly drafted any new master plans for these Bedouin. First, they were not offered plots for construction of residential buildings, because no new master plans were drafted as was done in the 1960s, based on the argument that most of these populations had relocated, so there was no need for additional programs or plans. Secondly, their land, which was left vacant, was not offered to Bedouin in Fellahin towns and villages at a reduced rate of 50%, as was offered to Bedouin in Bedouin-only localities. Since 1980s, Bedouin in Bedouin-only localities have enjoyed a 50% discount on plots they purchased. In addition, there are many government decisions relating to subsidy of infrastructure development expenses in the Bedouin sector.[48]

This discriminatory policy can be explained by government protocols from the end of the 1970s. In a 6 December 1978 Knesset session, Minister Moshe Nissim (Begin administration), presented the subject of planning and building the in Arab sector. In his response to questions of MK Shmuel Toledano (Prime Minister's Adviser on Arab affairs until 1977, and Head of State Comptroller Committee), said: "The government is aware of difficulties involved in drafting master plans in the Arab sector. Lack of master plans for Arab villages was apparently one of the reasons for violations of the Planning and Building Law".[49]

In same discussion, Nissim also referred to Bedouin population: "The current government allocated – and will allocate in the future – large resources for development of Bedouin communities [...]. This government adopted proposals of the previous government [first Rabin government] for Bedouin land and construction arrangements".[50]

From Nissim's words, as shown in the first quotation, it can be seen that government master plans for the Arab sector are not implemented, perhaps because of lack of interest, resulting in Arabs building without building permits. From Nissim's remarks, as quoted in the second quotation, we learn about establishment of a deliberate policy toward Bedouin, which had several reasons: Firstly, Judaizing the Galilee: preventing Bedouin from settling on state land; secondly, establishment of Bedouin-only settlements; thirdly, encouraging Bedouin to enlist in the IDF.[51]

While this does not mean that the State, through the ILA, has not taken steps on behalf of the Arab community regarding allocation of plots for building purposes, these measures were aimed at the entire Arab population, including the Bedouin.

Establishment of the Bedouin Councils Forum

In 1991, the state, at Bedouin local councils' initiative, decided to establish a forum for Bedouin councils in the Galilee, consisting of eight Bedouin villages: Bir al-Maksur, Zarzir, Bussmat Tab'un, Ka'abiya-Helf-Tabash-Hajajra, Shibli-Umm al-Ghanam, Bu'enie-Nujeidat, Tuba-Zangariah, and Al-Battuf Regional Council.[52] The purpose of the forum's establishment was to address their economic problems in particular, and the Bedouin sector as a separate entity from the Arab Fellahin. The member councils of this forum received benefits, privileges, and preferential treatment from the government.

Accordingly, the government began to budget this forum through five-year [*chomesh*] plans for training, nurturing, and developing the Bedouin sector. For example, in 2001, Housing and Construction

Minister Natan Sharansky funded this forum 36 million Shekels in order to establish public institutions, the implementation of a "build-your-own-home" plan, and development of older neighborhoods.[53]

However, administratively speaking, Bedouin living in Fellahin towns and villages belong to those jurisdictions. This category supported and identified politically and ideologically with the Higher Arab Monitoring Committee more than it did with the Bedouin Councils Forum, support being reflected in demonstrations, strikes, and membership in religious movements and political parties.

As aforementioned, the state did not relate to this Bedouin category of "Urban Bedouin" as it did to the Bedouin in Bedouin-only localities, as can be seen in funding to this sector under the *chomesh* plans. Pursuant to 1998 decision no. 1403, the government addressed the 2004/05 budget for the Bedouin Councils Forum, according to which it was budgeted 172 million Shekels for development of Bedouin-only settlements in the Galilee.[54] It included the Bedouin-only Bir al-Maksur, Zarzir, Bussmat Tab'un, Ka'abiya-Helf-Tabash-Hajajra, Shibli-Umm al-Ghanam, Bu'enie-Nujeidat, Tuba-Zangariah, and Al-Battuf Regional Councils, as well as Bedouin communities lying within boundaries of Jewish regional councils: Arab al-Aramsheh, an external committee in Mateh Asher Regional Council; Khawaled and Ibtin villages, members of Zevulun Regional Council; Wadi al-Hamam, members of Al-Batuf Regional Council; Manshiya Zabda, a member of Jezreel Valley Regional Council; Wadi Salameh, Dameida, Kamaneh, and Husayniyya, members of Misgav Regional Council.[55] Moreover, Umar Sawaed, a member of Shafa-Amer Council since the early 1980s, a consultant on Bedouin Affairs to Shafa-Amer's mayor, claimed: "Not only we did not receive budgetary aid from the government, but the Bedouin Councils Forum refused us some of this budget, as it would reduce their budget".[56]

Bedouin volunteers in the IDF

Before the establishment of Israel, Bedouin served in the Palmach and the Haganah (precursors to the IDF) on a voluntary basis only. This began in the mid-1930s, and increased during the 1948 war, after which a few Bedouin enlisted in the IDF.[57] This volunteering became more official and regulated when a dedicated company was formed for Galilee Bedouin called *Pal-heib* – Al-Heib Tribe Company.[58] This company participated in operations with the Palmach Brigade during occupation of the Galilee from Palestinians.[59]

At the end of the 1948 war, a minorities unit (Unit 300) was established, consisting of Bedouin recruits (some of whom had served in

Pal-heib), Druze, and Circassians. In 1955, a special force, Sayeret Shaked was established, comprised of Jewish and Bedouin soldiers,[60] whose main tasks were to combat intelligence infiltrations and sabotage by infiltrators on Egyptian border.[61]

At the same time, the state and its leadership viewed recruitment of Bedouin service into the IDF as a national mission of tactical and strategic importance.[62] Therefore, from the 1970s, defense figures began to consider recruiting Bedouin for compulsory military service.[63] Theretoward, internal military committees were established, but their conclusions did not obligate Bedouin population to be recruited, mainly for moral reasons, but they determined that it was possible to arrange service for those who chose it.[64]

In the early 1980s, a new trend began among young Bedouin who expressed their desire to enlist in the IDF, mainly, as trackers or border guards,[65] motivated by two factors: Firstly, to realize personal aspirations, as IDF service would help them obtain employment in the public sector; secondly, tracker positions were limited, pushing Bedouin youth to look to joining combat units.

These reciprocal interests – of Bedouin and of the state – contributed to maintenance of Israel's national missions. Former Defense Minister Moshe Arens described it thusly: "We are witnessing a process of Islamization and Palestinization among the Bedouin population. Regarding this, military service is a very important, if not decisive matter [...]. This national mission goes beyond classic tasks imposed on IDF".[66]

From the mid-1980s, dedicated recruiting of Bedouin for IDF service began taking shape. The idea was conceived in the IDF to establish a military framework based on enlisted Bedouin who would be trained as infantry soldiers to patrol the Egyptian border (Sinai border after the 1979 peace agreement between Israel and Egypt). Accordingly, in 1986, a Bedouin company, Patrol Unit 585, was established in the Southern Command, and by 1993 it reached a number that allowed it to become a battalion.[67]

Since the early 1990s, IDF attention to the Bedouin population has become more intense and even unique: The first step was an attempt to change the IDF's image from "the IDF kills and destroys" to "The IDF: Polite builder". In April 1991, Bedouin youth were invited to visit Nevatim Air Force Base, and were offered various maintenance and administrative positions. The second step was increasing Bedouin motivation to serve in the IDF.[68] IDF Head of Personnel Ran Goren instructed the army to act on several channels: Firstly, the *Gadna* ("youth brigade"),[69] began training Bedouin teenagers in first aid, physical fitness, and field trips around Israel. Secondly, it tried to raise awareness of IDF service by addressing Bedouin parents. Thirdly, it encouraged Bedouin to enlist in the *atuda'im* [pedagogic reserves] that would prepare young Bedouin for the teaching profession at the IDF's expense, after which they serve as teachers for a year in a military framework.[70]

In November 1998, the government approved the Program for Development of Bedouin Communities in the North, which aims to strengthen the Bedouin population's ties with the state.

The aforementioned programs contributed to increasing Bedouin soldiers' numbers and to expanding their options of military units offered to them by the IDF. Bedouin volunteers began serving as combatants in the core of the IDF's operational activity in all sectors, i.e., not only in their classic capacity as trackers. They began volunteering for combat units such as Unit 585, paratroopers, Golani, Givati, and the Armored Corps.[71]

As shown in Graph 5.2, A multi-year graph showing Bedouin IDF enlistees in the Galilee and the Naqab/Negev between the years 1998–2016,[7] Bedouin volunteer numbers who service in IDF has not always been consistent with proportionality of the Bedouin population in Israel. That local political events or government decisions affect the decrease or increase number of Bedouin recruits to IDF.

The graph shows the drastic decline of Bedouin recruits in 2001 (only 195 volunteers: 136 in the Galilee, and 95 in the Naqab). The reason therefor is the events of October 2000, during which 13 Arab citizens were killed.[73]

Nonetheless, we see an increase in number of recruits in 2004 (about 500 volunteers: 339 in the Galilee, and 161 in the Naqab). The reason therefor was Prime Minister Ehud Barak's directive of "maximum recruitment of Bedouin volunteers".[74] Between the years 1976–1978, Barak asked IDF Head of Personnel Major-General Rafael Vardi to establish a committee (the Vardi Commission) to examine the dual discrimination that Bedouin soldiers suffer.[75] The Vardi Commission recommended implementation of an affirmative action policy, whereby it was decided to build a dedicated service track for Bedouin in IDF. According thereto, the first three months of service include preparation for IDF service, providing basic knowledge and learning Hebrew; and the last six months of service include completion of basic education and vocational training in preparation for discharge.[76]

Nonetheless, three years later (2007) saw another drop in the number of Bedouin volunteers (222 volunteers: 148 in the Galilee, and 74 in the Naqab). The reason therefor can be attributed to several events: the 2007 pension reform (transition from budgetary to accrual pension); and lack

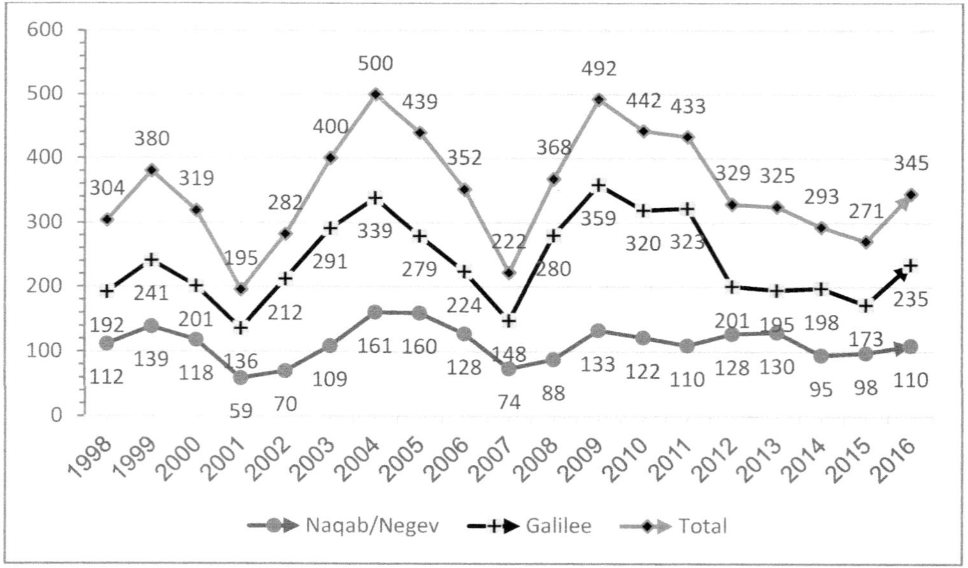

Graph 5.2 A multi-year graph showing Bedouin IDF enlistees in the Galilee and the Naqab/Negev between the years 1998–2016.

of desire among Bedouin youth to enlist in general, and to the Bedouin patrol battalion in particular following violent incidents in the battalion since the end of 2004, described in *Yediot Aharonot* on 10 September 2004: "The Bedouin patrol battalion is disintegrating. Two soldiers are suspected of murdering a Palestinian, and three of their commanders are suspected of murder, while other soldiers are accused of manslaughter, drug use, and smuggling dozens of kilograms of heroin".[77]

Following this report, and since 2008, we see another increase in the number of Bedouin recruits to the IDF (492 volunteers: 359 in the Galilee, and 133 in the Naqab). The reason was twofold: Firstly, the State Comptroller's report of 2005, which called for proper handling of Bedouin recruitment to the IDF. In its wake, a unit was established, called the Center for Activity in the Bedouin Sector", whose role is to strengthen the connection between the Bedouin sector and the State, and encourage Bedouin to enlist in the IDF.[78] Secondly, the Goldberg Commission's task of regulating Bedouin settlement in the Naqab, which published its report on 11 December 2008, recommending recognition of unrecognized Bedouin villages in the Naqab.[79]

Since 2016, there has been an increase in the number of Bedouin recruits to the IDF (345 volunteers: 235 in the Galilee, and 110 in the Naqab). The reasons for this rise were government programs designed to encourage enlistment among young Bedouin, including A. establishment of the IDF's first pre-military Bedouin preparatory program, *Ma'aseh* ["act"],[80] which graduated its first cohort of 15 teens in December 2016, most of whom enlisted in the IDF and were assigned to combat units). B. Sending "volunteer draft notices" to Bedouin youth, telling them of various roles they can fulfill. C. Giving a benefits package to Bedouin recruits, such as a significant discount on purchase of land for construction of a residential building, a 24-month shortened service, a free psychometric exam preparation course, subsidy on academic tuition, and a stipend for those who intend to pursue academic studies.[81] All of these have led to an increase in the number of Bedouin volunteers recruited from Bedouin-only communities, while there has been a decrease in the number of Bedouin volunteers from Fellahin towns and villages in the Galilee.

Recruiting Bedouins from Fellahin Villages and Towns in the Galilee to IDF

As aforementioned, Bedouin who reside in Fellahin towns and villages in the Galilee, like those in Bedouin-only communities, have volunteered

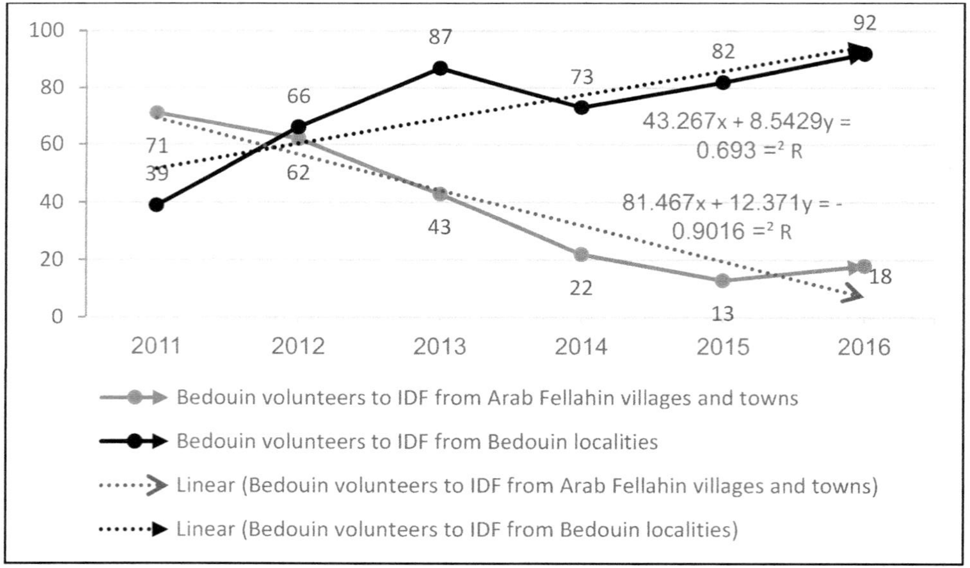

Graph 5.3 A comparative graph of the number of Bedouin volunteers in the IDF from Bedouin localities and from Fellahin villages and towns in the Galilee between the years 2011–2016.

for Israel's various security forces since before the state's establishment. As shown in Graph 5.3, the number of Bedouin volunteers in the IDF from Bedouin localities and from Fellahin villages and towns in the Galilee between the years 2011–2016,[82] demonstrates that every IDF recruitment cycle shows a significant number of Bedouins who hail from Fellahin villages and towns. Interestingly, these volunteers do not receive the same rights as volunteers who hail from Bedouin-only localities. Failure to grant equal rights to the former, together with their political identification with the Higher Arab Monitoring Committee, and their national and political connections with Fellahin, has resulted in a drop in the number of IDF volunteers from this category.

While the data in the graph indicate that Bedouin volunteers from Bedouin-only localities (from 39 in 2011 to 92 in 2016) have been trending and persistent (see black dotted line), there is a sharp decline in number of Bedouin recruits coming from Fellahin villages and towns (see dotted gray line), especially between 2011 and 2015, when the number of these volunteers dropped from 71 to 18 in 2016. A possible explanation for this decline emerged from my interviews with Bedouin inhabitants of Fellahin villages and towns,[83] in which it was expressed that the military framework does not contribute economically to the futures of young Bedouin: They do not receive discounts on plots of land for construction, and in any case, no plots for sale are offered by ILA due to the absence of master plans for these jurisdictions.

Another conclusion that emerges from this data is that the state does not differentiate between Bedouin living in Fellahin villages and towns and Bedouin living in Bedouin-only localities, despite the fact that some of the latter serve in the IDF. The state does not provide a benefit package such as five-year plans, as is the case for Bedouin living in Bedouin-only localities. In fact, the state is formulating five-year plans to assist the Bedouin sector, especially Bedouin-only communities, leading to significant economic and educational gaps between these two categories, despite the size of the Bedouin population in Fellahin villages and towns, estimated at 44,000.[84]

The resulting conclusion is that the Bedouin population living in Fellahin towns and villages, on the one hand is regarded as a Bedouin community by the surrounding society (i.e., the Fellahin); and on the other hand, government officials considered them to be one homogenous community. In other words, the policy that applies to the Fellahin population also applies to Bedouins living among and alongside Fellahin.

Nonetheless, it has been proven empirically that there is social and cultural flexibility and liquidity between the two communities within overall Arab culture. In other words, Bedouin do not regard Fellahin as foreign to them, and vice versa. In fact, Bedouin continue to move to Fellahin towns and villages, whether the state directs them to or not. This would seem to indicate that not only is there no dichotomy between two communities, but there are cultural elements that over time blend, especially during local elections, when we identify identity politics. This chapter addressed this population, which has "Fellahin between the cracks", tried to quantify it, and to identify social and demographic processes that influenced it in recent decades.

Summary and Conclusions

This study addressed the issue of "From Desert to Town: The integration of Bedouin into Arab Fellahin villages and towns in the Galilee, 1700–2020". To do so, it examined the process of Bedouin integration into Fellahin villages and towns in the Galilee, in its historical, social, and cultural aspects through three periods of rule: Ottoman, British, and Israeli. During these periods, a number of events took place that strongly affected the settlement and integration patterns of Bedouin in Fellahin villages and towns in the Galilee. Therefore, the book showed that the three aforementioned regimes had an interest in settling Bedouin in permanent locales stemming from administrative and other interests, and not out of concern and consideration for the Bedouin's circumstances.

The study also focused on the relationship between two categories, Bedouin and Fellahin. These relationships were based on interactions and practices that contribute to rapprochement between these two categories. According to the research assumption of social categorization of Bedouin and Fellahin that is based on flexibility, construction, and formation, rather than on a dichotomy or on a linear and inevitable process of complete assimilation of the Bedouin and their "becoming Fellahin" over time. While this does not mean that there are not essential differences that have become increasingly blurred over time, but rather that processes of assimilation and differentiation are parallel, structured processes.

The study showed that relationships between Bedouin and Fellahin should not be viewed as a war between desert and sown, as Ibn Khaldun claimed in the 14th century, but rather as symbiotic, characterized by daily interactions and practices between two communities. Therefore, due to the complexity of the subjects in this study, various methodologies and sources of information were used.

Thus, the book combined historical, sociological, and anthropological perspectives through use of primary and secondary sources, including public archives: State Archives of Israel (SAI), Central Zionist Archives (CZA), Valley of Maayanot Archives (VMA – *Emek Hamaayanot*), Jezreel Plain Regional Council Archives (JPRCA), Rosh Pina Archives (RPA), National Archives of London (NAL), and Ottoman State Archives of Istanbul (OSA). As per the ethnographic approach, 59 in-depth interviews were conducted with Bedouin and Fellahin men and women of various ages and from various locales in the Galilee.

Theretoward, the study was based on a theoretical framework of the construction and formation approach, characterized by a continuous process, and flexible and even fluid boundaries between two communities in all spheres: social, economic, political, and cultural. Another theoretical framework on which the study was based is that of identity politics, which evolved in the post-modern era as a reaction to the melting pot that Ben-Gurion advocated in the early years of the state. According to this new structural approach, various cultural identity groups in society maintain cultural and political distinctiveness, emphasizing their uniqueness, in order to promote primarily political and economic interests.

The work is divided into chapters based on the historical sequence of events, in three historical periods of rule, from the early 18th century until the early 21th century. The study shows that during Ottoman, British, and Israeli rule, there was settlement and integration of Bedouin in existing Fellahin towns and villages. The study also estimated the number of this Bedouin population during these three periods (see Summary Graph, opposite). At the end of Ottoman rule, they were estimated at 2,500. At the end of the British Mandate and the eve of the 1948 war, they were estimated at 11,702. In 1949: 13,048; in 1969, 22,062; in 1982, 29,332; and in 2020, 44,042. The summary graph accordingly shows an upward trend in the number of Bedouin inhabitants in relation to the independent variable of time. The graph summarizes the percentage of the Bedouin population living in Fellahin villages and towns in the Galilee, during the three periods of rule (Ottoman, British, and Israeli).

The summary graph above is an estimate of three categories of Bedouin: those living in Fellahin villages and towns; those living in Bedouin-only localities/villages, and those of nomads. Despite changes of government in Israel, enactment of laws and regulations, and government programs, the number of Bedouin living among and alongside Fellahin continued to increase in number.

While throughout the three periods, there was interaction between Bedouin and Fellahin, there are also dissonant characteristics and contradictions between two categories on a cultural, social, economic, and political level. However, these distinctions are fluid, dynamic, contextual, and in some cases interwoven into identity politics and social change processes.

The study's first conclusion is the policies of Bedouin settlement plans

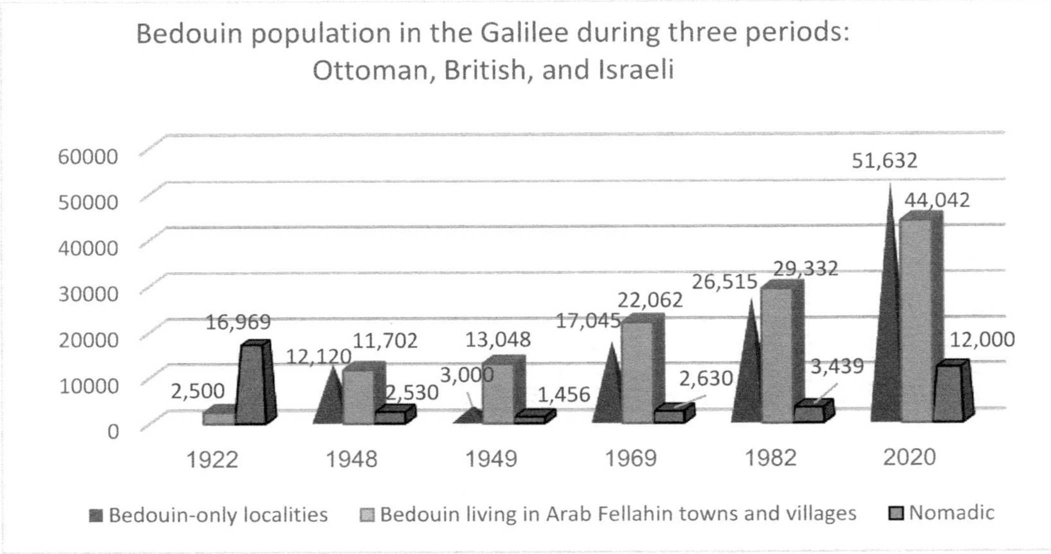

Bedouin population in the Galilee during three periods: Ottoman, British, and Israeli

Year	Bedouin-only localities	Bedouin living in Arab Fellahin towns and villages	Nomadic
1922	2,500	16,969	12,120
1948	2,530	11,702	3,000
1949	1,456	13,048	—
1969	2,630	17,045	22,062
1982	3,439	26,515	29,332
2020	12,000	44,042	51,632

adopted by all three governments – Ottoman, British, and Israeli – constituting factors in Bedouin settlement. The second conclusion is in the context of various aspects of relationships that, despite of moderating processes, special characteristics remain. In other words, despite economic, social, educational, religious, and cultural synergy between the two communities, they continue to preserve – and perhaps even create – economic, social, and cultural differences between them.

Accordingly, the insight in this study is that patterns of individual behavior in society wherein one lives, and acts are the result of values, norms, practices, and cultural codes that have certain unique characteristics that in most cases lead to one's habitus. These are, indeed, embodied, and self-contained in all individuals, and are expressed in both uniform and unique patterns of behavior (for each community separately), which pass intergenerationally, inter alia. However, they are not one rigid segment: While from looking at everyday dynamics, it appears as if there is a dichotomy between two communities, this is a false representation: In fact, this situation exists neither empirically nor anecdotally, but rather is an outgrowth of an ongoing structural process, based on flexible, fluid, and even permeable boundaries; and dependent upon circumstances of the two communities, Fellahin and Bedouin. As the study has shown, in some cases, Bedouin become Fellahin, and vice versa. However, the phenomenon does not occur in a vacuum; rather, it is strongly affected by outside – usually governmental – processes and historical events.

Appendix

Appendix A
Dynasty of Ottoman Governor Zahir Al-Umar in the Arab towns and villages in the Galilee
Source: Ziad al-Zidani, Nazareth. Private collection.

Appendix B
Record of land ownership (*miri* land) of the brothers Muhammad and Saleh Shibli (Ziadnah) in Deir Hanna, on 30 Haziran 1326 (13 July 1910). This document indicates a tithe (annual tax) of eight grush for Deir Hanna Valley lease – annual crop.
Source: Sa'id A. Shibli (Ziadnah), Deir Hanna. Private collection.

Appendix C
Example of a border pass related to an agreement signed on 2 February 1926 between United Kingdom and France concerning border crossings between Lebanon, Syria, and Palestine, obliging anyone wishing to move another territory to obtain approval of the district commissioner of that area.
Source: Government of Palestine, "The Laws of Palestine: Border Pass Agreement," *NAL*, CO 733/60/5-20; Government of Palestine, "Border crossings," *SAI*, PI: M 4349/34

Appendix D
A complaint filed by Galilee District Commissioner in Nazareth, C. T. Evans, on 3 September 1943 to High Commissioner of Palestine in Jerusalem, MacMichael, in which Evans complains about the "invasion" of the two Bedouin tribes, Al-Subayh and Al-Mazarib, into lands of others in Marj Ibn Amer.
Source: Government of Palestine, "Bedouin Control Ordinance, no. 18 of 1942," *SAI*, PI: 552/15, original symbol: Y/58/42

Appendix E
The High Commissioner's response to the Galilee District Commissioner on 21 September 1943, in which he seeks not to punish collectively, but

to punish individually and only in exceptional cases, in order to encourage Bedouin sedentarization.
Source: Government of Palestine, "Bedouin Control Ordinance, no. 18 of 1942," *SAI*, PI: 552/15, original symbol: Y/58/42

Appendix F (1–3)
Bedouin Control Ordinance of 1942, the purpose of which was to prevent Bedouin movement from one place to another
Source: High Commissioner of Palestine, "Bedouin Control Ordinance, no. 18 of 1942," *NAL*, CO 733/448. Government of Palestine, "Bedouin Control Ordinance, no. 18 of 1942," *SAI*, PI: 552/15, original symbol: Y/58/42

Appendix A

Appendix B

Appendix C

BORDER PASS

Issued under authority of Article 9 of
the Bon Voisinage Agreement of
2nd February, 1926,
between the
Governments of Palestine and Syria

PERMIS DE FRONTIERE

Prévu par l'Article 9 de la Convention
de Bon Voisinage
Libano-Syro-Palestinienne
de 2 Février 1926.

OPP. 8030—3000 Bks.—10.5.29   M. 242.

D R A F T

ASSISTANT DISTRICT COMMISSIONER'S OFFICE,

Date ....

BORDER PASS

.... of .... village,
.... Sub-District, is permitted to cross
the Frontier to .... to attend a ....
Valid for three days from the date of issue.

ASSISTANT DISTRICT COMMISSIONER
....

....
Photograph
overstamped
with stamp
of office
of issue.......

Appendix D

GOVERNMENT OF PALESTINE

IN REPLY PLEASE QUOTE
No. 929.

[Stamp: GOVERNMENT OF PALESTINE / CHIEF SECRETARY'S OFFICE / JERUSALEM / 7 SEP 1943 / Y/58/42]

DISTRICT COMMISSIONER'S OFFICE,
GALILEE AND ACRE DISTRICT,
NAZARETH.

3rd September, 1943.

CHIEF SECRETARY.

Subject :- Bedwin Control Ordinance No. 18 of 1942.

Reference :- Palestine Gazette No.1204, Supplement No. 1 of 25.6.1942.

I recommend that the Bedwin Control Ordinance be made applicable to the Arab Subeih and the Arab Mazareeb normally camping in the Nazareth Sub-District.

2. The Subeih are for the most part quiet and well-behaved but there are certain elements at feud with the Sheikh, and there are other families known to have been harbouring absconded offenders. They are already scheduled under the Collective Punishments Ordinance (Page 147 Drayton Vol.I) but the Control Ordinance will give me greater control over those families who live away from the tribe.

3. The Mazareeb, population about 250 souls, have, for many years, camped in the King George Fifth Forest, the registered owners of which are the Jewish National Fund. As you are aware the Jewish National Fund intend to have these Arabs evicted from the land; eventually it may be necessary to move the tribe and it will afford me greater control if the Ordinance has been applied to them.

I attach a draft order for consideration.

[signature]
DISTRICT COMMISSIONER
GALILEE DISTRICT.

Appendix E

Y/58/42.   2/September, 1943.

District Commissioner
 Galilee District.

        I am directed to refer to your letter No.929 of the 3rd September, 1943, requesting that the Beduin Control Ordinance be made applicable to the Arab Subeih and the Arab Mazareeb normally camping in the Nazareth sub-district.

2.   You will appreciate that the Beduin Control Ordinance is intended to be applied only to nomadic or semi-nomadic tribes and only in cases of real necessity, but not ad hoc in every case where there is only a small community of tent dwellers. In the circumstances I am to request you to be good enough to confirm that you are satisfied that the tribes mentioned in your letter do in fact fall within the category of nomads or semi-nomads for whom the Beduin Control Ordinance is designed, and that it would not be sufficient to make them amenable to the Collective Punishments Ordinance under which several of them are scheduled already.

CHIEF SECRETARY

Appendix F1

BEDUIN CONTROL ORDINANCE.
No. 18 of 1942.

AN ORDINANCE TO CONFER UPON DISTRICT COMMISSIONERS A GENERAL POWER OF CONTROL OVER NOMADIC TRIBES AND COMMUNITIES IN PALESTINE INCLUDING POWER TO INVESTIGATE AND PUNISH OFFENCES COMMITTED BY MEMBERS THEREOF.

BE IT ENACTED by the High Commissioner for Palestine, with the advice of the Advisory Council thereof :—

1. This Ordinance may be cited as the Beduin Control Ordinance, 1942. *Short title.*

2. In this Ordinance — *Interpretation.*

"Nomadic tribe" means any nomadic or semi-nomadic tribe or community in Palestine to which the provisions of this Ordinance have been applied by order of the High Commissioner under section 3.

"Nomadic tribesman" means a member of a nomadic tribe as defined in this section, whether or not such member is a Palestinian subject.

"Relative to the fifth degree" of any person means any lineal descendant of any of the great-great-great-grandparents of such person.

3. The High Commissioner may by order declare that the provisions of this Ordinance shall apply to any nomadic or semi-nomadic tribe or community in Palestine or to any nomadic or semi-nomadic tribe or community which, or any member of which, may enter Palestine from time to time. *Application of Ordinance to certain nomadic tribes.*

4. A District Commissioner may exercise within his district all or any of the following powers :— *General power of control and investigation by District Commissioner.*

(a) exercise general control and supervision over all or any nomadic tribes or tribesmen, superintend their movements, and wherever he considers it necessary direct them to go to, or not to go to, or to remain in, any specified area for any specified period;

(b) investigate any raid committed by any nomadic tribesman or tribesmen, or any other breach of the peace which they may commit, whether such raid or breaches of the peace took place in Palestine or elsewhere, arrest all persons suspected of complicity in such offence, impound their movable property until completion of investigation into the offence, and recover all loot and return it to the owners thereof;

Appendix F2

(e) in the event of the District Commissioner considering that reasonable grounds exist for supposing that a raid or breach of the peace is intended by any tribesman or tribesmen, he may seize so much of the movable property of such tribesman or tribesmen and of his or their relatives to the fifth degree, and retain it for so long, as he may consider necessary for the purpose of holding it as security for his or their good behaviour. If such raid or breach of the peace is committed by the tribesman or tribesmen whose property is being so retained, such property may be forfeited, and such forfeiture shall be in addition to the seizure and sale of any further movable property which may be ordered under section 5 and to any penalty which may be imposed under section 7.

Recovery of value of property lost or damaged, from tribesmen implicated and from their kinsmen.

5. If as a result of investigation by a District Commissioner into any offence committed or believed to have been committed within his district, or into any loss of or damage to property which has occurred therein, he has reason to believe that a nomadic tribesman or tribesmen —

(a) committed the offence or wilfully caused the loss or damage; or

(b) connived at or in any way abetted the commission of the offence or the loss or damage; or

(c) failed to render all the assistance in his or their power to discover the offender or offenders or to effect his or their arrest; or

(d) connived at the escape of, or harboured, any offender or person suspected of having taken part in the commission of the offence or implicated in the loss or damage; or

(e) combined to suppress material evidence of the commission of the offence or of the occurrence of the loss or damage.

he may, after holding an enquiry as provided for under section 6 and upon the conviction of such tribesman or tribesmen under section 7, order the seizure and sale of the movable property of such tribesman or tribesmen or of his or their relatives to the fifth degree for the following purposes :—

(i) to recover the value of looted property which has already been disposed of or cannot be seized, in order to compensate the owners of such looted property:

(ii) to collect the value of any fines imposed by him under the Ordinance.

Manner of enquiry into offences.

6. No nomadic tribesman shall be convicted of an offence against this Ordinance until an enquiry into his case has been held by the District Commissioner. Such enquiry shall be conducted, as far as is in the opinion of the District Commissioner practicable and

expedient, in the manner of a trial before a magistrate exercising summary jurisdiction, provided that no person shall have the right to be represented by an advocate thereat.

7. Where after holding an enquiry as provided for under section 6 the District Commissioner is satisfied that any nomadic tribesman — {Offences and penalties.}

(a) has been guilty of any of the acts or omissions set out in paragraphs (a) to (c) inclusive of section 5, or

(b) has failed, or is a sheikh or member of a nomadic tribe which has failed, to comply with any direction given by the District Commissioner in exercise of his powers under paragraph (a) of section 4,

such tribesman shall be deemed to be guilty of an offence against this Ordinance, and the District Commissioner may convict him of such offence accordingly and may punish him with a fine not exceeding £P.50 or with imprisonment for a term not exceeding one year or with both such penalties.

8.—(1) Any person sentenced by a District Commissioner under the preceding section to a fine exceeding £P.10 or to imprisonment for a term exceeding three months may appeal against his conviction or against such sentence by lodging with the District Commissioner within fifteen days of the sentence, a notice setting forth the grounds of appeal, and the District Commissioner shall transmit the same to the High Commissioner, who may either uphold the conviction and sentence, or uphold the conviction and reduce the sentence, or uphold the conviction and increase the sentence up to the maximum penalty provided under this Ordinance, or quash the conviction and order a fresh enquiry to be held under section 6, or quash the conviction without ordering such fresh enquiry. {Appeal.}

(2) A convicted person shall not be entitled to be released on bail pending the decision of the High Commissioner upon any appeal under this section; nor shall the collection of any fine imposed upon a convicted person, or the seizure and sale of any movable property under section 5, be stayed pending the decision of the High Commissioner upon any such appeal, unless the District Commissioner so directs.

8th June, 1942.

HAROLD MACMICHAEL
High Commissioner

Notes

Introduction

1 *Fellah* or *Falāh* (pl.: Fellahin or *Fallāhīn*) is a farmer or agricultural labourer in the Middle East and North Africa. Although the vast majority no longer engages in agriculture, the designation "fellahin" is still germane. The same applies to the Bedouin who self-ascribe and are referred to by others as "Bedouin" even though they now live-in permanent villages and towns, so the vast majority are non-nomadic.
2 This book is based largely on a dissertation that I wrote at Haifa University, titled: *The process of Bedouin integration into Arab towns and villages in the Galilee: Historical, Social, and Cultural Aspects, from the Beginning of the 18th to the End of the 20th Century*, 2016 [Hebrew]. Supervisors: Dr. Ido Shahar and Prof. Mahmoud Yazbak.
3 This study refers to both: Fellahin living in villages and towns, as Fellahin. Because until recently they were mainly engaged in the agricultural economics field. Therefore, to this day they are called Fellahin even though they live in villages and towns. But they continue to follow the Fallahi symbols and practices mode. as well as the Bedouin, continue to follow tribal symbols (as described in detail later in the book).
4 The term "sown" is the past participle of the verb "to sow", used to describe settlers who worked their own agricultural land, such as the Fellahin.
5 Abd al-Rahman Ibn Khaldun, *Muqaddimah Ibn Khaldun* (Cairo: Jazirat al-Ward Press, 2010 [Arabic]), 129–131.
6 Ibid.
7 Ibid., 131.
8 For more on relationships among these categories, see Cynthia Nelson (ed.), *The Desert and the Sown: Nomads in the Wider Society* (Berkeley, CA: Institute of International Studies, University of California Press, 1973).
9 John L. Burckhardt, *Travels in Syria and the Holy Land* (New York: AMS Press, 1995 [1822]), 285–309; Henry B. Tristram, *The Land of Israel: A Journal of Travels in Palestine* (London: Society for Promoting Christian Knowledge Press, 1865), 91–138, 485–504; James L. Buckingham, *Travels among the Arab tribes inhabiting the countries east of Syria and Palestine, including a journey from Nazareth to the mountains beyond the Dead Sea from thence through the plains* (London: Longman, Rees, Orme, Brown and Green, 1825), 1–597; Edward Robinson, *Biblical Researches in*

Palestine and the Adjacent Regions: A Journal of Travels in the Years 1838 to 1852 (Jerusalem: Universities' Booksellers Press, 1970 [1856]), 88–101; James Finn, *Stirring Times: Records from Jerusalem Consular Chronicles of 1853 to 1856* (London: C.K. Paul & Co., 1878), 11–144, 144–485.

10   Burckhardt, *Travels in Syria*, 299–302; Finn, *Stirring Times*, 186–189; Tristram, *The Land of Israel*, 120–124; Buckingham, *Travels among the Arab tribes*, 89–111; Robinson, *Biblical Researches*, 88–101.

11   Burckhardt, *Travels in Syria*, 317–345. The concept of *khawa* is the right of "brotherhood" between people, for example: "I give you *khawa* because you protect me or so you will not attack me or let someone else attack me".

12   Jibrall S. Jabbur, *The Bedouins and the Desert: Aspects of Nomadic Life in the Arab East*, trans. Lawrence I. Conrad (Albany: SUNY Press, 1995), 355–356, 516, 611; Alois Musil, *The Manners and Customs of the Rwala Bedouins* (New York: American Geographical Society, 1928), 59–60.

13   Finn, *Stirring Times*, 169–172.
14   Tristram, *The Land of Israel*, 112.
15   Ibid., 486–498.
16   Edward W. Said, *Orientalism* (New York: Pantheon Books, 1978).
17   Ibid., 149–166.
18   Ibid.
19   Ibid., 321.
20   Bernard Lewis, *The Middle East and the West* (Bloomington: Indiana University Press, 1964), 140.
21   Talal Asad, "The Concept of Cultural Translation in British Social Anthropology," in *Writing Culture: The Poetics and Politics of Ethnography*, eds. James Clifford and George E. Marcus (Berkeley: University of California Press, 1986), 141–164.
22   Ibid., 162.
23   Ibid., 163.
24   Khalid Furani, Dan Rabinowitz, "The Ethnographic Arriving of Palestine," *Annual Review of Anthropology*, Vol. 40, No. 1 (July 2011): 475–491.
25   Ibid., 478.
26   Emanuel Marx, "The Ecology and Politics of Nomadic Pastoralists in the Middle East," in *The Nomadic Alternative: Modes and Models of Interaction in the African-Asian Deserts and Steppes*, ed. Weissleder Wolfgang (Germany: Walter de Gruyter, 1978), 107–122; Ter Ellingson, *The Myth of the Noble Savage* (Berkeley, CA: University of California Press (2001); Yehoshua Ben-Arieh, "The Literature of Western Travelers to the Land of Israel in the Nineteenth Century as a Historical Source and as a Social Phenomenon," *Cathedra: The History of the Land of Israel and its Settlement*, Vol. 36, No. 2 (1986): 159–161; and other anthropologists as described in detail later in the book.

27   The use of the term "Culturism" became common in the neo-liberal era for cases where "tribalism" serves (the writer or the hegemon) as a

powerful element of identity or ascription (personal or collective), based on the answer to "Who you are?" and "Who are we?"
28 Moshe Ma'oz, *Ottoman Reform in Syria and Palestine 1840–1861: The Impact of the Tanzimat on Politics and Society* (Oxford: Clarendon Press, 1968), 134–148. Moshe Sharon, *The Bedouin in the Land of Israel from the Beginning of the Eighteenth Century to the End of the Crimean War* (M.A. thesis, Hebrew University, 1964 [Hebrew]).
29 Uriel Heyd, *Ottoman Documents on Palestine, 1552–1615: A Study of the Firman according to the Muhimme Defteri* (Oxford: Clarendon Press, 1960; Moshe Sharon, "The Political Role of the Bedouins in Palestine in the Sixteenth and Seventeenth Centuries," in *Studies on Palestine during the Ottoman Period*, ed. Moshe Ma'oz (Jerusalem: Magnes Press, 1975), 11–48; Ma'oz, *Ottoman Reform*; Adil Manna', "The Farrukh Governors of Jerusalem," in *Chapters in the History of Jerusalem at the Beginning of the Ottoman Period*, ed. Amnon Cohen (Jerusalem: Yad Yitzhak Ben Zvi, 1979 [Hebrew]).
30 Heyd, *Ottoman*, 91–92.
31 Ibid., 90–91.
32 Sharon, "The Political," 17–19.
33 Ma'oz, *Ottoman Reform*, 129.
34 Ibid., 131, 132, 133.
35 Manna', "The Farrukh," 202.
36 Adil Manna', *The History of Palestine in the Late Ottoman Period, 1700–1918 (A New Reading)]*, (Beirut: Mu'assat al-Dirasat al-Filastiniyah, 1999 [Arabic]).
37 Ibid., 13–15.
38 Dror Ze'evi, *An Ottoman Century: The District of Jerusalem in the 1600s* (New York: SUNY Press, 1996), 98.
39 Ibid.
40 Arnon Medzini, *The Distribution of Bedouin Settlement in the Galilee as a Product of Spontaneous Settlement and Government-Focused Policy*, (Haifa: University of Haifa Press, 1983 [Hebrew]). Arnon Medzini, "Bedouin Settlement in the Galilee," in *The States of the Galilee*, eds. Avshalom Shmueli, Arnon Sofer, and Nurit Kliot (Haifa: Society for Applied Scientific Research Press, 1983 [Hebrew]), 549–563; Yosef Ben-David, *The Bedouin in Israel: Social and Land Aspects* (Jerusalem: Ben Shimshi Institute for Land Policy and Land Use, 2004 [Hebrew]); Amnon Barkai and Yosef Ben David, "The Bedouin Lands in the North: A Struggle that Should Not Have Happened," *Ground-Journal of the Institute for Land Use Research*, Vol. 41, No. 1 (April 1996 [Hebrew]): 77–87; Avshalom Shmueli, *The End of the Nomads-Bedouin Societies in Settlement Processes* (Tel Aviv: Reshafim Press, 1980 [Hebrew]); Gil Kaufman, "The Bedouin Population in the Galilee: Processes and Changes, from Nomads to Permanent Settlements, 1963–2002," *National Security*, Vol. 4, No. 1 (April 2005 [Hebrew]): 76–97; Gideon Golani, *The Bedouin*

Settlement in the Alonim Hills-Shfaram (Jerusalem: Hebrew University Press, 1966 [Hebrew]).
41   The British Military Administration in Palestine began in December 1917 and continued until the establishment of civil government (under a British Mandate from the League of Nations) in July 1920. The Mandate continued until mid-May 1948 when the British withdraw from Palestine. This was immediately followed by the establishment of the state of Israel.
42   Shmueli, *The end of the Nomads-Bedouin*, 117.
43   Daniel G. Bates, "The Role of the State in Peasant-Nomad Mutualism," *Anthropological Quarterly*, Vol. 44, No. 3 (July 1971): 109–131.
44   Ibid.
45   Ashraf T. Abu al-Dahab, *Islamic Dictionary* (Cairo: Dar al-Shuruq, 1968 [Arabic]), 451; Yaacov Shimoni, *The Arabs of Palestine* (Tel Aviv: Am Oved, 1947 [Hebrew]), 169; Sultan bin M. Al-Qasemi, *Encyclopaedia of Islam*, Vol. 24 (Al-Sharjah: Markiz al-Sharjah lel-Abda'a al-Fikri, 1995 [Arabic]), 69–73.
46   Shimoni, *The Arabs*, 169.
47   Ibid., 157.
48   Henry Rosenfeld, *They Were Fellahin: Studies in the Social Development of the Arab Village in Israel* (Tel Aviv: Hakibbutz Hameuhad, 1964 [Hebrew]), 172.
49   Ibid., 173–181.
50   Ibn Khaldun, *Muqaddimah*, 130.
51   Ibid., 130–131.
52   Muhammad Ibn Iyas, *Wondrous Flowers of the Events of Time*, Vol. 2 (Cairo: Dar Ahiy'a al-Kutub al-Arabiya, 1960 [Arabic]), 300–303.
53   Said A. Al-Ashur, *The Mameluk Period in Egypt and Al-Sham* (Cairo: Dar al-Nahda al-Arabiya, 1976 [Arabic]), 325.
54   Ahmad Ibn A. Al-Maqrizi, *The Guide to the Knowledge of Royal Dynasties*, eds. Muhammad M. Ziyada and Said A. Al-Ashur, Vol. 4 (Cairo: Lajnat al-Ta'lif wa-al-Tarjamah wa-al-Nasher, 1957 [Arabic]), 1178–1190.
55   Ibid., 1181.
56   A fine levied by the Ottoman military and the police upon villagers for travel expenses. See Abd al-Rahman bin H. Al-Jabarti, *The Marvellous Compositions of Biographies and Events*, Vol. 3 (Cairo: Dar al-Kitab wa-al-Watha'iq al-Qawmiyya, 2009 [Arabic]), 317.
57   Ibid., 213.
58   The holder of an *iltizam* (a form of taxed farming that arose in the 15th century in the Ottoman Empire). The government sold off *iltizams* to wealthy notables, who would then reap up to five times the sum they had paid for this privilege, by taxing the peasants/farmers and taking a portion of their harvests).
59   Governor of Damascus under Ottoman rule, from 1742 up to his deposition in 1757.

60 Muhammad Kurd Ali, *Description of Syria*, Vol. 2 (Damascus: al-Ma ba'ah al-Hadithah, 1928 [Arabic]), 294.
61 Gabriel Baer, *The Arabs of the Middle East: Population and Society* (Tel Aviv: Zohar Press, 1973 [Hebrew]), 157.
62 Abraham Poliak, *Feudalism in Egypt, Syria, Palestine, and the Lebanon, 1250–1900* (Philadelphia: Porcupine Press, 1977), 64.
63 Burckhardt, *Travels in Syria*, 291–299.
64 Baer, *The Arabs*, 158.
65 *Tanzimat*: literally "ordering" and "organization", refers to a series of land reforms initiated by the Ottoman government.
66 The Ottoman Empire classified land into five categories: 1. Arazi *Mulk*, or lands held in complete ownership by an individual or group recognized as the private property of its cultivators or occupiers. This land was held in fee simple; 2. Arazi *Miri* or *Emiri*, or state lands whose actual ownership was that of the farmer, who was obliged to pay a tithe (10%); 3. Arazi *Waqf*, or lands that were an inalienable charitable endowment under Islamic law that typically involved donating a building, plot of land, or other assets for religious purposes; 4. Arazi *Matruke*, or abandoned lands not under cultivation and without any ostensible owner; such land was defined as public land of two categories: land that serves the public at large (for example, roads); and land designated for a specific group's use, such as grazing land that a certain village has used for many years; and 5. Arazi *Mawat*, or "dead lands", i.e., uncultivated and unappropriated land.
67 Al-Qasemi, *Encyclopaedia*, 7374–7375.
68 Abd al-Aziz M. Awad, *The Ottoman Administration in Syria, 1864–1914* (Cairo: Dar al-Ma'arif bi-Misr, 1969 [Arabic]), 236–237.
69 Kurd Ali, *Description*, 151–153.
70 Gabriel Baer, "The Surrender of the Egyptian Fallah," *The New East: Quarterly of the Israel Oriental Society*, Vol. 12 (Jerusalem: Merkaz Press, 1962 [Hebrew]), 55–63.
71 Ibid., 51–61.
72 Ibid., 61.
73 Awad, *The Ottoman*, 226–229; Al-Jabarti, *The Marvelous*, 220–225.
74 Rosenfeld, *They Were*.
75 Rosenfeld's approach relies heavily on the structural functionalism paradigm first formulated by Radcliffe Brown (1881–1955), a scholar who was deeply influenced by Emile Durkheim's sociology. To distinguish himself from Bronislaw Malinowski, Brown referred to his approach as "structuralist functionalism" and defined social anthropology as "comparative sociology", thus suggesting that it was not a discipline in its own right, with its own research methods and agenda. Malinowski argued that culture works to meet the needs of society rather than individuals. The drawback of this paradigm is its characteristic conservatism, i.e., in the absence of contradictions, it assumes social uniformity. For a critique of

structural functionalism, see Edmund R. Leach, *Rethinking Anthropology* (London: Athlone Press, 1971), 1–27.
76 Rosenfeld, *They Were*, 47–48.
77 Henry Rosenfeld, "Separation and Splitting Processes of the Extended Family in the Arab Village," *Megamot*, Vol. 8, No. 4 (April 1957 [Hebrew]): 411–418.
78 Ibid., 412.
79 Avner Cohen's advisor on his dissertation in the Department of Social Anthropology at the University of Manchester was Emrys Peters, whose research was mostly on the Cyrenaica tribes in Libya; and who applied the segmental principles of his mentor Evans-Prichard to his own work, subsequently used by Cohen.
80 Abner Cohen, *Arab Border-Villages in Israel: A Study of Continuity and Change in Social Organization* (Manchester, UK: University of Manchester Press, 1965).
81 Ibid., 5–9.
82 Little Triangle: the region of Arab localities between Umm el Fahm and Taiyibe (from Wadi Ara down the eastern edge of the Sharon plain to the northeast of the Tel Aviv metropolitan area.
83 Cohen, *Arab Border*, 15.
84 Ibid., 146–173.
85 Talal Asad, "Anthropological Texts and Ideological Problems: An Analysis of Cohen on Arab Villages in Israel," *Economy and Society*, Vol. 4, No. 3 (August 1975): 251–281.
86 Ibid., 271.
87 Ibid., 271–276.
88 Gil Eyal, "Between East and West: The Discourse about the Arab Village in Israel," *Theory and Criticism*, Vol. 3, No. 1 (Winter 1993 [Hebrew]): 39–55.
89 Objectification: The act of treating a person or anything other as an object or thing, like a tool that serves the desires and needs of the user.
90 Eyal, "Between East," 43.
91 Dan Rabinowitz, *Overlooking Nazareth: The Ethnography of Exclusion in Galilee* (Cambridge, UK: Cambridge University Press, 1997), 15.
92 Ibid., 16. "Elite" connotes in Hebrew both *spatial*-geographic superiority – in this case, overlooking-dominating Arab Nazareth from above – as well as *qualitative* superiority (elites, elite status, and "good quality").
93 Dan Rabinowitz, *Anthropology and Palestinians* (Raanana: Centre for the Study of Arab Society in Israel, 1998 [Hebrew]).
94 Ibid., 81.
95 Ibid., 85.
96 Lila Abu-Lughod, *Veiled Sentiments: Honor and Poetry in Bedouin Society* (Berkeley: California University Press, 1986).
97 Rabinowitz, *Anthropology*, 81.
98 Oren Yiftachel, *Watching over the Vineyard: The Example of Majd al-*

Krum (Raanana: The Institute for Israeli Arab Studies, 1997 [Hebrew]), 15–20.
99 Ibid., 14.
100 Ibid., 43.
101 Khalil Nakhleh, "Land Day," in *Palestinians in Israel: Reading in History, Politics, and Society*, eds. Nadin N. Rouhana and Areej Sabbagh-Khoury (Haifa: Mada al-Carmel Press, 2011 [Arabic]), 83–89.
102 Yiftachel, *Watching Over*, 56–58.
103 Ibid., 83.
104 I prefer to use the term "tribe" rather than *qabilah* [in Arabic] for convenience' sake, as all societies know this term. However, in the words of the Bedouin today and in the last centuries, Bedouin do not call themselves that; they call themselves "Arab" or *asherah* (is a group of people brought together by actual or imaginary kinship), and only very rarely call themselves *qabilah*, which was accepted-borrowed in later times, perhaps in imitation of colonial parlance. In other words, over time the term "tribe" became somewhat etic and ceased to be emic. For more details, see Edwin Segal's article on the hegemonic use of the term "tribe" by colonial powers and their administrations in Africa. The objective was, on one hand, to blur the overarching ethnic identity of the African countries (note that ethnic groups extend in many African countries, such as in South Africa, Kenya, and Malawi), and on the other hand to enhance the colonial powers' effectiveness by amplifying differences (a divide-and-control mechanism) between local populations. See Edwin S. Segal, "Intersections among Tribalism, Ethnicity, and Gender in Light of African Data," *Sociological Bulletin*, Vol. 49, No. 1 (March 2000): 1–17.
105 Mahmoud H. Zakzouk, *General Islamic Encyclopedia* (Egypt: Wizrt al-Awqaf, 2003 [Arabic]), 269.
106 Ibn Khaldun, *Muqaddimah*, 131–133.
107 Ibid., 131.
108 Anthropology in general, divided various-sized groups of origin in a lineal descent by lineage (tribe) and *hamula* [clan]. The difference between lineage and clan is that lineage is descent traced step-by-step from a common progenitor, progeny, race, descending line of offspring, or ascending line of parentage. By contrast, a clan is a group of people all descended from a common ancestor (in fact or belief). For more information, see Emanuel Marx, *The Bedouin Society in the Negev* (Tel Aviv: Reshafim Press, 1974 [Hebrew]), 57–59.
109 Robertson W. Smith, *Kinship and Marriage in Early Arabia* (Oosterhout, N.B, Netherlands: Anthropological Publications Press, 1966).
110 Ibid., 26.
111 Robert S. Pickett, "Review: Kinship and Marriage in Early Arabia," *The Family Coordinator*, Vol. 21, No. 3 (July 1972): 365; Jeanne Favret-Saada, "Review: Kinship and Marriage in Early Arabia," *Homme*, Vol. 10, No. 1 (March 1970): 107–110.

112 Evans Pritchard, *The Nuer: A Description of the Modes of Livelihood and Political Institutions of a Nilotic People* (Oxford: Oxford University Press, 1940).
113 Ibid., 151.
114 Evans Pritchard, *Kinship and Marriage among the Nuer* (Oxford: Clarendon Press, 1966), 3–5.
115 Emrys L. Peters, *The Bedouin of Cyrenaica: Studies in Personal and Corporate Power* (Cambridge: Cambridge University Press, 1990).
116 Ibid., 86–87.
117 Dale F. Eickelman, *The Middle East and Central Asia: An Anthropological Approach* (Hoboken, NJ: Prentice Hall, 1998).
118 Ibid., 124–125.
119 Dale F. Eickelman, *The Middle East: An Anthropological Approach* (Hoboken, NJ: Prentice Hall, 1981), 104.
120 Paul Dresch, "The Significance of the Course Events Take in Segmentary Systems," *American Ethnologist*, Vol. 13, No. 2 (May 1986): 309–324.
121 "Honour" in its broader meaning, *sharaf*, connotes or refers to moral values including autonomy, bravery, and generosity. In addition, "honour" is also tied to forbidden sexual relations, called *'ard* in Palestine *namus* in Turkey, and *hurma* in Algeria.
122 Dresch, "The Significance," 311.
123 Steven C. Caton, "Power, Persuasion, and Language: A Critique of the Segmentary Model in the Middle East," *International Journal of Middle East Studies*, Vol. 19, No. 1 (February 1987): 77–101.
124 Ibid., 96–99.
125 Talal Asad, *The Kababish Arabs: Power, Authority, and Consent in a Nomadic Tribe* (London: C. Hurst & Company Press, 1970).
126 Ibid., 103–104.
127 Marshall D. Sahlins, "The Segmentary Lineage: An Organization of Predatory Expansion," *American Anthropologist*, Vol. 63, No. 2 (April 1961): 322–345; Henry Munson, "On the Irrelevance of the Segmentary Lineage Model in the Moroccan Rif," *American Anthropologist*, Vol. 91, No. 2 (June 1989): 386–400.
128 Scott Atran and Dale F. Eickelman, "Thick Interpretation in the Middle East," *Current Anthropology*, Vol. 23, No. 6 (December 1982): 705–709.
129 Ibid., 706.
130 Ibid., 705.
131 Ibid.
132 Donald P. Cole, "Where Have the Bedouin Gone?" *Anthropological Quarterly*, Vol. 76, No. 2 (Spring 2003): 235–267.
133 Ibid., 238.
134 Francoise Metral, "Managing Risk: Sheep-rearing and Agriculture in the Syrian Steppe," in *The Transformation of Nomadic Society in the Arab East*, eds. Martha Mundy and Basim Musallam (Cambridge: Cambridge University Press, 2000), 127.

135 Emanuel Marx, "Economic Changes among the Bedouin in Recent Years," *The Bedouins: Notes and Articles*, Vol. 11 (Sde Boker: Midreshet Sde Boker Press, 1980 [Hebrew]), 3–11; Marx, *The Bedouin Society*, 57–59.
136 Julian Steward, "The Concept and Method of Cultural Ecology," in *Evolution and Ecology: Essays on Social Transformation*, eds. Jane Steward and Robert Murphy (Urbana: University of Illinois Press, 1977), 30–42.
137 Marvin Harris, "The Cultural Ecology of India's Sacred Cattle," *Current Anthropology*, Vol. 7, No. 1 (February 1966): 51–56.
138 The cultural ecology approach based on Marvin Harris' article in his study on the Indian population. He tried to prove that the cow had become sacred in India because of ecological changes in the Ganges, such as changes in ecological balance, dilution of land resources, population density, and the need as draft animals for hauling and ploughing, all of which led to the enactment of a law prohibiting eating cows in India. However, there are those who take issues with this claim.
139 Marx, "The Ecology," 107–122.
140 Marx, "Economic Changes among the Bedouin in Recent Years," 3.
141 Emanuel Marx, "Economic Change among Pastoral Nomads in the Middle East," in *The Changing Bedouin*, eds. Emanuel Marx and Avshalom Shmueli (New Brunswick, NJ: Transaction Books Press, 1984), 1–16.
142 Emanuel Marx, *Bedouin of Mount Sinai: An Anthropological Study of their Political Economy* (New York and Oxford, Bergahn Books Press, 2013), 82.
143 The term "binary oppositions" was coined by Lévi-Strauss, a French anthropologist who is most famous for his work as a structuralist. Lévi-Strauss found that there are many underlying structures in various societies that directly reflect on our work as writers. He found that the common ground that unites all of humanity is our ability to see the universe in terms of binary opposites, i.e., man/woman, black/white, earth/sky, and so forth. See Claude Lévi-Strauss, *The Story of Lynx*, trans. Catherine Tihanyi (Chicago: University of Chicago Press, 1995).
144 Gideon Kressel, *Individuality vs. Tribality: The Dynamic of an Israeli Bedouin Community in the Process of Urbanization* (Tel Aviv: Hakibbutz Hameuhad, 1975 [Hebrew]), 24–27. Kressel divided these families into 70 Bedouin-Fellahin families originating from the Naqab/Negev: 49 families originating from Libya-Morocco, 22 Fellahin families from the villages in the Southern Palestine coastal plain, 14 Sudanese-Fellahin families from the Naqab/Negev, and 11 Bedouin families from Sinai.
145 Ibid., 9.
146 Ibid., 94–98.
147 Joseph Ginat, *Blood Revenge: Family Honor, Mediation, Outcasting* (Brighton, UK: Sussex Academic Press, 1997).
148 Avinoam Meir, "Nomads and the State: The spatial dynamics of

centrifugal and centripetal forces among the Israeli Negev Bedouin," *Political Geography Quarterly*, Vol. 7, No. 3 (July 1988): 251–270; Ben David, *The Bedouin in Israel*; Ghazi Falah, *The Processes and Patterns of Sedentarization of the Galilee Bedouin, 1880–1982* (PhD diss., University of Durham, 1982). Ghazi Falah, "The Evolution of Semi-nomadism in Non-desert Environment: The Case of Galilee in the 19th Century," *GeoJournal*, Vol. 21, No. 4 (August 1990): 397–410. Ghazi Falah, "Pre-state Jewish Colonization in Northern Palestine and Impact on Local Bedouin Sedentarization 1914–1948," *Journal of Historical Geography*, Vol. 17, No. 3 (July 1991): 289–309.

149 For an introduction to this, see William H. Sewell, "A Theory of Structure: Duality, Agency, and Transformation," *American Journal of Sociology*, Vol. 98, No. 1 (July 1992), 1–29.

150 "Identity politics" is a term that has been accepted as a framework for discourse, strategy, and political practice that emphasizes the uniqueness of various communities in a society, and seeks to advance these communities' interests. See Yossi Yonah and Yehouda Shenhav, *What is Multiculturalism? On the Politics of Identity in Israel* (Tel Aviv: Babel Press, 2005 [Hebrew]), 13–51, as discussed further in Chapter 1.

151 The actual number of Bedouin villages in the Galilee is 20. However, the number of *recognized* Bedouin villages is only 17 (and three unrecognized villages in terms of Israeli authorities). Seven localities are located in separate municipal areas: Tuba-Zangariah, Nujeidat, Zarzir, Bir al-Maksur, Shibli (including Umm al-Ghanam), Ka'abiya-Helf Tabash-Hajajra, and Bussmat Tab'un. The remaining 10 settlements lie in the jurisdictions of the regional councils Arab al-Aramsheh, Khawlad and Ibtin, Wadi al-Hamam and Heib al-Farush, Manshiya, Wadi Salameh, Dameida, Kamaneh, and Husayniyya. The total population (of Bedouin villages) is estimated at 63,000 according to the CBSPC (2020).

152 Israeli Central Bureau of Statistics, Population Census (CBSPC) (Jerusalem: Government Press) 2020. The author was responsible for weighting the data.

153 The estimate was calculated by the author, as discussed further in Chapter 5.

154 "Unrecognized villages": Almost all land in Israel is state land held and administered by a central authority (the Israel Lands Authority), which not only leases land to those who live thereon; but it has been the Authority's policy to tightly control allocation of land for new communities and expansion of existing ones in an exhausting, drawn-out, byzantine process of pre-approval and lengthy pre-planning. Such management policies and practices (that affect Jews and Arabs alike) when coupled with gross neglect of the demographic needs of the Arab sector and discrimination in allocation of land, have driven widespread unapproved construction in the Arab sector, particularly by Bedouin who build unapproved clusters without permits, branded in Israeli discourse "unrecognized villages",

which range from small hamlets to sprawling towns (that being "unrecognized", often lack basic infrastructure and function off-grid in terms of public utilities).
155 According to a study of Bedouin population by demographer Arnon Soffer, there were approximately 20,000 Bedouin inhabitants in 2007, however, Sofer did not include in his estimate all veteran Bedouin families (such as Trabay and Ziadnah, etc., which are located in several towns and villages in the Galilee). See Arnon Soffer, "The Bedouins in Israel: Geographic Aspects," *Horizons in Geography*, Vol. 67–68, No. 1 (January 2007 [Hebrew]): 224–236.
156 CBSPC, 2020.

1 Historical Background: The Bedouin in Palestine, 1700–1918

1 While it can be assumed that even before the 18th century, there was Bedouin settlement in Arab villages and towns in the Galilee, this lies outside my research scope.
2 Bates, "The Role of the State," 109–131.
3 Ibid., 110–123.
4 Ahmed W. Zakariyya, *Tribes of Al-Sham* (Damascus: Dar al-Fikr, 1983 [Arabic]), 102–103; Tuvia Ashkenazi, *The Bedouin in the Land of Israel* (Jerusalem: Ariel, 2000 [Hebrew]), 29.
5 Al-Dimashqi al-Qurashi Ibn Kathir, *The Beginning and the End*, Vol. 1 (Cairo: Dar al-Fajr, 2004 [Arabic], 164–172; Abu Al-Hassan Ali Bin Al-Hussein Al-Masoudi, *The Meadows of Gold and Mines of Jawhar*, Vol. 2 (Cairo: Al-Amrah, 2007 [Arabic]). 106, https://dlib-eastview-com.ezproxy.haifa.ac.il/browse/book/read/16889/start.
6 Al-Masoudi, *The Meadows of Gold*, 109; Mustafa al-Dabbagh, *Arab Tribes and their Descendants in our Country Palestine* (Beirut: Dar al-Tali'a, 1979 [Arabic]), 151, https://archive.org/details/20190902_20190902_1906/page/n47/mode/2up.
7 Zakariyya, *Tribes of Al-Sham*, 102–103; Al-Dabbagh, *Arab tribes*, 196–201.
8 Ibn Khaldun, *Muqaddimah*, 111; Moshe Sharon, "The Bedouin and the Land of Israel under Islamic Rule," *The Bedouins: Notes and Articles*, Vol. 2 (Sde Boker: Midreshet Sde Boker Press, 1971 [Hebrew]), 17.
9 Frederick G. Peake, *A History of Trans-Jordan and its Tribes* (Jerusalem: Dar al-Aytam al-Islamiyya, 1934 [Arabic]), 83–160.
10 Hajj/Hadji is the Islamic pilgrimage to Mecca. Ma'oz, *Ottoman Reform*, 133.
11 Seth J. Frantzman, Ruth Kark, "Bedouin Settlement in Late Ottoman and British Mandatory Palestine: Influence on the Cultural and Environmental Landscape, 1870–1948," *New Middle Eastern Studies*, Vol. 1, No. 1 (January 2011): 1–24.
12 Ibid., 2–5.

13 Cengiz Orhonlu, *Osmanli Imparatorlugunda asiretleri iskan tesebbusu (1691–1696)* (Istanbul: Edebiyat Fakultesi Basimevi, 1963 [Turkey]), 39–98; Yasemin Avci, "The Application of Tanzimat in the Desert: The Bedouins and the Creation of a New Town in Southern Palestine 1860–1914," *Middle Eastern Studies*, Vol. 45, No. 6 (November 2009): 969–983.
14 Rasat Kasaba, *A Moveable: Ottoman Nomads, Migrants, and Refugees* (Seattle: University of Washington Press, 2009), 72–73.
15 Ali Rifa'at Abou-El-Haj, *Formation of the Modern State: The Ottoman Empire, Sixteenth to Eighteenth Centuries* (Albany: State University of New York Press, 1991).
16 Kasaba, *A Moveable*, 58.
17 The *derbend* system (literally referring to the guardians of mountain passes) was a network of guards and sentries enlisted by the Ottomans, including tribal communities, fleeing peasants, and migrants. Ottoman officials viewed the *derbend* as another method of sedentarizing itinerants while enhancing the security of roads and border areas.
18 Ibid., 71–72.
19 Ze'evi, *An Ottoman Century*, 98–114.
20 Ashkenazi, *The Bedouin*, 29; Al-Jabarti, *The Marvelous*, 321.
21 Ashkenazi, *The Bedouin*, 29–30.
22 Hussein Ibn Ghannam, *Ibn Ghannam's History*. Vol. 2, ed. Sulayman Al-Kharashi (Riyadh: Dar Al-Thuluthiyya, 2010 [Arabic]), https://archive.org/details/hamlaenglish_gmail_20180318_1430/page/n1/mode/2up.
23 Norman N. Lewis, "The Frontier of Settlement in Syria 1800–1950," *International Affairs*, Vol. 31, No. 1 (1955), 48–60, esp. 50.
24 See also: Falah, "The Evolution of Semi-nomadism," 402.
25 Clinton Bailey, "Dating the Arrival of the Bedouin Tribes in Sinai and the Negev," *Journal of the Economic and Social History of the Orient*, Vol. 28, No. 1 (January 1985): 20–49; Ashkenazi, *The Bedouin*, 29–30, 47–50.
26 Max V. Oppenheim, *The Bedouins: Palestine, Sinai, Jordan, and Al-Hejaz*, Vol. 2, trans. Mahmoud Kabibu (London: Dar Al-Warraq, 2004 [Arabic]), 99–105; Assaf Michael, *The Arabs under the Crusaders, the Mamelukes, and the Turks* (Tel Aviv: Davar Press, 1941 [Hebrew]), 263–268. On Bedouin settlement in Sinai and the Naqab prior to the 17th century, see Bailey, "Dating the Arrival of the Bedouin," 20–49; Aref Abu-Rabi'a, *A Bedouin Century: Education and Development among the Negev Tribes in the 20th Century* (New York: Berghahn Books, 2001), 1–16.
27 Clinton Bailey, "The Negev in the Nineteenth Century: Reconstructing History from Bedouin Oral Traditions," in *Asian and African Studies – Journal of the Israel Oriental Society*, ed. Gabriel Baer, Vol. 14, No. 1 (1980), 35–80.
28 Ibid., 37.
29 Ibid., 39–73.

30 Medzini, *The Distribution*, 28.
31 Oppenheim, *The Bedouin*, 19–80. See also a detailed description of the arrival of the Al-Subayh to Mount Tabor at the end of the 17th century: Aryeh Yitzhaki, "The Bedouin Tribes at the Foot of Mount Tabor," *Kedum*, Vol. 4, No. 20 (Jane 1982): 88–92.
32 Golani, *The Bedouin Settlement*, 6.
33 Ibid., 34–53; Oppenheim, *The Bedouin*, 36–40.
34 See also Tomer Mazarib, "The Settlement and Integration of the Bedouin into Arab Towns and Villages in the Galilee, 1700–1918," *The New East*, Vol. 60 (Haifa: Pardes Press, 2021 [Hebrew]), 99–126, esp. 110.
35 Frantzman and Kark, "Bedouin Settlement," 5; Donald Quataert, *Ottoman Empire, 1700–1922* (Cambridge, UK: Cambridge University Press, 2000), 37–44.
36 Sulaiman Abu Izz al-Din, *Ibrahim Pasha in Syria* (Beirut: Al-Muttaba al-Alamiyya, 1929 [Arabic]), 69.
37 Province [*iyalet* or *wilayat*]: administrative unit. This division was useful in the Ottoman Empire from the 16th century until shortly before the mid-19th century.
38 Abd al-Aziz M. Awad, *The Ottoman Administration in Syria, 1864–1914* (Cairo: Dar al-Ma'arif bi-Misr, 1969 [Arabic]), 212–214; Muhammad Kurd Ali, *Description of Syria*, Vol. 2 (Damascus: al-Ma ba'ah al-Hadithah, 1928 [Arabic]), 283; Oppenheim, *The Bedouin*, 28–29.
39 Quataert, *Ottoman Empire*, 124–129.
40 Ibid., 129.
41 Ibid., 128–130.
42 Bruce A. Masters, *The Arabs of the Ottoman Empire 1516–1918, A Social and Cultural History* (Cambridge, UK: Cambridge University Press, 2013), 95–96. Note: A few Fellahin raised animals; they used them mainly to aid in farming, such as oxen for plowing and planting crops.
43 Albert Hourani, *A History of the Arab Peoples* (London: Faber and Faber Press, 1991), 249–256; Kasaba, *A Moveable*, 93–122.
44 Ibid., 254; Manna', *The History*, 15–20.
45 Halil Inalcik with Donald Quataert, *An Economic and Social History of the Ottoman Empire*, Vol. 2 (Cambridge, UK: Cambridge University Press, 1997), 637–743.
46 Ibid., 681.
47 Ibid., 691.
48 Ibid., 672.
49 Ibid., 681.
50 Khalid M. Tarbiyeh, *The Tarbiyeh Tribe Throughout History* (Jerusalem: Dar al-Aytam, 1976 [Arabic]), 92–93.
51 Ibid., 93.
52 Muhammad A. Al-Suwaidi, *On Genealogy: The Gold Bars to Knowing the Arabian Tribes* (Egypt: Al-Maktaba al-Tijaria al-Kubra, 2008 [Arabic]), 34, 101; Ahmad Ibn Y. Al-Baladhuri, *Lineage of the Nobles*,

vol. 5 (Jerusalem: Hebrew University Press, 1958 [Arabic]); Zakariyya, *Tribes of Al-Sham*, 69.

53 Tarbiyeh, *Tarbiyeh Tribe*, 48; Adil Manna', *Sanjak of Jerusalem between Two Invasions (1798–1831): Administration and Society* (PhD diss., Hebrew University, 1986 [Hebrew]); Manna', *The History*, 11–12.
54 Shafiq Juha, Munir B'albak and Bahij Uthman, *The Illustrated History of Lebanon*, Vol. 7 (Beirut: Dar al-Malayin, 1999), 48–50.
55 Tarbiyeh, *Tarbiyeh Tribe*, 93; Manna', *The History*, 12.
56 Ahmad A. Al-Safadi, *Lebanon during the Reign of the Amir Fakhr al-Din al-Ma'ani II* (Beirut: al-Jami'ah al-Lubnaniya, 1969 [Arabic]), 140–201.
57 Ibid., 140.
58 Tarbiyeh, *Tarbiyeh Tribe*, 72–75; Al-Safadi, *Lebanon*, 198.
59 Tarbiyeh, *Tarbiyeh Tribe*, 102.
60 Muhammad Kh. Tarbiyeh. Interview by author. Sakhnin, 14 July 2014. He rejected the version claiming that members of Tarbiyeh tribe were of Fellahin or Turkmen origin.
61 Oppenheim, *The Bedouin*, 28–29.
62 Michael Sabbagh, *The History of Shaykh Zahir al-'Umar Al-Zaydani, governor of Acre and the Galilee* (Beirut: Harisa, 1950 [Arabic]), 15.
63 As'ad Mansur, *The history of Nazareth from its most ancient times to our present day* (Cairo: Maktabat al-Hilal, 1924 [Arabic]), 48–54.
64 Kurd Ali, *Description*, 294.
65 Sabbagh, *The History*, 15–163; Manna', *The History*, 48–75; Sa'id A. Shibli (Ziadnah). Interview by author. Deir Hanna, 30 August 2014.
66 Kurd Ali, *Description*, 301.
67 Jamil Arafat, *From our destroyed villages in the Galilee* (Nazareth: D.N, 1995 [Arabic]), 164; Walid al-Khalidi, *All That Remains: The Palestinian villages occupied and depopulated by Israel in 1948* (Beirut: Institute for Palestine Studies, 1997 [Arabic]), 474.
68 Ziad Al-Zidani. Interview by author. Nazareth, 19 July 2013; Muhammad A. Zidan. Interview by author. Kafr Manda, 13 July 2013. See also Abd Abd al-Halim, Walid Abd al-Halim, and others, *Kafr Manda between the past and present* (Kafr Manda: Local Council, 1985 [Arabic]), 29–44.
69 Ziad Al-Zidani. Interview by author. Nazareth, 19 July 2013.
70 Muhammad A. Zidan. Interview by author. Kafr Manda, 13 July 2013; Qasem Sh. Ziadnah. Interview by author. Deir Hanna, 30 August 2014.
71 David F. Lancy, *Playing on the Mother Ground: Cultural Routines of Children's Development* (New York: Guildford Press, 1996), 1–30, 72–93; Esben Leifsen, "Childhoods in Shifting Analytical Spaces: Cross-Cultural, Biocultural, and Human Ecological Perspectives," *Reviews in Anthropology*, Vol. 38, No. 3 (August 2009): 197–216.
72 John A. Clausen, *Socialization and Society* (Boston: Little Brown, 1968).
73 Pierre Bourdieu, *Outline of a Theory of Practice*, trans. Richard Nice (Cambridge, UK: Cambridge University Press, 1977), 72.

74 James Reilly, "The Peasantry of Late Ottoman Palestine," *Journal of Palestine Studies*, Vol. 10, No. 4 (Summer 1981): 82–97.
75 Herbert Bodman, *Political Factions in Aleppo, 1760–1826* (Chapel Hill: University of North Carolina Press, 1963), 5.
76 Roger E. Owen, *The Middle East in the World Economy, 1800–1914* (London: Methuen Press, 1981), 44.
77 Abbas Mohammed, "The Nomadic and the Sedentary: Polar Complementaries, not Polar Opposites," in *The Desert and the Sown: Nomads in the Wider Society*, ed. Cynthia Nelson (Berkeley: Institute of International Studies, University of California, 1973), 97–112.
78 Owen, *The Middle East*, 43.
79 Yitzhak Hofman, "The Administration of Syria and Palestine under Egyptian Rule (1831–1840)," in *Studies on Palestine during the Ottoman Period*, ed. Moshe Ma'oz (Jerusalem: Magnes Press, 1975), 311–333.
80 Oppenheim, *The Bedouin*, 54.
81 Sharon, *The Bedouin in the Land*, 84.
82 Yehoshua Ben-Arieh, *A City Reflected in its Times: Jerusalem in the Nineteenth Century* (Jerusalem: Yad Yitzhak Ben Zvi, 1977 [Hebrew]), 131.
83 Ibid., 133.
84 Sharon, *The Bedouin in the Land*, 85.
85 Oppenheim, *The Bedouin*, 54; Sharon, *The Bedouin in the Land*, 88.
86 Avigdor Levy, "The Officer Corps in Sultan Mahmoud II's New Ottoman Army, 1826–1839," *International Journal of Middle East Studies*, Vol. 2, No. 1 (January 1971): 21–39.
87 Ma'oz, *Ottoman*, 135.
88 Ibid., 142.
89 Ben Aryeh, *A City Reflected*, 135.
90 Ahmad Amara, "Civilizational Exceptions: Ottoman Law and Governance in Late Ottoman Palestine," *Law and History Review*, Vol. 36, No. 4 (November 2018): 915–941, esp. 928; Selim Deringil, "They Live in A State of Nomadism and Savagery: The Late Ottoman Empire and the Post-Colonial Debate," *Comparative Studies in History and Society*, Vol. 45, No. 2 (April 2003): 311–342, esp. 312; Ussama Makdisi, "Ottoman Orientalism," *American Historical Review*, Vol. 107, No. 3 (2002), pp. 768–796.
91 Ma'oz, *Ottoman Reform*, 129–148; Erik J. Zucher, *Turkey: A Modern History*, trans. Adi Ginzburg-Hirsch (Tel Aviv: Tel Aviv University Press, 2005 [Hebrew]), 69; Bernard Lewis, *The Emergence of Modern Turkey*, trans. Moshe Singer and Rivka Gottlieb (Jerusalem: Magnes Press 1977 [Hebrew]), 60–103.
92 Muhammad S. Taqosh, *The Ottomans from the establishment of the state to the overthrow of the caliph* (Beirut: Dar beit al-Mhrusa, 1995 [Arabic]), 408–417.
93 Carter Findley, "The Evolution of the System of Provincial Administration

as Viewed from the Center," in *Palestine in the Late Ottoman Period: Political, Social, and Economic Transformation*, ed. David Kushner (Jerusalem: Yad Yitzhak Ben Zvi, 1986), 5.
94 Haim Gerber, "A New Look at the Tanzimat: The Case of the Province of Jerusalem," in *Palestine in the Late Ottoman Period: Political, Social, and Economic Transformation*, ed. David Kushner (Jerusalem: Yad Yitzhak Ben Zvi, 1986), 31.
95 Findley, "Evolution," 3–29; Iris Agmon, "The Bedouin Tribes of the Hula and Baysan Valleys at the End of Ottoman Rule," *Cathedra*, Vol. 45, No. 1 (September 1987 [Hebrew]), 88; Emile Touma, *Palestine in the Ottoman Period* (Al-Quds: Dar al-Fajr, 1983 [Arabic]), 106.
96 Awad, *The Ottoman Administration*, 159.
97 Deringil, "They Live," 311–342; Avci, "The Application," 970.
98 Ahmad Amara, "Beyond Stereotypes of Bedouins as 'Nomads' and 'Savages': Rethinking the Bedouin in Ottoman Southern Palestine, 1875–1900," *Journal of Holy Land and Palestine Studies*, Vol. 15, No. 1 (May 2016): 59–77.
99 Ibid., 61.
100 Amara, "Civilizational Exceptions," 915–941.
101 Ibid., 920.
102 Serif Mardin, "Center-Periphery Relations: A Key to Turkish Politics?" *Daedalus*, Vol. 102, No.1 (Winter 1973): 169–190.
103 See also the definition of this term "Culturism" in Oxford Dictionary: "Belief in the relative superiority or inferiority of certain cultures; discrimination or prejudice based on assumptions about culture," https://www.lexico.com/definition/culturism.
104 See Michael F. Brown, "Cultural Relativism 2.0," *Current Anthropology*, Vol. 49, No. 3 (June 2008): 363–383.
105 Amara, "Civilizational Exceptions," 919.
106 Frantzman and Kark, "Bedouin Settlement," 5; Clinton Bailey, "The Ottomans and the Bedouin Tribes of the Negev," in *Ottoman Palestine, 1800–1914: Studies in Economic and Social History*, ed. Gad G. Gilbar (Leiden: E. J. Brill, 1990), 321–332.
107 Arif Al-Arif, *The History of Beersheba and its Confederations* (Cairo: Madbuli Library, 1934).
108 Amara, "Beyond Stereotypes," 66.
109 Ibid., 67.
110 Dotan Halevy, "Drinking (Beer) from the Sea of Gaza: The Rise and Fall of Gaza's Maritime Trade in the Late Ottoman Period," *The New East*, Vol. 55 (2016 [Hebrew]), 35–59.
111 Yosef Ben-David and Gideon Kressel, "The Bedouin Market: The Cornerstone of Beer Sheba," *Cathedra*, Vol. 77, No. 1 (October 1997 [Hebrew]), 39–65.
112 Halevy, "Drinking (Beer)," 41.
113 Muhammad R. Al-Tamimi and Muhammad Bahjat, *The Province of*

Notes to Chapter 1

Beirut: Its Southern Part: The sub-districts of Beirut, Acre, and Nablus (Beirut: Dar Lahd Khatir, 1987 [Arabic]), 395–415.
114 Ibid., 400; Agmon, "The Bedouin Tribes," 97.
115 Similar to the Bedouin market in Beer Sheva. See Ben David and Kressel, "The Bedouin Market," 39–55; Halevy, "Drinking (Beer)," 35–59; it is like other places in the Middle East; see also Bates, *Role*, 109–131.
116 Ottoman Empire, Shura Council, "Lands of Al-Hanadi tribe," (Istanbul: OSA, 1874–1907), File No. DH-ID, 2/135/43[Ottoman].
117 Ibid.
118 Muhammad S. Al-Abbadi, "Aqil Agha al-Hasi (1820–1870)," *Eternal from History* (Amman: Jam'iyt Aumal al-Mata'a al-Tawniya 1987 [Arabic]), 75–82; Mansur, *The History of Nazareth*, 73–80.
119 Muhammad Y. Sawaed, *The Bedouins in Palestine: The Ottoman Period, 1516–1914* (Amman: Zahran Press, 2008 [Arabic]), 139–158.
120 Ibid., 140.
121 Al-Tamimi and Bahjat, *The Province of Beirut*, 397–401.
122 Halevy, "Drinking (Beer)," 35–59; Marx, *The Bedouin Society*, 68.
123 The villages: Shuna (southern Safed), Nuqib (named after the Bedouins who came from the Naqab/Negev, east of Tiberias), Al-Safa, Ashrafia, Al-Khunayzir, Umm 'Ajara, Al-Hamra, Al-Ghazzawiyya, Frunh (in Besan Valley), Al-Mansi (Baniha, Turkmen, on southern Mount Carmel). See Seth J. Frantzman, *The Arab Settlement of Late Ottoman and Mandatory Palestine: New Village Formation and Settlement Fixation, 1871–1948* (PhD dissertation Hebrew University, 2010), 190; Claude. R. Conder and Horatio H. Kitchener, *The Survey of Western Palestine: Memoirs of the Topography, Orography, Hydrography, and Archaeology*, Vol. 1, London: Committee of the Palestine Exploration, 1881, Map; Frantzman and Kark, "Bedouin Settlement", 11.
124 Agmon, "The Bedouin Tribes," 100; Al-Arif, *The History of Beer Sheva*, 31; Avci, "The Application," 969.
125 Between 5,000 and 8,000 Jews immigrated to Palestine, see: Yehoshua Kaniel, "The Size of the Negative Immigration from Palestine in the First and Second *Aliyot* (1882–1914)," *Cathedra*, Vol. 73, No. 1 (January 1994 [Hebrew]): 115–138.
126 Map prepared by the author, which was edited in accordance with the literature reviewed in this book; see also Mazarib, "The Settlement," 125.
127 For further details, see Umar al-Barghouti and Khalil Totah, *The History of Palestine* (Cairo: Al-Thaqafa al-Diniya, 2001 [Arabic]), 236–241; Marwan al-Madi, *Ijzim village: The white dove* (Damascus: Al-Ahali, 1996 [Arabic]), 74; Labyeb Qudsiya, *Ijzim village in Haifa district* (Amman: Dar Wael Lil-Nasher, 2010 [Arabic]). Efrat Ben-Ze'ev, "The Palestinian Village of Ijzim in 1948: A Historical-Anthropological View," *The New East*, Vol. 43 (2002 [Hebrew]), 65–82.
128 Ottoman Empire, Shura Council, "Lands of Al-Hanadi tribe," (Istanbul: OSA, 1874–1907), file No. DH-ID, 2/135/43.

129 Alexander Scholch, "The Decline of Local Power in Palestine After 1856: The Case of Aqil Aga," *Die Welt des Islamic*, Vol. 23, No. 1 (April 1984): 458–475.
130 Mansur, *The History of Nazareth*, 73–74; Mustafa Al-Dabbagh, *Encyclopedia: Palestine, Our Homeland*, Vol. 1 (Kafr Qar'a: Dar al-Shafq, 1988 [Arabic]), 180.
131 William F. Lynch, *Narrative of the United States Expedition to the River Jordan & the Dead Sea* (Philadelphia: Lea and Blanchard Press, 1849), 79–282; Mansur, *The History of Nazareth*, 73–74; Al-Abbadi, "Aqil", 75–82.
132 Muhammad al-Hasi. Interview by author. Ibillin, 28 August 2014.
133 Al-Abbadi, "Aqil," 75–82; Shukri Arraf, *Bedouin of Marj Ibn Amer and the two Galilees: Between the past and the present* (Tarshiha: Makhoul Press, 2001 [Arabic]) 377; Sulaiman Musa, "Aqila al-Hasi," *Jordanian Wings Magazine* (Dairah Al-Alaqat Al-Amma, no date): 8–11.
134 Arraf, *Bedouin of Marj Ibn Amer*, 118.
135 Gottlieb Schumacher, "Population list of the Liva of Akka," *Palestine Exploration Fund Quarterly Statement*, Vol. 19, No. 1 (July 1887): 169–191.
136 Oppenheim, *The Bedouin*, 40.
137 Ibid., 39.
138 Al-Dabbagh, *Encyclopedia*, Vol. 6, 389.
139 Arraf, *Bedouin of Marj Ibn Amer*, 339–347.
140 Hussein Shawahdeh. Interview by author. Eilabun, 6 August 2014.
141 Mahmoud Ghazalin. Interview by author. Yafa, 16 February 2013; Musa Ghazalin. Interview by author. Yafa, 26 February 2013, who is the son of the mukhtar of this tribe during the British Mandate until 1948; see also Hussein Khalil, *Iksal is the daughter of the Plain* (Taybeh: Markiz Iha'a al-Turath al-Arabi, 1991[Arabic]), 303–304.
142 Qasem Zubeidat. Interview by author. Sakhnin, 14 July 2014. The term *hamula* referred to Fellahin families.
143 Arieh Bitan, *Settlement Changes in the Eastern Lower Galilee, 1800–1978* (PhD diss., Hebrew University, 1969 [Hebrew]).
144 Yones Masharqa. Interview by author. Nazareth, 23 October 2014.
145 Muhammad S. Al-Taib, *Encyclopedia of Arab tribes, field and historical research*, vol. 2 (Cairo: Dar al-Fikr al-Arabi, 2005 [Arabic]), 266.
146 Arraf, *Bedouin of Marj Ibn Amer*, 377; Al-Taib, *Encyclopedia*, 277.
147 Al-Taib, *Encyclopedia*, 278.
148 Arraf, *Bedouin of Marj Ibn Amer*, 377; Mansur, *The History of Nazareth*, 204; Al-Abbadi, "Aqil," 75–82.
149 This figure shows a Bedouin district in the Wadi al-Saki'a neighborhood; you can also see the fortress of Zahir Al-Umar in the background. Photo processed by the author.
150 Anis Karawi, director of Shafa-Amer's archive, photographs, and architecture box.
151 See also Medzini, *The Distribution*, 33.

152 Arraf, *Bedouin of Marj Ibn Amer*, 163.
153 Khalid N'arani. Interview by author. Bussmat Tab'un, 17 May 2015; Al-Dabbagh, *Encyclopedia*, Vol. 3, 130.
154 Muhammad A. Masarwa. Interview by author. Hajajra, 25 July 2014.
155 See also Yosef Ben-David and Amnon Barkai, *The Bedouin in Northern Israel as Reflected by Changes* (Jerusalem: Ariel Press, 2012 [Hebrew]), 126.
156 Yazid Zubeidat. Interview by author. Bussmat Tab'un, 24 April 2015.
157 Yosef Waschitz, *The Arabs of Palestine* (Jerusalem: Sifriat Poalim, 1947 [Hebrew]), 71.
158 Shimoni, *The Arabs*, 132.
159 Turkey, *Salanameh* (Ottoman Administrative Yearbook) *Wilayat* Syria, Vol. 3 (Haifa: University of Haifa: Abba Hushi Archives, 1871), 237–250.
160 Ibid., upon which Schumacher also relied in his 1887 estimate. See Schumacher, "Population list of the Liva of Akka," 169–191.
161 Awad, *The Ottoman Administration*, 341.
162 Tarbiyeh, *Tarbiyeh Tribe*, 48; Nassir Tarbiyeh. Interview by author. Sakhnin, 6 June 2013; Muhammad Kh. Tarbiyeh. Interview by author. Sakhnin, 14 July 2014; Saleh O. Hujeirat. Interview by author. Shafa-Amer, 10 July 2014; Awad Al-Muhameidat. Interview by author. Shafa-Amer, 18 September 2014. See also Schumacher, "Population list of the Liva of Akka," 169–191.
163 Khalid N'arani. Interview by author. Bussmat Tab'un, 17 May 2015; Muhammad A. Masarwa. Interview by author. Hajajra, 25 July 2014.
164 Medzini, "Bedouin," 553; Ben David, *The Bedouin in Israel*, 66; Ashkenazi, *The Bedouin*, 52.

2 Galilee Bedouin under British Rule, 1918–1948

1 Note that Britain conquered Palestine in October 1917. This occupation put an end to Ottoman rule after 402 years, and after completion of occupation (in September 1918), a temporary British military government was imposed in Palestine. In 1920 (San Remo Committee), the League of Nations granted the British a mandate to rule Palestine. The Mandate was characterized as a civilian government entrusted to the British High Commissioner, whose seat was in Jerusalem.
2 Robert S. G. Fletcher, *British Imperialism and "The Tribal Question": Desert Administration and Nomadic Societies in the Middle East, 1919–1936* (Oxford: Oxford University Press, 2015), 282.
3 Cecil J. Edmonds, report JQ1825.M4, Box 3, File 1, *Middle East Centre Archive* (MECA), St Antony's College, Oxford, 1928.
4 John B. Glubb, "a letter from Glubb to Kitching [in the home office]," J. B. Glubb collection, *MECA*, 5 June 1926.
5 Amin Sa'id, *The Great Arab Revolt: A Detailed History of the Arab Cause in a Quarter Century*, Vol. 2 (Cairo: Maktabat Madbuli, 1990 [Arabic]).
6 In the McMahon–Hussein Correspondence (1915–1916), Hussein sets out

the borders of one large Arab kingdom that includes the Arabian Peninsula (with the exception of Aden port area in Yemen), Iraq, Syria (including Lebanon), and Palestine, in fact the entire region inhabited by Arabs at that time. Also, Sharif Hussein demanded of the British to be appointed as king of the new Arab kingdom, and to be called "King of the Arabs".

7 The San Remo Conference (1920), signed on 16 May 1916, approved the Sykes–Picot Agreement between France and Britain for partition of the Arab region. On 24 April 1920, the Conference decided to grant Britain Mandatory (civil) rule over Palestine, part of which was separated in 1922 and included Transjordan, which became independent in 1947 and changed its name to the Hashemite Kingdom of Jordan.

8 Zvi Elpeleg, *The Disturbances of 1936–1939: Riots? Or Rebellion?* (Tel Aviv: Shiloah Institute, 1979 [Hebrew]); Nakdimon Rogel, *Tel Hai: A Front without a Rear* (Tel Aviv: Yariv-Hadar, 1979 [Hebrew]). IDF, "A Review of Arab Villages in the Galilee," *HHA* (Tel Aviv, 1948 [Hebrew]), file no. 105/226.

9 Subhi Yasin, *Guerilla Warfare in Palestine* (Cairo: Dar al-Katab al-Arabi, 1967 [Arabic]).

10 Ibid., 24–25.

11 Emile Touma, *The origins of the Palestinian cause* (Haifa: M'ahad Emile Touma, 1995 [Arabic]).

12 Mustafa Kabha and Nimer Sarhan, *A Record of Leaders, Revolutionaries and Volunteers in the Revolt, 1936–1939* (Kafr Qara: Maktabat Al-Huda'a, 2009 [Arabic]).

13 Mustafa Tlass, *The Great Arab Revolt* (Damascus: Dar Tlass, 1984 [Arabic]), 231–246. For further details, see Edward T. Lawrence, *Seven Pillars of Wisdom: A Triumph* (New York: Doubleday Doran, 1938), 99–101.

14 Al-Fadl tribe originated in Iraq. In the 15th century, some of this tribe moved to the Golan Heights, and from there some reached the Marj Ibn Amer. See Sawaed, *The Bedouin in Palestine*, 31; Mahmoud Fadeli. Interview by author. Al-Jadida-Al-Makr, 21 July 2014.

15 George Antonius, *The Arab Awakening: The Story of the Arab National Movement* (Beirut: Dar al-Elem Lilmlayein, 1978 [Arabic]), 320.

16 Rogel, *Tel Hai*, 94–97.

17 Yasin, *Guerilla Warfare*, 75–76; Kabha and Sarhan, *A Record of leaders*, 74.

18 Baruch Kimmerling and Joel S. Migdal, *Palestine: The Making of a People* (Cambridge, MA: Harvard University Press, 1993), 108; John Marlowe, *Rebellion in Palestine* (London: Cresset Press, 1946), 147.

19 Subhi Yasin, *The Great Arab Revolt in Palestine, 1936–1939* (Cairo: Dar Al-Nhada Ll-tiba'a, 1967), 34.

20 Kimmerling and Migdal, *Palestine*, 111.

21 Yasin, *The Great Arab Revolt*, 63.

22 Ibid., 50.

23 Ezra Danin, *Documents and portraits from the archives of the Arab gangs, 1936–1939* (Jerusalem: Magnes, 1981 [1944, Hebrew]), 16–17.
24 Government of Palestine, "Kadoorie Agricultural School, 20 August 1933," *VMA* (Beit Shean [Hebrew]) Physical Identification (PI): 560/313/77.
25 Government of Palestine, "Arab Higher Committee: Sarona Lands," *SAI*, PI: P/320/28.
26 Bitan, *Settlement Changes*, 80.
27 Ben David, *The Bedouin in Israel*, 66.
28 Falah, "The Evolution," 397–410.
29 Fletcher, *British Imperialism and "The Tribal Question,"* 232.
30 Ibid., 233.
31 Eugene Rogan, "Neither Pro-Zionist nor Pro-Arab but Pro-Empire: A Reassessment of British Policy in the Palestine Mandate," https://balfourproject.org/eugene-rogan.
32 Government of Palestine, "The Laws of Palestine: Border Pass Agreement," *NAL*, CO 733/60/5-20.
33 Government of Palestine, "Border crossings," *SAI*, PI: M 4349/34.
34 Ibid.
35 Government of Palestine, "The Laws of Palestine: Expropriation Land Ordinance, 1926," *NAL*, CO 733/60/59971; Government of Palestine, "Land Settlement Ordinances, 1928–1930," *Official Gazette of the Government of Palestine* (Jerusalem: Government of Palestine Press, May 1932), 323.
36 Government of Palestine, "Public works, civil Haifa," *SAI*, PI: RG/12/M/5141/2.
37 Government of Palestine, "Expropriation land for public purposes," *VMA*, PI: 560/313/60.
38 Government of Palestine, "The Laws of Palestine: Forests Ordinance, 1926," *NAL*, CO 733/60/5-20; Government of Palestine, "Forests Ordinance, 1926," *Official Gazette of the Government of Palestine* (Jerusalem: Government of Palestine Press, September 1926).
39 Government of Palestine, "The Laws of Palestine: Forests Ordinance, 1926," *NAL*, CO 733/60/5-20.
40 Ibid.
41 Ahmed Mazarib. Interview by author. Zarzir, 14 July 2015; Muhammad A. Masarwa. Interview by author. Hajajra, 25 July 2014.
42 Government of Palestine, "The Laws of Palestine: Collective Punishments Ordinances," *NAL*, CO 733/303/3.
43 Government of Palestine, "The Laws of Palestine: Collective Punishment Ordinance, 16 May 1926," *NAL*, CO 733/303/chapter 20.
44 Ibid.
45 High Commissioner of Palestine, "Bedouin Control Ordinance, no. 18 of 1942," *NAL*, CO 733/448.
46 Government of Palestine, "Bedouin Control Ordinance, no. 18 of 1942,"

SAI, PI: 552/15, original symbol: Y/58/42; High Commissioner of Palestine, "Bedouin Control Ordinance, no. 18 of 1942," NAL, CO 733/448.
47 Government of Palestine, "Land Settlement Ordinances, 1928–1930," NAL, CO 733/60/59971; Government of Palestine, "Land Settlement Ordinances, 1928–1930," *Official Gazette of the Government of Palestine* (Jerusalem: Government of Palestine Press, May 1932), 323–328.
48 Ahmed Mazarib. Interview by author. Zarzir, 14 July 2015.
49 Government of Palestine, "Settlement survey in 1928," SAI, PI: 4349/35.
50 Government of Palestine, "Bedouin Control Ordinance, no. 18 of 1942," SAI, PI: 552/15, original symbol: Y/58/42; High Commissioner of Palestine, "Bedouin Control Ordinance, no. 18 of 1942," NAL, CO 733-448.
51 Ibid.
52 Agency arises from the actor's knowledge of schemas, which means her ability to apply them to new contexts. Alternatively, to put the same thing the other way around, agency arises from the actor's control of resources, which means her capacity to reinterpret or mobilize an array of resources in terms of schema other than those that constituted the array. See Sewell, "A Theory of Structure," 20.
53 Yones Masharqa. Interview by author. Nazareth, 23 October 2014; Samir H. Nujeidat. Interview by author. Bu'enie-Nujeidat, 6 August 2014.
54 Knesset Plenum, "Law to repeal the Bedouin Control Ordinance, 6 February 1963," *Government of Israel: Knesset Minutes*, Vol. 36, (Jerusalem: Government Press, 1963), 1064–1066.
55 Muhsin N. Sawaed. Interview by author. Shafa-Amer, 10 July 2014.
56 Lewis N. Norman, *Nomads and Settlers in Syria and Jordan 1800–1980* (Great Britain: Cambridge University Press, 1987), 17–44.
57 Government of Palestine, "Veterinary Service, 16 January 1944," VMA, PI: 560/313/09.
58 Government of Palestine, "Abdullah Al-Khair Public ad, 13 February 1937," VMA, PI: 560/313/12.
59 This kind of tax was collective rather than individual. The lands of each village were valued based on the type of produce grown and the expected annual yield. See Assaf Likhovski, *Tax Law and Social Norms in Mandatory Palestine and Israel* (Cambridge, UK: Cambridge University Press, 2017), 56.
60 The Palestinian Pound (LP) consisted officially of 1,000 mils, equal to one British pound sterling. See Government of Palestine, "Revenue tax receptions, 1937," VMA, PI: 560/310/7.
61 The actual rate of the animal tax varied from village to village, depending upon the hardships each village was experiencing. See also Martin Bunton, *Colonial Land Policies in Palestine, 1917–1936* (Oxford, UK: Oxford University Press, 2007), 140–141, 150–155; Roza I. M. El-Eini,

"Government Fiscal Policy in Mandatory Palestine in the 1930s," *Middle Eastern Studies*, Vol. 33, No. 3 (July 1997): 570–596.
62 The rate of the tithe also changed, especially in the 1930s when a series of poor harvests ultimately compelled the British to enact a law to commute and remit large amounts of the tithe.
63 Government of Palestine, "Summons to Defendants, 1946," VMA, PI: 560/310/3.
64 Ibid.
65 Al-Taib, *Encyclopedia*, 93–106.
66 Yitzhaki, "The Bedouin," 88–92.
67 Khalid A. Manasra. Interview by author. Reina, 23 October 2014; See also Arraf, *Bedouin of Marj Ibn Amer*, 197–198; Yitzhaki, "The Bedouin," 88.
68 Samir H. Nujeidat. Interview by author. Bu'enie-Nujeidat, 6 August 2014; Dhahir Nujeidat, *Olive Roots* (Bu'enie-Nujeidat: Al-Madrasa Al-Ibtidayia, 2008 [Arabic]), 3; Arraf, *Bedouin of Marj Ibn Amer*, 350–356.
69 Hussein Shawahdeh. Interview by author. Eilabun, 6 August 2014.
70 Ibid.
71 Jihad Marisat. Interview by author. Iblin, 28 August 2014; Arraf, *Bedouin of Marj Ibn Amer*, 324–327.
72 Oppenheim, *The Bedouin*, 36.
73 Mahmoud Kallam, *Tribes of Acre region: Their uprooting from their land began during the British occupation* (Beirut: Dar Beisan Press, 2016 [Arabic]); Arraf, *Bedouin of Marj Ibn Amer*, 245.
74 Nassir A. al-Fawaz. Interview by author. Eilabun, 27 August 2014.
75 Hussein Shawahdeh. Interview by author. Eilabun, 6 August 2014. See next chapter on members of this tribe during the 1948 war.
76 Arraf, *Bedouin of Marj Ibn Amer*, 267.
77 Khalil, *Iksal is the daughter of the plain*, 304.
78 IDF, "A Review of Arab Villages in the Galilee," file no. 105/226; Hussein Mahmoud Abu Shahab (son of the neighborhood's establisher). Interview by author. Shafa-Amer, 10 July 2014.
79 Mahmoud Ramih. Interview by author. Maghar, 27 August 2014.
80 Ibid.; Oppenheim, *The Bedouin*, 39.
81 Kayid Sweitat. Interview by author. Abu Snan, 17 July 2014.
82 Muhammad Sh. Sweitat. Interview by author. Isfiya, 27 July 2015.
83 Oppenheim, *The Bedouin*, 37.
84 Arraf, *Bedouin of Marj Ibn Amer*, 269–277.
85 These tribes considered themselves Bedouins.
86 Alia Khatib, *The Turkmen Arabs: Sons of Marj Ibn Amer*, Vol. 1 (Amman: Dar al-Jalil, 1987), 31–36; Arraf, *Bedouin of Marj Ibn Amer*, 41–42, and 385–401. In another version, of Frederick Gerard Peake, the Turkmens arrived in Haifa region from Turkey in 1870. See Frederick G. Peake, Peake, *A History of Trans-Jordan*, 373.
87 Khatib, *The Turkmen Arabs*, 37.
88 Ibid., 51–61.

89 Abdallah Said (Abu Kulib). Interview by author. Haifa, 29 July 2015.
90 Arraf, *Bedouin of Marj Ibn Amer*, 371.
91 Yusuf Maslama. Interview by author. Nazareth, 16 October 2014.
92 Oppenheim, *The Bedouin*, 39.
93 Ibrahim al-Hindawi. Interview by author. Shafa-Amer, 18 September 2014.
94 Oppenheim, *The Bedouin*, 38.
95 See also Al-Dabbagh, *Encyclopedia*, Vol. 1, 153.
96 Map prepared by the author, who processed new data and added it to the map of Claude R. Conder, *Palestine Exploration Map* (London: Committee of Palestine Exploration Fund, 1880).
97 This data is based on my knowledge of those families above, as I reside in this region. Moreover, I am familiar with the oral history and source of those families.
98 Atef Sa'ida. Interview by author. Manshiya Zabda, 16 August 2016.
99 See also Ben David and Barkai, *The Bedouin in Northern Israel*, 127.
100 Ibid.
101 Eric Mills, *Census of Palestine, 1931* (Jerusalem: Messrs, 1932), 34–44.
102 The estimate was of the general population, men, and women.
103 John B. Barron, *Palestine: Report and General Abstracts of the Census of 1922* (Jerusalem: Ptd. at Greek Convent Press, 1923).
104 Mills, *Census of Palestine, 1931*, 50.
105 Ibid., 56.
106 Barron, *Palestine: Report and General Abstracts of the Census of 1922*.
107 The estimate made for the general population, men, and women over 18 years old.
108 Mills, *Census of Palestine, 1931*, 50.
109 Ibid.
110 Ibid. 56. See also Anglo-American Committee of Inquiry, *A Survey of Palestine: Prepared in December 1945 and January 1946 for the information of the Anglo-American Committee of Inquiry*, Vol. 1 (Jerusalem: Government Press, 1947), 148.
111 Government of Palestine, "The Laws of Palestine: Collective Punishments," *NAL*, CO 761/344/chapter 20; Mills, *Census of Palestine, 1931*, 18.
112 Ibid; see also Medzini, *The Distribution*, 27.
113 Shimoni, *The Arabs*, 153, in the footnote.
114 The concept of "Nomadic Bedouin" during the British Mandate was mainly: Bedouins who migrate for short distances, e.g., from their permanent residence (*dirah*) to their pastures, according to the seasons of the year.
115 Roger Owen, "Economic Development in Mandatory Palestine 1918–1948," in *The Palestinian economy: Studies in development under prolonged occupation*, ed. George T. Abed (Routledge: London & New York, 1988), 15.

Notes to Chapter 2

116 Anglo-American Committee of Inquiry, *A Survey of Palestine*, 50–53.
117 United Nations (UN), *A Survey of Palestine: Supplement to Survey of Palestine, Notes Compiled for the Information of the United Nations Special Committee on Palestine* (Jerusalem: Government Press, 1947), 12.
118 Anglo-American Committee of Inquiry, *A Survey of Palestine*, 12.
119 Ibid., 1–24.
120 Ibid., 6–8.
121 A letter from Ahmed Musa (Mukhtar Arab Al-Rarmil) to the Arab Higher Committee, "The lands of Arab al-Ramil in Haifa District, 19 October 1946," *SAI*, PI: P/339/26; Government of Palestine, "Arab Higher Committee: Sarona Lands," *SAI*, PI: P/320/28.
122 JAI, "The number of the Bedouin," CZA (Jerusalem [Hebrew]), file no. kkl9/193/28.
123 Government of Palestine, "Mandatory files, 1941–1947," *SAI*, PI: 559/8.
124 IDF, "A Review of Arab Villages in the Galilee," file no. 105/226.
125 Al-Dabbagh, *Encyclopedia: Palestine, Our Homeland*.
126 Oppenheim, *The Bedouin*, 39.
127 Al-Khalidi, *All That Remains*.
128 Al-Dabbagh, *Encyclopedia: Palestine, Our Homeland*, Vol. 1, 193.
129 JAI, "The number of the Bedouin," file no. kkl9/193/28; Al-Dabbagh, *Encyclopedia: Palestine, Our Homeland*; Al-Khalidi, *All That Remains*.
130 JAI, "The number of the Bedouin," file no. kkl9/193/28.
131 Al-Dabbagh, *Encyclopedia: Palestine, Our Homeland*, Vol. 1, 197; Al-Khalidi, *All That Remains*, 67.
132 Abdallah Said (Abu Kulib). Interview by author. Haifa, 29 July 2015.
133 Incidentally, the pronunciation "Igzim", rather than "Ijzim" stems from the fact that some of these residents were Egyptians who came with the occupation of Ibrahim Pasha (1831–1840).
134 Al-Dabbagh, *Encyclopedia: Palestine, Our Homeland*, Vol. 1, 197.
135 Ibid., 198.
136 Muhammad Sh. Sweitat. Interview by author. Isfiya, 27 July 2015.
137 Al-Dabbagh, *Encyclopedia: Palestine, Our Homeland*, Vol. 1, 199.
138 Abdallah Said (Abu Kulib). Interview by author. Haifa, 29 July 2015.
139 Al-Dabbagh, *Encyclopedia: Palestine, Our Homeland*, Vol. 1, 200; Khatib, *The Turkmen Arabs*, 25–28.
140 Medzini, *The Distribution*, 37; Abdallah Said (Abu Kulib). Interview by author. Haifa, 29 July 2015.
141 Al-Dabbagh, *Encyclopedia: Palestine, Our Homeland*, Vol. 1, 200.
142 Khalid N'arani. Interview by author. Bussmat Tab'un, 17 May 2015.
143 Abdallah Said (Abu Kulib). Interview by author. Haifa, 29 July 2015.
144 During this period, the Bedouin in Palestine began referring to themselves as "Arab" and less by the word "tribe", as it appears in the written and oral sources. It also gave the same meaning of "tribe". For more detailed information, see documents on the Bedouin tribes in the *Jezreel Plain*

Regional Council Archives (JPRCA) (Kibbutz Mizra: Jezreel Plain Regional Council, 2005 [Hebrew]), file no. 578/01.

145 Al-Dabbagh, *Encyclopedia: Palestine, Our Homeland*, Vol. 1, 202.
146 A letter from Ahmed Musa (Mukhtar Arab Al-Rarmil) to the Arab Higher Committee, "The lands of Arab al-Ramil in Haifa District, 19 October 1946," SAI, PI: P/339/26.
147 Ibid. See also Arraf, *Bedouin of Marj Ibn Amer*, 119–120.
148 Al-Dabbagh, *Encyclopedia: Palestine, Our Homeland*, Vol. 1, 152–153, and Vol. 7, 440.
149 Arraf, *Bedouin of Marj Ibn Amer*, 546; Al-Dabbagh, *Encyclopedia: Palestine, Our Homeland*, Vol. 7, 440.
150 Al-Dabbagh, *Encyclopedia: Palestine, Our Homeland*, Vol. 1, 150.
151 Mahmoud Fadeli. Interview by author. Al-Jadida-Al-Makr, 21 July 2014.
152 Ibid.
153 Al-Dabbagh, *Encyclopedia: Palestine, Our Homeland*, Vol. 7, 149.
154 Kitan Al-Na'im. Interview by author. Tarshiha, 23 July 2014.
155 Al-Dabbagh, *Encyclopedia: Palestine, Our Homeland*, Vol. 1, 146.
156 Kayid Sweitat. Interview by author. Abu Snan, 17 July 2014.
157 Al-Dabbagh, *Encyclopedia: Palestine, Our Homeland*, Vol. 1, 150.
158 Sa'id A. Shibli (Ziadnah). Interview by author. Deir Hanna, 30 August 2014.
159 Al-Dabbagh, *Encyclopedia: Palestine, Our Homeland*, Vol. 1, 149.
160 Ahmed Marisat. Interview by author. Tamra, 29 August 2014.
161 Al-Dabbagh, *Encyclopedia: Palestine, Our Homeland*, Vol. 1, 144–164; JAI, "The number of the Bedouin," file no. kkl9/193/28.
162 Qasem Zubeidat. Interview by author. Sakhnin, 14 July 2014.
163 Al-Dabbagh, *Encyclopedia: Palestine, Our Homeland*, Vol. 1, 150.
164 Sa'id A. Shibli (Ziadnah). Interview by author. Deir Hanna, 30 August 2014.
165 Al-Dabbagh, *Encyclopedia: Palestine, Our Homeland*, Vol. 1, 152.
166 Muhsin N. Sawaed. Interview by author. Shafa-Amer, 10 July 2014.
167 Al-Dabbagh, *Encyclopedia: Palestine, Our Homeland*, Vol. 1, 199.
168 Muhsin N. Sawaed. Interview by author. Shafa-Amer, 10 July 2014.
169 Al-Dabbagh, *Encyclopedia: Palestine, Our Homeland*, Vol. 1, 202–203; JAI, "The number of the Bedouin," file no. kkl9/193/28.
170 Al-Dabbagh, *Encyclopedia: Palestine, Our Homeland*, Vol. 1, 197.
171 Muhsin N. Sawaed, Interview by author. Shafa-Amer, 10 July 2014.
172 Al-Dabbagh, *Encyclopedia: Palestine, Our Homeland*, Vol. 1, 174.
173 Saleh O. Hujeirat. Interview by author. Shafa-Amer, 10 July 2014.
174 Oppenheim, *The Bedouin*, 36; Al-Dabbagh, *Encyclopedia: Palestine, Our Homeland*, Vol. 1, 164 (in footnote).
175 JAI, "The number of the Bedouin," file no. kkl9/193/28; Al-Dabbagh, *Encyclopedia: Palestine, Our Homeland*, Vol. 1, 158–164; Arraf, *Bedouin of Marj Ibn Amer*, 372.
176 Al-Dabbagh, *Encyclopedia: Palestine, Our Homeland*, Vol. 1, 158–164.

177 Ibid., 162.
178 Ibid., 158–159.
179 Ibid., 177.
180 Mahmoud Ramih. Interview by author. Maghar, 27 August 2014.
181 JAI, "The number of the Bedouin," file no. kkl9/193/28; Al-Dabbagh, *Encyclopedia: Palestine, Our Homeland*, Vol. 1, 180–181.
182 IDF, "A Review of Arab Villages in the Galilee," file no. 105/226; Mahmoud Ramih. Interview by author. Maghar, 27 August 2014.
183 JAI, "The number of the Bedouin," file no. kkl9/193/28; Al-Dabbagh, *Encyclopedia: Palestine, Our Homeland*, Vol. 1, 180–181.
184 Government of Palestine, "Arab Higher Committee: Sarona Lands," PI: P/320/28.
185 Yones Masharqa. Interview by author. Nazareth, 23 October 2014.
186 Al-Dabbagh, *Encyclopedia: Palestine, Our Homeland*, Vol. 6, 388.
187 Ibid., Vol. 1, 169.
188 Sa'id A. Shibli (Ziadnah). Interview by author. Deir Hanna, 30 August 2014.
189 JAI, "The number of the Bedouin," file no. kkl9/193/28; Al-Dabbagh, *Encyclopedia: Palestine, Our Homeland*, Vol. 1, 170–174.
190 JAI, "The number of the Bedouin," file no. kkl9/193/28; Al-Dabbagh, *Encyclopedia: Palestine, Our Homeland*, Vol. 1, 202–203.
191 Mahmoud Ghazalin. Interview by author. Yafa, 16 February 2013; Musa Ghazalin. Interview by author. Yafa, 26 February 2013.
192 Al-Dabbagh, *Encyclopedia: Palestine, Our Homeland*, Vol. 1, 174; Atef Khalidi. Interview by author. Nazareth, 23 October 2014.
193 Al-Dabbagh, *Encyclopedia: Palestine, Our Homeland*, Vol. 1, 173; Saleh O. Hujeirat. Interview by author. Shafa-Amer, 10 July 2014.
194 Al-Dabbagh, *Encyclopedia: Palestine, Our Homeland*, Vol. 1, 171; Saleh O. Hujeirat. Interview by author. Shafa-Amer, 10 July 2014.
195 JAI, "The number of the Bedouin," file no. kkl9/193/28.
196 Al-Dabbagh, *Encyclopedia: Palestine, Our Homeland*, Vol. 1, 174; Mahmoud Ghazalin. Interview by author. Yafa, 16 February 2013; Musa Ghazalin. Interview by author. Yafa, 26 February 2013.
197 Al-Dabbagh, *Encyclopedia: Palestine, Our Homeland*, Vol. 1, 170; Samir H. Nujeidat. Interview by author. Bu'enie-Nujeidat, 6 August 2014.
198 JAI, "The number of the Bedouin," file no. kkl9/193/28; Al-Dabbagh, *Encyclopedia: Palestine, Our Homeland*, Vol. 1, 170–174; Muhammad A. Zidan. Interview by author. Kafr Manda, 13 July 2013.
199 JAI, "The number of the Bedouin," file no. kkl9/193/28.
200 Oppenheim, *The Bedouin*, 64.
201 JAI, "The number of the Bedouin," file no. kkl9/193/28.
202 Oppenheim, *The Bedouin*, 64. See also Agmon, "The Bedouin Tribes," 87–102.
203 Al-Dabbagh, *Encyclopedia: Palestine, Our Homeland*, Vol. 1, 185–189.
204 Ibid., 189; Oppenheim, *The Bedouin*, 60.

205 Arraf, *Bedouin of Marj Ibn Amer*, 29–34; Government of Palestine, "Mandatory files, 1941–1947," *SAI*, 559/8.

206 Mills, *Census of Palestine, 1931*, 56: Natural increase in the Galilee during the British Mandate was high. In Nazareth District: 69.4%; Beit Shean: 79.5%; Tiberias: 68.1%; Haifa: 44.3%; Acre: 82.5%; Safed: 76.2%, for a total natural increase on average of 70%.

207 Haganah: a Jewish paramilitary organization during the British mandate, between the years 1921–1948; see IDF, "A Review of Arab Villages in the Galilee", file no. 105/226.

208 Oppenheim, *The Bedouin*, 36–40; Al-Dabbagh, *Encyclopedia: Palestine, Our Homeland*, Vol. 1, 141–202.

209 JAI, "The number of the Bedouin," file no. kkl9/193/28.

210 Ibid., 54–56.

211 According to estimates: of Government of Palestine, Survey: 1922, 1931, and 1945 with weighting with archives, books, and in-depth interviews.

212 Barron, *Palestine: Report and General Abstracts of the Census of 1922*; Mills, *Census of Palestine, 1931*, 56; Anglo-American Committee of Inquiry, *A Survey of Palestine*, 50–53.

3 Impact of the 1948 War on the Bedouin

1 Benny Morris, *1948: A History of the First Arab–Israeli War*. Trans. Yaakov Sharett (Tel Aviv: Am Oved, 2010 [Hebrew]), 15–36.

2 Rashid Khalidi, "Palestinians and 1948: The underlying causes of failure," in *The War for Palestine: Rewriting the History of 1948*, eds. Eugene L. Rogan and Avi Shlaim (Cambridge, UK: University of Cambridge Press, 2001), 12–36.

3 Morris, *1948: A History*, 95, 405.

4 Issah Nakhleh, *Encyclopedia of the Palestine Problem* (New York: Intercontinental Books, 1991).

5 Husni A. Jarar, *The Nakba of Palestine, the Year of 1947–1948: Conspiracies and Sacrifices* (Amman: Dar al-Furqan, 1995 [Arabic]); Al-Madi, *Ijzim village*.

6 Nir Man, *Rock of Controversy: Studies in Historiography of the War of Independence* (Jerusalem: Carmel, 2015 [Hebrew]); Zerubbabel Gilad and Mati Meged, *The Book of the Palmach* (Tel Aviv: Hakibbutz Hameuhad, 1957 [Hebrew]).

7 Morris, *1948: A History*; Khalidi, "Palestinians and 1948;" Al-Khalidi, *All That Remains*.

8 Khalidi, "Palestinians and 1948," 21. He means the fall of the ruling elite: the Husseini family in Jerusalem.

9 Akram Zu'aytir, *Diary of Akram Zu'aytir: The Palestinian National Movement, 1935–1939* (Beirut: Mu'assat al-Dirasat al-Filastiniyah, 1980 [Arabic]), 608–609.

10 Yasin, *Guerilla Warfare*, 142.

Notes to Chapter 3

11 Morris, *1948: A History*, 305–312, 367–404; Al-Khalidi, *All That Remains*, 66–144, 372–502.
12 Yasin, *Guerilla Warfare*, 142–171.
13 David Horowitz, "The Story of Rosh Pina and its History," *Rosh-Pina Archives (RPA)* (no date [Hebrew]), file no. 3.
14 David Horowitz, "Neighbors' Relationships: The Case of Yigal Allon and Al-Heib tribe," *RPA* (8 April 1925 [Hebrew]), file no. 4.
15 Saul Dagan and Avner Kozviner, *Palheib: Bedouin in the Palmach in 1948*, (Tel Aviv: Irgun Chevrei ha-Haganah, 1993 [Hebrew]), 25.
16 Hillel Cohen, *Good Arabs: The Israeli Security Agencies and the Israeli Arabs, 1948–1967* (Jerusalem: Keter, 2006 [Hebrew]), 35.
17 Ben David and Barkai, *The Bedouin in Northern Israel*, 77. The Black Hand was a Palestinian underground organization established in the 1930s after fall of Izz al-Din al-Qassam on 20 November 1935. Its objective organization was to fight British forces and Zionist settlement in Palestine, as well as Arabs who cooperated with the British or with Zionists.
18 Morris, *1948: A History*, 183.
19 Dagan and Kozviner, *Palheib*, 1–79.
20 Ibid., 9.
21 Mola Cohen, "The raid on the Syrian Customs House on the night of 18–19 May 1948," *RPA* (8 April 1925, no date [Hebrew]), file no. 4.
22 Operation Yiftach [*Mivtza Yiftah*] was a Palmach offensive carried out between 28 April and 23 May 1948, the objectives of which were to capture Safad and to secure the eastern Galilee before the British Mandate ended in May 1948.
23 Operation Matateh [*Mivtza Matateh*] was a Haganah offensive launched over ten days beginning on 4 May 1948, with objectives of capturing the flatlands between Lake Tiberias and Lake Hula, the main purpose of which was to expel Bedouin living in the area between the Tiberias–Rosh Pina Road in the west and the Jordan River in the east. See Benny Morris, *The Birth of the Palestinian Refugee Problem Revisited 1947–1949* (Cambridge, UK: Cambridge University Press, 2004).
24 Dagan and Kozviner, *Palheib*, 17–24; Gilad and Meged, *The Book of the Palmach*, 30–31.
25 Uri Milstein and Dov Doron, *Shaked Reconnaissance Unit: Prevention and routine security in the IDF's history* (Tel Aviv: Yediot Aharonot Press, 1994 [Hebrew]), 32.
26 Ibid.
27 Ibid., 51.
28 Ibid., 52; Mike Elder, *Unit 424: The Story of the Shaked Reconnaissance Unit* (Tel Aviv: Sayeret Shaked Press, 1994 [Hebrew]).
29 Milstein and Doron, *Shaked Reconnaissance Unit*, 51–55.
30 Muhammad Y. Sawaed, *Bedouin-Jewish Relations in Mandatory Palestine 1918–1948* (PhD diss., Bar-Ilan University, 1998 [Hebrew]).
31 Ibid., 215–296.

32 Ibid., 278.
33 Moti Golani, *Last Days: The Mandatory Government – Evacuation and War* (Jerusalem: Zalman Shazar Center Press, 2009 [Hebrew]), 80–89; Al-Madi, *Ijzim village*, 104.
34 Sawaed, *Bedouin-Jewish Relations*, 296; Medzini, *The Distribution*, 36.
35 Arif al-Arif, *The Catastrophe: The Catastrophe of Jerusalem and the Lost Paradise* (Beirut: Dar al-Huda Press, 1956 [Arabic]), 79–80.
36 Al-Dabbagh, *Encyclopedia: Palestine, Our Homeland*, Vol. 7, 122–123.
37 Al-Arraf, *Al-Nakba*, 80.
38 Al-Dabbagh, *Encyclopedia: Palestine, Our Homeland*, Vol. 7, 124.
39 Morris, *1948: A History*, 305–308.
40 Khatib, *The Turkmen Arabs*, 84–85.
41 Morris, *1948: A History*, 158; Khatib, *The Turkmen Arabs*, 82; Al-Khalidi, *All That Remains*, 137.
42 Morris, *1948: A History*, 161.
43 Arraf, *Bedouin of Marj Ibn Amer*, 114.
44 Morris, *1948: A History*, 161.
45 Arraf, *Bedouin of Marj Ibn Amer*, 114.
46 Morris, *1948: A History*, 183.
47 Tel el-Husn, Ancient Beisan, northern modern-day Beisan.
48 Ahmad al-Marashali and Hasham Abd al-Hadi, *The Palestinian Encyclopedia*, Vol. 1, part one (Damascus: Al-Mu'assa al-Filastiniyah Press, 1990).
49 Morris, *1948: A History*, 183–184.
50 Ibid., 183.
51 Oppenheim, *The Bedouin*, 64.
52 Al-Dabbagh, *Encyclopedia: Palestine, Our Homeland*, Vol. 6, 498–500; Sawaed, *Bedouin-Jewish Relations*, 289.
53 Muhammad Sh. Sweitat. Interview by author. Isfiya, 27 July 2015.
54 Ibid.
55 Abdallah Said (Abu Kulib). Interview by author. Haifa, 29 July 2015.
56 Al-Dabbagh, *Encyclopedia: Palestine, Our Homeland*, Vol. 7, 586; Al-Khalidi, *All That Remains*, 67.
57 Abdallah Said (Abu Kulib). Interview by author. Haifa, 29 July 2015.
58 Morris, *1948: A History*, 158.
59 Khatib, *The Turkmen Arabs*, 84–85.
60 Morris, *1948: A History*, 158.
61 Al-Madi, *Ijzim village*, 118; Al-Dabbagh, *Encyclopedia: Palestine, Our Homeland*, Vol. 7, 658.
62 Al-Madi, *Ijzim village*, 118.
63 Ibid., 68; Qudsiya, *Ijzim village*, 222–223.
64 Morris, *1948: A History*, 325; Qudsiya, *Ijzim village*, 481–497.
65 Al-Dabbagh, *Encyclopedia: Palestine, Our Homeland*, Vol. 1, 197.
66 Muhammad Sh. Sweitat. Interview by author. Isfiya, 27 July 2015.
67 Morris, *1948: A History*, 169.

68 Al-Dabbagh, *Encyclopedia: Palestine, Our Homeland*, Vol. 1, 197; Al-Khalidi, *All That Remains*, 77–80.
69 Al-Dabbagh, *Encyclopedia: Palestine, Our Homeland*, Vol. 1, 199; Al-Khalidi, *All That Remains*, 101.
70 Jamil Arafat, *From the memory of the homeland: The displaced Palestinian villages in Haifa district* (Nazareth: D.N, 2000 [Arabic]), 143–148.
71 Morris, *1948: A History*, 158.
72 Abdallah Said (Abu Kulib). Interview by author. Haifa, 29 July 2015.
73 Morris, *1948: A History*, 155.
74 Khatib, *The Turkmen Arabs*, 84–85; Al-Khalidi, *All That Remains*, 137; Morris, *1948: A History*, 158.
75 Khadra Banu Rabiah. Interview by author. Nazareth, 16 October 2015.
76 Al-Dabbagh, *Encyclopedia: Palestine, Our Homeland*, Vol. 1, 200.
77 Khalid N'arani. Interview by author. Bussmat Tab'un, 17 May 2015.
78 Ibid.
79 Al-Dabbagh, *Encyclopedia: Palestine, Our Homeland*, Vol. 1, 202.
80 Al-Khalidi, *All That Remains*, 116; Morris, *1948: A History*, 155–159.
81 JAI, "The entry of refugees into asylum villages," CZA (Jerusalem, 1948 [Hebrew]), file no. kkl9/193/28.
82 The number of these Bedouins was taken from a letter from Ahmed Musa (Mukhtar Arab Al-Rarmil) to the Arab Higher Committee titled "The lands of Arab Al-Ramil in Haifa District, 19 October 1946," SAI, PI: P/339/26.
83 Muhammad Sh. Sweitat. Interview by author. Isfiya, 27 July 2015.
84 Ibid.; Transfer Committee, "Arab Refugees," SAI, PI: G 1322/22. Noting that, the "Trans Committee" was formed unofficially by non-Cabinet members of the first government of Israel in May 1948, with the aim of overseeing the expulsion of Palestinian Arabs from their towns and villages, and preventing their return. See also Morris, *The Birth of the Palestinian Refugee Problem*, 312–315.
85 Muhammad Sh. Sweitat. Interview by author. Isfiya, 27 July 2015.
86 Abdallah Said (Abu Kulib). Interview by author. Haifa, 29 July 2015. Notably, the interviewee is from the Abu Kulib family; he moved to Haifa when he was 4 years old.
87 Muhsin N. Sawaed. Interview by author. Shafa-Amer, 10 July 2014.
88 JAI, "The entry of refugees into asylum villages," file no. kkl9/193/28.
89 Arraf, *Bedouin of Marj Ibn Amer*, 119–121.
90 Al-Dabbagh, *Encyclopedia: Palestine, Our Homeland*, Vol. 7, 372.
91 Ibid., 440.
92 Muhsin N. Sawaed. Interview by author. Shafa-Amer, 10 July 2014.
93 Transfer Committee, "Arab Refugees," SAI, PI: G 1322/22.
94 Fawaziah Majdoub. Interview by author. Iblin, 28 August 2014.
95 Al-Dabbagh, *Encyclopedia: Palestine, Our Homeland*, Vol. 1, 152–153, and Vol. 7, 440.
96 Fawaziah Majdoub. Interview by author. Iblin, 28 August 2014.

97 Arraf, *Bedouin of Marj Ibn Amer*, 121–122.
98 Khalid Kh. Sawaed. Interview by author. Iblin, 28 August 2014.
99 Al-Khalidi, *All That Remains*, 485; Arraf, *Bedouin of Marj Ibn Amer*, 596.
100 JAI, "The entry of refugees into asylum villages," file no. kkl9/193/28.
101 Jihad Marisat. Interview by author. Iblin, 28 August 2014; Arraf, *Bedouin of Marj Ibn Amer*, 324–327.
102 JAI, "The entry of refugees into asylum villages," file no. kkl9/193/28.
103 Al-Dabbagh, *Encyclopedia: Palestine, Our Homeland*, Vol. 7, 580.
104 Ibid.
105 Arraf, *Bedouin of Marj Ibn Amer*, 546; Al-Dabbagh, *Encyclopedia: Palestine, Our Homeland*, Vol. 7, 440.
106 Ibid., 367–370.
107 Mahmoud Fadeli. Interview by author. Al-Jadida-Al-Makr, 21 July 2014.
108 Ibid.
109 Al-Dabbagh, *Encyclopedia: Palestine, Our Homeland*, Vol. 7, 420.
110 Kitan Al-Na'im. Interview by author. Tarshiha, 23 July 2014.
111 Ibid.
112 Al-Dabbagh, *Encyclopedia: Palestine, Our Homeland*, Vol. 1, 146.
113 Kayid Sweitat. Interview by author. Abu Snan, 17 July 2014.
114 Al-Dabbagh, *Encyclopedia: Palestine, Our Homeland*, Vol. 1, 150.
115 Sa'id A. Shibli (Ziadnah). Interview by author. Deir Hanna, 30 August 2014.
116 Al-Khalidi, *All That Remains*, 475.
117 Al-Dabbagh, *Encyclopedia: Palestine, Our Homeland*, Vol. 1, 149.
118 Ahmed Marisat. Interview by author. Tamra, 29 August 2014.
119 Ibid.
120 Al-Dabbagh, *Encyclopedia: Palestine, Our Homeland*, Vol. 1, 144–164; JAI, "The number of the Bedouin," file no. kkl9/193/28.
121 Qasem Zubeidat. Interview by author. Sakhnin, 14 July 2014.
122 Ibid.
123 Al-Dabbagh, *Encyclopedia: Palestine, Our Homeland*, Vol. 7, 287.
124 Al-Dabbagh, *Encyclopedia: Palestine, Our Homeland*, Vol. 1, 150.
125 Sa'id A. Shibli (Ziadnah). Interview by author. Deir Hanna, 30 August 2014; Hussein Shawahdeh. Interview by author. Eilabun, 6 August 2014.
126 Al-Dabbagh, *Encyclopedia: Palestine, Our Homeland*, Vol. 1, 152.
127 Muhsin N. Sawaed. Interview by author. Shafa-Amer, 10 July 2014.
128 Al-Dabbagh, *Encyclopedia: Palestine, Our Homeland*, Vol. 1, 199.
129 Muhsin N. Sawaed. Interview by author. Shafa-Amer, 10 July 2014; Fahed Marisat. Interview by author. Tamra, 29 October 2014.
130 Hussein Mahmoud Abu Shahab. Interview by author. Shafa-Amer, 10 July 2014.
131 Muhammad Gh. Hujeirat. Interview by author. Bir al-Maksur, 15 July 2015.
132 Hussein Mahmoud Abu Shahab. Interview by author. Shafa-Amer, 10 July 2014.

133 Al-Dabbagh, *Encyclopedia: Palestine, Our Homeland*, Vol. 1, 202–203; JAI, "The number of the Bedouin," file no. kkl9/193/28.
134 Ibid.
135 Amnon Barkai, "Demography between 1901–2001," *JPRCA*, file no. 578/01.
136 Shukri Arraf, *Kaukab Abu Al-Hija: Its roots in the earth and its branches in the sky* (Kaukab Abu Al-Hija Local Council Press, 2008 [Arabic]), 159.
137 Al-Dabbagh, *Encyclopedia: Palestine, Our Homeland*, Vol. 1, 197.
138 Muhsin N. Sawaed. Interview by author. Shafa-Amer, 10 July 2014.
139 Atta Mawasi. Interview by author. Iblin, 28 August 2014. See also Saber A. Sakran, *Iblin Roots* (Nazareth: M.D, 1986 [Arabic]), 80.
140 Al-Dabbagh, *Encyclopedia: Palestine, Our Homeland*, Vol. 1, 174.
141 Saleh O. Hujeirat. Interview by author. Shafa-Amer, 10 July 2014.
142 Sakran, *Iblin Roots*, 127.
143 Muhammad Gh. Hujeirat. Interview by author. Bir al-Maksur, 15 July 2015.
144 Al-Dabbagh, *Encyclopedia: Palestine, Our Homeland*, Vol. 1, 164 (in footnote); Oppenheim, *The Bedouin*, 36.
145 Al-Dabbagh, *Encyclopedia: Palestine, Our Homeland*, Vol. 1, 164.
146 Ibid., 158–164.
147 Morris, *1948: A History*, 178.
148 Ibid.
149 Ibid.
150 Barkai, "Demography between 1901–2001", file no. 578/01; Morris, *1948: A History*, 179.
151 Al-Khalidi, *All That Remains*, 355–357.
152 Ibid.; see also Suleiman Khawalde, "Changes among the Krad al-Khait tribe in the Galilee, from 1858 to our present," *The Bedouins-Notes and Articles*, Vol. 27 (Sde Boker: Midreshet Sde Boker Press, 1995 [Hebrew]), 24–39. Khawalde assumed that the total number of Krad al-Khait during this period was about 785. Ibid. 33.
153 Yusuf Hajaj (Krad al-Baqqra). Interview by author. Shafa-Amer, 18 September 2014.
154 Dan Rabinowitz and Suleiman Khawalde, "Demilitarized, then Dispossessed: The Kirad Bedouin of the Hula Valley in the Context of Syrian-Israeli Relations," *International Journal of Middle East Studies*, Vol. 32, No. 4 (2000): 530–551.
155 Also called the Tripartite Aggression in the Arab world.
156 Khawalde, "Changes among the Krad al-Khait tribe," 33; Yusuf Hajaj. Interview by author. Shafa-Amer, 18 September 2014.
157 Cohen, *Good Arabs*, 126.
158 Mahmoud Azayzah. Interview by author. Sha'ab, 28 July 2015. Note: 4.2 Israel pounds was worth $1.00, https://documents1.worldbank.org/curated/en/325221468285341444/text/multi0page.txt

159 Khawalde, "Changes among the Krad al-Khait tribe," 33; Yusuf Hajaj. Interview by author. Shafa-Amer, 18 September 2014.
160 See Map 2.1, which shows the Bedouin tribes' locations in this region.
161 Dawn Chatty, "Changing Sex Roles in Bedouin Society in Syria and Lebanon," in *Women in the Muslim World*, eds. Lois Beck and Nikki Keddie (Cambridge, MA: Harvard University Press, 1978), 399–433; Ghazi Falah, *The Role of the British Administration in the Sedenterization of the Bedouin Tribes in Northern Palestine 1918–1948* (England: University of Durham Press, 1983).
162 Al-Dabbagh, *Encyclopedia: Palestine, Our Homeland*, Vol. 6, 141–235.
163 Morris, *1948: A History*, 367–378.
164 Arraf, *Bedouin of Marj Ibn Amer*, 245–246.
165 Mahmoud Fadeli. Interview by author. Al-Jadida-Al-Makr, 21 July 2014.
166 Awad Al-Muhameidat. Interview by author. Shafa-Amer, 18 September 2014.
167 Atta Mawasi. Interview by author. Iblin, 28 August 2014.
168 Al-Dabbagh, *Encyclopedia: Palestine, Our Homeland*, Vol. 6, 179.
169 Arraf, *Bedouin of Marj Ibn Amer*, 372, 392.
170 Al-Dabbagh, *Encyclopedia: Palestine, Our Homeland*, Vol. 1, 158–164.
171 Ibid., 162.
172 Al-Khalidi, *All That Remains*, 368–369.
173 Al-Dabbagh, *Encyclopedia: Palestine, Our Homeland*, Vol. 1, 158–159.
174 Ibid., Vol. 6, 151–154; Morris, *1948: A History*, 178–183.
175 Al-Dabbagh, *Encyclopedia: Palestine, Our Homeland*, Vol. 1, 151.
176 Mahmoud Azayzah. Interview by author. Sha'ab, 28 July 2015.
177 Morris, *1948: A History*, 178.
178 Mustafa A. Abbasi, *Safad during the Mandate Period 1917–1948: Arabs and Jews in a Mixed City* (Jerusalem: Yad Yitzhak Ben-Zvi, 2015 [Hebrew]), 212–213; Morris, *1948: A History*, 181.
179 Morris, *1948: A History*, 160–161; Mahmoud Ramih. Interview by author. Maghar, 27 August 2014.
180 Morris, *1948: A History*, 160–161.
181 IDF, "A Review of Arab Villages in the Galilee," file no. 105/226.
182 Mahmoud Ramih. Interview by author. Maghar, 27 August 2014.
183 Al-Dabbagh, *Encyclopedia: Palestine, Our Homeland*, Vol. 1, 180–181; JAI, "The number of the Bedouin," file no. kkl9/193/28.
184 Jihad Marisat. Interview by author. Iblin, 28 August 2014; Arraf, *Bedouin of Marj Ibn Amer*, 324–327.
185 Hussein Shawahdeh. Interview by author. Eilabun, 6 August 2014; Atta Mawasi. Interview by author. Iblin, 28 August 2014.
186 Sa'id A. Shibli (Ziadnah). Interview by author. Deir Hanna, 30 August 2014; Hussein Shawahdeh. Interview by author. Eilabun, 6 August 2014.
187 Nassir A. al-Fawaz. Interview by author. Eilabun, 27 August 2014.
188 Government of Palestine, "Arab Higher Committee: Sarona Lands," PI: P/320/28.

Notes to Chapter 3

189 Yones Masharqa. Interview by author. Nazareth, 23 October 2014.
190 Ibid.
191 Al-Dabbagh, *Encyclopedia: Palestine, Our Homeland*, Vol. 6, 388.
192 Ibid.; Al-Khalidi, *All That Remains*, 396.
193 Ziad al-Zidani. Interview by author. Nazareth, 19 July 2013; Sa'id A. Shibli (Ziadnah). Interview by author. Deir Hanna, 30 August 2014.
194 Khalid A. Manasra. Interview by author. Reina, 23 October 2014. See also JAI, "Arab and Bedouin Refugees in 1948," CZA (Jerusalem [Hebrew]), file no. kkl9/329/1–15.
195 Atef Khalidi. Interview by author. Nazareth, 23 October 2014.
196 Barkai, "Demography between 1901–2001," file no. 578/02.
197 JAI, "The number of the Bedouin," file no. kkl9/193/28.
198 Al-Dabbagh, *Encyclopedia: Palestine, Our Homeland*, Vol. 7, 122.
199 Morris, *1948: A History*, 308.
200 JAI, "Arab and Bedouin Refugees in 1948," file no. kkl9/329/1-15; Barkai, "Demography between: 1901–2001," file no. 578/02; Al-Dabbagh, *Encyclopedia: Palestine, Our Homeland*, Vol. 1, 202–203.
201 JAI, "Arab and Bedouin Refugees in 1948," file no. kkl9/329/1-15.
202 Mahmoud Ghazalin. Interview by author. Yafa, 16 February 2013; Musa Ghazalin. Interview by author. Yafa, 26 February 2013.
203 Al-Dabbagh, *Encyclopedia: Palestine, Our Homeland*, Vol. 1, 174.
204 Ibid.; Atef Khalidi. Interview by author. Nazareth, 23 October 2014.
205 Al-Dabbagh, *Encyclopedia: Palestine, Our Homeland*, Vol. 1, 173.
206 Saleh O. Hujeirat. Interview by author. Shafa-Amer, 10 July 2014.
207 Al-Dabbagh, *Encyclopedia: Palestine, Our Homeland*, Vol. 1, 171.
208 JAI, "The number of the Bedouin," file no. kkl9/193/28; Morris, *1948: A History*, 309; Saleh O. Hujeirat. Interview by author. Shafa-Amer, 10 July 2014.
209 JAI, "The number of the Bedouin," file no. kkl9/193/28.
210 Atef Sa'ida. Interview by author. Manshiya Zabda, 16 August 2016.
211 Al-Dabbagh, *Encyclopedia: Palestine, Our Homeland*, Vol. 1, 174.
212 Mahmoud Ghazalin. Interview by author. Yafa, 16 February 2013.
213 Al-Dabbagh, *Encyclopedia: Palestine, Our Homeland*, Vol. 1, 170.
214 Samir H. Nujeidat. Interview by author. Bu'enie-Nujeidat, 6 August 2014.
215 JAI, "The number of the Bedouin," file no. kkl9/193/28; Al-Dabbagh, *Encyclopedia: Palestine, Our Homeland*, Vol. 1, 170–174.
216 Morris, *1948: A History*, 309.
217 Muhammad A. Zidan. Interview by author. Kafr Manda, 13 July 2013.
218 Al-Dabbagh, *Encyclopedia: Palestine, Our Homeland*, Vol. 7, 113; JAI, "Arab and Bedouin Refugees in 1948," file no. kkl9/329/1-15. In this file, it is mentioned that 33 refugees from Al-Subayh tribe fled to Reina. The families are Muhsin Ali Mansur (8 refugees); Ahmed Ali Mansur (2); Hamad Ali Mansur (3); Mahmoud Saleh Mansur (7); Ahmed Saleh Mansur (8); and Ahmed Hussein (5).
219 Ibid; Khalid A. Manasra. Interview by author. Reina, 23 October 2014.

220 Al-Dabbagh, *Encyclopedia: Palestine, Our Homeland*, Vol. 7, 93; JAI, "Arab and Bedouin Refugees in 1948," file no. kkl9/329/1-15.
221 Khalid A. Manasra. Interview by author. Reina, 23 October 2014.
222 JAI, "The number of the Bedouin," file no. kkl9/193/28. According to Al-Dabbagh, *Encyclopedia: Palestine, Our Homeland*, Vol. 6, 491. Bedouin residents estimated in Beisan region to be 6,000–7,000 in 1948 (before the war).
223 Oppenheim, *The Bedouin*, 64.
224 Government of Palestine, "Mandatory files, 1941–1947," *SAI*, 559/8.
225 JAI, "The number of the Bedouin," file no. kkl9/193/28; Morris, *1948: A History*, 183–184.
226 Oppenheim, *The Bedouin*, 64; Al-Dabbagh, *Encyclopedia: Palestine, Our Homeland*, Vol. 6, 495; Al-Khalidi, *All That Remains*, 36; see also Agmon, "The Bedouin Tribes," 87–102.
227 Government of Palestine, "Mandatory files, 1941–1947," *SAI*, 559/8; Al-Dabbagh, *Encyclopedia: Palestine, Our Homeland*, Vol. 6, 494–497; Al-Khalidi, *All That Remains*, 36; Morris, *1948: A History*, 183–184.
228 Oppenheim, *The Bedouin*, 60; Al-Dabbagh, *Encyclopedia: Palestine, Our Homeland*, Vol. 6, 493.
229 Government of Palestine, "Mandatory files, 1941–1947," *SAI*, 559/8.
230 Al-Khalidi, *All That Remains*, 12–24; Arraf, *Bedouin of Marj Ibn Amer*, 29–34.
231 Moshe Carmel, *Northern Battles* (Tel Aviv: Ma'arachot Press, 1949 [Hebrew]), 40; Morris, *1948: A History*, 183–184.
232 Samir Mjali. Interview by author. Nazareth, 16 October 2014. Morris, *1948: A History*, 184, mentioned that the remaining residents of Beisan were estimated at between 1,000 and 1,200, who were expelled to Jordan, and only a few, mainly Christian families, were transferred to Nazareth.
233 Ibid.
234 Khadra Banu Rabiah. Interview by author. Nazareth, 16 October 2015.
235 Ibid.
236 Transfer Committee, "Arab Refugees: third Session, 15 December 1948," *SAI*, PI: G 1322/22.
237 Ibid.
238 Cohen, *Good Arabs*, 120–121.
239 Ibid., 121; Transfer Committee, "Arab Refugees," *SAI*, PI: G 1322/22.
240 Transfer Committee, "Arab Refugees: third session, 15 December 1948," *SAI*, PI: G 1322/22; JAI, "Arab and Bedouin Refugees in 1948," file no. kkl9/329/1-15.
241 Ahmed Mazarib. Interview by author. Zarzir, 14 July 2015.
242 Dagan and Kozviner, *Palheib*, 1–79.
243 Mahmoud Ghazalin. Interview by author. Yafa, 16 February 2013; Musa Ghazalin. Interview by author. Yafa, 26 February 2013.
244 Ibid; Ahmed Mazarib. Interview by author. Zarzir, 14 July 2015.
245 Barkai, "Demography between 1901–2001," file no. 578/07; Ben David,

The Bedouin in Israel, 507; Ahmed Mazarib. Interview by author. Zarzir, 14 July 2015.
246 Transfer Committee, "Arab Refugees: third session, 15 December 1948," *SAI*, PI: G 1322/22.
247 Khalid A. Manasra. Interview by author. Reina, 23 October 2014.
248 Atef Khalidi. Interview by author. Nazareth, 23 October 2014.
249 Kayid Sweitat. Interview by author. Abu Snan, 17 July 2014.
250 Mahmoud Azayzah. Interview by author. Sha'ab, 28 July 2015.
251 Morris, *1948: A History*, 305–312.
252 Said Mahmoud, *The Integration and Assimilation of the Arab Internal Refugees in the Arab Sanctuary Villages in Northern Israel 1948–1986* (M.A. Thesis, Hebrew University, 1990 [Hebrew]), 28.
253 Ibid., 26–28.
254 Hillel Cohen, *The Present Absentees: Palestinian Refugees in Israel Since 1948* (Jerusalem: Van Leer Institute, 2000 [Hebrew]), 27–32.
255 Estimate of the number of Arab villagers expelled to Syria and Lebanon in 1948: 935,000. This constituted 54% of the total Palestinian population of Mandatory Palestine. See more extensively at Salman Abu Sitta, *Record of the Catastrophe* (London: Centre of Palestinian Return, 1998 [Arabic]), 14.
256 Estimation of the Bedouin population's distribution in the Galilee was done by compiling statistics from various sources, including the Anglo-American Committee of Inquiry, *A Survey of Palestine: Prepared in December 1945 and January 1946 for the information of the Anglo-American Committee of Inquiry*, Vol. 1 (Jerusalem: Government Press, 1947), 148. Weighed with Abu Sitta, *Record of the Catastrophe*; Al-Dabbagh, *Encyclopedia: Palestine, Our Homeland*, Vol. 1, 6, 7; Al-Khalidi, *All That Remains*; Arraf, *Bedouin of Marj Ibn Amer*; Transfer Committee, "Arab Refugees," *SAI*, PI: G 1322/22; JAI, "Arab and Bedouin Refugees in 1948," file no. kkl9/329/1-15; Barkai, "Demography between: 1901–2001," file no. 578.
257 Ibid.
258 Medzini, *The Distribution*, 38. Sawaed, *Bedouin–Jewish Relations*, 297.
259 Ghazi Falah, "The Processes and Patterns of Sedentarization," 126.
260 Medzini, *The Distribution*, 36.
261 Barkai, "Demography between 1901–2001," file no. 578/01; Shadi Heib. Interview by author. Heib al-Frush-Rumana, 31 July 2014.

4 Israeli Military Rule, 1948–1966: Chain Migrations and Government Plans

1 Ghazi Falah, "Development of the 'Planned Bedouin Settlement' in Israel 1964–1982: Evaluation and Characteristics," *Geoforum*, Vol. 14, No. 3 (1983): 311–323.
2 The new areas were referred to as *siyeg*. A few English writers spell the

term "siyagh", hinting at an Arab source, as Arabic has a similar word, *sayej*, also meaning "fence"; but the term is Hebrew and means "fencing in" or "delimiting". See Ghazi Falah, "Israeli State Policy toward Bedouin Sedentarization in the Negev," *Journal of Palestine Studies*, Vol. 18, No. 2 (1989): 71–79.

3 Falah, "Development of the Planned Bedouin Settlement," 313–321.
4 For more on this policy, see Arnon Y. Degani, "The decline and fall of the Israeli Military Government, 1948–1966: A case of settler-colonial consolidation?" *Settler Colonial Studies*, Vol. 5, No. 1 (May 2014): 84–99.
5 Mahmoud Ghazalin. Interview by author. Yafa, 16 February 2013.
6 Muhsin N. Sawaed. Interview by author. Shafa-Amer, 10 July 2014.
7 Kayid Sweitat. Interview by author. Abu Snan, 17 July 2014.
8 Saleh O. Hujeirat. Interview by author. Shafa-Amer, 10 July 2014.
9 Kitan Al-Na'im. Interview by author. Tarshiha, 23 July 2014.
10 Muhsin N. Sawaed. Interview by author. Shafa-Amer, 10 July 2014.
11 Cohen, *The Present Absentees*, 45–60.
12 Umar Sawaed (Advisor Mayor of Shafa-Amer). Interview by author. Shafa-Amer, 09 July 2014; Cohen, *The Present Absentees*, 45–60.
13 Khadra Banu Rabiah. Interview by author. Nazareth, 16 October 2015.
14 Yazid Zubeidat. Interview by author. Bussmat Tab'un, 24 April 2015.
15 Yusuf Maslama. Interview by author. Nazareth, 16 October 2014.
16 Ibrahim al-Hindawi. Interview by author. Shafa-Amer, 18 September 2014.
17 Uri Ben-Eliezer, *Trough the Sight: The Development of Israeli Militarism, 1936–1956* (Tel Aviv: Dvir, 1995 [Hebrew]), 280; Baruch Kimmerling, "Patterns of Militarism in Israel," *Archive of European Sociology*, Vol. 34, No. 2 (1993): 196–223.
18 Ben-Eliezer, *Through the Sight*, 285.
19 Yosef Weitz, "Judaization of the Galilee: Sakhnin Areas," CZA (Jerusalem, 11 June 1958 [Hebrew]), file no. kkl/5/24727.
20 Pinhas Sapir, "Judaization of the Galilee: Sakhnin areas," CZA (Jerusalem, 8 October 1958 [Hebrew]), file no. kkl/5/24727.
21 Barkai, "Demography between 1901–2001," file no. 578/07. The ideology of *geulat ha-karka* became a central motivating force in all avenues of Zionist politics. See Robert Friedman, *Zealots for Zion: Inside Israel's West Bank Settlement Movement* (New York: Random House, 1992) and David Kretzmer, *The Occupation of Justice* (Albany: SUNY Press, 2002). The concept of *geula* is a religious one meaning redeeming something, usually the soul or the land from foreign occupation and exploitation. In Zionist terms, the conquest of most of Palestine and expulsion of most of its inhabitants in the areas that were controlled by the IDF during the Nakba (1948–1949) has been and still is viewed as liberating it from its inhabitants and restoring it to its original owners. See Ilan Pappe, *The Ethnic Cleansing of Palestine* (Oxford, UK: One World, 2006); Nur

Masalha, *The Bible and Zionism: Invented Traditions, Archaeology, and Post-Colonialism in Palestine-Israel* (London: Acumen, 2007).
22 Yair Boimel, *A Blue White and Shadow: The Israeli Establishment's Policy and Actions among its Arab Citizens, the Formative Years: 1958–1968* (Haifa: Pardes Press, 2007 [Hebrew]), 201.
23 Tawfiq Toubi, "A Plan for Expulsion of Arab Al-Sawaed and Arab Al-Sweitat," *Government of Israel: Knesset Minutes*, Vol. 36 (Jerusalem: Government Press, December 2, 1964 [Hebrew]), 504.
24 See correspondence documents between IDF Operations Division and JNF representatives in 1958, JNF, "The Concentration of Bedouin in the Galilee," CZA (Jerusalem, 1958 [Hebrew]), file no. kkl/5/24727.
25 ILA, "The Bedouin in the Galilee," *SAI* (1962) PI: 43/6405/13.
26 Medzini, *The Distribution*, 39.
27 ILA, "The Bedouin in the Galilee," *SAI* (1962) PI: 43/6405/13.
28 Ibid. document name: "Illegal Buildings in the Galilee."
29 Ibid.
30 ILA, "The Bedouin in the Galilee," *SAI* (1962) PI: 43/6405/13.
31 These areas, deemed "vital to the state", are mainly intended for establishment of Jewish settlements, such as Karmiel, Nazareth Illit (today Nof haGalil), and others.
32 ILA, "The Bedouin in the Galilee," *SAI* (1962) PI: 43/6405/13. Document name: Parcels for construction in Arab villages.
33 Ibid.
34 Baruch Uziel, "Preventing Illegal Construction in the Galilee," *Government of Israel: Knesset Minutes*, Vol. 38 (Jerusalem: Government Press, November 1963 [Hebrew]), 213.
35 Shlomo Ben-Meir, "Preventing Illegal Construction in the Galilee," *Government of Israel: Knesset Minutes*, Vol. 38 (Jerusalem: Government Press, November 1963 [Hebrew]), 213.
36 Ahmed Sawaed. Interview by author. Al-Rama, 28 July 2015. This interviewee lived in Area 9 with his family, and were transferred from there to Al-Rama, a Fellahin village.
37 ILA, "The Bedouin in the Galilee," *SAI* (1962) PI: 43/6405/13. Document name: Survey and field summaries for Area 9.
38 Ibid.
39 Ibid.
40 Toubi, "A Plan for Expulsion of Arab," 504.
41 ILA, "The Bedouin in the Galilee," *SAI* (1962) PI: 43/6405/13. Document: "Survey and field summaries for Area 9."
42 Hassan Al-Na'im. Interview by author. Abu Snan, 17 July 2014. This interviewee lived in *Al-Zinar* area with his family, and moved from there to Abu Snan, a Fellahin village.
43 Kitan Al-Na'im. Interview by author. Tarshiha, 23 July 2014.
44 Ibid.
45 Ahmed Sawaed. Interview by author. Al-Rama, 28 July 2015.

46 Saleh Sawaed. Interview by author. Al-Rama, 28 July 2015.
47 Muhammad Al-Heib. Interview by author. Al-Rama, 28 July 2015.
48 Hussein Al-Hamdun. Interview by author. Abu Snan, 17 July 2014.
49 Jihad Marisat. Interview by author. Iblin, 28 August 2014; Sakran, *Iblin Roots*, 72.
50 Ahmed Marisat. Interview by author. Tamra, 29 August 2014.
51 Umar Sawaed. Interview by author. Shafa-Amer, 9 July 2014.
52 Salim Al-Na'im. Interview by author. Nazareth, 23 October 2014.
53 Al-Dabbagh, *Encyclopedia: Palestine, Our Homeland*, Vol. 1, 173.
54 Salim Al-Na'im. Interview by author. Nazareth, 23 October 2014.
55 Arraf, *Bedouin of Marj Ibn Amer*, 367.
56 Adel Al-Heib. Interview by author. Nazareth, 16 October 2014.
57 Sa'id Quzli. Interview by author. Isfiya, 27 July 2015.
58 Ibid. Muhammad Sh. Sweitat. Interview by author. Isfiya, 27 July 2015.
59 Yones Masharqa. Interview by author. Nazareth, 23 October 2014.
60 Atef Khalidi. Interview by author. Nazareth, 23 October 2014.
61 Awad Al-Muhameidat. Interview by author. Shafa-Amer, 18 September 2014.
62 Atta Mawasi. Interview by author. Iblin, 28 August 2014.
63 Salim Al-Na'im. Interview by author. Nazareth, 23 October 2014.
64 Ibid.
65 Nimer Al-Na'im. Interview by author. Al-Na'im Abu Grad, 2 November 2015.
66 ILA, "The Bedouin in the Galilee," *SAI* (1962) PI: 43/6405/13. Document no. 155: "Survey of Shafa-Amer area."
67 Muhsin N. Sawaed. Interview by author. Shafa-Amer, 10 July 2014.
68 Anis Karawi (director of Shafa-Amer's archive). Interview by author. Shafa-Amer, 10 July 2014.
69 ILA, "The Bedouin in the Galilee," *SAI* (1962) PI: 43/6405/13. Document no. 155: "Survey of Shafa-Amer area." Appendix given to MKs during their tour of the Galilee, 1962.
70 Ibid.
71 Medzini, *The Distribution*, 53–54.
72 Ian Lustick, *Arabs in the Jewish State: Israel's Control of a National Minority* (Austin and London: University of Texas Press, 1980), 67–70.
73 JNF, "The Concentration of Bedouin in the Galilee," file no. kkl/5/24727.
74 Notably, there were Bedouin who did not agree to the state proposals, such as Arab Al-Na'im Abu Garad (south Karmiel), Ramia, Husayniyya, and others. The reasons for their refusal differed, but most importantly were economic, i.e., in terms of cost/benefit. These Bedouins remained in their locations until the present.
75 Barkai, "Demography between 1901–2001," JPRCA, files no. 578/1-15.
76 Falah estimated this population in 1968 at 10,243. See Falah, "The Processes and Patterns of Sedentarization," 126. This estimate was inaccurate, as it did not include all Bedouin communities in the Galilee, nor

does it include the Bedouin who living in Fellah towns and villages. In addition, the 1961 ILA estimate of Bedouin in the Galilee was 9,267. See ILA, "The Bedouin in the Galilee," *SAI*, PI: 43/6405/13. This estimate is also incomplete, as it did not include all Bedouin living in Bedouin localities, such as the Arab Al-Aramsheh; nor did it include Bedouin living in Fellah towns and villages.

5 Governmental and Civilian Events, 1966–2020: Bedouin Settlement in Fellahin Villages and Towns

1. Hassan Al-Na'im. Interview by author. Abu Snan, 17 July 2014.
2. Ibid.
3. Ibid.
4. Oren Yiftachel, "Land Day," *Theory and Criticism*, Vol. 12–13, No. 1 (April 1990 [Hebrew]): 279–290.
5. For more information, see Government of Israel, "The authorities, their residents, and budgets," *Israel Government Yearbook* (Jerusalem: Government of Israel Press, 1963/4 [Hebrew]), 316–317.
6. Jacob Landau, *The Arab Minority in Israel, 1967–1991: Political Aspects* (Tel Aviv: Am Oved, 1993 [Hebrew]), 45.
7. Boimel, *A Blue White and Shadow*, 186.
8. Emanuel Alenkvh and Shraga Eshel, "Curfews in 3 Galilee villages; one Arab killed; 13 police and soldiers injured," *Yediot Aharonot* (Tel Aviv: Yediot Aharonot Press, 31 March 1976 [Hebrew]). The reporters further reported that Sakhnin, Deir Hanna, and Araba residents rioted and attacked IDF units with stones, bottles, and olive oil cans. Dozens were arrested.
9. Yiftachel, "Land Day," 279.
10. Yeshayahu Ben-Porat, "A retreat to 1948," *Yediot Aharonot* (Tel Aviv: Yediot Aharonot Press, 31 March 1976 [Hebrew]). The reporter noted, "Yesterday's events necessitate an immediate revision of policy toward the Arab minority, and its implementation by new people with a different mentality. What happened [Land Day] should not be assumed to be a passing phenomenon".
11. Yiftachel, "Land Day," 279.
12. Mohanad Mustafa, *The decline of Arab parties in local government: 1978–1998* (Umm el Fahm: Markiz Al-Dirasat Al-Muasirah, 2000 [Arabic]), 36–37.
13. Ben David, *The Bedouin in Israel*, 307–314.
14. See sub-chapter: Government plans for Bedouin settlement in the Galilee in the early 1960s and its implications for integration of Bedouin into Arab towns and villages in the Galilee.
15. Shmueli, *The End of the Nomads-Bedouin*, 102.
16. Khalid Kh. Sawaed. Interview by author. Iblin, 28 August 2014; Sakran, *Iblin roots*, 72.

17　Muhsin N. Sawaed. Interview by author. Shafa-Amer, 10 July 2014.
18　Ali Sawaed. Interview by author. Ba'ana, 23 July 2014; Ahmed Sawaed. Interview by author. Al-Rama, 28 July 2015.
19　Hassan Al-Na'im. Interview by author. Abu Snan, 17 July 2014; Kayid Sweitat. Interview by author. Abu Snan, 17 July 2014.
20　Arraf, *Bedouin of Marj Ibn Amer*, 367; Salim Al-Na'im. Interview by author. Nazareth, 23 October 2014.
21　Barkai, "Demography between 1901–2001," file no. 578/2. Falah estimated this population one year prior (1981) at about 30,295 Falah in "The Processes and Patterns of Sedentarization," 126.
22　This graph depicts natural growth of the Bedouin population.
23　As'ad Ghanem and Sarah Ozacky-Lazar, *The Al-Aqsa Intifada among the Palestinian citizens of Israel: Motives and Results* (Givat Haviva: Arab-Jewish Center for Peace Studies, 2001 [Hebrew]).
24　Established on 8 November 2000.
25　Shimon Shamir, *The Arabs in Israel: Two Years after the Or Commission Report* (Tel Aviv: Tel Aviv University, Moshe Dayan Center for Oriental and North African Studies, 2005 [Hebrew]), 6.
26　Ghanem and Ozacky-Lazar, *The Al-Aqsa Intifada*.
27　As'ad Ghanem and Sarah Ozacky-Lazar, *A year after the October Riots: What has changed?* (Givat Haviva: Arab-Jewish Center for Peace Studies, 2001 [Hebrew]), 26; Lustick, *Arabs in the Jewish State*, 54–56; Boimel, *A Blue White and Shadow*, 82–86.
28　Ghanem and Ozacky-Lazar, *A year*, 26.
29　Eyal Shahar and Amir Gilat, "Al-Sana demands: A minute of silence in memory of the 13 rioters killed," *Maariv* (Tel Aviv: Maariv Press, 29 October 2000 [Hebrew]), 12.
30　Ibid.
31　Amir Gilat, "Higher Committee of Arab Citizens of Israel: The government drowned with blood our just struggle," *Maariv* (Tel Aviv: Maariv Press, 29 October 2000 [Hebrew]), 12.
32　Sliman Khawalde, "The Bedouin Component of the Shafa-Amer Urban Community," *The Bedouins: Notes and Articles*, Vol. 30 (Sde Boker: Midreshet Sde Boker Press, April 1998 [Hebrew]), 61.
33　Sa'id Quzli, *The State of Israel and the Negev Bedouin (1948–2012): Policy and Reality on the Issue of Land, Settlement, and Military Recruitment* (PhD diss., Haifa University, 2014 [Hebrew]), 247.
34　Ibid., 248–249.
35　Shamir, *The Arabs in Israel*, 27.
36　Al-Haj claimed that the Arab minority is undergoing a dual process of marginalization: On one hand, the Jewish majority marginalizes the Arab minority inside Israel; and on the other hand, Palestinians who live on the other side of the Green Line equally marginalize their fellow Arabs who reside "inside". According to Al-Haj, this dual marginalization experience enables Arabs in Israel to define their identities in national, Palestinian,

and civic Israeli terms, without fully committing to either reference group. See Majid Al-Haj, "Identity and Orientation among Arabs in Israel: The case of a dual periphery," *State, Government, and International Relations*, 41–42 (1997 [Hebrew]): 103–122.
37 Dan Rabinowitz and Khawla Abu Bakir, *The Upright Generation* (Jerusalem: Keter, 2002 [Hebrew]).
38 Ibid., 14–16.
39 Mazarib, *The process of Bedouin integration*, 201–211.
40 Rinat Zafrir, "Zeldstein's Tent," *Haaretz* (Tel Aviv: Haaretz Press, 16 March 1997 [Hebrew]).
41 Rinat Zafrir, "The Government will Promote Lone/Single-Household Settlement in the Negev and North," *Haaretz* (Tel Aviv: Haaretz Press, 4 May 2003 [Hebrew]), https://www.haaretz.co.il/misc/1.879777.
42 This photograph shows the Bedouin neighborhood of Wadi Al-Saki'a (Sawaed family) on the outskirts of Shafa-Amer. Moreover, this photograph can be compared with Fig. 5.1 of 1910 in Chapter 1, showing the difference between the two periods (1910, 2020) and due to the addition of the Bedouin population to Shafa-Amer. The author took this photograph on 10 July 2020.
43 The comparison estimate was made between CBSPC censuses in December 2020, with data from in-depth interviews with Bedouins in the years 2013/14/15. This estimate was cross-referenced with 2013 voter registration data.
44 CBSPC, 2020.
45 ILA, "The Bedouin in the Galilee," *SAI* (1962) PI: 43/6405/13. Document no. 155: "Survey of Shafa-Amer area;" Medzini, *The Distribution*, 41.
46 Barkai, "Demography between 1901–2001," files no. 578/7.
47 See chapter 4.
48 See: Government of Israel, "Subsidizing Infrastructure Development Expenses for the Bedouin Sector," *Israel Government Yearbook* (Jerusalem: Government of Israel Press, between 1980–2011 [Hebrew]).
49 Moshe Nissim, "Knesset debate of 12 December 1978, on the Arab sector in Israel," these documents are in *JPRCA*, file no. 572/2.
50 Ibid., 6.
51 In the 1960s and 1970s, military units such as Sayeret ["patrol"] Shaked increased the number of Bedouin recruits to their ranks, and other small subunits were established, such as Atalef and Sayeret 525, which included dozens of Bedouin volunteers. For more information, see Mike Elder, *Unit 424*, 95–102.
52 Barkai, "Demography between 1901–2001," files no. 572/10.
53 See Construction and Housing Ministry, "Multi-year Programs for the Development and Empowerment of Bedouin Communities in the North, 2001," *JPRCA*, file no. 572/7. See also Ofer Petersburg, "Construction and Housing Ministry will allocate 36 million Shekels to the Bedouin

authorities in the north," *Yediot Aharonot* (Tel Aviv: Yediot Aharonot Press, 14 May 2001 [Hebrew]).
54 Construction and Housing Ministry, "A plan to develop the Bedouin communities in the north for 2004/5," *JPRCA*, file no. 572/1.
55 Ibid.
56 Umar Sawaed. Interview by author. Shafa-Amer, 9 July 2014.
57 Randall S. Geller, *Minorities in the Israeli military, 1948–1958* (Lanham, MD: Lexington Books, 2017), 137–162.
58 Dagan and Kozviner, *Palheib*, 1–79.
59 See sub-chapter "Bedouin division into three camps."
60 Milstein and Doron, *Shaked Reconnaissance Unit*, 13.
61 Ibid., 28.
62 State Comptroller and Ombudsman of Israel, "Bedouin Sector Service in the IDF," *Government of Israel* (Jerusalem: Government of Israel, State Comptroller's Office, 2004 [Hebrew]), Annual Report 55A, 129–142. See also https://www.mevaker.gov.il/he/Reports/Report_576/7c2ff7bb-86de-4d5a-9ff5-66647efb17bb/2004-55a-240-Beduim.pdf.
63 Quzli, *The State of Israel and the Negev Bedouin*, 212–214.
64 IDF, "The Bedouin in Israel," *SAI* (1972) PI: 43/6405. Document no. 17093.
65 Quzli, *The State of Israel and the Negev Bedouin*, 223.
66 Moshe Arens, "Civil Rights and National Duties," in *Dilemmas in Jewish-Arab Relations in Israel*, ed. Yitzhak Reiter (Tel Aviv: Schocken, 2005 [Hebrew]), 150–151.
67 Quzli, *The State of Israel and the Negev Bedouin*, 229.
68 Lia Eshet, "The Bedouin Recruitment Process will be Shortened," *BaMahane* [IDF magazine] (Tel Aviv: Israel Defense Forces Press, 1 May 1991 [Hebrew]), 10.
69 *Gadna* [Hebrew: "]: is a weeklong IDF training simulation in which nearly all (Jewish) 11th graders participate.
70 Eshet, "The Bedouin Recruitment Process," 11.
71 Ibid. 131.
72 IDF, *Personnel Division, Population Manager* (Tel Aviv, 2016).
73 As'ad Ghanem and Sarah Ozacky-Lazar, *The Al-Aqsa Intifada*, 1–20.
74 Amos Harel, "The number of Bedouin recruits to the IDF has dropped by more than half," *Haaretz* (Tel Aviv: Haaretz Press, 14 June 2001 [Hebrew]), https://www.haaretz.co.il/misc/1.709309.
75 Ibid.
76 Ibid. 2.
77 Yossi Yehoshua and Shahar Ginosar, "Martial Ethics 101: Soldier, commander suspected in murder: What happens in the Bedouin Reconnaissance Battalion, which has received the President's Medal of Honor," *Yediot Aharonot* (Tel Aviv: Yediot Aharonot Press, 10 September 2004 [Hebrew]).
78 State Comptroller and Ombudsman, "Special Population Frameworks:

Minorities, Youth at Risk," *Government of Israel: State Comptroller's Office* (Jerusalem: Government Press, 2007 [Hebrew]), Annual Report 58A, 561. See also https://www.mevaker.gov.il/he/Reports/Report_293/97177910-9f8c-48c7-8b65-99b36865900f/155-ver1.pdf.

79 Construction and Housing Ministry, "Report of Committee on the Resolution of Bedouin Settlement in the Negev," *Government of Israel: Construction and Housing Ministry* (Jerusalem: Government Press, 11 December 2008 [Hebrew]). See also http://www.moch.gov.il/SiteCollectionDocuments/odot/doch_goldberg/Doch_Vaada_Shofet_Goldberg.pdf.
80 Http://maase.org.il.
81 Tali Stambulchik, "IDF Calls for Bedouin to Join," *IDF Website*, 1 October 2017, https://www.idf.il.
82 IDF, *Personnel Division, Population Manager* (Tel Aviv, 2016). Trend lines are most accurate when an R-value squared (a number ranging from 0 to 1 that reveals the degree of compatibility of the estimated values of the trend line with actual data) is equal to 1 or close to 1. In addition, using the Y equation, the adjustment can be calculated by the least squares for a line at $Y = MX + b$, where M is the slope, and b is the point of intersection.
83 Umar Sawaed. Interview by author. Shafa-Amer, 09 July 2014; Ali Sawaed. Interview by author. Ba'ana, 23 July 2014; Ahmed Sawaed. Interview by author. Al-Rama, 28 July 2015; Hassan Al-Na'im. Interview by author. Abu Snan, 17 July 2014; Muhammad Sh. Sweitat. Interview by author. Isfiya, 27 July 2015.
84 Ibid.

Bibliography

GOVERNMENT PUBLICATIONS AND ARCHIVAL MATERIALS

Israel Government Publications, Jerusalem [Hebrew]

Construction and Housing Ministry: Report of Committee on the Resolution of Bedouin Sedentarization in the Negev, 11 December 2008, *Israel Government Yearbook*: The authorities, their residents, and budgets, 1963/4, 316–317.

Government of Israel: Knesset Minutes: Uziel, Baruch, Preventing Illegal Construction in the Galilee, Vol. 38, November 1963.

Government of Israel: Knesset Minutes: Ben-Meir, Shlomo, Preventing Illegal Construction in the Galilee, Vol. 38, November 1963.

Government of Israel: Knesset Minutes, Law to repeal the Bedouin Control Ordinance, 6 February 1963, Vol. 36, 1963.

Government of Israel: Knesset Minutes, Toubi, Tawfiq, A Plan for Expulsion of Arab Al-Sawaed and Arab Al-Sweitat, Vol. 36, 2 December 1964.

Israel Government Yearbook: Subsidizing infrastructure development expenses for the Bedouin sector, 1980–2011.

State Comptroller and Ombudsman of Israel: Special Population Frameworks: Minorities, Youth at Risk, Annual Report, 58A, 2007, https://www.mevaker.gov.il/he/Reports/Report_293/97177910-9f8c-48c7-8b65-99b36865900f/155-ver1.pdf

State Comptroller and Ombudsman of Israel: Bedouin Sector Service in the IDF, Annual Report 55A, 2004, https://www.mevaker.gov.il/he/Reports/Report_576/7c2ff7bb-86de-4d5a-9ff5-66647efb17bb/2004-55a-240-Beduim.pdf; www.moch.gov.il/SiteCollectionDocuments/odot/doch_goldberg/Doch_Vaada_Shofet_Goldberg.pdf

IDF Personnel Division, Population Manager, Tel Aviv [Hebrew]

IDF Website: Stambulchik, Tali, IDF Calls for Bedouin to Join, 1 October 2017, https://www.idf.il

Personnel Division, Population Manager

Central Bureau of Statistics, Population, Census (CBSPC), Jerusalem

Census, 2020 Agriculture Census, 1981

British Government Publications

Anglo-American Committee of Inquiry: *A Survey of Palestine: Prepared in December 1945 and January 1946 for the information of the Anglo-American Committee of Inquiry*, Vol. 1 (Jerusalem: Government Press, 1947). Government of Palestine, "The Laws of Palestine: Forests Ordinance, 1926," *Official Gazette of the Government of Palestine* (Jerusalem: Government of Palestine Press, September 1926). Government of Palestine, "Land Settlement Ordinances, 1928–1930," *Official Gazette of the Government of Palestine* (Jerusalem: Government of Palestine Press, May 1932), 323–328.

Public Archives

The National Archives (NAL), London

CO, File no	File name
CO 733/60/5-20	Government of Palestine: The Laws of Palestine: Border Pass Agreement, 1926
CO 733/303/3 and 761/344/chapter 20	Government of Palestine: The Laws of Palestine: Collective Punishments Ordinances, 1926
CO 733/60/59971	Government of Palestine: The Laws of Palestine: Expropriation Land Ordinance, 1926
CO 733/60/5-20	Government of Palestine: The Laws of Palestine: Forests Ordinance, 1926
CO 733/60/5-20	Government of Palestine: The Laws of Palestine: Forests Ordinance, 1926
CO 733/452/4	Government of Palestine: Telegrams, 1922
CO 733/60/5-20	Government of Palestine: The Laws of Palestine: Forests Ordinance, 1926
CO 733/448	High Commissioner of Palestine: Bedouin Control Ordinance, no. 18, 1942
CO 733/60/59971	Government of Palestine: Land Settlement Ordinances, 1928–1930

Middle Eastern Center Archive (MECA), Private Papers Collection, St Antony's College, Oxford

File name/no	File name
J. B. Glubb collection	John Bagot Glubb Papers
JQ1825.M4	Cecil J. Edmonds, 1928

Ottoman State Archives (OSA), Istanbul [Ottoman]

File no	File name
DH-ID, 2/135/43	Ottoman Empire, Shura Council: Lands of Al-Hanadi tribe, 1907

Central Zionist Archives (CZA), Jerusalem [Hebrew]

File no	File name
kkl9/193/28	JAI: The entry of refugees into asylum villages, 1948
kkl5/24727	JAI: Weitz Yosef: Judaization of the Galilee: Sakhnin areas, 11 June 1958
kkl9/329/1-15	JAI: Arab and Bedouin Refugees in 1948, 1948
kkl9-193	JAI: Survey 1922, 1922
kkl5/24727	JNF: The Concentration of Bedouin in the Galilee, 1958 Sapir, Pinhas: Judaization of the Galilee: Sakhnin areas, 8 October 1958
kkl9/193/28	JAI: The number of the Bedouin, 1948

Haganah Historical Archives (HHA), Tel Aviv [Hebrew]

File no	File name
105/226	IDF: A Review of Arab Villages in the Galilee, 1948

Jezreel plain Regional Council Archives (JPRCA), Kibbutz Mizra [Hebrew]

File no	File name
572/1	Housing and Construction Ministry: A plan to develop the Bedouin communities in the north for 2004/5
572/2	Knesset session minutes: Nissim, Moshe, On the Arab sector in Israel, 12 December 1978
572/7	Construction and Housing Ministry: Multi-year Programs for the Development and Empowerment of Bedouin Communities in the North, 2001, 2001
578/1-15	Barkai, Amnon: demography between 1901–2001, 2005

Rosh Pina Archives (RPA), Rosh-Pina [Hebrew]

File no   File name
3   Horowitz, David: The Story of Rosh Pina and its History, no date
4   Cohen, Mola: The raid on the Syrian Customs House on the night of 18–19 May 1948
4   Horowitz, David, Neighbors' Relationships: The case of Yigal Allon and Al-Heib tribe, no date

State Archives of Israel (SAI), Jerusalem

File no	File name
43/6405	IDF: The Bedouin in Israel, Document no. 17093, 1972 [Hebrew]
43/6405/13	ILA: The Bedouin in the Galilee, 1962 [Hebrew]
4349/35	Government of Palestine: Settlement survey, 1928
552/15/ Y/58/42	Government of Palestine: Bedouin Control Ordinance, no. 18 of 1942
559/8	Government of Palestine: Mandatory files, 1941–1947

G 1322/22	Transfer Committee: Arab Refugees, 1948
M 4349/34	Government of Palestine: Border crossings, 1926
P/320/28	Government of Palestine: Arab Higher Committee: Sarona Lands, 18 May 1947 [Arabic].
P/339/26	Ahmed Musa (Mukhtar Arab al-Rarmil) to Arab Higher Committee: The lands of Arab al-Ramil in Haifa District, 19 October 1946 [Arabic].
RG/12/M/5141/2	Government of Palestine: Public works, Civil Haifa, 1934

Valley of *Maayanot* Archives (VMA), Beisan

File no	File name
560/310/3	Government of Palestine: Summons to defendants, 1946
560/310/7	Government of Palestine: Revenue tax receptions, 1937
560/313/09	Government of Palestine: Veterinary service, 16 January 1944
560/313/12	Government of Palestine: Abdullah Al-Khair public ad, 13 February 1937
560/313/60	Government of Palestine: Expropriation land for public purposes, 1933
560/313/77	Government of Palestine: Kh/Kadoorie Agricultural School, 20 August 1933

Abba Hushi Archives, Haifa [Ottoman]

File no	File name
DR436/S9	Turkey, *Salanameh* (Ottoman Administrative Yearbook) *Wilayat* Syria, Vol. 3, 1871

Shafa-Amer Municipality Archives, Shafa-Amer

File no	File name
C45	Photographs and architecture

Private Archives [Arabic]

File name	Archivist name
Documents	Shibli A. (Ziadnah) Sa'id, Deir Hanna
Photographs/ architecture	Al-Zidani Ziad, Nazareth

PRINTED SOURCES: PRIMARY AND SECONDARY SOURCES

Abbas, Mohammed, "The Nomadic and the Sedentary: Polar Complementaries, not Polar Opposites," in *The Desert and the sown: Nomads in the wider society*, ed. Nelson, Cynthia (Berkeley: Institute of International Studies, University of California, 1973), 97–112.

Abbasi, Mustafa A., *Safad during the Mandate Period 1917–1948: Arabs and Jews in a Mixed City* (Jerusalem: Yad Yitzhak Ben-Zvi, 2015 [Hebrew]).

Abd al-Halim, Abd and Abd al-Halim, Walid et al., *Kafr Manda between the past and present* (Kafr Manda: Local Council, 1985 [Arabic]).

Abou-El-Haj Rifa'at, Ali, *Formation of the Modern State: The Ottoman Empire, Sixteenth to Eighteenth Centuries* (Albany: State University of New York Press, 1991).

Abu al-Dahab, Ashraf T., *Islamic Dictionary* (Cairo: Dar al-Shuruq, 1968 [Arabic]).

Abu Izz al-Din, Sulaiman, *Ibrahim Pasha in Syria* (Beirut: Al-Muttaba al-Alamiyya, 1929 [Arabic]).

Abu Sitta, Salman, *Record of the Catastrophe* (London: Centre of Palestinian Return, 1998 [Arabic]).

Abu-Lughod, Lila, *Veiled Sentiments: Honor and Poetry in Bedouin Society* (Berkeley: University of California Press, 1986).

Abu-Rabi'a, Aref, *A Bedouin Century: Education and Development among the Negev Tribes in the 20th Century* (New York: Berghahn Books, 2001).

Agmon, Iris, "The Bedouin tribes of the Hula and Baysan Valleys at the end of Ottoman rule," *Cathedra: The History of the Land of Israel and its Settlement*, Vol. 45, No. 1 (September 1987 [Hebrew]): 87–102.

Al-Abbadi, Muhammad S., "Aqil Agha al-Hasi (1820–1870)," *Eternal from History*, Vol. 1, No. 1 (Amman: Jam'iyt Aumal al-Mata'a al-Tawniya 1987 [Arabic]): 75–82.

Al-Arif, Arif, *The Catastrophe: The Catastrophe of Jerusalem and the Lost Paradise* (Beirut: Dar al-Huda Press, 1956 [Arabic]).

Al-Arif, Arif, *The History of Beer Sheva and its Confederations* (Cairo: Madbuli Library, 1934 [Arabic]).

Al-Ashur, Said A., *The Mameluk Period in Egypt and Al-Sham* (Cairo: Dar al-Nahda al-Arabiya, 1976 [Arabic]).

Al-Baladhuri, Ahmad Ibn Y., *Lineage of the Nobles*, Vol. 5 (Jerusalem: Hebrew University Press, 1958 [Arabic]).

Al-Barghouti, Umar and Totah, Khalil, *The History of Palestine* (Cairo: Al-Thaqafa al-Diniya, 2001 [Arabic]).

Al-Dabbagh, Mustafa, *Arab tribes and their descendants in our country Palestine* (Beirut: Dar al-Tali'a, 1979 [Arabic]), https://archive.org/details/20190902_20190902_1906/page/n47/mode/2up.

Al-Dabbagh, Mustafa, *Encyclopedia: Palestine, Our Homeland*, Vol. 1, 6, 7 (Kafr Qar'a: Dar al-Shafq, 1988 [Arabic]).

Al-Haj, Majid, "Identity and Orientation among Arabs in Israel: The Case of a Dual Periphery," *State, Government, and International Relations*, Vol. 41–42 (1997 [Hebrew]): 103–122.

Kurd, Ali Muhammad, *Description of Syria*, Vol. 2 (Damascus: al-Ma ba'ah al-Hadithah, 1928 [Arabic]).

Al-Jabarti bin Abd al-Rahman H., *The Marvelous Compositions of Biographies and Events*, Vol. 3 (Cairo: Dar al-Kitab wa-al-watha'iq al-Qawmiyya, 2009 [Arabic]).

Al-Khalidi, Walid, *All That Remains: The Palestinian Villages Occupied and*

Depopulated by Israel in 1948 (Beirut: Institute for Palestine Studies, 1997 [Arabic]).

Al-Madi, Marwan, *Ijzim village: The white dove* (Damascus: Al-Ahali, 1996 [Arabic]).

Al-Masoudi, Abu Al-Hassan Ali Bin Al-Hussein, *The Meadows of Gold and Mines of Jawhar*, Vol. 2 (Cairo: Al-Amrah, 2007 [Arabic]), https://dlib-eastview-com.ezproxy.haifa.ac.il/browse/book/read/16889/start.

Al-Maqrizi, Ahmad Ibn A., *The Guide to the Knowledge of Royal Dynasties*, eds. Ziyada M. Muhammad and Al-Ashur A. Said, Vol. 4 (Cairo: Lajnat al-Ta'lif wa-al-Tarjamah wa-al-Nasher, 1957 [Arabic]).

Al-Marashali, Ahmad and al-Hadi Hasham, Abd, *The Palestinian Encyclopedia*, Vol. 1 (Damascus: Al-Mu'assa al-Filastiniyah Press, 1990 [Arabic]).

Alois, Musil, *The Manners and Customs of the Rwala Bedouin* (New York: American Geographical Society, 1928).

Al-Qasemi, Sultan bin M., *Encyclopaedia of Islam*, Vol. 24 (Al-Sharjah: Markiz Al-Sharjah lel-Abda'a Al-Fikri, 1995 [Arabic]).

Al-Safadi, Ahmad A., *Lebanon during the Reign of the amir Fakhr al-Din al-Ma'ani II* (Beirut: al-Jami'ah al-Lubnaniya, 1969 [Arabic]).

Al-Suwaidi, Muhammad A., *On genealogy: The gold standard to knowing the Arabian tribes* (Egypt: Al-Maktaba al-Tijaria al-Kubra, 2008 [Arabic]).

Al-Taib, Muhammad S., *Encyclopedia of Arab tribes, Field and Historical Research*, Vol. 2 (Cairo: Dar al-Fikr al-Arabi, 2005 [Arabic]).

Al-Tamimi, Muhammad R. and Bahjat, Muhammad, *The Province of Beirut: Its Southern Part: The Provinces of Beirut, Acre, and Nablus* (Beirut: Dar Lahd Khatir, 1987 [Arabic]).

Amara, Ahmad, "Beyond Stereotypes of Bedouin as 'Nomads' and 'Savages': Rethinking the Bedouin in Ottoman Southern Palestine, 1875–1900," *Journal of Holy Land and Palestine Studies*, Vol. 15, No. 1 (May 2016): 59–77.

Amara, Ahmad, "Civilizational Exceptions: Ottoman Law and Governance in Late Ottoman Palestine," *Law and History Review*, Vol. 36, No. 4 (November 2018): 915–941.

Arafat, Jamil, *From the memory of the homeland: The displaced Palestinian villages in Haifa district* (Nazareth: D.N, 2000 [Arabic]).

Arafat, Jamil, *From our destroyed villages in the Galilee* (Nazareth: D.N, 1995 [Arabic]).

Arens, Moshe, "Civil Rights and National Duties," in *Dilemmas in Jewish-Arab Relations in Israel*, ed. Yitzhak Reiter (Tel Aviv: Schocken, 2005 [Hebrew]).

Arraf, Shukri, *Bedouin of Marj Ibn Amer and the two Galilees between the past and the present* (Tarshiha: Makhoul Press, 2001 [Arabic]).

Arraf, Shukri, *Kaukab Abu Al-Hija: Its roots in the earth and its branches in the sky* (Kaukab Abu Al-Hija Local Council Press, 2008 [Arabic]).

Asad, Talal, "Anthropological Texts and Ideological Problems: An Analysis of

Cohen on Arab Villages in Israel," *Economy and Society*, Vol. 4, No. 3 (August 1975): 251–281.

Asad, Talal, "The Concept of Cultural Translation in British Social Anthropology," in *Writing Culture: The Poetics and Politics of Ethnography*, eds. Clifford James and Marcus E. George (Berkeley: University of California Press, 1986), 141–164.

Asad, Talal, *The Kababish Arabs: Power, Authority, and Consent in a Nomadic Tribe* (London: C. Hurst & Company Press, 1970).

Ashkenazi, Tuvia, *The Bedouin in the Land of Israel* (Jerusalem: Ariel, 2000 [Hebrew]).

Atran, Scott and Eickelman Dale F., "Thick Interpretation in the Middle East," *Current Anthropology*, Vol. 23, No. 6 (December 1982): 705–709.

Avci, Yasemin, "The Application of Tanzimat in the Desert: The Bedouin and the Creation of a New Town in Southern Palestine 1860–1914," *Middle Eastern Studies*, Vol. 45, No. 6 (November 2009): 969–983.

Awad, Abd al-Aziz M., *The Ottoman Administration in Syria, 1864–1914* (Cairo: Dar al-Ma'arif bi-Misr, 1969 [Arabic]).

Baer, Gabriel, *The Arabs of the Middle East: Population and Society* (Tel Aviv: Zohar Press, 1973 [Hebrew]).

Baer, Gabriel, "The Surrender of the Egyptian Fallah," *The New East: Quarterly of the Israel Oriental Society*, Vol. 12 (Jerusalem: Merkaz Press, 1962 [Hebrew]), 55–63.

Bailey, Clinton, "Dating the Arrival of the Bedouin Tribes in Sinai and the Negev," *Journal of the Economic and Social History of the Orient*, Vol. 28, No. 1 (January 1985): 20–49.

Bailey, Clinton, "The Negev in the Nineteenth Century: Reconstructing History from Bedouin Oral Traditions," in *Asian and African Studies-Journal of the Israel Oriental Society*, ed. Baer, Gabriel, Vol. 14, No. 1 (1980), 35–80.

Bailey, Clinton, "The Ottomans and the Bedouin tribes of the Negev," in *Ottoman Palestine, 1800–1914: Studies in Economic and Social History*, ed. Gilbar G. Gad (Leiden: E. J. Brill, 1990), 321–332.

Barkai, Amnon and Ben-David, Yosef, "The Bedouin Lands in the North: A Struggle that Should Not Have Happened," *Ground-Journal of the Institute for Land Use Research*, Vol. 41, No. 1 (April 1996 [Hebrew]): 77–87.

Barron, John B., *Palestine: Report and General Abstracts of the Census of 1922* (Jerusalem: Ptd. at Greek Convent Press, 1923).

Bates, Daniel G., "The Role of the State in Peasant-Nomad Mutualism," *Anthropological Quarterly*, Vol. 44, No. 3 (July 1971): 109–131.

Ben-Arieh, Yehoshua, *A City Reflected in its Times: Jerusalem in the Nineteenth Century* (Jerusalem: Yad Yitzhak Ben Zvi, 1977 [Hebrew]).

Ben-Arieh, Yehoshua, "The Literature of Western Travelers to the Land of Israel in the Nineteenth Century as a Historical Source and as a Social Phenomenon," *Cathedra*, Vol. 36, No. 2 (1986 [Hebrew]): 159–161.

Ben-David, Yosef and Barkai, Amnon, *The Bedouin in Northern Israel as Reflected in Changes* (Jerusalem: Ariel Press, 2012 [Hebrew]).

Ben-David, Yosef and Kressel, Gideon, "The Bedouin Market: The Cornerstone of Beer Sheva," *Cathedra*, Vol. 77, No. 1 (October 1997 [Hebrew]): 39–65.

Ben-David, Yosef, *The Bedouin in Israel: Social and Land Aspects* (Jerusalem: Ben Shimshi Institute for Land Policy and Land Use, 2004 [Hebrew]).

Ben-Eliezer, Uri, *Through the Sight: The Development of Israeli Militarism, 1936–1956* (Tel Aviv: Dvir, 1995 [Hebrew]).

Ben-Ze'ev, Efrat, "The Palestinian Village of Ijzim in 1948: A Historical-Anthropological View," *The New East*, Vol. 43 (Jerusalem: Hebrew University Press, 2002 [Hebrew]), 65–82.

Bodman, Herbert, *Political Factions in Aleppo, 1760–1826* (Chapel Hill: University of North Carolina Press, 1963).

Boimel, Yair, *A Blue White and Shadow: The Israeli Establishment's Policy and Actions among its Arab Citizens, the Formative Years: 1958–1968* (Haifa: Pardes, 2007 [Hebrew]).

Bourdieu, Pierre, *Outline of a Theory of Practice*, trans. Nice, Richard (Cambridge, UK: Cambridge University Press, 1977).

Brown, Michael F., "Cultural Relativism 2.0," *Current Anthropology*, Vol. 49, No. 3 (June 2008): 363–383.

Buckingham, James L., *Travels among the Arab tribes inhabiting the countries east of Syria and Palestine, including a journey from Nazareth to the mountains beyond the Dead Sea from thence through the plains* (London: Longman, Hurst, 1825).

Bunton, Martin, *Colonial Land Policies in Palestine, 1917–1936* (Oxford, UK: Oxford University Press, 2007).

Burckhardt, John L., *Travels in Syria and the Holy Land* (New York: AMS, 1995 [1822]).

Carmel, Moshe, *Northern Battles* (Tel Aviv: Ma'arachot, 1949 [Hebrew]).

Caton, Steven C., "Power, Persuasion, and Language: A Critique of the Segmentary Model in the Middle East," *International Journal of Middle East Studies*, Vol. 19, No. 1 (February 1987): 77–101.

Chatty, Dawn, "Changing Sex Roles in Bedouin Society in Syria and Lebanon," in *Women in the Muslim World*, eds. Beck, Lois and Keddie, Nikki (Cambridge, MA: Harvard University Press, 1978), 399–433.

Clausen, John A., *Socialization and Society* (Boston: Little Brown, 1968).

Cohen, Abner, *Arab Border-Villages in Israel: A Study of Continuity and Change in Social Organization* (Manchester, UK: University of Manchester Press, 1965).

Cohen, Hillel, *Good Arabs: The Israeli Security Agencies and the Israeli Arabs, 1948–1967* (Jerusalem: Keter, 2006 [Hebrew]).

Cohen, Hillel, *The Present Absentees: Palestinian Refugees in Israel Since 1948* (Jerusalem: Van Leer Institute, 2000 [Hebrew]).

Cole, Donald P., "Where Have the Bedouin Gone?" *Anthropological Quarterly*, Vol. 76, No. 2 (Spring 2003): 235–267.

Conder, R. Claude, *Palestine Exploration Map* (London: Committee of Palestine Exploration Fund, 1880).

Conder, Claude R. and Kitchener, Horatio H., *The Survey of Western Palestine: Memoirs of the Topography, Orography, Hydrography, and Archaeology*, Vol. 1, London: Committee of the Palestine Exploration, 1881.

Dagan, Saul and Kozviner, Avner, *Palheib: Bedouin in the Palmach in 1948* (Tel Aviv: Irgun Chevrei ha-Haganah, 1993 [Hebrew]).

Danin, Ezra, *Documents and portraits from the archives of the Arab gangs, 1936–1939* (Jerusalem: Magnes, 1981 [1944, Hebrew]).

Degani, Arnon Y., "The decline and fall of the Israeli Military Rule, 1948–1966: A case of settler-colonial consolidation?" *Settler Colonial Studies*, Vol. 5, No. 1 (May 2014): 84–99.

Deringil, Selim, "They Live in A State of Nomadism and Savagery: The Late Ottoman Empire and the Post-Colonial Debate," *Comparative Studies in History and Society*, Vol. 45, No. 2 (April 2003): 311–342.

Dresch, Paul, "The Significance of the Course Events Take in Segmentary Systems," *American Ethnologist*, Vol. 13, No. 2 (May 1986): 309–324.

Eickelman, Dale F., *The Middle East and Central Asia: An Anthropological Approach* (Hoboken, NJ: Prentice Hall, 1998).

Eickelman, Dale F., *The Middle East: An Anthropological Approach* (Englewood Cliffs, NJ: Prentice Hall, 1981).

Elder, Mike, *Unit 424: The Story of the Shaked Reconnaissance Unit* (Tel Aviv: Amutat Sayeret Shaked Press, 1994 [Hebrew]).

El-Eini, Roza M. I., "Government Fiscal Policy in Mandatory Palestine in the 1930s," *Middle Eastern Studies*, Vol. 33, No. 3 (July 1997): 570–596.

Ellingson, Ter, *The Myth of the Noble Savage* (Berkeley, CA: University of California Press (2001).

Elpeleg, Zvi, *The Disturbances of 1936–1939: Riots? Or Rebellion?* (Tel Aviv: Shiloah Institute, 1979 [Hebrew]).

Evans-Pritchard, Edward E., *Kinship and Marriage among the Nuer* (Oxford, UK: Clarendon Press, 1966).

Evans-Pritchard, Edward E., *The Nuer: A Description of the Modes of Livelihood and Political Institutions of a Nilotic People* (Oxford, UK: Oxford University Press, 1940).

Falah, Ghazi, "Development of the 'Planned Bedouin Settlement' in Israel 1964–1982: Evaluation and Characteristics," *Geoforum*, Vol. 14, No. 3 (1983): 311–323.

Falah, Ghazi, "Israeli State Policy toward Bedouin Sedentarization in the Negev," *Journal of Palestine Studies*, Vol. 18, No. 2 (1989): 71–79.

Falah, Ghazi, "Pre-state Jewish Colonization in Northern Palestine and [its] Impact on Local Bedouin Sedentarization 1914–1948," *Journal of Historical Geography*, Vol. 17, No. 3 (July 1991): 289–309.

Falah, Ghazi, "The Evolution of Semi-nomadism in [a] Non-Desert Environment: The Case of the Galilee in the 19th Century," *GeoJournal*, Vol. 21, No. 4 (August 1990): 397–410.

Falah, Ghazi, *The Role of the British Administration in the Sedenterization of the Bedouin Tribes in Northern Palestine 1918–1948* (England: University of Durham Press, 1983).

Favret-Saada, Jeanne, "Review: Kinship and Marriage in Early Arabia," *Homme*, Vol. 10, No. 1 (March 1970): 107–110.

Findley, Carter, "The Evolution of the System of Provincial Administration as Viewed from the Center," in *Palestine in the late Ottoman period: Political, social, and economic transformation*, ed. Kushner, David (Jerusalem: Yad Yitzhak Ben Zvi, 1986), 3–29.

Finn, James, *Stirring Times: Records from Jerusalem Consular Chronicles of 1853 to 1856* (London: C.K. Paul & Co. Press, 1878).

Fletcher, Robert S. G., *British Imperialism and "The Tribal Question": Desert Administration and Nomadic Societies in the Middle East, 1919–1936* (Oxford, UK: Oxford University Press, 2015).

Frantzman, Seth J. and Kark, Ruth, "Bedouin Settlement in Late Ottoman and British Mandatory Palestine: Influence on the Cultural and Environmental Landscape, 1870–1948," *New Middle Eastern Studies*, Vol. 1, No. 1 (January 2011): 1–24.

Friedman, Robert *Zealots for Zion: Inside Israel's West Bank Settlement Movement* (New York: Random House, 1992).

Furani, Khalid and Rabinowitz, Dan, "The Ethnographic Arriving of Palestine," *Annual Review of Anthropology*, Vol. 40, No. 1 (July 2011): 475–491.

Geertz, Clifford, *The interpretation of cultures: Selected essays* (New York: Basic Books, 1973).

Geller, Randall S., *Minorities in the Israeli military, 1948–1958* (Lanham, MD: Lexington Books, 2017).

George, Antonius, *The Arab Awakening: The Story of the Arab National Movement* (Beirut: Dar al-Elem Lilmlayein, 1978 [Arabic]).

Gerber, Haim, "A New Look at the Tanzimat: The Case of the Province of Jerusalem," in *Palestine in the late Ottoman period: Political, social, and economic transformation*, ed. David Kushner (Jerusalem: Yad Yitzhak Ben Zvi, 1986), 30–45.

Ghanem, As'ad and Ozacky-Lazar, Sarah, *The Al-Aqsa Intifada among the Palestinian citizens of Israel: Motives and Results* (Givat Haviva: Arab-Jewish center for Peace Studies, 2001 [Hebrew]).

Ghanem, As'ad and Ozacky-Lazar, Sarah, *A Year after the October Riots: What Has Changed?* (Givat Haviva: Arab-Jewish center for Peace Studies, 2001 [Hebrew]).

Gil, Eyal, "Between East and West: The Discourse about the Arab Village in Israel," *Theory and Criticism*, Vol. 3, No. 1 (Winter 1993 [Hebrew]): 39–55.

Gilad, Zerubbabel and Meged, Mati, *The Book of the Palmach* (Tel Aviv: Hakibbutz Hameuhad, 1957 [Hebrew]).

Ginat, Joseph, *Blood Revenge: Family Honor, Mediation, Outcasting* (Brighton, UK: Sussex Academic Press, 1997).

Golani, Gideon, *The Bedouin Settlement in the Alonim Hills-Shfaram* (Jerusalem: Hebrew University Press, 1966 [Hebrew]).

Golani, Moti, *Last Days: The Mandatory Government – Evacuation and War* (Jerusalem: Zalman Shazar Center, 2009 [Hebrew]).

Halevy, Dotan, "Drinking (Beer) from the Sea of Gaza: The Rise and Fall of Gaza's Maritime Trade in the Late Ottoman Period," *The New East*, Vol. 55 (Haifa: Pardes Press, 2016 [Hebrew]), 35–59.

Harris, Marvin, "The Cultural Ecology of India's Sacred Cattle," *Current Anthropology*, Vol. 7, No. 1 (February 1966): 51–56.

Heyd, Uriel, *Ottoman Documents on Palestine, 1552–1615: A Study of the Firman According to the Muhimme Defteri* (Oxford, UK: Clarendon Press, 1960).

Hofman, Yitzhak, "The Administration of Syria and Palestine under Egyptian Rule (1831–1840)," in *Studies on Palestine during the Ottoman Period*, ed. Ma'oz Moshe (Jerusalem: Magnes Press, 1975), 311–333.

Hourani, Albert, *A History of the Arab Peoples* (London: Faber and Faber Press, 1991).

Ibn Ghannam Hussein, *Ibn Ghannam's History*. Vol. 2, ed. Sulayman Al-Kharashi (Riyadh: Dar Al-Thuluthiyya, 2010 [Arabic]), https://archive.org/details/hamlaenglish_gmail_20180318_1430/page/n1/mode/2up.

Ibn Iyas, Muhammad, *Wondrous Flowers of the Events of Time*, Vol. 2 (Cairo: Dar Ahiy'a al-Kutub al-Arabiya, 1960 [Arabic]).

Ibn Kathir, al-Qurashi Al-Dimashqi, *The Beginning and the End*, Vol. 1 (Cairo: Dar al-Fajr, 2004 [Arabic]).

Ibn Khaldun, Abd al-Rahman, *Muqaddimah Ibn Khaldun* (Cairo: Jazirat Al-Ward Press, 2010 [Arabic]).

Inalcik, Halil and Quataert, Donald, *An Economic and Social History of the Ottoman Empire*, Vol. 2 (Cambridge, UK: Cambridge University Press, 1997).

Issah, Nakhleh, *Encyclopedia of the Palestine Problem* (New York: Intercontinental Books, 1991).

Jabbur, Jibrall S., *The Bedouins and the Desert: Aspects of Nomadic Life in the Arab East*, trans. Conrad I. Lawrence (Albany: State University of New York, 1995).

Jarar, Husni A., *The Nakba of Palestine, the Year of 1947–1948: Conspiracies and Sacrifices* (Amman: Dar al-Furqan, 1995 [Arabic]).

Juha, Shafiq, B'albak, Munir, and Uthman, Bahij, *The Illustrated History of Lebanon*, Vol. 7 (Beirut: Dar al-Malayin, 1999 [Arabic]).

Kabha, Mustafa and Sarhan, Nimer, *A Record of Leaders, Revolutionaries and Volunteers in the Revolt, 1936–1939* (Kafr Qara: Maktabat Al-Huda'a, 2009 [Arabic]).

Kallam, Mahmoud, *Tribes of Acre region: Their uprooting from their land began during the British occupation* (Beirut: Dar Beisan Press, 2016 [Arabic]).

Kaniel, Yehoshua, "The Size of the Negative Immigration from Palestine in the First and Second *Aliyot* (1882–1914)," *Cathedra*, Vol. 73, No. 1 (January 1994 [Hebrew]): 115–138.

Kasaba, Rasat, *A Moveable: Ottoman Nomads, Migrants, and Refugees* (Seattle, WA: University of Washington Press, 2009).

Kaufman, Gil, "The Bedouin Population in the Galilee: Processes and Changes, from Nomads to Permanent Settlements, 1963–2002," *National Security*, Vol. 4, No. 1 (April 2005 [Hebrew]): 76–97.

Khalidi, Rashid, "Palestinians and 1948: The underlying causes of failure," in *The War for Palestine: Rewriting the History of 1948*, eds. Rogan, L. Eugene and Shlaim, Avi (Cambridge, UK: University of Cambridge Press, 2001), 12–36.

Khalil, Hussein, *Iksal is the daughter of the Plain* (Taybeh: Markiz Iha'a al-Turath al-Arabi, 1991[Arabic]).

Khatib, Alia, *The Turkmen Arabs: Sons of Marj Ibn Amer*, Vol. 1 (Amman: Dar al-Jalil, 1987 [Arabic]).

Khawalde, Suleiman, "The Bedouin Component of the Shafa-Amer Urban Community," in *The Bedouin: Notes and Articles*, Vol. 30 (Sde Boker: Midreshet Sde Boker Press, April 1998 [Hebrew]), 42–64.

Khawalde, Suleiman, "Changes among the Krad al-Khait tribe in the Galilee, from 1858 to our present," in *The Bedouin: Notes and Articles*, Vol. 27 (Sde Boker: Midreshet Sde Boker Press, 1995 [Hebrew]), 24–39.

Kimmerling, Baruch and Migdal, Joel S., *Palestine: The Making of a People* (Cambridge, MA: Harvard University Press, 1993).

Kimmerling, Baruch, "Patterns of Militarism in Israel," *Archive of European Sociology*, Vol. 34, No. 2 (1993): 196–223.

Kressel, Gideon, *Individuality vs. Tribality: The Dynamic of an Israeli Bedouin Community in the Process of Urbanization* (Tel Aviv: Hakibbutz Hameuhad, 1975 [Hebrew]).

Kretzmer, David, *The Occupation of Justice* (Albany, NY: SUNY Press, 2002).

Lancy, David F., *Playing on the Mother Ground: Cultural Routines of Children's Development* (New York: Guildford Press, 1996).

Landau, Jacob, *The Arab Minority in Israel, 1967–1991: Political Aspects* (Tel Aviv: Am Oved, 1993 [Hebrew]).

Lawrence, Edward T., *Seven Pillars of Wisdom: A Triumph* (New York: Doubleday Doran, 1938).

Leach, Edmund R., *Rethinking Anthropology* (London: Athlone Press, 1971).

Leifsen, Esben, "Childhoods in Shifting Analytical Spaces: Cross-Cultural, Biocultural, and Human Ecological Perspectives," *Reviews in Anthropology*, Vol. 38, No. 3 (August 2009): 197–216.

Lévi-Strauss, Claude, *The Story of Lynx*, trans. Tihanyi, Catherine (Chicago: University of Chicago Press, 1995).

Levy, Avigdor, "The Officer Corps in Sultan Mahmoud II's New Ottoman Army, 1826–1839," *International Journal of Middle East Studies*, Vol. 2, No. 1 (January 1971): 21–39.

Lewis, Bernard, *The Middle East and the West* (Bloomington, IN: Indiana University Press, 1964).

Lewis, Bernard, *The Emergence of Modern Turkey*, trans. Singer, Moshe and Gottlieb, Rivka (Jerusalem: Magnes Press 1977 [Hebrew]).

Lewis, Norman N. "The Frontier of Settlement in Syria 1800–1950," *International Affairs*, Vol. 31, No. 1 (1955): 48–60.

Lewis, Norman N. *Nomads and Settlers in Syria and Jordan 1800–1980* (Great Britain: Cambridge University Press, 1987).

Likhovski, Assaf, *Tax Law and Social Norms in Mandatory Palestine and Israel* (Cambridge, UK: Cambridge University Press, 2017).

Lustick, Ian, *Arabs in the Jewish State: Israel's Control of a National Minority* (Austin and London: University of Texas Press, 1980).

Lynch, William F., *Narrative of the United States Expedition to the River Jordan & the Dead Sea* (Philadelphia: Lea and Blanchard Press, 1849).

Makdisi, Ussama, "Ottoman Orientalism," *American Historical Review*, Vol. 107, No. 3 (2002): 768–796.

Ma'oz, Moshe, *Ottoman Reform in Syria and Palestine 1840–1861: The Impact of the Tanzimat on Politics and Society* (Oxford, UK: Clarendon Press, 1968).

Man, Nir, *Rock of Controversy: Studies in Historiography of the War of Independence* (Jerusalem: Carmel, 2015 [Hebrew]).

Manna', Adil, "The Farrukh Governors of Jerusalem," in *Chapters in the History of Jerusalem at the Beginning of the Ottoman Period*, ed. Cohen, Amnon (Jerusalem: Yad Yitzhak Ben Zvi, 1979 [Hebrew]).

Manna', Adil, *The History of Palestine in the Late Ottoman Period, 1700–1918 (A New Reading)* (Beirut: Mu'assat al-Dirasat al-Filastiniyah, 1999 [Arabic]).

Mansur, As'ad, *The history of Nazareth from its most ancient times to our present day* (Cairo: Maktabat al-Hilal, 1924 [Arabic]).

Mardin, Serif, "Center-Periphery Relations: A Key to Turkish Politics?" *Daedalus*, Vol. 102, No.1 (Winter 1973): 169–190.

Marlowe, John, *Rebellion in Palestine* (London: Cresset Press, 1946).

Marx, Emanuel, *Bedouin of Mount Sinai: An anthropological study of their political economy* (New York and Oxford: Bergahn Books Press, 2013).

Marx, Emanuel, "Economic Change among Pastoral Nomads in the Middle East," in *The Changing Bedouin*, eds. Marx, Emanuel and Shmueli, Avshalom (New Brunswick, NJ: Transaction Books, 1984), 1–16.

Marx, Emanuel, *The Bedouin Society in the Negev* (Tel Aviv: Reshafim Press, 1974 [Hebrew]).

Marx, Emanuel, "Economic Changes among the Bedouin in Recent Years," in *The Bedouin: Notes and Articles*, Vol. 11 (Sde Boker: Midreshet Sde Boker Press, 1980 [Hebrew]), 3–11.

Marx, Emanuel, "The Ecology and Politics of Nomadic Pastoralists in the Middle East," in *The Nomadic Alternative: Modes and Models of Interaction in the African-Asian Deserts and Steppes*, ed. Wolfgang Weissleder (German: Walter de Gruyter, 1978), 107–122.

Masalha, Nur, *The Bible and Zionism: Invented Traditions, Archaeology, and Post-Colonialism in Palestine-Israel* (London: Acumen, 2007).

Masters, Bruce A., *The Arabs of the Ottoman Empire 1516–1918: A Social and Cultural History* (Cambridge, UK: Cambridge University Press, 2013).

Mazarib, Tomer, "The Settlement and Integration of the Bedouin into Arab Towns and Villages in the Galilee, 1700–1918," *The New East*, Vol. 60 (Haifa: Pardes Press, 2021 [Hebrew]), 99–126.

Medzini, Arnon, "Bedouin Settlement in the Galilee," in *The States of the Galilee*, eds. Shmueli, Avshalom, Sofer, Arnon, and Kliot, Nurit (Haifa: Society for Applied Scientific Research, 1983 [Hebrew]), 549–563.

Medzini, Arnon, *The Distribution of Bedouin Settlement in the Galilee as a Product of Spontaneous Settlement and Government-Focused Policy* (Haifa: University of Haifa Press, 1983 [Hebrew]).

Meir, Avinoam, "Nomads and the state: The spatial dynamics of centrifugal and centripetal forces among the Israeli Negev Bedouin," *Political Geography Quarterly*, Vol. 7, No. 3 (July 1988): 251–270.

Metral, Francoise, "Managing Risk: Sheep-rearing and Agriculture in the Syrian Steppe," in *The Transformation of Nomadic Society in the Arab East*, eds. Mundy, Martha and Musallam, Basim (Cambridge, UK: Cambridge University Press, 2000).

Michael, Assaf, *The Arabs under the Crusaders, the Mamelukes, and the Turks* (Tel Aviv: Davar Press, 1941 [Hebrew]).

Mills, Eric, *Census of Palestine, 1931* (Jerusalem: Messrs, 1932).

Milstein, Uri and Doron, Dov, *Shaked Reconnaissance Unit: Prevention and routine security in the IDF's history* (Tel Aviv: Yediot Aharonot Press, 1994 [Hebrew]).

Morris, Benny, *1948: A History of the First Arab–Israeli War*, trans. Sharett, Yaakov (Tel Aviv: Am Oved, 2010 [Hebrew]).

Morris, Benny, *The Birth of the Palestinian Refugee Problem Revisited 1947–1949* (Cambridge, UK: Cambridge University Press, 2004).

Munson, Henry, "On the Irrelevance of the Segmentary Lineage Model in the Moroccan Rif," *American Anthropologist*, Vol. 91, No. 2 (June 1989): 386–400.

Musa, Sulaiman, "Aqila al-Hasi," *Jordanian Wings Magazine* (Dairah Al-Alaqat Al-Amma, no date [Arabic]): 8–11.

Mustafa, Mohanad, *The decline of Arab parties in local government: 1978–1998* (Umm El Fahm: Markiz Al-Dirasat Al-Muasirah, 2000 [Arabic]).

Nakhleh, Khalil, "Land Day," in *Palestinians in Israel: Readings in History, Politics, and Society*, eds. Nadin N. Rouhana and Areej Sabbagh-Khoury (Haifa: Mada al-Carmel Press, 2011 [Arabic]).

Nelson, Cynthia (ed.), *The desert and the sown: Nomads in the wider society* (Berkeley: Institute of International Studies, University of California, 1973).

Nujeidat, Dhahir, *Olive Roots* (Bu'enie-Nujeidat: Al-Madrasa Al-Ibtidayia, 2008 [Arabic]).
Oppenheim, Max V., *The Bedouins: Palestine, Sinai, Jordan, and Al-Hejaz*, Vol. 2, trans. Mahmoud Kabibu (London: Dar Al-Warraq, 2004 [Arabic]).
Orhonlu, Cengiz, *Osmanli Imparatorlugunda asiretleri iskan tesebbusu (1691–1696)* (Istanbul: Edebiyat Fakultesi Basimevi, 1963 [Turkey]), 39–98.
Owen, Roger E., "Economic Development in Mandatory Palestine 1918–1948," in *The Palestinian economy: Studies in development under prolonged occupation*, ed. Abd T. George (Routledge: London & New York, 1988), 13–35.
Owen, Roger E., *The Middle East in the World Economy, 1800–1914* (London: Methuen Press, 1981).
Pappe, Ilan, *The Ethnic Cleansing of Palestine* (Oxford: One World, 2006).
Peake, Frederick G., *A history of Trans-Jordan and its tribes* (Jerusalem: Dar al-Aytam al-Islamiyya, 1934 [Arabic]).
Peters, Emrys L., *The Bedouin of Cyrenaica: Studies in Personal and Corporate Power* (Cambridge, UK: Cambridge University Press, 1990).
Pickett, Robert S., "Review: Kinship and Marriage in Early Arabia," *The Family Coordinator*, Vol. 21, No. 3 (July 1972): 365.
Poliak, Abraham, *Feudalism in Egypt, Syria, Palestine, and the Lebanon, 1250–1900* (Philadelphia: Porcupine Press, 1977).
Quataert, Donald, *Ottoman Empire, 1700–1922* (Cambridge, UK: Cambridge University Press, 2000).
Qudsiya, Labyeb, *Ijzim village in Haifa district* (Amman: Dar Wael Lil-Nasher, 2010 [Arabic]).
Rabinowitz, Dan and Abu Bakir, Khawla, *The Upright Generation* (Jerusalem: Keter, 2002 [Hebrew]).
Rabinowitz, Dan and Khawalde, Suleiman, "Demilitarized, then Dispossessed: The Kirad Bedouin of the Hula Valley in the Context of Syrian-Israeli Relations," *International Journal of Middle East Studies*, Vol. 32, No. 4 (2000): 530–551.
Rabinowitz, Dan, *Anthropology and Palestinians* (Raanana: Center for the Study of Arab Society in Israel, 1998 [Hebrew]).
Rabinowitz, Dan, *Overlooking Nazareth: The Ethnography of Exclusion in Galilee* (Cambridge, UK: Cambridge University Press, 1997).
Reilly, James, "The Peasantry of Late Ottoman Palestine," *Journal of Palestine Studies*, Vol. 10, No. 4 (Summer 1981): 82–97.
Robinson, Edward, *Biblical Researches in Palestine and the Adjacent Regions: A Journal of Travels in the Years 1838 & 1852* (Jerusalem: Universities' Booksellers Press, 1970 [1856]).
Rogan, Eugene, "Neither Pro-Zionist nor Pro-Arab, but Pro-Empire: A Reassessment of British policy in the Palestine Mandate," https://balfourproject.org/eugene-rogan/.
Rogel, Nakdimon, *Tel Hai: A Front without a Rear* (Tel Aviv: Yariv-Hadar, 1979 [Hebrew]).

Rosenfeld, Henry, "Separation and splitting processes of the extended family in the Arab village," *Megamot*, Vol. 8, No. 4 (April 1957 [Hebrew]): 411–418.

Rosenfeld, Henry, *They Were Fellahin: Studies in the Social Development of the Arab Village in Israel* (Tel Aviv: Hakibbutz Hameuhad, 1964 [Hebrew]).

Sa'id, Amin, *The Great Arab Revolt: A Detailed History of the Arab Cause in a Quarter Century*, Vol. 2 (Cairo: Maktabat Madbuli, 1990 [Arabic]).

Sabbagh, Michael, *The History of Shaykh Zahir al-'Umar Al-Zaydani, Governor of Acre and the Land of Galilee* (Beirut: Harisa, 1950 [Arabic]).

Sahlins, Marshall D., "The Segmentary Lineage: An Organization of Predatory Expansion," *American Anthropologist*, Vol. 63, No. 2 (April 1961): 322–345.

Said, Edward W., *Orientalism* (New York: Pantheon Books, 1978).

Sakran, Saber A., *Iblin roots* (Nazareth: M.D, 1986 [Arabic]).

Sawaed, Muhammad Y., *The Bedouins in Palestine: The Ottoman Period, 1516–1914* (Amman: Zahran Press, 2008 [Arabic]).

Scholch, Alexander, "The Decline of Local Power in Palestine After 1856: The Case of Aqil Aga," *Die Welt des Islamic*, Vol. 23, No. 1 (April 1984): 458–475.

Schumacher, Gottlieb, "Population list of the Liva of Akka," *Palestine Exploration Fund Quarterly Statement*, Vol. 19, No. 1 (July 1887): 169–191.

Segal, Edwin S., "Intersections among Tribalism, Ethnicity, and Gender in Light of African Data," *Sociological Bulletin*, Vol. 49, No. 1 (March 2000): 1–17.

Sewell, William H., "A Theory of Structure: Duality, Agency, and Transformation," *American Journal of Sociology*, Vol. 98, No. 1 (July 1992), 1–29.

Shamir, Shimon, *The Arabs in Israel: Two Years after the Or Commission Report* (Tel Aviv: Tel Aviv University, Moshe Dayan Center for Oriental and North African Studies, 2005 [Hebrew]).

Sharon, Moshe, "The Bedouin and the Land of Israel under Islamic Rule," in *The Bedouin: Notes and Articles*, Vol. 2 (Sde Boker: Midreshet Sde Boker Press, 1971 [Hebrew]), 8–24.

Sharon, Moshe, "The Political Role of the Bedouin in Palestine in the Sixteenth and Seventeenth Centuries," in *Studies on Palestine during the Ottoman Period*, ed. Ma'oz Moshe (Jerusalem: Magnes Press, 1975), 11–48.

Shimoni, Yaacov, *The Arabs of Palestine* (Tel Aviv: Am Oved, 1947 [Hebrew]).

Shmueli, Avshalom, *The End of the Nomads-Bedouin Societies in Settlement Processes* (Tel Aviv: Reshafim Press, 1980 [Hebrew]).

Smith, Robertson W., *Kinship and Marriage in Early Arabia* (Oosterhout, N.B, Netherlands: Anthropological Publications Press, 1966).

Soffer, Arnon, "The Bedouins in Israel: Geographic Aspects", *Horizons in Geography*, Vol. 67–68, No. 1 (January 2007 [Hebrew]): 224–236.

Steward, Julian, "The concept and method of cultural ecology," in *Evolution and Ecology: Essays on Social Transformation*, eds. Steward, Jane and Murphy, Robert (Urbana, IL: University of Illinois Press, 1977), 30–42.

Taqosh, Muhammad S., *The Ottomans from the establishment of the state to the overthrow of the caliph* (Beirut: Dar beit al-Mhrusa, 1995 [Arabic]).

Tarbiyeh, Khalid M., *Tarbiyeh tribe throughout history* (Jerusalem: Dar al-Aytam, 1976 [Arabic]).

Tlass, Mustafa, *The Arab Rebellion* (Damascus: Dar Tlass, 1984 [Arabic]).

Touma, Emile, *Palestine in the Ottoman Period* (Al-Quds: Dar al-Fajr, 1983 [Arabic]).

Touma, Emile, *The origins of the Palestinian cause* (Haifa: M'ahad Emile Touma, 1995 [Arabic]).

Tristram, Henry B., *The Land of Israel: A journal of travels in Palestine* (London: Society for Promoting Christian Knowledge, 1865).

United Nations (UN), *A Survey of Palestine: Supplement to Survey of Palestine, Notes Compiled for the Information of the United Nations Special Committee on Palestine* (Jerusalem: Government Press, 1947).

Waschitz, Yosef, *The Arabs of Palestine* (Jerusalem: Sifriat Poalim, 1947 [Hebrew]).

Yasin, Subhi, *The Great Arab Revolt in Palestine, 1936–1939* (Cairo: Dar Al-Nhada Ll-tiba'a, 1967 [Arabic]).

Yasin, Subhi, *Guerilla Warfare in Palestine* (Cairo: Dar al-Katab al-Arabi, 1967 [Arabic]).

Yiftachel, Oren, "Land Day," *Theory and Criticism*, Vol. 12–13, No. 1 (April 1990 [Hebrew]): 279–290.

Yiftachel, Oren, *Watching Over the Vineyard: The Example of Majd al-Krum* (Raanana: Institute for Israeli Arab Studies, 1997 [Hebrew]).

Yitzhaki, Aryeh, "The Bedouin Tribes at the Foot of Mount Tabor," *Kedum*, Vol. 4, No. 20 (January 1982 [Hebrew]): 88–92.

Yonah, Yossi and Shenhav, Yehouda, *What is Multiculturalism? On the Politics of Identity in Israel* (Tel Aviv: Bavel Press, 2005 [Hebrew]).

Zakariyya, Ahmed W., *Tribes of Al-Sham* (Damascus: Dar al-Fikr, 1983 [Arabic]).

Zakzouk, Mahmoud H., *General Islamic Encyclopedia* (Egypt: Wizrt al-Awqaf, 2003 [Arabic]).

Zu'aytir, Akram, *Diary of Akram Zu'aytir: The Palestinian National Movement, 1935–1939* (Beirut: Mu'assat al-Dirasat al-Filastiniyah, 1980 [Arabic]).

Zucher, Erik J., *Turkey: A Modern History*, trans. Ginzburg-Hirsch, Adi (Tel Aviv: Tel Aviv University Press, 2005 [Hebrew]).

UNPUBLISHED THESES AND DISSERTATIONS

Bitan, Arieh, *Settlement Changes in the Eastern Lower Galilee, 1800–1978* (PhD diss., Hebrew University, 1969 [Hebrew]).

Falah, Ghazi, *The Processes and Patterns of Sedentarization of the Galilee Bedouin, 1880–1982* (PhD diss., University of Durham, 1982).

Frantzman, Seth J., *The Arab Settlement of Late Ottoman and Mandatory*

Palestine: New Village Formation and Settlement Fixation, 1871–1948 (PhD diss., Hebrew University, 2010).

Manna', Adil, *Sanjak of Jerusalem between two invasions (1798–1831): Administration and society* (PhD diss., Hebrew University, 1986 [Hebrew]).

Mazarib, Tomer, *The process of Bedouin integration into Arab towns and villages in the Galilee: Historical, social, and cultural aspects, from the beginning of the 18th century to the end of the 20th century* (PhD diss., Haifa University, 2016 [Hebrew]).

Quzli, Sa'id, *The State of Israel and the Negev Bedouin (1948–2012): Policy and Reality on the Issue of Land, Settlement, and Military Recruitment* (PhD diss., Haifa University, 2014 [Hebrew]).

Said, Mahmoud, *The Integration and Assimilation of the Arab Internal Refugees in the Arab Sanctuary Villages in Northern Israel 1948–1986* (M.A. thesis, Hebrew University, 1990 [Hebrew]).

Sawaed, Muhammad Y., *Bedouin–Jewish Relations in Mandate Palestine 1918–1948* (PhD diss., Bar-Ilan University, 1998 [Hebrew]).

Sharon, Moshe, *The Bedouin in the Land of Israel from the beginning of the eighteenth century to the end of the Crimean War* (M.A. thesis, Hebrew University, 1964 [Hebrew]).

PERIODICALS

Alenkvh, Emanuel and Eshel, Shraga, "Military Curfews in 3 villages in the Galilee; 1 Arab killed; 13 police and soldiers injured," *Yediot Aharonot* (Tel Aviv: Yediot Aharonot Press, 31 March 1976 [Hebrew]).

Ben-Porat, Yeshayahu, "A retreat to 1948," *Yediot Aharonot* (Tel Aviv: Yediot Aharonot Press, 31 March 1976 [Hebrew]).

Eshet, Lia, "Bedouin Recruitment Process to be Shortened," *Bamahane* (Tel Aviv: Israel Defense Forces Press, 1 May 1991 [Hebrew]).

Gilat, Amir, "Higher Follow-Up Committee of Arab Citizens of Israel: The Government Drowned Our Just Struggle in Blood," *Maariv* (Tel Aviv: Maariv Press, 29 October 2000 [Hebrew]).

Harel, Amos, "Number of Bedouin recruits to the IDF has dropped by more than half," *Haaretz* (Tel Aviv: Haaretz Press, 14 June 2001 [Hebrew]), https://www.haaretz.co.il/misc/1.709309.

Petersburg, Ofer, "Housing and Construction Ministry will allocate 36 million Shekels to the Bedouin authorities in the north," *Yediot Aharonot* (Tel Aviv: Yediot Aharonot Press, 14 May 2001 [Hebrew]).

Rinat, Zafrir, "The Government Will Promote Single-Household Settlement in the Negev and North," *Haaretz* (Tel Aviv: Haaretz Press, 4 May 2003 [Hebrew]), https://www.haaretz.co.il/misc/1.879777.

Rinat, Zafrir, "Zeldstein's Tent," *Haaretz* (Tel Aviv: Haaretz Press, 16 March 1997 [Hebrew]).

Shahar, Eyal and Gilat, Amir, "Al-Sana demands: A minute of silence in memory of the 13 rioters killed," *Maariv* (Tel Aviv: Maariv Press, 29 October 2000 [Hebrew]).

Yehoshua, Yossi and Ginosar, Shahar, "Martial Ethics 101: Soldiers, Commander Suspected in Murder: What Happens in the Bedouin Reconnaissance Battalion, which received the President's Medal of Honor," *Yediot Aharonot* (Tel Aviv: Yediot Aharonot Press, 10 September 2004 [Hebrew]).

Ze'evi, Dror, *An Ottoman Century: The District of Jerusalem in the 1600s* (New York: SUNY Press, 1996).

INTERVIEWS

Abu Shahab, M. Hussein (son of the neighborhood's founder). Interview by author. Shafa-Amer, 10 July 2014.
Al-Fawaz, A. Nassir. Interview by author. Eilabun, 27 August 2014.
Al-Hamdun, Hussein. Interview by author. Abu Snan, 17 July 2014.
Al-Hasi, Muhammad. Interview by author. Ibillin, 28 August 2014.
Al-Heib, Adel. Interview by author. Nazareth, 16 October 2014.
Al-Heib, Muhammad. Interview by author. Al-Rama, 28 July 2015.
Al-Hindawi, Ibrahim. Interview by author. Shafa-Amer, 18 September 2014.
Al-Muhameidat, Awad. Interview by author. Shafa-Amer, 18 September 2014.
Al-Na'im, Hassan. Interview by author. Abu Snan, 17 July 2014.
Al-Na'im, Kitan. Interview by author. Tarshiha, 23 July 2014.
Al-Na'im, Nimer. Interview by author. Al-Na'im Abu Grad, 2 November 2015.
Al-Na'im, Salim. Interview by author. Nazareth, 23 October 2014.
Al-Zidani, Ziad. Interview by author. Nazareth, 19 July 2013.
Azayzah, Mahmoud. Interview by author. Sha'ab, 28 July 2015.
Banu Rabiah, Khadra. Interview by author. Nazareth, 16 October 2015.
Fadeli, Mahmoud. Interview by author. Al-Jadida-Al-Makr, 21 July 2014.
Ghazalin, Mahmoud. Interview by author. Yafa, 16 February 2013.
Ghazalin, Musa. Interview by author. Yafa, 26 February 2013.
Hajaj, Yusuf (Krad al-Baqqra). Interview by author. Shafa-Amer, 18 September 2014.
Heib, Shadi. Interview by author. Heib al-Frush-Rumana, 31 July 2014.
Hujeirat, Gh. Muhammad. Interview by author. Bir al-Maksur, 15 July 2015.
Hujeirat, O. Saleh. Interview by author. Shafa-Amer, 10 July 2014.
Karawi, Anis (director of Shafa-Amer's archive). Interview by author. Shafa-Amer, 10 July 2014.
Khalidi, Atef. Interview by author. Nazareth, 23 October 2014.
Majdoub, Fawaziah. Interview by author. Iblin, 28 Augus, 2014.
Manasra, A. Khalid. Interview by author. Reina, 23 October 2014.
Marisat, Ahmed. Interview by author. Tamra, 29 August 2014.
Marisat, Fahed. Interview by author. Tamra, 29 October 2014.
Marisat, Jihad. Interview by author. Iblin, 28 August 2014.
Masarwa, A. Muhammad. Interview by author. Hajajra, 25 July 2014.
Masharqa, Yones. Interview by author. Nazareth, 23 October 2014.

Maslama, Yusuf. Interview by author. Nazareth, 16 October 2014.
Mawasi, Atta. Interview by author. Iblin, 28 August 2014.
Mazarib, Ahmed. Interview by author. Zarzir, 14 July 2015.
Mjali, Samir. Interview by author. Nazareth, 16 October 2014.
N'arani, Khalid. Interview by author. Bussmat Tab'un, 17 May 2015.
Nujeidat, H. Samir. Interview by author. Bu'enie-Nujeidat, 6 August 2014.
Quzli, Sa'id. Interview by author. Isfiya, 27 July 2015.
Ramih, Mahmoud. Interview by author. Maghar, 27 August 2014.
Said, Abdallah (Abu Kulib). Interview by author. Haifa, 29 July 2015.
Saida, Atef. Interview by author. Manshiya Zabda, 16 August 2016.
Sawaed, Ahmad. Interview by author. Acre, 16 August 2014.
Sawaed, Ahmed. Interview by author. Al-Rama, 28 July 2015.
Sawaed, Ali. Interview by author. Ba'ana, 23 July 2014.
Sawaed, Kh. Khalid. Interview by author. Iblin, 28 August 2014.
Sawaed, N. Muhsin. Interview by author. Shafa-Amer, 10 July 2014.
Sawaed, Saleh. Interview by author. Al-Rama, 28 July 2015.
Sawaed, Umar (Advisor to Mayor of Shafa-Amer). Interview by author. Shafa-Amer, 9 July 2014.
Shawahdeh, Hussein. Interview by author. Eilabun, 6 August 2014.
Shibli (Ziadnah), A. Sa'id. Interview by author. Deir Hanna, 30 August 2014.
Sweitat, Kayid. Interview by author. Abu Snan, 17 July 2014.
Sweitat, Muhammad. Interview by author. Al-Jadida-Al-Makr, 21 July 2014.
Sweitat, Sh. Muhammad. Interview by author. Isfiya, 27 July 2015.
Tarbiyeh, Kh. Muhammad. Interview by author. Sakhnin, 14 July 2014.
Tarbiyeh, Nassir. Interview by author. Sakhnin, 6 June 2013.
Ziadnah, Sh. Qasem. Interview by author. Deir Hanna, 30 August 2014.
Zidan, A. Muhammad. Interview by author. Kafr Manda, 13 July 2013.
Zubeidat, Qasem. Interview by author. Sakhnin, 14 July 2014.
Zubeidat, Yazid. Interview by author. Bussmat Tab'un, 24 April 2015.

Index

A

Abu Kulib, 78, 93, 95, 200, 201, 206, 207, 241
Abu Snan, 26, 62, 65, 78, 95, 97, 102, 103, 109, 114, 121, 122, 134, 140, 152, 199, 202, 208, 213, 214, 215, 216, 217, 218, 221, 240, 241
Acre, 17, 27, 29, 35, 37, 42, 45, 48, 51, 56, 65, 66, 68, 69, 70, 71, 73, 74, 75, 76, 78, 79, 94, 95, 96, 97, 98, 99, 122, 149, 152, 190, 193, 199, 204, 227, 232, 237, 241
Al-Anezzah, 31, 50
Al-B'ena, 26, 152
Al-Bashatwa, 32, 37, 45, 76, 82, 91, 107
Al-Bawati, 45
Al-Dalaika, 48, 52, 58, 80, 91, 104, 141
Al-Dalhamiya, 44, 46, 52, 81, 105
Al-Damun, 49, 78, 97, 98, 110
Al-Fadl, 55, 78, 80, 97, 102, 103, 196
Al-Fawawza, 65
Al-Ghazalin, 48, 52, 65, 73, 81, 106, 109, 114
Al-Ghazzawiyya, 32, 37, 45, 82, 91, 107, 193
Al-Ghrefat, 60, 81, 106, 109
Al-Hamdun, 73, 77, 80, 94, 121, 122, 142, 216, 240
Al-Hanadi, 32, 40, 44, 46, 68, 81, 115, 149, 193
Al-Hasi, 46, 48, 52, 79, 100, 240
Al-Hawara, 40, 48, 49, 52, 79
Al-Hejaz, 37, 188, 236
Al-Howeitat, 32, 40, 55, 64, 73
Al-Jadida, 26, 78, 97, 152, 196, 202, 208, 210, 240, 241
Al-Jawamees, 60, 73, 109, 141
Al-jbarat, 40
Al-Ka'abiya-Helf, 96
Al-Khalidi, 77, 105, 109, 123, 201, 204, 205, 206, 207, 208, 209, 210, 211, 212, 226
Al-Khalsa, 55, 57, 66, 80, 103
Al-Madi, 46, 77, 94, 206, 227

Al-Maghar, 26, 152
Al-Makr, 26, 97, 103, 196, 202, 208, 210, 240, 241
Al-Mansi, 49, 66, 69, 77, 91, 94, 110, 193
Al-Mazarib, 60, 61, 73, 81, 89, 90, 106, 109, 167
Al-Muhameidat, 80, 102, 103, 123, 195, 210, 216, 240
Al-N'arani, 50
Al-Na'im, 31, 32, 66, 77, 78, 80, 81, 97, 101, 104, 106, 121, 122, 123, 124, 134, 140, 152, 202, 208, 214, 215, 216, 217, 218, 221, 240
Al-Najmiyya, 48, 52, 100
Al-Naora, 58, 66, 81, 89, 106, 115, 123, 129, 139
Al-Rama, 26, 120, 122, 129, 139, 151, 152, 215, 216, 218, 221, 240, 241
Al-Sa'diyya, 50, 52
Al-Saqer, 45, 63, 91, 92
Al-Sawaed, 73, 79, 96, 97, 114, 126
Al-Sayyid, 32, 45, 80, 101
Al-Sindiyana, 77, 94, 110
Al-Subayh, 32, 37, 57, 60, 61, 64, 73, 75, 76, 81, 91, 93, 105, 106, 107, 109, 167, 189, 211
Al-Ta'amra, 40
Al-Ziadnah, 28, 35, 37, 38, 78, 79, 98
anthropology, 4, 5, 16, 19, 181
Aqil Agha, 3, 40, 45, 46, 79, 193, 226
Arab Al-Abidiyya, 78, 95
Arab Al-Araqiya, 78, 95
Arab Al-Ghrefat, 78, 95
Arab Al-Hanbuzi, 78, 95
Arab Al-Sawaed, 78, 79, 95, 121, 131, 215, 222
Arab al-Shkirat, 49
Arabal-Tawatha, 49
Arab Al-Wazaoza, 78, 95
Arab Turkmens, 49
ayan, 12, 35
Azazmah, 32, 55, 88

Index

B

Banu Rabiah, 108, 114, 207, 212, 214, 240
Banu Saqer, 4, 32, 37, 81, 92, 107, 108
Beer Sheva, 32, 42, 43, 88, 146, 193, 226, 229
Beisan, 12, 3, 4, 26, 29, 31, 32, 37, 39, 40, 44, 59, 63, 69, 70, 71, 74, 76, 77, 81, 82, 91, 92, 107, 108, 110, 199, 206, 212, 225, 232
Bir al-Maksur, 100, 107, 111, 125, 131, 141, 142, 153, 154, 155, 186, 208, 209, 240
Bu'enie-Nujeidat, 26, 81, 152, 154, 155, 198, 199, 203, 211, 236, 241

C

Chain Migrations, 5, 113, 114, 115, 213
Circassians, 156
colonialism, 29, 41
cultural translation, 4
Culturism, 5, 43, 178, 192

D

Daliyat Al- Carmel, 26
Damascus, 11, 30, 31, 34, 35, 37, 39, 41, 42, 180, 181, 187, 189, 193, 196, 206, 226, 227, 238
Deir Hanna, 26, 37, 38, 65, 79, 98, 105, 120, 131, 136, 142, 152, 167, 190, 202, 203, 208, 210, 211, 217, 225, 241
desert, 1, 2, 6, 18, 20, 29, 30, 31, 34, 36, 53, 58, 163, 186, 235
dirah, 58, 61, 64, 120, 133, 200
Druze, 11, 36, 50, 66, 97, 102, 156

E

effendis, 22, 44, 46, 50, 61
Egyptian occupation, 41
Eilabun, 26, 48, 52, 64, 65, 80, 98, 104, 105, 152, 194, 199, 208, 210, 240, 241

G

Gaza, 6, 34, 36, 42, 44, 46, 192, 232
geographical researchers, 7, 8
Ghawarna, 55, 66, 68, 73, 76, 78, 80, 91, 95, 96, 97, 103, 141, 149
Golan Heights, 29, 32, 34, 55, 66, 78, 99, 102, 196
Government Plans, 5, 113, 115, 117, 213
grazing lands, 23

H

habitus, 38, 166
Hajajra, 50, 51, 52, 60, 68, 78, 81, 96, 106, 107, 122, 141, 153, 154, 155, 186, 195, 197, 240
hamula, 14, 16, 111, 183, 194
Hauran, 11, 41, 55
Heib, 32, 52, 56, 60, 65, 73, 80, 81, 87, 88, 89, 91, 101, 104, 105, 106, 109, 111, 122, 129, 131, 139, 141, 142, 151, 155, 186, 205, 213, 216, 224, 240
historical scholars, 5
Hujeirat, 56, 68, 73, 79, 81, 99, 100, 106, 114, 124, 126, 129, 131, 139, 140, 141, 142, 149, 151, 195, 202, 203, 208, 209, 211, 214, 240
Hula Valley, 26, 52, 65, 80, 89, 91, 101, 102, 103, 209, 236

I

Iblin, 26, 45, 46, 48, 49, 52, 56, 65, 79, 96, 97, 100, 122, 123, 131, 140, 142, 152, 199, 207, 208, 209, 210, 216, 217, 237, 240, 241
Ibn Khaldun, 2, 10, 18, 23, 163, 177, 180, 183, 187, 232
Ibrahim Pasha, 32, 34, 39, 40, 46, 48, 49, 50, 64, 68, 94, 189, 201, 226
identities remain, 22
Ijzim, 46, 52, 77, 94, 110, 193, 201, 204, 206, 227, 229, 236
Iksal, 26, 48, 52, 65, 81, 106, 114, 129, 139, 151, 152, 194, 199, 233
iltizam, 11, 41, 180
integration, 6, 1, 2, 7, 8, 14, 16, 25, 27, 52, 53, 54, 58, 84, 86, 87, 93, 112, 113, 115, 117, 132, 133, 163, 164, 177, 217, 219, 239
Isfiya, 4, 26, 94, 95, 97, 123, 129, 139, 151, 152, 199, 201, 206, 207, 216, 221, 241

J

Jenin, 7, 34, 36, 42, 44, 50, 69, 91, 94, 95
Jordan Valley, 26, 58, 68, 82, 107
Juarish, 24

K

Kabul, 26, 49, 90, 137, 151, 152
Kafr Kana, 15, 26, 91, 139, 151, 152
Kafr Manda, 26, 37, 38, 56, 81, 106,

Kafr Manda *(continued)*
    107, 129, 139, 151, 152, 190, 203, 211, 226, 241
Kafr Maser, 26, 151, 152
Kafr Qasem, 14, 137
khawa, 3, 4, 35, 178
Khawaled, 56, 62, 79, 100, 126, 131, 140, 141, 142, 153, 155
kinship, 18, 20, 21, 55, 183
Krad al-Baqqra, 52, 80, 101, 102, 103, 209, 240
Krad al-Ghannama, 52, 80, 101

L
Land Day, 17, 124, 133, 134, 136, 137, 144, 146, 183, 217, 235, 238
Libya, 20, 22, 182, 185
Lod, 27, 44

M
Maghar, 65, 80, 104, 120, 199, 203, 210, 241
Majd al-Krum, 16, 17, 79, 98, 120, 238
Mameluk, 10, 180, 226
Manshiya Zabda, 26, 68, 69, 81, 106, 129, 139, 151, 152, 153, 155, 200, 211, 241
Masarwa, 50, 52, 195, 197, 240
Masharqa, 48, 52, 62, 80, 104, 105, 123, 194, 198, 203, 211, 216, 240
Maslama, 58, 66, 114, 129, 139, 200, 214, 241
Mawasi, 48, 52, 64, 65, 73, 79, 80, 91, 92, 98, 99, 100, 102, 103, 104, 105, 123, 149, 151, 209, 210, 216, 241
Military Rule, 5, 15, 27, 110, 113, 114, 127, 132, 133, 134, 213, 230
mixed settlements, 8, 133
Mjali, 108, 149, 212, 241
modernization discourse, 41
Muhammad Ali, 11, 13
mukhtars, 12, 42, 52, 61
multiz, 11
Muslims, 4, 29, 30, 45, 66, 70, 71, 74, 81

N
Nablus, 3, 34, 42, 44, 69, 193, 227
Nahaf, 26, 120, 122, 139, 151, 152
Nahalal, 69, 89, 90
nomads, 2, 6, 7, 10, 26, 30, 34, 43, 53, 59, 61, 75, 93, 116, 132, 164
North Africa, 9, 13, 29, 30, 177

Nujeidat, 62, 64, 81, 106, 129, 131, 139, 142, 151, 186, 198, 199, 203, 211, 236, 241
Numeirat, 32, 78, 80, 95, 101, 102, 103

O
October 2000 events, 144, 145, 146
Orientalist, 3, 4, 7, 8, 43
Ottoman Orientalism, 41, 191

P
Palestinian, 16, 54, 55, 57, 85, 86, 87, 90, 91, 92, 93, 94, 112, 113, 114, 133, 134, 136, 137, 144, 145, 146, 159, 190, 193, 196, 198, 200, 204, 205, 206, 207, 213, 218, 226, 227, 229, 231, 235, 236, 238
Pal-heib unit, 89
permanent settlers, 7

Q
Qlitat, 66, 73, 77, 78, 94, 95, 96, 97, 123, 129, 139, 151
Quzli, 123, 126, 129, 139, 146, 151, 216, 218, 220, 239, 241

R
Ramle, 24, 27, 29
Reina, 15, 26, 81, 106, 107, 129, 139, 151, 152, 199, 211, 212, 213, 240
relations, 1, 2, 6, 8, 9, 12, 20, 21, 25, 34, 44, 45, 49, 57, 87, 88, 93, 109, 115, 184
relationships, 2, 3, 5, 6, 15, 18, 21, 50, 56, 90, 97, 137, 144, 163, 166, 177
Rmihat, 65, 80, 104
Rumana, 81, 106, 111, 129, 139, 151, 213, 240
Rwala, 55, 178, 227

S
Sa'id Zaglul, 12
Sabarja, 32, 73, 81, 106
Safad, 3, 17, 34, 36, 37, 42, 51, 65, 69, 70, 71, 74, 75, 76, 79, 80, 87, 91, 101, 102, 103, 104, 205, 210, 225
Saffuriya, 50, 68, 111
Sahl Al-Battuf, 64, 65, 68, 111
Sakhnin, 27, 36, 37, 48, 52, 79, 98, 111, 114, 115, 120, 122, 124, 134, 136, 149, 152, 190, 194, 195, 202, 208, 214, 217, 224, 241
Samkia, 32, 62, 80, 104, 149

Index

Samniyya, 68, 73, 77, 78, 79, 94, 95, 96, 97, 99, 100, 114, 124, 126, 149, 151
Sarona, 48, 52, 58, 80, 105, 197, 201, 203, 210, 225
Sawaed, 60, 62, 65, 79, 90, 98, 99, 100, 102, 109, 111, 114, 116, 121, 122, 123, 124, 125, 129, 131, 139, 140, 141, 142, 149, 151, 155, 193, 196, 198, 202, 205, 206, 207, 208, 209, 213, 214, 215, 216, 217, 218, 219, 220, 221, 237, 239, 241
Sawilat, 65, 77, 94, 102
sedentarizaion, 6, 7, 25, 29, 39, 52, 58, 63, 74, 113, 127
semi-nomads, 7, 61
Sha'ab, 26, 49, 65, 101, 102, 103, 109, 120, 121, 152, 209, 210, 213, 240
Shamalana, 32
Shammar, 30, 31
Shawahdeh, 48, 64, 80, 104, 194, 199, 208, 210, 241
Shibli, 64, 69, 98, 105, 107, 141, 154, 155, 167, 186, 190, 202, 203, 208, 210, 211, 225, 241
Sursock, 44, 49, 57, 64
Sweitat, 62, 65, 66, 73, 77, 78, 79, 80, 94, 95, 97, 98, 100, 104, 105, 109, 114, 116, 123, 129, 139, 140, 149, 151, 199, 201, 202, 206, 207, 208, 213, 214, 215, 216, 218, 221, 222, 241

T

Tab'un, 48, 49, 50, 51, 77, 95, 96, 106, 107, 111, 114, 125, 153, 154, 155, 186, 195, 201, 207, 214, 241
Tamra, 27, 37, 38, 49, 65, 79, 94, 95, 96, 97, 98, 122, 136, 140, 149, 152, 202, 208, 216, 240
Tanzimat, 11, 12, 29, 41, 42, 179, 181, 188, 192, 228, 231, 234
Tarshiha, 26, 68, 78, 95, 97, 114, 122, 123, 152, 194, 202, 208, 214, 215, 227, 240
taxes, 10, 11, 12, 34, 35, 40, 41, 42, 63, 70
the Land Code, 13

Tiberias, 3, 29, 32, 34, 37, 38, 40, 42, 44, 46, 48, 51, 52, 58, 61, 65, 69, 70, 71, 74, 76, 80, 81, 89, 91, 92, 101, 104, 105, 107, 110, 122, 146, 193, 204, 205
Trabay, 7, 28, 35, 36, 37, 40, 79, 98, 149, 187
Transjordan, 7, 32, 55, 95, 196
travelers, 3, 4, 5, 44
Triangle, 14, 26, 182
tribalism, 23, 178
Tuba-al- Zangariah, 52
Turan, 9, 13, 16, 26, 107, 129, 139, 151, 152
Turkmens, 66, 73, 91, 93, 199

U

umm al-Ghanam, 107
Uzair, 26, 68, 81, 106, 111, 129, 131, 139, 142, 151, 152

W

Wadi Al-Hamam, 80, 125, 141, 153
Wahhabis, 31
Western, 3, 4, 5, 8, 10, 11, 41, 178, 193, 228, 230
Western travelers, 3, 4, 5, 8
Wilayats, 13, 41, 42

Y

Yafa, 15, 26, 65, 81, 106, 109, 114, 122, 123, 136, 152, 194, 203, 211, 212, 214, 240

Z

Zahir Al-Umar, 37, 38, 40, 167, 194
Zarzir, 95, 96, 107, 114, 141, 153, 154, 155, 186, 197, 198, 212, 213, 241
Zinati, 88
Zionist, 12, 5, 15, 54, 57, 59, 77, 90, 92, 163, 197, 205, 214, 224, 236
Zubeidat, 48, 50, 52, 56, 73, 77, 79, 80, 95, 98, 100, 105, 108, 114, 126, 129, 139, 141, 149, 151, 194, 195, 202, 208, 214, 241